Fundamentals of Commercial Banking

AN APPLIED APPROACH

First Edition

Dr. Kent S. Belasco
Marquette University, Milwaukee, Wisconsin

Bassim Hamadeh, CEO and Publisher
Angela Schultz, Senior Field Acquisitions Editor
Alisa Munoz, Project Editor
Susana Christie, Senior Developmental Editor
Rachel Kahn, Production Editor
Emely Villavicencio, Senior Graphic Designer
Greg Isales, Licensing Coordinator
Natalie Piccotti, Director of Marketing
Kassie Graves, Senior Vice President, Editorial
Jamie Giganti, Director of Academic Publishing

Printed in the United States of America.

To my family, the inspiration and motivation for everything I do.

To my students, my commercial banking program students, and my graduates, who provide the foundation and need for this book, and who remind me every day of the importance and necessity for continued education and the demand for careers in commercial banking.

CONTENTS

CHAPTER 1

Commercial Bank Basics and Foundations

From the dawn of commerce and the growth of mediums of exchange for goods and services, the need for people and organizations to handle these mediums of exchange as well as a means of funding has been a constant. Literally, for hundreds of years—from primitive society, to the Medici's of Italy, to JPMorgan Chase—the need for money managers has been continuous.

In the United States, formalized banking began in 1791 with the first central bank for the new country. Begun by Alexander Hamilton, the first Treasury secretary, it unfortunately was closed in 1811. Following Alexander Hamilton's death in 1804, in a duel with Aaron Burr, support for the central bank waned. Although another central bank was attempted later, it also failed. It wasn't until 1913 that the central bank was revived by President Woodrow Wilson. Although this was the case, banks existed throughout that period in the United States. In many ways, it was this almost 100-year period that created the necessity for the Federal Reserve bank. With a variety of financial and market crises during this period, the need for stability in the financial sector was clear.

This chapter focuses on the foundation of the commercial banking industry in the United States and the importance of this industry in the economy.

Key Terms

Deposits subject to withdrawal
Loans
Economic functions
Economic cycle
Interest income
Fee income
Money supply
Payment
Risk protection
Liquidity services
Community banks
Regional banks
Money center banks
Retail banks
Correspondent banks
Systemically important financial institution (SIFI)
Domestically systemically important bank (D-SIB)
Globally systemically important bank (G-SIB)

Learning Objectives

By the end of this chapter, the student will:

- Understand the origins of banking in the United States.
- Know the definition of the word "bank."
- Understand the impact banks have on society.
- Know how banks make money.
- Know the role of commercial banks in the financial system.
- Understand the economic cycle and the relationship commercial banking has with it.
- Differentiate banks by size, category, and regulatory category.

Definition and Foundation of Commercial Banks

Commercial banks are defined by two major attributes: (1) They offer **deposits subject to withdrawal on demand,** and (2) they make **loans** of a business nature. There are many organizations that provide loans, but one of the most identifying factors of a bank is the ability to obtain deposits from customers. This is truly a critical function, as this becomes the primary source for the loans that banks make.

Economic Functions

Banks also are defined by the **economic functions** they perform. Banks are integral to the economy. Commercial banks and the ability to provide loans to businesses clearly affects how the economy functions. This was a major concern during the financial crisis of 2008, with banks no longer lending at the same level as previously. In many ways, some would say, that prolonged the crisis. The economic functions that banks perform predominantly include making loans and taking deposits, but they play an important intermediary role in the economy.

- making loans
  - » The major role of banks in the economy is making loans to businesses. Businesses need to grow. Often, they do not have the ready resources to expand a plant, buy new equipment, or develop new products. As such, commercial banks fill this role by providing the needed funds so that the businesses can grow. When this occurs, expansion and growth create jobs as well as prosperity (i.e., higher salaries).
- taking deposits
  - » Commercial banks accept deposits via various products available to the public. These include checking and savings accounts and time deposits. This is the source of the funds used to lend. As discretionary funds become available, consumers and businesses deposit these in commercial banks for investment and transactional purposes.
- intermediary role
  - » Commercial banks are at the center of the economy, receiving deposits and lending out the money. This receipt and disbursement function does not exist without commercial banks, by definition.

Range of Services

In addition to the economic functions, commercial banks offer a wide range of services to clients that facilitate a variety of needs that consumers have. These services range from retail consumers, businesses, and wealth management services.

Legal Basis

Commercial banks are defined by a legal basis. Banks are chartered by regulatory bodies that provide them the legal basis to offer loans and take deposits. These regulatory bodies include the Office of the Comptroller of the Currency and state regulatory bodies. These organizations derive their authority from the law (regulations) (Ross and Hudgins, 2013). Regulatory agencies will be outlined in a later chapter.

In addition to the above, commercial banks hold approximately 20% of the assets in the country. This is significant and is the cause of concern when banks are having trouble, as it has a huge effect on the economy in general. The following quote sums up well the purpose and importance of commercial banking in the economy.

> It can be argued that the genius of modern banking, while imperfect and subject at times to nefarious manipulation, has been the single greatest contributor to human progress, putting a serious dent in the crushing widespread poverty that was, even in western civilizations, the norm rather than the exception before the modern banking system took hold. Academics have long noted the strong correlation between modern banking systems and national wealth, allowing businesses to take on more risks in their efforts to grow. Prudent risks can lead to faster economic growth, more jobs, and greater innovation in all fields of human endeavor. (Trennert, 2015, p.178)

Economic Cycle

The **economic cycle**, depicted in Figure 1.1, is an important rendition of the importance of commercial banking in the economy. The graphic shows how the stakeholders involved in the economy are affected and interact with one another. The nature of the cycle is round and is continually functioning in a circuitous fashion. As long as the circuitous flow continues, unimpeded, the economy will operate efficiently. If any part does not function, the flow will be broken. The primary stakeholders include:

- commercial banks (financial intermediary)
- firms (businesses)
- households (consumers) (Rose & Marquis, 2011).

Stakeholders are reflected in the color green in Figure 1.1. The role commercial banks play is that of a financial intermediary, one that facilitates the movement of money among the stakeholders. This role that commercial banks play is not arbitrary, but critical to the functioning of the economy and the reason for their existence. In fact, commercial banks must exist and throughout history have performed this role in some fashion.

Firms, or businesses, are companies that generally exist within the community. These businesses, small and large, are the lifeblood of the economy. They create products for sale, offer services to households and others, and, most importantly, create jobs for the public.

Households are generally consumers. They "consume" by purchasing products and services from the businesses. Their source of income for this consumption is salaries they receive from businesses for the jobs they perform. In addition, households accumulate funds for investment (savings) and deposits those additional funds in commercial banks.

Commercial banks, then, are at the center of the cycle. They facilitate the movement of money from households and firms and provide valuable services. If commercial banks were to be eliminated from the cycle, the flow of money would cease and the economy would not function.

In order to understand this flow and the relationship of the stakeholders, consider the following sequence, beginning at the bottom of the cycle, with commercial banks, and moving counterclockwise.

1. commercial banks
   » Commercial banks are intermediaries. They take in money and pay out in loans. Therefore, the cycle begins with the commercial bank and through their role the cycle begins.
2. loans
   » Commercial banks make loans to firms: small- and medium-sized businesses. Loans are borrowings and are a key component in the flow.
3. firms
   » Firms receive this money from the bank, via a loan, for the purpose of growing their business. This means the purchase of equipment, raw materials, physical plant, or other needed assets. Firms must continually focus on growth for their existence, performing an increasingly vital role in the community.
4. goods, services, and expenditures
   » With this money, firms will produce more goods and services (center of the cycle in blue) and make capital expenditures (property, plant, and equipment).
5. salaries
   » As firms grow and prosper, they will need more employees. They, therefore, will create jobs and hire more workers. In addition to that, based upon their earnings, salaries will grow for employees to share in the prosperity of the firm.
6. households
   » As salaries and jobs grow, employees have more disposable income. This additional money is vested in the household. Households, then, have an opportunity to either spend it or save/invest it as discretionary funds.

7. goods, services, and expenditures
   » With additional discretionary funds available, households will consume more products and services offered by the firms (arrows to the right of the households).
   » As these products and services are purchased, at higher levels, the firms benefit by additional revenues, and therefore, the flow is back to the firms, in part.
8. firms
   » Firms will then take the additional revenue and profit and invest in more goods and services, requiring the hiring, potentially, of more workers, thus resulting in more salaries, or money, to the household, and the flow continues.
9. savings
   » With additional discretionary funds, after consuming products and services, additional funds will remain. These funds will be invested by putting the money into savings at commercial banks.
10. commercial banks
   » Commercial banks receive the additional deposits, for savings, from households. Since the purpose of the bank is to make loans, they will take these additional funds and loan them to firms (businesses), who then invest in products and services, jobs, salaries, and so on, and the cycle continues.

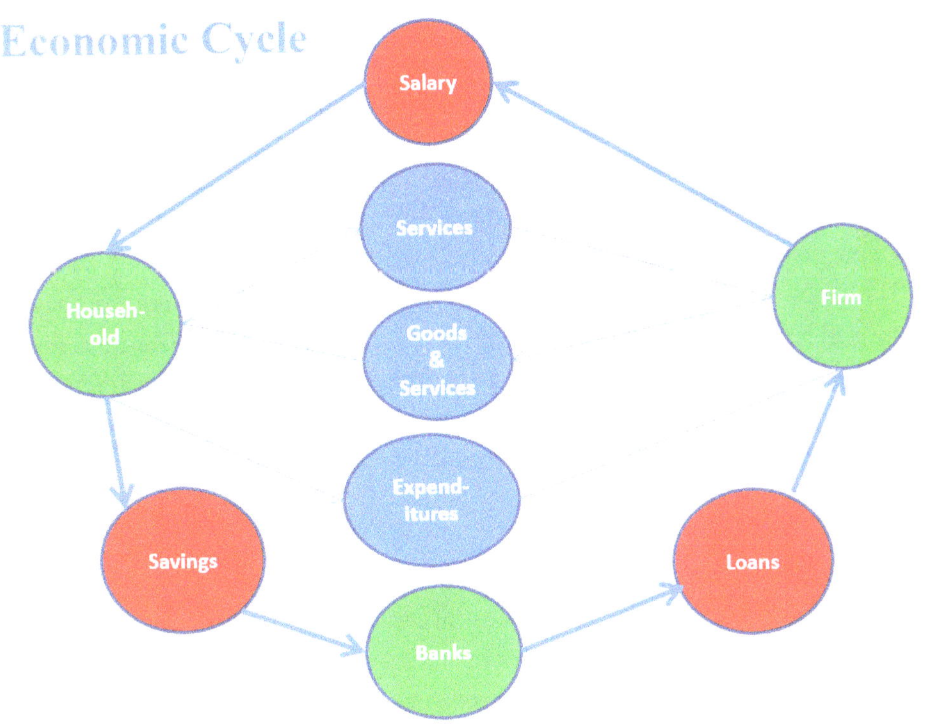

FIGURE 1.1 Economic Cycle

How Banks Make Money

As demonstrated by the economic cycle, a major part of this flow is making loans. Although this is integral to the economy, it must be remembered that commercial banks are corporations. Similar to other businesses, banks are independent enterprises and are accountable to shareholders who invest in them. Therefore, maximizing shareholder value is as important to a bank as it is to a for-profit corporation. So how do banks make money?

Most corporations produce products or services that they sell to generate revenue or sales. Revenue, to a corporation, is their objective and ultimately results in bottom-line net income. For a commercial bank, this is similar, but the products that produce this revenue are different. Commercial banks generate revenue from two sources, **interest income** and **fee income.**

Interest Income

Interest income is generated, predominantly, from making loans. When a bank makes a loan, it charges an interest rate (percentage). This interest rate is affected by activities of the Federal Reserve, which will be discussed in a later chapter, but nevertheless is a percentage of the amount of the loan made, charged annually.

Since the job of commercial banks is to make loans, loans become the primary source of revenue for a bank. Loans represent the largest item on a bank's balance sheet and produce the greatest amount of revenue. In order for a bank to be profitable, their primary product is loans, and therefore, they employ a large staff of commercial lenders to make these loans to firms. The source of the funds used to make loans is from deposits received from households, placed into savings, checking, and time deposit accounts. Commercial banks lend out a large percentage of the deposits they receive.

The deposits banks receive, literally, become their cost of sales. Banks must pay interest to households for the use of the funds, which are used to make loans. This rate of interest is lower than the bank charges for loans to firms. The difference between the interest received on loans and the interest paid on deposits equals the profit that the bank earns. This is called the *net interest margin*. The higher the margin, the more the profit. This is the largest source of revenue and profit for the bank.

Fee Income

Banks also charge various fees for the financial services they perform for firms and households. Although this is relatively small compared with interest income from loans, it nevertheless is another important source of revenue. Unlike interest income, this source of income does not relate to interest, and it is called *noninterest income.*

In general, fee income is generated from three basic categories in the bank (not exhaustive). These include service charges, cash management fees, and wealth management fees:

- service charges: Banks have a wide variety of service charges that are assessed. Although they will be outlined in detail in a later chapter, they include fees for overdrafts, nonsufficient funds, stop payments, minimum balance fees, wire transfers, and many others that relate to the depository accounts, as well as others.
- cash management fees: Banks generate a variety of services that they perform for businesses. These services, in addition to generating fee income, attract large deposits from businesses, a source of funding for loans. These services include lockbox services, automated clearing house, remote deposit capture, controlled disbursement, and others.
- wealth management fees: Commercial banks offer investment management services to consumers and households. This is a relatively large source of income of all the fees. These services include trust management fees, retirement and financial planning fees, and portfolio and investment management fees. Fees are typically assessed as a percentage of the amount of funds under management.

Role of the Bank in the Financial System

Commercial banks provide a number of key functions that are unique among the stakeholders and the economy in general. It is this role they play that sets them apart from other enterprises. This role is most important, and banks are at the center of it. One need only reread the quote earlier in the chapter to understand the magnitude of the role they play and the dynamic facilitation of financial activities that occur as a result.

Primary Purpose

One of the major roles that banks perform is to encourage savings. They perform this role by offering a variety of depository products and providing incentive to the public by way of interest rates paid on these accounts. Along with regular marketing and advertising of these rates, banks attract deposits and help households to save and plan for their future. These funds, as previously outlined, become the source of money for lending. This is credit and is invested in people and firms to allow them to buy homes, pay for college, and other discretionary needs.

Savings growth is a sign that households have additional discretionary funds, due to the availability of jobs, increased salaries, and general prosperity. In the economy this is desirable because it not only increases the funds available for loans but also provides a cushion for households for future expenditures or longer term savings and investments—all good things for society—and banks are at the center of encouraging this. A good example is the piggy bank that young children are given as a way to encourage savings by putting pennies in the bank. This modeling of future behavior helps society in many ways. One such way is the expansion of the **money supply**, or M1 and M2. M1 consists of checking accounts (deposits) and currency in the economy, and M2 adds savings and time deposits. The expansion of the money supply through increased deposits is a positive economic indicator of growth and prosperity.

The expansion of the money supply and the growth of savings provides the foundation for making loans. As outlined in the economic cycle (Figure 1.1), making loans provides the fuel for businesses to grow, which stimulates the economic cycle. However, this is not just to businesses; households also seek loans for homes, automobiles, boats, vacation homes, and so forth. The major role that banks play is to allow people to reasonably improve their way of life, and perpetuate this, through credit. Without this role that banks play, households and businesses alike would have to save the considerable amounts of money necessary to grow and improve their lives, which could take years or not be possible at all. Consider the cost of college education: Without the ability to take out student loans, considerably fewer students would enter college, which would be detrimental to the country.

Other Purposes

Beyond the primary role of commercial banks, they perform other valuable purposes for the economy. These include **payment**, **risk protection**, and **liquidity services**.

- payment: Commercial banks are facilitators of payments. Payment functions include cash, checking accounts, debit cards, ATMs, merchant services, and the like. These important services allow for the exchanges of money for goods and services, which is necessary for daily life. These services and functions permit transactions to occur and streamline this process for businesses and personal consumption. This role is very important to an effective economy, allowing it to function on a day-to-day basis.
- risk protection: As already discussed, a primary role of banks is to encourage savings. As consumers save and invest, these important assets must be secure from theft and loss. Commercial banks offer many services to provide—and, in some cases, virtually guarantee—safety. FDIC insurance protects households from loss of their savings (up to $250,000) in the event that the bank itself fails. This protection provides considerable comfort for bank clients and helps to ease their fears, encouraging them to deposit in the bank as a much safer repository than the home, or anywhere else for that matter. In addition, banks have vaults, safe deposit boxes, and secure accounts that cannot easily be breached by hackers. It is no wonder that commercial banks over the years have physical facades that are substantial, with heavy pillars, and that are classical in appearance to demonstrate both strength and security. Because banks themselves are engaged in risk every day, they understand well how to mitigate that risk, which they pass on to consumers and businesses.

- liquidity services: Another function that is performed by commercial bank is liquidity. Liquidity is the ability to have the cash available to cover current obligations. This is a necessary function for banks and businesses on a day-to-day basis, but also for consumers. Banks provide services such as credit cards, overdrafts, short-term loans, lines of credit, and others. These services provide clients with the necessary cash to satisfy current obligations. In addition, these tools are available for that purpose and are designed to maintain the flow of cash. Cash flow is the lifeblood of the consumer, and also for businesses. At certain times of the year or due to other events, businesses may find themselves short of cash while they await cash inflows from customers. To shore up this deficit, tools such as working capital loans, standby letters of credit, unsecured revolving credit, and others satisfy this need and make it possible for businesses to continue to function without the risk of going out of business.

Size and Categories of Commercial Banks

Now that the role and functions of commercial banks have been established, an understanding of how banks are categorized by size helps to deepen the understanding of the many thousands of banks that exist in the United States.

Banks are independent corporations. Like other corporations, size is an important indicator of the breadth of products, services, and delivery mechanisms that are circulated. Unlike other businesses, however, commercial banks are always measured on the basis of asset size to understand how they are categorized and to understand the limitations of products and services they can sell. Since making loans is the major function banks perform and since loans are assets, they are typically the largest asset on the balance sheet. Therefore, asset size is indicative of the amount of loans being made and is a measure of organic growth for the bank

Asset size is the bottom-line total assets on the balance sheet of a bank. However, merely knowing the amount of assets does not effectively differentiate banks without an understanding of the meaning of this size. Commercial banks are categorized in two forms—functional and regulatory—and then further within those two broad categories.

Functional

Asset size is an important differentiator for understanding the functional type of bank. Three types of banks fall under this broad category: **community banks**, **regional banks**, and **money center banks** (Rose & Hudgins, 2013).

Community Banks

Community banks are the basic form of bank and, in terms of size, are where banks started. Early in the history of the United States, as towns were formed out West or elsewhere, people came together as a community, supporting themselves based upon their needs. These needs typically included grocery stores, hotels, houses of worship, taverns, hardware stores, and post offices—all to support the needs of a community that was limited to the confines of the boundaries of the town. With all of these needs for commerce, banks were also needed to handle the financial needs of the community and almost always were found in every small town. In the early days, and to an extent today, these community banks accepted deposits from the people in that community and made loans to small businesses in the same community. They also performed risk protection services for valuables by providing vaults and other means of secure protection. In short, they served the needs of the community, hence the term "community banks."

Community banks tend to be the smaller banks in regard to assets and today are categorized as having less than $10 billion in assets. Banks in this functional category can range anywhere from less than $500 million up to the $10 billion threshold. As with their predecessors of years past, they still focus on servicing a local community or town. Given the branching laws and electronics today, this can be more expansive than the confines of a single town, but generally is more limited in geographic range. These banks have more limited product lines and offer more personalized services (the latter of which is the appeal for these banks). Clients in a community enjoy the familiarity with the bankers, and this adds to the trust and safety level of the assets they have.

Community banks may also be referred to as **retail banks**. The reason for this is that many of their services are direct to consumers (households) and designed to facilitate those needs. This does not mean they do not work with businesses (they do), but their overall mission may be to service the needs of the consumers. Structurally, community banks have more of a limited organizational structure (i.e., flatter) and are not as deep as some larger banks. This can be a benefit from an employee standpoint, as there typically is closer contact with top management in the organization. Community bankers tend to be more broadly focused, having knowledge of and performing many of the basic banking functions the bank offers, as generalists.

Unfortunately, the smaller sized banks, particularly at the lower end of the range, are definitely more susceptible to market and economic fluctuations. Volatility in the economy and the market can financially impair the banks in these categories and affect their longevity. This also occurs with regulatory changes. These too can be onerous to a smaller entity and put undue strain on the resources they have. Nevertheless, banks of larger sizes and in different categories strive to be called "community banks" simply because this moniker is indicative of a focus on the community, which is valued.

Regional Banks

Regional Banks are the next tier of banks, ranging in size from over $10 billion to $50 billion in assets. Unlike community banks, these banks service a much wider range. This can include a specific region, such as the Midwest, the Northeast, or even a specific group of states. Obviously, as the service area expands, delivery mechanisms, such as electronics, branch expansion, and others, must occur.

Regional banks, since they have more resources, are an acquirer of smaller community banks, to expand their size and footprint. Many of the banks that failed during the financial crisis were acquired by regional banks. Products and services for this category are definitely more expansive, growing beyond loans and deposits. Wealth management, credit cards, investment services, trust services, and others are not unusual for banks of this size range. This expands their revenue sources. They may also be a **correspondent bank** for a smaller bank, providing financial services to the smaller bank that may be beyond their scope.

Finally, regional banks are much more sophisticated in function. Employees tend to be less generalist and more specialist, focusing on specialized areas, such as commercial lending, or retail banking, or operations only, whereas in a community bank a single employee may have knowledge of and perform all of these functions. Organizationally, the internal structure is more complex and deeper, being less flat and more hierarchical. This defines not only the sophistication in products and services but also the specialization needed to perform these duties.

Money Center Banks

The last functional category is money center banks. These represent the largest of all banks in the country and are above $50 billion in assets. Obviously, banks in this category can range well above the $50 billion size, as evidenced by banks such as JPMorgan Chase, which now has more than $3 trillion in assets. Banks in this category are the industry leaders. They are typically located in very large cities, and their span of service ranges from regions to other countries and different continents. They are truly global in scope and provide products and services to many countries, governments, and industries. In addition, they offer a very wide range of services that are highly specialized and, in some cases, tailored to individual needs.

One of the benefits of banks in this category is that they have enormous resources and are very well diversified. As a result, they are generally capable of withstanding many risks and a high degree of economic stability—much more than the smaller banks can.

Finally, organizationally, they are extremely sophisticated, having thousands of employees in very specialized roles. Internal structures are deeply hierarchical, with many business lines and functions to effectively manage a worldwide organization, from a span of control standpoint. These organizations impact the economy and the broader global economy.

Regulatory

The other important category of banks also relates to the size of the bank (asset size) but for different reasons. There are three types of banks in this category, all of which relate to the relative risk the bank presents to the economy in the United States and to the world at large. After the financial crisis of 2008 and beyond, much focus was directed to banks that were considered "too big to fail." In general, these banks were classified this way because they controlled a vast amount of the financial resources in the country. Should the bank fail, it could create a significant impairment to the economy and thus trigger another financial crisis of the magnitude experienced in 2008.

To avoid this, banks have now been categorized into three designations that cover the country and the world at large. These designations include **systemically important financial institutions (SIFIs), domestically systemically important banks (D-SIBs)**, and **globally systemically important banks (G-SIBs)**.

Systemically Important Financial Institutions (SIFIs)

During the financial crisis, due to the strains on the banking system, attention was focused on the biggest banks that actually had difficulty during this time. Citibank and Bank of America, in particular, had challenges and were at risk during this period of time, especially with the collapse of Lehman Brothers and Bear Stearns, among others. The Dodd-Frank Wall Street Reform and Protection Act of 2009 (FinReg) addressed the concept of "too big to fail" by prohibiting its application to big banks for abusive practices. The concept of "too big to fail" was focused on making sure that the biggest banks in the country would not go out of business (fail), which in itself could put the economy at risk due to the amount of resources they manage and control. As part of the regulations that resulted and in an effort to prevent this, the largest banks were required to pass stringent stress tests to make sure they had sufficient capital to continue lending to businesses in the event of a significant economic downturn.

According to the Basel Accord (discussed in detail later), banks must hold an adequate amount of capital to prevent failure. Failure can occur when businesses can no longer make payments on their loans, due to loss in earnings, which would cause banks to take losses due to write-offs. When loans are written off, they are considered expenses to the bank and reduce the overall net income. If this results in a loss (negative amount), retained earnings will be negative, which will reduce common stock equity, or capital of the enterprise. When this occurs, the bank's capital ratios will drop and may not be in compliance with regulations. If this occurs, the bank must immediately obtain funding externally to bring this back into compliance. If this does not occur, the bank will ultimately be closed by the regulators; in short, it will fail.

Because the biggest banks in the country were the ones causing the most concern, the regulators identified thresholds from which banks were designated as "statistical important" and deemed significant in that they had the most potential to impair the economy or create a financial crisis. For this designation, the original threshold was $50 billion in assets. Any bank at or above that size fell within this definition and was therefore subject to additional scrutiny, including stress tests. Over the years, and within the most recent administration, amendments were made to this threshold due to the impact on banks more toward the lower end of the threshold. The concern was that the additional requirements to banks toward the lower end of the range may put undue stress on them and actually put them at risk of failure. As a result, the threshold was increased to $100 billion and then increased to $250 billion after a phase-in period of 18 months from the passage of this amendment in 2018. Ultimately, this changed the number of banks qualifying for SIFI status from 29 to 21 and finally to approximately 11, as it stands today. Banks such as JPMorgan Chase, Bank of America, Citibank, Wells Fargo, Morgan Stanley, and so on would all continue to be deemed SIFI banks and subject to the annual stress tests. Annual stress tests subject these banks to "adverse" and "extremely adverse" economic questions to determine whether they can still meet regulatory capital requirements, liquidity, and other measures and continue to function, lending money. In addition to annual stress tests, these institutions are subject to incremental increases in Tier 1 and Tier 2 capital requirements for compliance.

Domestically Systemically Important Banks (D-SIBs)

Somewhat different than SIFI designated banks, D-SIBs are identified differently and not necessarily by asset size. D-SIBs include broader financial institutions, such as insurance firms and payment firms (e.g., American Express). Unlike SIFI banks, D-SIBs are identified by a national regulator. Typically, this would be from the Office of the Comptroller of the Currency who regulates the largest banks that hold national charters. These organizations are identified as having "domestic" systemic importance, or within the country, such as the United States.

Even though D-SIB designated banks typically would be SIFI banks, they do not have to be. Based upon the regulator's determination, a smaller bank could be given this status based upon their clientele, the markets they serve, or their impact on certain segments of the economy. Therefore, this is more of a subjective designation. Similar to SIFI banks, however, they are subjected to stringent annual stress tests to assess their resilience. The list of these organizations were in the range of 19 entities, not all of which were banks, but subject to adjustment based upon regulatory determination.

Globally Systemically Important Banks (G-SIBs)

The final regulatory category is similar to D-SIBs and is referred to as G-SIBs. Globally systemically important banks expand beyond the country boundaries and stretch around the world. Each country participating is responsible for identifying institutions within their country that would qualify (similar to how D-SIBs are selected). Once identified, they are combined with other countries' selections to form the full G-SIB. In addition to being held to higher capital requirements for compliance, they are also subjected to annual stress tests.

The primary reason for this regulatory category is the recognition that we live in a global economic environment and that the impairment of banks in other parts of the world can have a significant impact on the world economy. For this reason, the number of organizations is higher than either SIFIs or D-SIBs, reaching 30 entities. In addition, like D-SIBs, these include banks, insurance firms, and other financial entities that are determined to be important. Organizations such as JPMorgan Chase, Bank of China, Barclays, Credit Suisse, Deutsche Bank, Mitsubishi, Santander, and so on are examples of those included.

Overall, these categories and subcategories help to identify and define what banks do and how they impact the economy. This renewed attention requires continual diligence to ensure and guard against the challenges experienced during the financial crisis to, hopefully, prevent this from happening again.

CHAPTER SUMMARY

Commercial banks are more than just financial businesses. Although they perform a number of important services on behalf of customers, they exist for a higher reason, which is part and parcel to the economy. All businesses play a role in the economy, but there are none as central to the functioning of the economy as commercial banks in its intermediary role of facilitating the movement of money. The primary objective of this chapter has been to establish the important role that commercial banks play in the economy. Students should be able to understand the economic cycle and the flow of money to and from businesses and consumers and why this is needed. Commercial banks are critical to a well-functioning economy, predominantly due to the loan function they perform. Aside from the economic focus, an understanding of the different types of banks, functional and regulatory, is necessary to define the breadth and scope of services performed as well as the supervisory attention garnered. Overall, a basic understanding of commercial banks is the goal of this chapter and is used as the foundation for deeper analysis.

END OF CHAPTER QUESTIONS

1. Identify the three economic functions commercial banks perform.
2. Name the two attributes that make a commercial bank a bank.
3. Who are the three stakeholders in the economic cycle?
4. Outline the primary way in which commercial banks make money.
5. Differentiate between interest and fee income.
6. Name the three functional categories of banks and what they do.
7. Identify the three regulatory classifications of commercial banks and how they are different.

CHAPTER 2

Structure of Commercial Banks

Commercial banks have evolved in structure over the years, from mammoth classical edifices to virtual banks. Nevertheless, there remains much confusion on how banks are structured and organized. There is a tendency, today and in the recent past, to lump commercial banks and investment banks in the same category. This is just one example of some of the confusion, but an important one, as the average person regards them all as "banks," which could not be further from the truth.

The purpose of this chapter is to clarify what commercial banks are, what they are not, and how they are identified. Although many different designations are identified in this chapter, the first point of clarity is the distinction between commercial banks and investment banks. Commercial banks are not investment banks, although a commercial bank may own an investment bank. Historically, investment banks are, for the most part, Wall Street. These are organizations such as Bear Stearns, Goldman Sachs, Lehmann Brothers, and so forth. Their primary function is buying and selling securities, managing portfolios of investments, private equity, and performing third-party merger and acquisition activities. The most significant difference between an investment bank and a commercial bank is that investment banks do not have customer deposits or make loans, which, as defined in Chapter 1, is the definition of a commercial bank. Commercial banks are characterized as "Main Street" in contrast to "Wall Street." This distinction defines the "community" aspect

Key Terms

Charter	Virtual bank
Member bank	Channels
Unit banks	Call center
Branch bank	ATM
Bank holding company	Executive committee
Financial holding company (FHC)	Risk committee
	Asset liability committee
Electronic banking	Credit committee

Learning Objectives

By the end of this chapter, the student will:

- Understand the legal structures of banks and their meaning.
- Know the physical structural distinctions of commercial banks and their evolution.
- Define the primary channels for delivering services from commercial banks.
- Understand the internal committee structure and their purposes within banks.

of commercial banks: working with consumers and businesses in the community, taking in deposits, and making loans.

Now that these differences have been established, the remainder of this chapter will focus on commercial banks, their legal structure, physical structure, and their delivery structure as well as internal structures within a bank.

Structure and Organization of Commercial Banks

The look and feel of commercial banks can be relatively complex. There are many terms that are in the news or you have heard about through conversations that help to identify a bank, not only physically but also through other broader terms that may be more nebulous. This section will help to demystify some of these general descriptors and provide you with the nomenclature important for commercial banks.

Commercial banks can be categorized within two broad headings. These are outlined below, along with the subheadings that will be outlined in more detail in the following pages.

- legal structure
    - insured banks
    - state chartered banks
    - nationally chartered banks
    - member banks
- physical structure
    - unit banks
    - branch banks
    - holding companies
    - electronic banks

Legal Structure

The legal structure of commercial banks is generally defined by legal authority that allows the commercial bank to operate and conduct business as well as to be affiliated with the key government agencies necessary for operation. Within this structure there are four key items to understand:

- chartering
- deposit insurance
- Federal Reserve membership
- national and state charters

Chartering

Banks must apply for and receive a **charter** that allows them to legally operate as a commercial bank. Principals of a potential bank must apply for a bank charter from the governing agency or structure. Two types of charters exist, national charters and state charters:

- national charters: The National Currency and Bank Act of 1863 was enacted to provide for the chartering of new national banks. This law also created the Office of the Comptroller of the Currency (OCC), which is the agency that is responsible for assessing the need for charters and providing them for new national banks. Additionally, the OCC regulates these national banks. Generally, the largest banks are usually nationally chartered and supervised by the OCC.
- state charters: Regional and smaller community banks generally receive their charter to operate from the state in which they reside. Each state in the United States has the authority to provide these charters to banks. Of the total number of banks in the United States, the vast majority are state charted institutions. In addition to chartering, the states also perform a supervisory role of these banks as part of the regulatory oversight.

Deposit Insurance

In 1933 President Franklin Roosevelt signed into law the Banking Act, known as Glass-Stegall. In addition to other aspects of this law, which will be explained later, the act created the Federal Deposit Insurance Corporation (FDIC), a government agency. This agency, in addition to performing supervisory services for most of the commercial banks in the country, provides insurance to depositors in the event the bank should fail. During the Great depression in the early 1930s, many banks failed, and customers literally lost their savings that they had in these banks. To prevent this from happening again, the FDIC provides insurance coverage to depositors. Initially, in 1933, this was $2,500, which grew to $100,000 and then to $250,000 during the financial crisis of 2008. For the most part, most of the commercial banks in the country are insured by the FDIC. Banks must purchase this insurance and pay an annual premium to offer this coverage.

FIGURE 2.1 FDIC Official Sign

This is shown on signage near the bank's entrance (see Figure 2.1). Most customers seek this coverage when contemplating a banking relationship. Nevertheless, this is optional. Banks do not have to be insured; however, without it they likely will not get the customer deposits they need to operate. Therefore, this becomes another layer of membership that defines most of the banks in the United States.

Member Banks

The last area under the legal structure is membership with the Federal Reserve bank. The Federal Reserve (Fed) is the central bank for the United States. The Federal Reserve provides many services to commercial banks beyond monetary policy and supervisory services. Although these will be discussed more fully in Chapter 4, eligibility for these services requires membership with the Federal Reserve. Most commercial banks are members of the Fed. As a practical matter, all nationally chartered commercial banks are required to be members of the Federal Reserve system. State chartered banks are not required to be members, but many become members. State chartered banks applying for membership must meet several requirements, including a CAMELS rating of 1 or 2, profitability, capital adequacy, and satisfactory CRA ratings to expedite the application. Once approved they become members of the Federal Reserve district to which they geographically belong.

Membership requires the purchase of capital stock (equity) in the Fed, holding 6% of the bank's paid-in capital and surplus, with half of this (3%) paid and the rest on call. Member banks will receive a 6% dividend annually on the stock. Although they receive stock in the Fed, this does not allow them to control any of the activities of the Federal Reserve. This permits the bank to indicate that they are a **member bank** in the Federal Reserve and can avail themselves of these services, such as Fedwire (wire transfers), Automated Clearinghouse (ACH), and so on.

Physical Structure

Commercial banks take many forms that may not be obvious to the casual viewer or even the bank's customer. Physically, banks are obvious, as they are distinctive in design, signage, and location. However, understanding the nuances of what one is looking at is an important requirement for truly understanding commercial banks. Today, there are approximately 5,000 banks in the United States. These are independently chartered institutions (down from approximately 7,800 in 2002, which has been the pattern of consolidation in the recent past). This section will help the student to understand what this means and to help differentiate the various aspects of the generic term "bank."

Physical structure is somewhat a misnomer. Some of the types discussed are hardly physical but may be virtual, or even a financial structure. Nevertheless, these distinctions are important for understanding commercial banks. Four distinct areas are important for discussion:

- unit banks
- branch banks
- holding companies
- electronic, or virtual, banks

Unit Banks

Unit banks are one of the oldest kinds of banks. These banks are a single location, physical structure, and have no other locations affiliated with it. Earlier in the 20th century and prior to this, most commercial bank were unit banks. To help to envision this, the banks that were robbed by the likes of Butch Cassidy and the Sundance Kid and Bonnie and Clyde were unit banks, as they proliferated throughout the country.

Since they are one of the oldest types, they generally were very distinctive in their façade. One cannot miss unit banks, as their physical buildings still exist. Most are imposing facades with classical pillars, and a very solid, stable presence is conveyed. This is by design, as bankers want to convey to customers that the bank is a safe, solid, and prosperous stronghold to store their money. This helps to provide confidence and trust in the bank. Today, many of these old unit banks are no longer commercial banks but have been relegated to antique shops in some of the smaller towns.

What is unique about a unit bank is that literally all their products and services are offered through a single office. Although these structures may have an attached drive-up, or even an ATM in the lobby vestibule or drive-up, they are a single physical unit. Many new banks, or *de novo banks*, which are newly chartered banks, begin as unit banks. This is the origin of the community bank. These banks were prominent in the local community and were typically positioned on the main street of the town where customers and businesses could easily access them. Customers within a community generally prefer this structure, as the employees of the bank get to know their customers and there is a sense of trust and comfort with the staff, along with a sense of community. Today, many of the unit banks of the past do not exist, given the changes in banking laws over recent years. However, remnants of this will be seen as you travel through small towns across the country. As will be shown, unit banks have evolved over time, and the remaining types in this section will demonstrate that phenomenon. Unit banks have relatively simple and flat organizational structures, generally, all within the confines of a solitary entity, as demonstrated below.

FIGURE 2.2 Unit Bank Example

Branch Banks

As discussed, unit banks fulfilled a specific purpose: to have a physical location within a town, servicing the financial needs of the town. In short, they did not service customers outside of the boundaries of the community or town. This was somewhat limiting as banks sought to grow and attract deposits. Since deposits represent the source of funds for loans, this became an important driver of expansion. Commercial banks then began to build branch structures in neighboring towns or other remote locations to provide easier access for people in the locations rather than requiring them to come into the town. So, in a sense, branch banks became a strategy to help attract deposits.

Branch banks, then, are physical offices that may only offer limited services and not all of those that are offered at the main bank. Additionally, branch banks are part of the same charter as the main bank, so they are not counted as a bank, but only as an extension of the main bank in town.

From an organizational standpoint, bank branches may have a branch manager, tellers, a personal banker or two, and possibly an office for business banking. Employees will report up to the bank organizational structure.

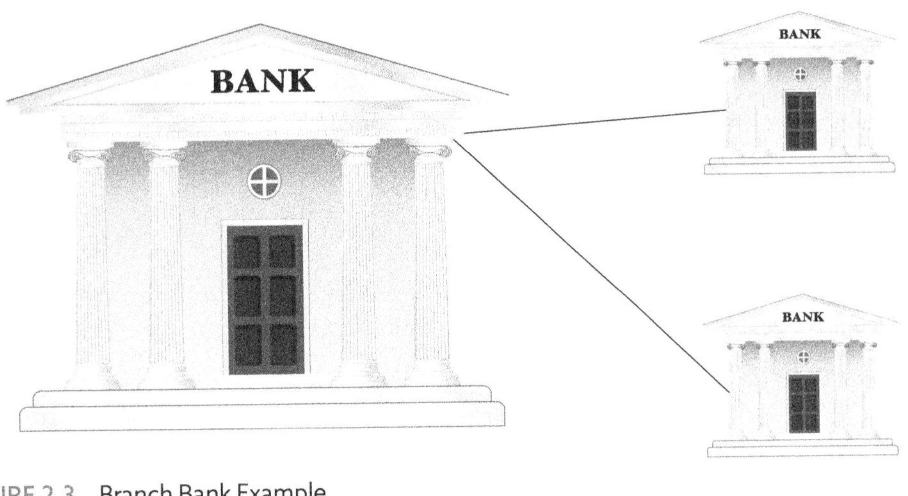

FIGURE 2.3 Branch Bank Example

Branch banking is regulated by state law. Originally, some states were considered *unit-bank states*—that is, only unit banks were permitted with no branching ability. Illinois is a good example of this, as the state remained a unit-bank state until the 1980s, and that is the reason for the large number of chartered banks within the state. Once state laws changed, banks were permitted to open branches within the state and/or within certain proximity to the main bank. This change in legislation began to change the reach of unit banks, which allowed them to grow much quicker. As of 2018 there were 77,647 branches in the United States. When compared to the number of chartered banks in the United States at approximately 5,000, this indicates that, on average, there are about 15.5 branches per chartered bank. Although this is a large number of branches, their numbers have been declining over the years. Since 2010 branches have declined by 3,537. This, in part, is due to some of the bank failures that occurred during the financial crisis of 2008, as well as due to growth of technology and electronic access to banks. It is anticipated that this trend will continue.

Another important change that resulted in the proliferation of branches was the passage of the Riegle-Neal Interstate Branch Banking Law of 1994. This law, for the first time, permitted banks to open branches outside of state boundaries, thus allowing for greater competition and growth and the creation of some of the largest banks that have been seen in this country, with assets over $3 trillion. Growth in overall branches since the passage of Riegle-Neal has been about 50%. This law had a tremendous impact on the proliferation of branches while, at the same time, chartered banks were declining in number due to acquisitions and other factors.

Holding Companies

As banks continued to grow and expand their branch networks and as regulations changed that allowed banks to offer more expanded services, the concept of **bank holding**

companies evolved. In 1956 the Bank Holding Company Act defined this concept as "any company that has control over a bank" (Bank Holding Company Act, 1956). Holding companies are corporations that are chartered for the purpose of holding stock in one or more banks or other businesses. The holding company itself is a corporation and not a commercial bank. Their role is that of a parent company that owns banks and other businesses: They do not run the banks that they own but influence management and policy formulation governing the banks. This structure has allowed corporations to diversify and provide centralized services that help affiliate banks to operate much more efficiently.

Over the recent past, holding companies have grown in popularity. In part the reasons for this include:

- better access to capital markets to raise funds for further acquisition and growth as well as major projects
- tax advantages
- ability to use higher leverage
- ability to expand into businesses outside banking

Obviously, the last item is the most expansive and allows these corporations to be more competitive in the industry. Today, there are many organizations that are holding companies. These can either be multibank or single bank holding companies. Multibank holding companies hold stock in several affiliate banks that are independently chartered but are owned by the holding companies. Some of the largest entities fall into this category.

The original Bank Holding Company Act of 1956 prohibited bank holding companies from owning insurance companies. In 1999 the Gramm-Leach-Bliely Act changed this when it was signed into law by President Bill Clinton. This law not only repealed the Glass-Stegall Act of 1933 but also defined a new type of holding company, called a **financial holding company (FHC).** This special type of holding company allows holding companies to offer a broader range of services, including:

- dealing in and underwriting securities
  - » Glass-Stegall prohibited banks from being involved with investment banking activities. However, with this act, holding companies are now able to offer these services within this structure.
- selling and underwriting insurance
  - » Insurance organizations are also considered financial institutions and provide another means of income by way of insurance premiums, which can provide greater income and funding to help holding companies and, in turn, the banks owned by them.

Within the structure of a financial holding company, affiliates maintain their own capital, have their own management teams, and manage their own profit and loss results.

They benefit from protection against losses, however, as the holding company itself can provide support as needed. One of the major results of bank holding companies and financial holding companies was consolidation in the industry. This allowed bank holding companies to purchase commercial banks and roll them into the family as separately chartered institutions or merge them into the single bank that the bank corporation owns. Nevertheless, the concept changed the overall footprint of banks in the United States.

Organizationally, holding companies are structured such that the corporation has its own board of directors and chief executive officer, and each affiliate bank would have its own board of directors and chief executive officer as well. The structure is more complex and hierarchical, dependent upon how large and diverse the entity is (see Figure 2.4).

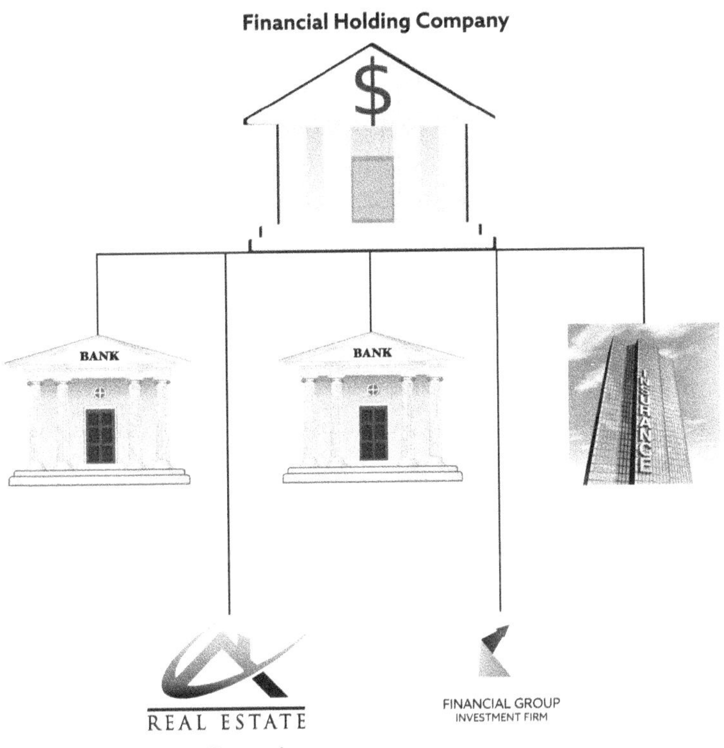

FIGURE 2.4 Holding Company Example

Electronic/Virtual Banks

The look and feel of commercial banks have evolved considerably over the years, but not as much as has occurred with the evolution of technology and electronics. Within the realm of electronics, most banks have taken advantage of the advancements that have been made in the recent past, and these are now well integrated into the fabric of commercial banking. Whereas in the past clients had to physically visit a bank branch or main location to conduct banking business, now many of these services are offered in a variety of electronic means. **Electronic banking** involves several different types, and the following are among the most common:

- automated teller machines (ATMs): These devices have proliferated over the past 4 decades. Originally designed to dispense cash rather than physically going to a teller, they have evolved to taking deposits, making payments, completing loan applications, and real-time interactive banking.
- point-of-sale terminals (merchant banking): Business clients selling retail products can obtain terminals from banks to allows debit/credit card purchases at their stores. These machines are integrated with the bank's systems and network, allowing for automated payment processing and deposit into business accounts.
- call center banking: Call centers have evolved over the years and allow a wide variety of banking services over the telephone.
- remote deposit capture: In the past, business merchants had to deposit physical checks received at their banks through drop boxes. Remote deposit capture provides an image capture device that allows the merchant to scan and send checks to the bank electronically.
- online banking: The internet has created the opportunity whereby many of the bank's services can be performed by visiting the bank's website.

Electronic banking expands the window for conducting bank transactions. Instead of worrying about getting to the bank before it closes, customers can perform transactions when it is convenient for them. The utilization of electronics allows the bank to expand its reach without having to deploy physical branches, thus enabling the opportunity to attract and retain deposits and customers.

With the advent of the various electronics outlined, a new concept evolved several years ago, identified as a **virtual bank**. Virtual banks are institutions that have no physical structure (offices or branches) but offer bank products and services mostly online through the electronic means described above. Although virtual banks have been around over the last three decades, their acceptance in the marketplace can be challenging. One major benefit of a virtual bank is efficiency. Since they do not have to contend with the costs of building and maintaining branches, which is a major part of noninterest expense, they can be more competitive on pricing loan and deposit products, among other services. Although this is positive, clients—particularly, older clients—tend to want to physically meet with bank employees in a bank environment. Another challenge is that without the physical edifice, some clients view this as a lack of strength and security, two very important requirements of successful banks.

Today, virtual banks have rebounded, as clients also are more tech savvy and price conscious. Since many of these clients seldom enter a bank, the need for the physical structure becomes moot. Furthermore, the younger generation has grown up with the technology and utilize it very effectively without the need to physically visit a bank. As more and more services become available electronically, virtual banks may further proliferate. A good example of this is fintech companies that have grown recently that provide many of these services electronically and without the need for a physical presence. Although fintechs have not yet obtained bank charters, the likelihood of this occurring soon is high.

Delivery of Bank Products and Services

As was referenced in the electronic banking section, these mechanisms have helped to expand how products and services are delivered to clients. Mechanisms for product and service delivery are known as **channels**, or conduits of bank activities. Channels not only deliver products but also provide information, resolve issues, impart financial advice, and process transactions for bank clients.

Delivery channels fall within five broad categories, some of which are more traditional:

- branch
- telephone
- internet
- mobile
- ATM

Bank Channels

Each of the bank channels identified above provides the avenues of access to the bank. An illustration of these channels is shown below and represents the myriad of ways that a client can access the bank. It is extremely important that commercial banks offer all these channels in today's banking environment; to offer anything less or the full range of channels would be deemed a "limited" service bank. In addition, maintaining the continual accessibility of the channels is critical to retaining customers. Today's bank client desires anytime access to their information. Continual downtime or other inaccessibility would cause bank customers to potentially leave the bank.

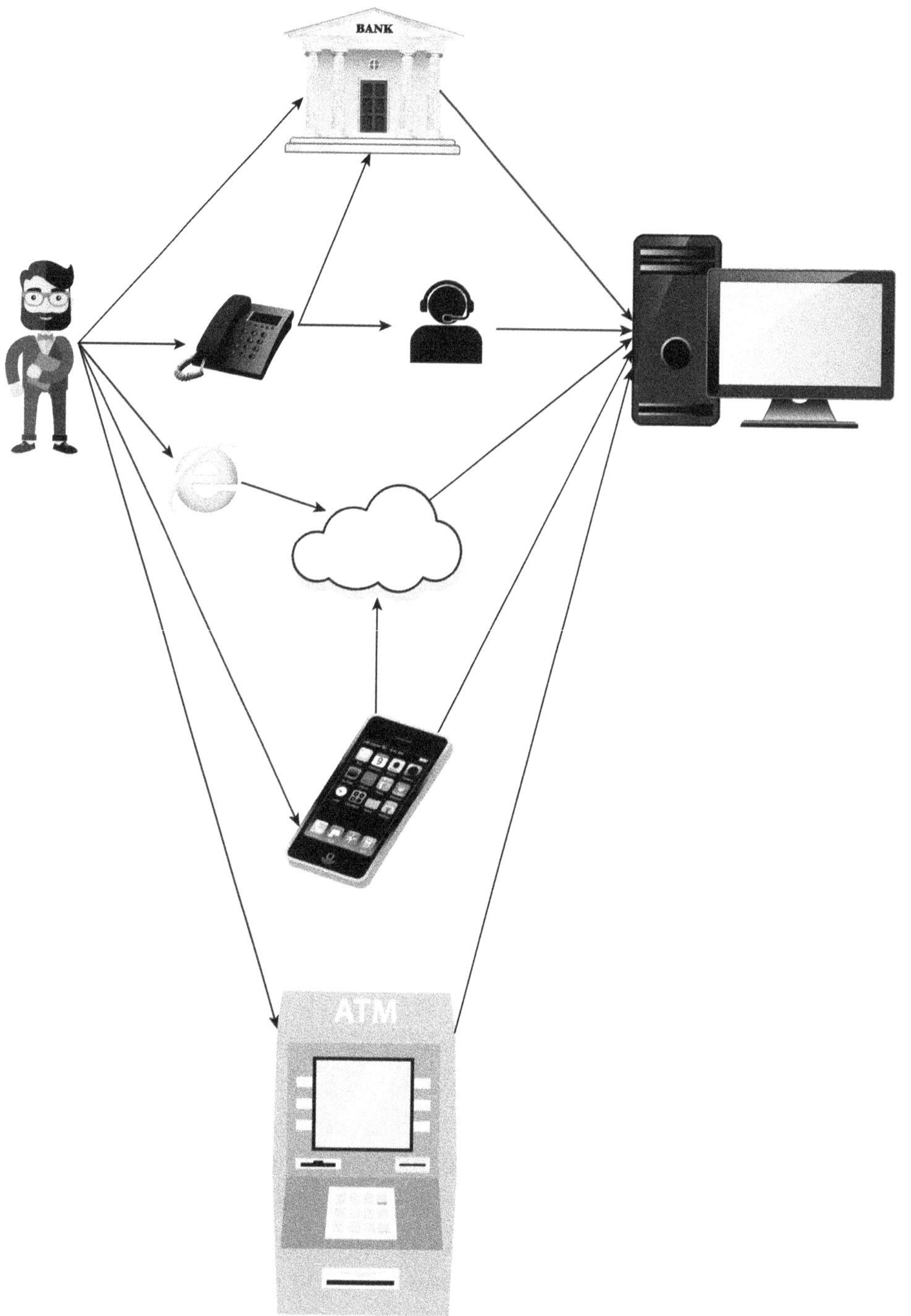

FIGURE 2.5 Bank Delivery Channel Illustration

Branch

The first delivery channel illustrated is the physical branch. This is, by far, the most traditional of the banking channels. Clients would visit the bank or branch and talk face to face with a banker to conduct business. In addition, clients could use the drive-thru facility at the bank or branch as well, which is still a physical interaction. Although this delivery channel is diminishing in volume, it nevertheles remains. Within the next 5–10 years, however, many physical branches will be eliminated in lieu of more electronic access. Obviously, this mode of delivery is subject to hours of operation; therefore, it is more limited than the others. Within the branch, tellers and personal bankers are the usual residents. Business bankers, wealth management representatives, and other client-contact individuals may also be available.

Telephone

Telephone usage to conduct business has been in existence for over 100 years and continues, to this day, as a viable channel to conduct business. As a bank channel, the telephone provides direct access to bank personnel without having to physically visit the bank or branch location. Although generally a traditional channel, if one simply contacts the bank to speak to bank personnel, this is similar to the branch channel. The reason for this is that this channel is limited to hours of operation to speak with someone and is therefore somewhat limiting. In addition, dependent upon the need, this may necessitate visiting the branch anyway to sign documents or deliver or receive funds.

Call Center

Although the telephone continues to be a traditional bank channel, what is newer that utilizes this channel is the **call center**. Call centers are, as the name implies, a central point or points where calls are directed to conduct bank business. These centers are centrally located and may be geographically placed to take advantage of time zones. The centers can consist of a handful of call representatives to hundreds of representatives. The primary benefit of the call center is generally 24/7 access. Dependent upon the size of the bank, 24/7 access may be with live representatives utilizing multiple centers at various time zones or electronic access afterhours. Most call centers have interactive voice response (IVR) systems (sometimes called VRUs or voice response systems) to handle client access for automated 24/7 access. These systems direct the calls via an "auto attendant," which asks the client various questions and, upon selection of the number, directs the caller to the area of service desired. Automated systems like these provide a wide range of services and these are growing in sophistication today. Loan applications, in some cases, can be taken through this automated system. Although one can speak to a live agent in most cases, the growing demand for and sophistication of the automation make this a very viable bank delivery channel.

Internet

The advent of the internet and the personal computer has revolutionized many organizations, including banks. This is a very sophisticated, self-activated channel for clients to conduct banking business. This is accomplished through online banking. The internet provides the vehicle for online access to account information, products, and services at the fingertips of the user. Since most customers today have laptop and desktop computers, tablets, and mobile phones, online banking becomes a very easy means of conducting bank business.

All banks have websites today, and these sites provide a wealth of products and services for the client to access using their internet connection. Online banking, via the internet, is one of the most viable channels that clients access. As a result of online banking, the amount of customer traffic and bank branches has diminished significantly. Some of the primary information and services that are available through online banking are outlined below.

- account information
  - » Clients can log in and view the status of their checking, savings, time deposits, and investments that they may have with the bank.
- transactions
  - » Transfer of money between accounts can occur easily at the push of a button.
- bill payment
  - » Clients can set up automated bill payment, which, once established, will automatically produce payments to recurring invoices (e.g., utilities, mortgage or rent payments, loan payments, auto payments, etc.). This is an excellent service and is accomplished through automated clearing house (ACH) transactions or through physical check generation and mailing.
- payments
  - » Payment for loans with the bank can be made through online banking.
- loan applications
  - » Applications for loans can be made online, in some cases, to be evaluated for approval.
- bank information
  - » Financial statements, earnings releases, annual reports, bank management, and news about the bank are all available online.
- products and services
  - » The breadth of products and services that the bank offers are all readily available on the bank website to evaluate and consider utilization.

Mobile Banking

One of the latest arrivals on the scene, as a bank channel, is mobile banking. Mobile banking takes advantage of both the cellular network services and the internet. Although this is the case, it has unique capabilities, which is the reason it has grown tremendously in popularity. Using a smartphone, clients can access the bank's website, like they would be using their computer, but generally, the mobile phone is used for unique services, which are described further on. The main advantage of this channel is the mobility feature. Smartphones are easy to use; they are always accessible and generally with you. This allows one to truly take advantage of the benefits of this mode of delivery. In addition to the services that can be performed using online banking, some of the more unique features of this capability are described below.

- remote deposit
  - Using the smartphone and the mobile app, clients can take a picture of the front and back of a check and deposit it without having to go anywhere.
- alerts
  - Mobile banking can be set up to alert the client if a balance on a checking account (or other account) is nearing zero or running the risk of overdrawing. Other alerts can be established as well.
- payments
  - Payments can be made to outstanding loans.
- purchases
  - Purchases can be made by swiping the phone through a scanner.
- pay bills
  - Customers can direct the payment of recurring or ad-hoc bills directly using the phone.
- person-to-person payments
  - Individuals can take advantage of Venmo or Zelle for person-to-person payments.

ATM

ATMs, or automated teller machines, are another channel of delivery. This delivery channel does require travelling physically to a branch, drive-up, or to another remote location to access the device. So, to some degree, this is somewhat traditional in that a physical visit is required. However, when it first arrived, it was a revolutionary channel because it is totally self-activated and does not require a live attendant. The objective of ATMs, at the onset, was to reduce the amount of traffic in the lobby of a bank, which, in fact, it has accomplished. Today, traffic within branches, particularly tellers' lines, is at an absolute minimum. Banks must belong to the networks that transmit the transactions back to the bank, which also provide for expanded services of ATMs. As a result of this, a significant benefit of ATMs is their availability throughout the world. Rather than having to carry a fair amount of cash with oneself, ATMs are strategically placed, making them very convenient to access, such that cash can be obtained easily, when needed.

Originally, banks did not charge for this service. However, several years ago the laws changed, permitting banks to surcharge for usage by a noncustomer of the bank at their "owned" ATMs. These costs have helped banks to offset the significant costs of these devices and the interchange fees required to process transactions. Also, banks can join broader networks, allowing customers a wider range of ATM availability, and these become selling points for attracting bank clients.

In addition to sources of cash, deposits can be made to ATMs, and loan payments can be made as well. ATMs are placed within bank lobbies, in their vestibules, at drive-up locations, in gas stations, in convenient stores, in grocery stores, and a wide variety of other locations. This makes ATMs a very versatile and much used delivery channel for bank customers.

Internal Bank Structure

The internal structure of commercial banking is extensive and involves a number of areas. For students who are planning to enter the profession but are uncertain what to consider, almost any discipline that exists outside of banking can be found within the banking industry. Banks are corporations and they involve a wide variety of disciplines that one can enter, rotate to, and remain in all throughout their career. Commercial banks generate revenue and must sell products and services to achieve the desired level of revenue. Simplistically, bank functions can be divided between sales, support, and administration. The following pages provides a high-level overview of the various departments and functions as well as key positions in a bank in order to orient students to their internal structure and roles.

Sales

The sales functions within a bank involve selling the products and services that the bank offers. These products and services will fall into commercial, retail, and wealth sales, in general. Their function, the primary roles and responsibilities, consist of the following.

Commercial

The commercial sales area of a bank is focused on business banking needs. This can be small, medium, and large businesses, depending upon the size of the bank. A commercial sales position is predominantly focused on making loans to businesses; however, generating deposits and cross-selling to other services is very important. The following are the key roles and responsibilities, at a high level, for these positions.

- chief lending officer: This is the most senior officer in this area, responsible for all commercial activities. This is also an executive-level position and would be a part of the executive committee of the bank. This position is filled from experienced business bankers, with a number of years' experience and results. Although many people report to this position, it is not the largest in the bank. However, the amount of financial resources that are controlled by this role are the largest in the bank.
- commercial lender/relationship manager: This position is responsible for making commercial loans to businesses. Their objective is not only to generate interest income from making the loan but also to build relationships with the entity to guide them to other services that the bank offers. Commercial lenders usually have a portfolio of accounts (customers) whom they work with and are in continual communication. They make physical calls on the business, meaning they visit the headquarters of the business and meet with key executives to uncover banking needs and learn about the business. For this reason, individuals in this position are in the field, by design, rather than in the office. Golfing, dinner engagements, entertainment events, luncheons, and other activities are the province of the commercial lender. Commercial lending is highly competitive, and individuals in these roles must be well versed in understanding and reading the economy and must be knowledgeable of finance and accounting. Preparatory to this role, lenders spend time as credit analysts to learn how to analyze business credits before they are charged with a portfolio. The size of a commercial lender's portfolio may not be a large number of clients; however, the amount of money that is managed is sizeable within each portfolio.
- cash (treasury) managers: Another sales function in the commercial area that is not focused on making loans is the cash manager, now called treasury managers. The focus of this position is still sales to businesses, but their objective is to obtain deposits and generate fee income. Although they work closely with commercial lenders and may accompany a commercial lender on a call with an existing client, their objective is different. Generating deposits for the bank is critical for the lending force, as this is the source of funds for loans. Since businesses have the ability to maintain very large deposits, they are very attractive to the bank. Another objective of this role is to generate noninterest or fee income. This is accomplished by selling a variety of services to the business client for a defined fee. These services include lockbox services, remote deposit capture, ACH, merchant card services, wire transfer services, cash vault services and many more. These services are outlined in detail in Chapter 10 of this text.
- credit analysts: Credit analysts are generally entry-level roles, preparatory for careers in commercial lending. Their primary role is to complete credit analyses on potential business clients for presentation to the credit committee. The skills required in this role are rather

heavy in the accounting and finance disciplines. The reason for this is that credit analysts will review the company's financial statements, complete a ratio analysis and a cash flow analysis, review tax information, and potentially join in on a call to the potential client. The analyses they perform will result in the preparation of a loan package for presentation to the credit committee. Although this can be an entry-level role, a number of banks have now recognized that some individuals are very adept at performing these credit analyses, and therefore, this can become a permanent role with a path toward credit management.

Retail

Retail banking involves the largest volume of clients for a bank. Rather than a focus on businesses, the focus in this area is the individual consumer. Positions within the retail area work with a wide range and volume of clients. The focus of retail banking is generating deposits, generating fee income, and building household relationships. Although there can be many roles in the retail area, some of the primary roles are defined below.

- chief retail officer: This is a newer title. This could also be called the chief deposit officer. This position is the executive or C-level officer that is the head of all retail activities in the bank. This employee would likely report to the CEO and would be a member of the executive committee. The chief retail officer is responsible for the largest number of employees in the bank. Ultimately, this position is responsible for branches and branch activities, tellers, personal bankers, consumer lending, mortgage lending, call center (customer services), and other services offered directly to consumers.
- branch manager: Retail staff are housed in the main bank location as well as at all branches. Usually, there is a branch manager who is responsible for the staff at the branch appointed. This is a management position; however, the branch manager is also a banker and will have a portfolio of customers that they work with.
- personal banker: Personal bankers are individuals responsible for opening accounts, attracting deposit accounts for the bank, and maintaining overall relationships with the bank consumers. Personal bankers typically have a large number of clients in their portfolios, in contrast to business bankers who may have much fewer clients. This position is located in the retail branch and is available to meet with clients directly. Personal bankers handle many duties and provide advice to clients regarding types of accounts to open, forms of ownership (e.g., joint, common ownership, etc.), certificates of deposits, checking accounts, account issues, errors, financial needs, issuing cashier's checks, applications for consumer loans, opening ATM accounts, mobile accounts, online accounts, and many more. They are the primary consumer representative for the bank, with the primary goal of obtaining deposits.
- teller: Tellers are located in each of the branches of a bank. Their primary role is to handle transactions. This would include cashing checks, processing payments, accepting deposits to accounts, and processing withdrawals. Often, they are the first, and sometimes the only,

in-person contact a client might have with the bank. They are responsible for a cash drawer that is used for cashing checks and other transactions. At the close of the day, one of the primary jobs of a teller is to balance the cash drawer. This is a client-contact position and a key representative of the bank's mission. Tellers also are charged with cross-selling services to clients where the needs make sense.

- call center representative: Call center representatives are also client-contact positions, but not face to face. These employees are located at central or regional call centers and handle all communications over the telephone. Call centers are very sophisticated and operate for extended hours, beyond the hours of a branch and, in some cases, 24/7, dependent upon the size of the bank. Call center representatives, today, handle more than just customer complaints or issues. They take loan applications, open savings accounts, set up ATM and debit card accounts, provide client balances, and research transactions for support. This is a very busy role for a bank, with representatives talking with hundreds of customers during their normal work day.

Wealth Management

Wealth management is the last of the primary sales function in a bank. Not all banks have a wealth management function, but this has grown in the recent past. Bankers work with a wide variety of clients. Clients have financial needs beyond the traditional loans and deposits (e.g., investments, trusts, safekeeping, etc.). Unlike the commercial and retail roles, which are focused on interest income and expense, wealth management is a fee-income business. Wealth managers work closely with businesses and retail bankers. The reason for this is to build the overall financial relationship with a client. The key roles in wealth management are outlined in the following pages.

- chief wealth officer: This is the top position responsible for all wealth management services and may report to the CEO or chief sales position. Their primary objective is to generate fee income for the bank (noninterest income).

Support

Operations

Operations is the back office. These are generally non client-contact positions. Their primary role is to support the sales effort. They accomplish this by performing the documentation, setting up accounts, inputting data into the systems, and processing transactions that occur from clients. These positions are also responsible for ensuring compliance with laws and regulations and following the detailed policies of the bank. To some degree they are sort of a maintenance function in that they fix issues, complete research, and ensure that client accounts are properly handled at all times to retain client satisfaction and good will. As a result they have a very close relationship with the sales force, which can, at times, be adversarial.

- chief operations officer: This is the top officer in charge of all of operations for the bank. This is an executive officer position and reports to the CEO, in most cases. The three operational areas that may report to this position provide support for the three primary sales forces: commercial, retail, and wealth management. The chief operations officer is charged with maintaining compliance, security, productivity, efficiency, and, above all, accuracy in the roles that report to them. This can become a balancing act at times to ensure protection of the bank and client privacy while meeting the timing and requirements of the sales force.
- loan operations manager: Loan operations is a major role in the bank. The functions performed within this department focus on the processing and handling of commercial and consumer loans. The manager of this department is typically a senior-level officer of the bank and reports to the chief operations officer. Their primary job is to process loans from start to finish. This is truly a "production" function where time and accuracy are of paramount importance. Loan operations is responsible for all aspects of loan processing (e.g., recording and processing loan applications, producing loan documentation, booking the loan on the core loan system, managing and maintaining loan files, scanning documents, maintaining collateral documents, processing loan payments and statements, and closing loans and releasing collateral).
- deposit operations manager: Different than the loan operations function, this back-office role is to work toward the processing of deposits and transactions for the retail sales area, for the most part. Included under this role may be the item-processing function (check processing), lockbox, and other cash management services. In this regard they are accountable, and support, the commercial sales area as well through business deposits and cash management services. The role of deposit operations manager is also a senior-level officer skilled in managing the production of a large staff of employees. The position reports to the chief operations officer. In addition to processing new account set up (deposit accounts), they are involved with reconciliations of key general ledger accounts, processing checks, processing lockbox payments, performing research, and other functions. Like loan operations, this is a "production" department where timeliness, efficiency, security, and accuracy are the key objectives.
- trust operations manager: Trust operations is the back-office support of the wealth management sales area. Similar to the previous two operations areas, this group is responsible for maintaining important legal documents, safekeeping of securities, providing key documents to trust and wealth officers, and ensuring the client needs (and sales force needs) are met in a timely fashion. In some organizations the trust operations manager reports to the chief wealth or trust officer. In other banks this position is centralized under the chief operations officer. The primary reason for this is that the skills of operations officer are focused on production, efficiency, compliance, accuracy, and security more so than those of the sales force. This is evolving and varies by bank.

- branch operations manager: This operational role is responsible for the physical maintenance of the branch structure of the bank. Although this role typically reports to the chief retail officer, it may in some cases report to the chief operations officer. This back-office function is different than the others in that it is not necessarily a production operation. Branch operations includes snow plowing parking lots in the winter; mowing grass and maintaining landscaping in the summer; painting, building, and remodeling branches; buying and selling branches; maintaining internal décor, signage, lighting, vaults, safe deposit boxes, and drive-ups; among others. This operations area carries a significant budget that includes taxes and all of the physical upkeep of branches; therefore, effective and prudent management of these costs is one of the major objectives of the branch operations manager. This position is typically a senior-level officer in the bank and one with building and real estate background.

Marketing

The marketing role in a bank is generally the same as that of a business. Their primary role is to promote the bank, its products and services, in the most attractive and unique way to attract as many clients as possible. Since banks are corporations, accountable to shareholders, generating revenue is extremely important. To do this, the marketing role must differentiate the bank from others since there is a considerable amount of competition with other banks. Advertising, communications, and product development are some of the major duties of this important area.

- chief marketing officer: The primary role in this department is the chief marketing officer (CMO). This role may or may not report to the CEO, but in many cases to the chief retail officer. The reason for this is that the vast majority of the banking relationships are more retail or consumer based than business. Further, the attraction of deposit dollars is vital to the bank, which is the primary role of the retail sales area. Nevertheless, regardless of where it reports, it is responsible to meet the needs of all customers, commercial, retail, and wealth. Banks are notorious for continual advertising on billboards, television, radio, and online. Every avenue is important to advance the bank and its products and services. Marketing is further responsible for understanding and managing households, to build long-lasting relationships that utilize many of the bank's services. In addition, they are responsible for product brochures, the language in these brochures, signage, and maintaining the advertising and brand standards of the bank. In some organizations, communications may be a subfunction within this department. This would include a social media presence.

Credit Administration

The credit department of a bank is a support function. Its primary role is to support and provide oversight over the extension of credit, through loans. This function is responsible for maintaining a formal credit policy, or rules, for the extension of credit for the bank.

Typically, part of the responsibility of this role is to manage troubled credits through the workout and collections functions. The objective is to attempt to prevent losses; however, this is not always possible. Therefore, they continually review some of the largest business credits to ensure that the quality of the client and their businesses is closely monitored to avoid losses. This department is closely involved with developing reserves for loan losses and projecting the probability of future losses.

- chief credit officer: The role of the chief credit officer is an executive officer position and reports to the CEO. The importance of this is to ensure that independence between the sales areas and credit exists. The chief credit officer typically chairs the credit committee and carries significant weight in the approval of commercial loans. In addition, this is considered a risk management role, managing credit risk. The CCO would be accountable for the overall asset quality of the loan portfolio and works closely with the regulators during their safety and soundness examinations to ensure that the quality of the bank's credits (loans) are of a high quality and adhere to the credit policy.
- loan workout: Loan workout is a department reporting to the chief credit officer. The primary purpose of this department is to work with troubled loans to work out or restructure the deal effectively such that the bank will be repaid and not take a loss. The manager and officer is this area would be skilled in commercial lending and credit analysis. They would work directly with clients to negotiate effectively and reach amicable relationships that avoid losses and potentially maintain the relationship. As loans ultimately become losses and need to be written off, opportunities for recoveries still exist. Outside attorneys and agencies exist who continue to attempt collection of amounts written off. These must be monitored to obtain any recoveries that would mitigate the impact of the losses.

Administrative

Aside from sales and support efforts, an administrative category is the final part of the internal structure. These functions are neither client-contact nor directly supporting or dedicated to specific sales functions. The primary role of this category is the management of the bank, which includes strategy and planning, personnel, accounting and finance, information technology, risk management, and legal. All of these functions are performed for all aspects of the bank, not just specific departments.

Executive

The executive role is oversight and management of the bank, from the top down. This is the leadership of the bank, and although focused on the chief executive officer, it also includes the executive committee, comprised of executive officers responsible for each of the functions within the bank. The primary role or responsibilities of the executive category is setting the vision and strategy for the bank, managing the performance and profitability of the bank, maintaining compliance, and effectively managing all risks that the bank faces. This is the province of the executive team, led by the chief executive officer and the chief operating officer.

- chief executive officer: The chief executive officer (CEO) is the top officer of the bank. They report directly to the chairman of the board or to the board directly. In some cases the CEO may also be the chairman of the board. In addition to setting the strategic direction of the bank, the primary administrative functions in this segment report directly to the CEO, including finance, technology, risk management, human resources, and legal. If the bank does not have a chief operating officer, this may be vested in the CEO together with the additional direct reports. The CEO is ultimately responsible for the reporting of performance and status to the bank's examiners and to the public. This is a legal responsibility. The CEO is accountable to the bank's shareholders as well as the performance of the bank's stock.
- chief operating officer: If the bank has this role, separate from the CEO, it is to divide the responsibilities for expertise and span of control. The responsibility of the chief operating officer (COO) is to manage the day-to-day banking. This, typically, involves the sales and the support functions. Client contact and the results from those interactions along with the generation of revenue is the primary objective. In other words, they provide banking products and services to clients. This focuses the role on the issues attendant to these jobs and not on the myriad of administrative duties of the bank. The COO may also be the president of the bank, or this may remain with the CEO. Often, individuals in this role have a background in sales and have grown from these ranks. This role's performance metrics would include achievement of sales growth goals, efficiency levels, and credit risk.

Finance

The finance function of the bank is responsible for all accounting, reporting, finance, and budgeting activities. In addition, the purchase, sale, and management of securities is an important revenue-generating function for the bank. This is typically the province of the bank's treasurer. A major function in this area is the production of the financial statements and call reports of the bank. This involves the management of the general ledger. The finance function is involved in all aspects of the bank, at some level.

- chief financial officer: This is one of the top three to five positions in the bank and reports directly to the CEO. The chief financial officer (CFO) regularly reports to the board of directors on the financial status of the bank. The roles and functions that report to this position, generally, would include accounting, finance/treasurer, budgeting, and possibly planning. The CFO participates in many of the key meetings of the bank. One of the most important is the asset/liability committee (ALCO). The CFO typically chairs this meeting and is very closely involved in managing the bank's liquidity position, capital compliance, and interest sensitivity. In addition, the reserve account at the Fed is managed under the responsibilities of the CFO. The position, further, works closely with the external auditor of the bank, particularly on the assessment of the financial statements for the independent opinion. CFOs typically hold CPA certifications as one of the requirements of the position.

- treasurer: Dependent upon the size of the bank, they may or may not have a treasurer position. If not, the duties of this office would be performed by the CFO. Overall, the bank's treasurer is responsible mostly for management of the investment portfolio for the bank. This will include investments held to maturity as well as the trading account and income-related investments. This position closely monitors and advises the bank on the yield curve and the direction of interest rates. This is most important when planning revenue and expenses from interest. The securities portfolio, alone, can account for significant gains, dependent upon the skill of the treasurer and staff, and can make a big difference in the bank's overall profitability for a given quarter. This position reports to the CFO.

Legal

All banks require legal services for a variety of reasons. Banks may be parties to lawsuits and require preparation of legal documents, such as customized loan documents, corporate secretarial matters, contract analysis and preparation, and product and external communications legal reviews. The size of the bank will make a difference as to whether they employ an attorney on staff or outsource the legal function. Regardless, outsourcing legal services will continue regardless of size for more specialized services, such as mergers and acquisitions.

- chief legal officer: If the bank employs an in-house attorney, this individual would usually fill the role of chief counsel. The chief legal officer will coordinate all relationships with in-house or outsourced legal staff for a variety of purposes. This position would report regularly to the risk committee and board of directors on legal liabilities, or legal risk, that the bank faces. In addition, the person filling this role may assume the role of corporate secretary as well. The duties for this would involve corporate statements in all external reporting as well as external communications, including public relations.

Human Resources

Human resources is the department that manages all services to the employees of the bank. They are responsible for the array of corporate benefits made available to employees, as well as payroll. In addition to existing employee benefits, the department also coordinates retirement benefits for all retirees, to include pensions, 401(k) plans, profit sharing, and other programs. Another major role is employee relations, including hiring, exit interviews, recruiting, and dealing with staff complaints and issues.

- chief human resources officer: This position reports, generally, to the CEO of the bank and is a key position for the attainment of satisfactory employee contentment and motivation.

Chief human resource officers (CHROs) have strong people skills, working closely with individuals within the bank. Reporting to this position would include the benefits, employee relations, recruiting, and payroll functions of the bank. CHROs work closely with all employees of the bank and therefore is a very people-oriented position. Their primary objectives are to ensure that all key positions are filled with qualified talent (i.e., recruiting) in a timely manner and that employees are paid on time. Benefits, today, are quite complex, and this is a key recruiting incentive, so it behooves the bank to ensure that the CHRO is well versed in the latest benefit opportunities that may be available to organizations.

Information Technology

This department involves all of the technological functions that a bank may use. Today, online tools and resources are critical requirements of every bank client. These must be managed effectively, focusing on uptime, system speed, state-of-the-art tools and applications, information security, and back-up and recovery. All departments and customers rely on the systems and network of the bank, and these functions are managed under this department. Primary departments that occur in this area include core processing (mainframe system), data network, voice network and telephony, hardware, software, system development, information security, technical support, help desk, and the internet (web servers and applications). There are many opportunities for roles in this area of the bank, particularly today, as the demands for online services and mobile banking are the direction of the future.

- chief information officer: The top role responsible for information technology in the bank is the chief information officer (CIO). This is an executive-level position and is a critical role for any bank today. In addition to managing all of the departments reporting to this position (network, information security, technical support, core services, hardware and software, development, and internet), the CIO works closely with all peer positions to ensure that technical services are provided timely, accurately, and efficiently. In addition, making sure that systems are available at all times and that the frequency of downtime is at an absolute minimum is a major requirement and expectation of users. In this regard, the CIO is not a client-contact position but more an internally focused position. Although technical knowledge and skills are at a high level, the ability to listen to, satisfy, and manage internal client challenges are critical tools to have for any CIO. The CIO generally reports to the CEO of the bank.

Risk Management

Risk management is a relatively new role for banks. Because the nature of banking is fraught with risk, the need to manage these effectively to minimize losses to the bank has become acute. Today the expectations of the regulators has demanded the need for a department focused solely on the many risks banks face. One need only look at the beginning of a 10K report to see the litany of risks identified and disclosed in this report. Under this function, banks have included a variety of roles that relate to these risks, including compliance, audit, loan review, physical security, information security (in some cases), and BSA (Bank Secrecy Act) and fraud. This is an oversight role and provides the vehicles to identify, understand, and manage the risks that the bank faces. This is one of the fastest growing departments in banks today and an area of significant employment opportunities.

- chief risk officer: The chief risk officer (CRO) is an executive-level position and reports directly to the CEO or the board of directors, which is the preference of the regulators. The CRO works with and establishes a variety of control mechanisms to identify these risks and ensures that these are reported to management and the board. They establish the procedures for risk assessments and educating the departments to identify the risks in their respective areas. In addition, the CRO works closely with the regulators and coordinates the timing and compilation of information for safety and soundness exams, as well as response reporting. The province of this role is to understand and manage all of the risks facing a bank to include financial, regulatory, compliance, reputation, operational, technology, capital, strategic, and credit. The position of CRO has become very important of the executive-level positions and is a major requirement in all banks.

Committees

Although banks are known for conducting a plethora of meetings on a day-to-day basis, there are a handful of critical meetings that all banks utilize to make most of their decisions and set policy. Students of commercial banking must be aware of these significant meetings and what they do to understand how the decision-making process works.

From an internal structure standpoint, decision making and oversight occurs in two broad areas, board of directors and management. The types of meetings that occur within each of these areas include:

- board of directors
  - nominating committee
  - compensation committee
  - risk committee
  - audit committee
- management
  - executive committee
  - risk committee
  - asset liability committee
  - credit committee

Board of Directors

The board of directors of a bank provides oversight of the bank's operations. Boards do not make management decisions but typically approve actions, policies, and personnel directions. Bank board members are engaged to provide expertise to management of the bank and are typically hired because they may possess expertise that would benefit the management of the bank. Boards provide oversight through four primary committee meetings, defined below.

Nominating Committee

Board members fill designated terms and must be elected by the shareholders of bank. Terms can be three years or more, but generally fall within that range. The nominating committee is charged with identifying candidates to fill vacating (retiring) board positions, evaluating their credentials and fit, and making recommendations for addition to the board. In this way there is an ongoing process to populate the board with effective talent that can be a true benefit to the bank ensure there are no significant gaps in board compensation. The committee is a select few members of the board.

Compensation Committee

Although members on this committee do not make individual compensation decisions for the bank, with the exception of the CEO and chairman of the board, they do provide oversight and approval of the merit increase thresholds and other short- and long-term compensation benefits to officers of the bank. Given the officer structure of banks, this committee provides approval of management's recommendation for promotion of officers to various levels. They do not recommend individuals for promotion but provide approval based upon management's recommendation. As indicated, bonuses and other short- and long-term benefits are approved by this committee, as recommended by management.

Risk Committee

Banks face a wide variety of risks; in fact, they are in business to take risks. Although management also has a risk committee, so too does the board. This committee provides oversight of the efforts of the work of the chief risk officer of the bank. In some cases, the chief risk officer reports directly to the board, which would be to this committee. Nevertheless, the role of the board is to review how management is assessing risks, understanding the risks they face, and what they are doing to mitigate these risks. The federal regulators generally require that management effectively risk assess processes and activities to ensure that the risks have been clearly and accurately identified so that they could be properly mitigated. Board members, through this committee, must make sure that they are addressed effectively, from an oversight standpoint, as they face liability to shareholders if not properly understood and reviewed. Regulators also want to continually make sure that board members are not only aware of but also that they approve of management's actions as they relate to risk identification and mitigation.

Audit Committee

The final committee identified is the audit committee of the board. This committee is responsible for reviewing the results of both the internal and external auditors' evaluations and reports. The chief risk officer and/or chief audit officer participate, with the internal and external auditors, to render the status of the most recent audits. In addition, this committee may also review internal compliance review results to assess the level of compliance with regulation. Again, this is an oversight role and assesses management's attention and response to audit comments. Finally, the committee also receives the examiner's safety and soundness audits to understand the bank's rating and the level of findings produced as a result. The audit committee is focused not only on the results but also on the timeliness and quality of management's responses to the results.

Management

Management, in this context, is comprised of the executive officers of the bank. These typically are the most senior officers who head the business units within the bank. Management includes the chief executive officer, chief financial officer, chief information officer, chief operations officer, chief risk officer, chief lending officer, chief credit officer, chief retail officer, chief wealth management officer, chief legal officer, and chief human resources officer. These officers, generally, are responsible for developing policies, managing processes, and executing on the bank's mission and strategy. Similar to the board, management makes these decisions through four key committees.

Executive Committee

One of the most important committees of the bank is the **executive committee**. This is a decision-making body and is accountable to the board of directors. This committee manages the bank and all attendant staff.

- purpose: The committee has decision-making responsibility and is the primary committee that focuses on the bank's overall mission, strategy, issues, plans, and budgets. The current year's progress to plan on both budget and tactical plans are regularly evaluated. All policies are reviewed and approved by this committee prior to going to the board of directors for overall approval.
- leadership: chaired by the CEO
- composition: The committee includes all C-level officers of the bank that are the heads of all functional areas of the bank. This would include sales areas (commercial, retail, and

wealth management), information technology, operations, finance and treasury, credit, legal, human resources, and risk. These individuals are all executive officers of the bank and are the legal officers that can bind the bank in terms of contracts and other decisions. In general, these are the individuals that are deemed "management" when referred to by the federal regulators. Many of these officers regularly report to the full board of directors on a quarterly basis on the status of initiatives.

- frequency: quarterly

Risk Committee

The **risk committee**, or strategic risk committee, is a bit newer than the other three key committees of the bank. Nevertheless, it has become an increasingly important committee given the myriad of risks banks face today.

- purpose: The purpose of the committee is to regularly review all the primary risks the bank faces by way of the functional areas where risks may arise. Risk assessments are presented and reviewed by each committee member, including the inherent risk, risk mitigation strategies, and residual risks, as well as the severity rating of each. The committee is empowered to identify and approve actions that are required if the residual risks remain high and need further mitigation. Finally, the group is empowered to recommend acceptance of residual risks deemed relatively low in severity. These ultimately would be reviewed by the board of directors for final acceptance.
- leadership: Although the CEO of the bank is the de facto risk officer, this is delegated to the chief risk officer, who chairs this committee.
- composition: Although most of the same C-level officers from the executive committee are members of the strategic risk committee, other senior officers are also included. In general, composition includes the areas of information technology, operations, credit, legal, financial, loan review, sales, human resources, physical security, BSA/AML, information security, and so on. In general, the composition is focused on the primary risks all banks face and the departments where these risks originate, including capital risk, operations risk, liquidity risk, interest rate risk, reputation risk, technology risk, credit risk, and compliance risk.
- frequency: quarterly

Asset Liability Committee

Commercial banks operate on relatively narrow margins, and due to the nature of financial change and client traffic fluctuations in interest rates, liquidity and thusly capital occur minute by minute, day by day. To track these fluctuations and their impact to the bank, the **asset liability committee (ALCO)** was formed.

- purpose: Banks operate and earn their profitability predominantly based upon their interest rate margin. This is the difference between the rate received from loans and the rate paid on deposits. Therefore, interest rate fluctuations will make a difference in future planning and decision making. In addition, the bank must always be liquid, which is mandated by Basel III. Since there is a constant flow of cash in and out of a bank every day, this liquidity level must be constantly monitored to ensure enough source of funding is available, or can be obtained, almost instantly. Finally, capital ratios will fluctuate based upon the level of risk in the asset structure (mostly loans) of the bank and requires monitoring to ensure compliance with regulatory standards. These three areas identify the need for the ALCO committee to meet to make pricing decisions, review capital compliance, and manage liquidity and funding levels and to take appropriate actions to maintain these areas effectively.

- leadership: chaired by the chief financial officer (CFO)
- composition: The committee is comprised of several key C-level and other officers of the bank. These include the CEO, chief credit officer, chief risk officer, treasurer, chief retail officer, and chief lending officer. These individuals manage interest rate fluctuations, product pricing and margins, and capital levels and the decisions required.
- frequency: Monthly or ad hoc, as required. Given the speed with which interest rates, cash in, and outflows and margins change, it is necessary to make modifications to directions frequently, as demanded by the environment.

Credit Committee

Because most of a bank's income is derived from interest income, which is earned through making loans, particularly business loans, a significant risk the bank faces is the inherent risk of lending money, or *credit risk*. Although this is the fourth of the key committees of the bank, it has been in existence for quite some time, as one of the fundamental requirements of a bank is to loan money.

- purpose: The **credit committee** is designed to review all potential loans that are being considered and proposed by lending officers for approval. The primary risk that banks face relative to credit risk is whether the bank will be repaid or not. As such, much due diligence is required to effectively analyze business loans to ensure that they have the wherewithal to repay the loan in the time frame proposed by the lender. The committee's job is to review the loan detail, listen to the officer's rationale for making the loan, and to ensure, based upon the expertise of the committee, that the business is a "going-concern" and is financially able to repay the loan. Credit committees have a considerable responsibility in that loans that do not get repaid impact the capital of the bank and, should considerable losses be obtained, could impair the bank's ability to function.
- leadership: chief credit officer
- composition: The committee is comprised of, in addition to the chief credit officer, the chief lending officer, chief retail lending officer, loan operations manager, loan review manager, chief financial officer, and CEO (for loans requiring that level of approval).

- frequency: Similar to the urgency with ALCO, credit committees would meet monthly and, in some cases, ad hoc, dependent upon the urgency of the deal. This will depend upon the bank and the volume of loans being proposed.

CHAPTER SUMMARY

Most consumers and clients of banks are seldom aware of the nuances of commercial banks. Although the terms used in this chapter are frequently mentioned in the news media, most would not be aware of their meanings or understand their derivation or purpose. Banking is an ancient discipline, stemming back to the earliest history of mankind. As a result, the depth of the thought that has evolved over the years into the modern banking system we know today is borne out of necessity, risk, and opportunity. For the student of commercial banking, a foundation in the structure and terminology of banks, both externally and internally, lays a foundation from which an appreciation of the reasons for the concepts that are defined within this chapter can be achieved.

Banking is and has been evolving. Understanding some of the origins will help the student of commercial banking in participating and recommending the direction for commercial banking as it continues to evolve. Although still scratching the surface, commercial banking is one of the more complex financial disciplines and structures that has existed for some time. Its importance in the economy has been defined in the prior chapter, and this chapter establishes the importance of its structure for understanding the depth of its legal foundations, memberships, physical evolution, and internal oversight. These concepts will aid in understanding the next layers of commercial banking, from a building block standpoint, and appreciating the foundations that will enable more effective bank decision making for future commercial bankers.

Now that this foundation has been established, the next chapter will outline the products and services that commercial banks offer and how they generate revenue and profitability for the bank. These foundations are important for future understanding of the central bank and how the regulatory structure and laws evolved and are enforced.

END OF CHAPTER QUESTIONS

1. What governmental agency provides insurance protection to depositors for deposits placed in commercial banks?
2. Who is the chartering agency for national banks?

3. What is the primary difference between a bank holding company and a financial holding company?
4. What is a unit bank, and what are its defining characteristics?
5. What was the purpose for banks to open branches?
6. Which management committee of the bank monitors liquidity and capital requirements?
7. Who typically chairs the credit committee of the bank?
8. What is the purpose of the nominating committee of the board?
9. What is the oldest and the newest delivery channel of banks?
10. What is the cost of membership in the Federal Reserve system?

Figure Credits

Fig. 2.1: Source: https://www.fdic.gov/consumers/banking/facts/.
Fig. 2.2: Copyright © 2013 Depositphotos/rixipix.
Fig. 2.3: Copyright © 2013 Depositphotos/rixipix.
Fig. 2.4a: Copyright © by Laieta30 (CC BY-SA 4.0) at https://commons.wikimedia.org/wiki/File:Bank(1).svg.
Fig. 2.4b: Copyright © 2013 Depositphotos/rixipix.
Fig. 2.4c: Copyright © 2011 Depositphotos/lucadp.
Fig. 2.4d: Copyright © 2013 Depositphotos/Mictoon.
Fig. 2.4e: Copyright © 2013 Depositphotos/artbutenkov.
Fig. 2.5a: Copyright © 2013 Depositphotos/rixipix.
Fig. 2.5b: Copyright © 2015 Depositphotos/VisualGeneration.
Fig. 2.5c: Copyright © 2012 Depositphotos/mitay20.
Fig. 2.5d: Copyright © 2015 Depositphotos/Icon_Craft_Studio.
Fig. 2.5e: Copyright © 2012 Depositphotos/Lumumba.
Fig. 2.5f: Source: https://commons.wikimedia.org/wiki/File:Internet_Explorer_9.png.
Fig. 2.5g: Source: https://pixabay.com/vectors/cloud-thought-weather-153992/.
Fig. 2.5h: Source: https://pixabay.com/vectors/iphone-cellphone-smartphone-mobile-37856/.
Fig. 2.5i: Copyright © 2017 Depositphotos/Axsimen.

CHAPTER 3

Bank Products and Services

To understand the foundation of commercial banking, like any business, one must understand the products and services they sell. With the structure of banking and delivery channels defined, what is delivered, why, and how they are used in society is important for understanding how commercial banks differ from other corporations.

Commercial banks are in the business of money; therefore, the nature of the products and services they sell are not tangible objects, but financial instruments. These instruments vary in complexity, dependent upon the bank. This chapter will provide the student with an understanding of the core types of products and services that banks offer to establish the foundation from which other more unique products might evolve. This is not an exhaustive list of every product a bank could offer but rather the core types of instruments that most, if not all, banks would typically offer.

Sources and Uses

Banks are driven by their balance sheets. In other words, the balance sheet identifies the predominant (core) products that they sell. These will fall under assets and liabilities. By definition, banks take deposits, and from these deposits, they make loans. Therefore, these become the sources of funds and the uses of the funds.

Key Terms

Transaction deposit
NOW accounts
Super NOW accounts
Money market deposit accounts (MMDAs)
Demand deposit accounts (DDAs)
Passbook savings
Statement savings accounts
Certificates of deposit
Individual retirement accounts
Roth IRA
Keogh
Payment system
Cash/currency
Money supply
Cash distribution System
Liquidity
Checks
Routing and transit number
Branch capture
Bitcoin
Core deposits
Stable funds
Senior debt
Interbank loans/deposits
Commercial and industrial loans
Facilities
Lines of credit
Working capital
Term loans
Construction loans
Mortgage loans
Bridge loans
Installment loans
Noninstallment loans
Home equity loans
Fiduciary capacity
Trust

Learning Objectives

By the end of this chapter, the student will:

- Know the difference between transaction and nontransaction accounts.
- Identify the core deposits of a bank.
- Identify the primary types of commercial and consumer loans.
- Know the type of products and services offered under wealth management.

For a commercial bank to operate, they must have funding; otherwise, they cannot loan those funds out. In this regard, understanding the sources of funds, as the starting point, is the focus. Banks derive most of their income from making loans; therefore, they must have funds to do that. Funds are, for the most part, deposits. Although banks utilize other nondeposit sources of funds, these will be discussed in a later chapter.

For our purposes and very broadly speaking, these sources and uses are outlined as follows:

- uses (assets)
  - » loans
    - ▹ interbank loans
    - ▹ commercial loans
    - ▹ consumer loans
    - ▹ credit cards
    - ▹ mortgage loans
- sources (liabilities)
  - » deposits
    - ▹ checking accounts
    - ▹ savings accounts
    - ▹ time accounts

In addition, banks also sell products and services in the wealth management area. Unlike the traditional loans and deposits, wealth management services generate fee income, not interest income or expense.

Deposits

Banks regularly advertise to attract deposits. For example, signs advertising "free checking accounts" are not unusual along the highway. The reason for this is that they need funds to loan to customers to generate income. Banks need deposits as their lifeblood, and deposits define the role they play in the economy. Unfortunately, obtaining deposits can be difficult and requires constant attention. These instruments take many forms and are structured for different reasons. However, there are two basic categories of deposits:

- transaction deposits
- nontransaction deposits

Both categories can further be refined into two subcategories. These categories and subcategories are expanded upon below.

- interest bearing
- noninterest bearing

Transaction Deposits

Transaction deposits are more fluid and more frequently used accounts. Their primary purpose is for making payments for goods and services to various individuals and corporations. In addition, another distinctive feature is that the provider is required to honor withdrawals immediately, or upon demand (when presented for payment). Rather than having to use cash, transaction accounts provide a payment mechanism for the movement of money, usually in the form of checks, but also using debit cards. This is also one of the oldest types of accounts and services provided and grew out of need to have a vehicle to pay bills, for the most part.

Transaction deposits can be either interest bearing or noninterest bearing. Interest-bearing accounts pay a rate of interest monthly to the depositor. This amount is added to the account and is one of the reasons that customers "shop" different banks, to determine the highest paid provider. Noninterest-bearing transaction accounts pay no interest. This is an account that is set up for the convenience of the depositor with the intent that significant balances will not be maintained in the account. Although there can be a wide variety of unique types, account types will fall into the following generic deposits.

- interest bearing
  - » negotiable orders of withdrawal account (NOW)
  - » super NOW accounts
  - » money market accounts
- noninterest bearing
  - » demand deposit account (DDA)

Negotiable Orders of Withdrawal (NOW) Accounts

NOW accounts have been in existence for several decades. These were designed as a means of attracting deposits to a bank, as they paid an interest rate. In addition, clients who maintained significant balances in their transaction accounts where no interest was paid needed the convenience that transaction accounts afford while at the same time earning interest on balances maintained. NOW accounts carry some restrictions. Generally, the amount of checks that can be written per month is limited to a specified cap. In this way, balances do not vary as significantly as in a demand deposit account, which allows the bank to count on the availability of funds.

Super NOW Accounts

Super NOW accounts are a variation on a theme. Although not used much any longer, they are very similar to NOW accounts. The primary difference is that they limit the amount of checks written more so than NOW accounts, but in return, they pay a higher rate of interest. Again, this hybrid satisfied a need, at the time, but then evolved into the last type, money market deposit accounts.

Money Market Deposit Accounts (MMDAs)

Money market deposit accounts evolved from the prior to instruments. These accounts were revolutionary, at the time, and evolved with Super NOW accounts because of the Garn–St. Germain Depository Institution Act of 1982. MMDAs were designed to provide the highest amount of interest of the transaction accounts. Restrictions on this account are at the highest level, limiting the amount of checks that can be written per month. This account is used as a quasi-savings account, due to the amount of interest it pays. When they originally began in the 1980s, the amount of interest paid, at the time, was very high and they were billed as the fastest way to gain wealth. To this day, MMDAs are still popular and pay the best rates of transaction accounts. Banks want to attract money market deposit accounts because the balance are higher and they are retained longer, due to the restrictions. This aids in the bank's funding needs.

Demand Deposit Accounts (DDA)

Demand deposit accounts (DDA), or checking accounts, are the ultimate in transaction accounts and one of the most-used type of accounts for bank customers. These accounts do not pay interest, which was originally prohibited by the Glass-Stegall Act. They are used predominantly for making payments for goods and services. Since they are used so frequently, they are one of the most volatile accounts, as balances fluctuate very frequently. Once a bank makes a loan to a new customer, the first step in disbursing the loan is to open a checking account at the bank, to which loan proceeds are deposited. Finally, these accounts are the primary drivers of checks in the industry, which is the predominant transaction vehicle (see Figure 3.1). Today, the volume of checks in the system are diminishing in lieu of other methods of payment, such as debit cards. Nevertheless, the foundation account behind this is a demand deposit account.

FIGURE 3.1 Checkbook Example

Nontransaction Deposits

Nontransaction accounts are precisely what the name implies. These instruments are not designed to be used to pay for goods and services, but rather as vehicles to save money and accumulate wealth. These are a good source of funding for the bank mainly because these balances do not fluctuate since they are not used to make payments. Nontransaction accounts are a benefit to bank clients because they provide the client with a place to put savings and have it grow from the interest payments made. These accounts benefit significantly from compounding, over time, and are very valuable to bank customers.

All nontransaction accounts are interest bearing and will pay a rate of interest that is commensurate with the market to remain competitive. There are several types of basic nontransaction deposits, although many variations exist. The key types of nontransaction deposits include:

- savings
  - » passbook savings
  - » statement savings
- time deposits
  - » certificates of deposit (CDs)
  - » independent retirement accounts (IRAs)

Passbook Savings

One of the oldest, and seldom used today, nontransaction accounts is that of the **passbook savings** (see Figure 3.2). These accounts are basic savings accounts—that is, the most primary of the savings instruments. These are interest bearing, but generally at a relatively low rate. As the name suggests, these are deposits accounts that rely on a small booklet to record deposits and withdrawals. These transactions were date-stamped and recorded in writing or updated from a machine. Many a youngster of the past opened these as the first bank account they owned. Rather than putting money in the piggy bank, kids opened these to save for future purchases and earn interest. In this regard, the balances were generally not high. However, collectively, the balances add up for a bank, and since they are not transaction accounts, the balances remain stable, which is good for bank funding and at lower interest rates. These types of accounts are generally more historical than anything; few banks use these any longer.

DATE	DESCRIPTION	WITHDRAWALS	DEPOSITS	BALANCE
03-10-16	ATMW	**21.25		**474.11
03-10-16	ATMF	**1.50		**472.61
03-10-20	DEBP	**2.99		**469.62
03-10-21	WEBP	**300.00		**169.62
03-10-22	ATMW	**100.00		**69.62
03-10-23	DEBP	**29.08		**40.54
03-10-24	DEBR		**2.99	**43.53
03-10-27	TELP	**6.77		**36.76
03-10-28	PYRL		**694.81	**731.57
03-10-30	WEBT		**50.00	**781.57

Please refer to the back cover for the list of common transaction codes.

Please verify your account activity regularly. If there is an error, notify the bank within 45 days.

FIGURE 3.2 Passbook

Statement Savings Accounts

Passbook savings accounts were replaced by **statement savings accounts** (see Figure 3.3). These accounts carry all the characteristics of the passbook savings, except for the booklet. Now transactions are recorded electronically by the bank and rendered in a monthly statement to the client. In general, these are lumped into the general category of savings deposits. Commercial banks, many times, have a variety of methods to attract depositors. These can be special purposes savings accounts to save for travel or school expenses or even Christmas savings accounts for gifts. Each of these specialty accounts may have a variation in interest paid and/or other benefits to attract customers.

FIRST BANK OF WIKI
1425 JAMES ST. PO BOX 4000
VICTORIA BC V8X 3X4 1-800-555-5555

CHEQUING ACCOUNT STATEMENT
Page : 1 of 1

JOHN JONES
1643 DUNDAS ST W APT 27
TORONTO ON M6K 1V2

Statement period	Account No.
2003-10-09 to 2003-11-08	00005-123-456-7

Date	Description	Ref.	Withdrawals	Deposits	Balance
2003-10-08	Previous balance				0.55
2003-10-14	Payroll Deposit - HOTEL			694.81	695.36
2003-10-14	Web Bill Payment - MASTERCARD	9685	200.00		495.36
2003-10-16	ATM Withdrawal - INTERAC	3990	21.25		474.11
2003-10-16	Fees - Interac		1.50		472.61
2003-10-20	Interac Purchase - ELECTRONICS	1975	2.99		469.62
2003-10-21	Web Bill Payment - AMEX	3314	300.00		169.62
2003-10-22	ATM Withdrawal - FIRST BANK	0064	100.00		69.62
2003-10-23	Interac Purchase - SUPERMARKET	1559	29.08		40.54
2003-10-24	Interac Refund - ELECTRONICS	1975		2.99	43.53
2003-10-27	Telephone Bill Payment - VISA	2475	6.77		36.76
2003-10-28	Payroll Deposit - HOTEL			694.81	731.57
2003-10-30	Web Funds Transfer - From SAVINGS	2620		50.00	781.57
2003-11-03	Pre-Auth. Payment - INSURANCE		33.55		748.02
2003-11-03	Cheque No. - 409		100.00		648.02
2003-11-06	Mortgage Payment		710.49		-62.47
2003-11-07	Fees - Overdraft		5.00		-67.47
2003-11-08	Fees - Monthly		5.00		-72.47
	*** Totals ***		1,515.63	1,442.61	

FIGURE 3.3 Statement Savings

Certificates of Deposit (CDs)

This is the first of the time deposits. Time deposits are different than savings accounts in that they specify a term, a length of time before the account matures. **Certificates of Deposit** are exactly that: These accounts are opened for a specified term, with a rate of interest that is fixed over the term of the account (see Figure 3.4). Customers are presented with a certificate once a CD is opened. This is a form of contract that specifies the initial amount deposited, the fixed interest rate, the compounding period, and the term or maturity of the account. CDs are generally desired, as they usually will pay the highest interest rate. The reason for this is that the bank is willing to pay more for a commitment from the client that the balance will remain at the bank for the specified term. This is beneficial to the bank, from a funding standpoint, and from the client side, they benefit from a guaranteed interest rate, regardless of whether interest rates fall or not. Since this is contractual, if any amount is withdrawn prior to maturity, a penalty is assessed. The penalty is due to the commitment to a higher interest rate, so clients are penalized by the amount of the premium they earned on the account for the period the balance was held. Certificates of deposit are frequently advertised by banks and frequently shopped by customers.

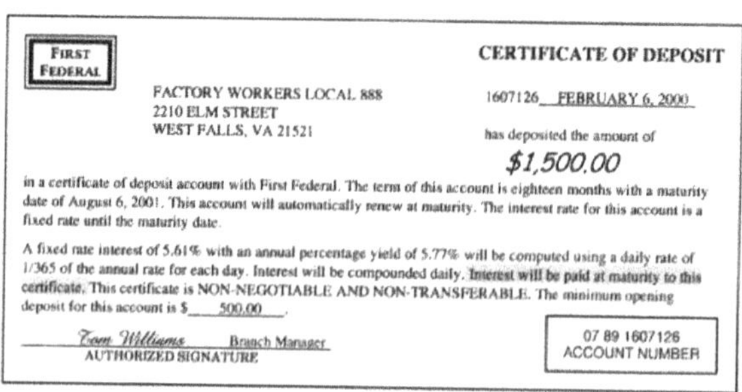

FIRST FEDERAL

CERTIFICATE OF DEPOSIT

FACTORY WORKERS LOCAL 888
2210 ELM STREET
WEST FALLS, VA 21521

1607126 FEBRUARY 6, 2000

has deposited the amount of

$1,500.00

in a certificate of deposit account with First Federal. The term of this account is eighteen months with a maturity date of August 6, 2001. This account will automatically renew at maturity. The interest rate for this account is a fixed rate until the maturity date.

A fixed rate interest of 5.61% with an annual percentage yield of 5.77% will be computed using a daily rate of 1/365 of the annual rate for each day. Interest will be compounded daily. Interest will be paid at maturity to this certificate. This certificate is NON-NEGOTIABLE AND NON-TRANSFERABLE. The minimum opening deposit for this account is $ 500.00 .

Tom Williams Branch Manager
AUTHORIZED SIGNATURE

07 89 1607126
ACCOUNT NUMBER

FIGURE 3.4 Example of a CD

Individual Retirement Account (IRA)

In 1981 another revolutionary instrument emerged with the passage of the Economic Recovery Tax Act. This is the **individual retirement account** part of the time deposit family. IRAs were revolutionary, as they carried significant benefits for clients that no other instruments had. First, interest was earned, tax deferred, on the account. Since IRAs compound interest, balances grow from interest earned and no taxes are paid on these earnings until withdrawn or by age 72. Initially, amounts deposited in IRAs also received favorable tax benefits. Like CDs, however, there are very specific rules for IRAs, and there are penalties in the event money is withdrawn prior to the term. In the case of IRAs, the term is generally retirement. Nevertheless, IRAs remain very effective retirement planning instruments for clients today. The concept behind tax-deferred status of interest was that taxation does not occur until one is retired, at which time they are likely to be in a lesser tax bracket since they would no longer be employed, thus paying less tax on these earnings.

In 1997 **Roth IRAs** emerged because of the Tax Relief Act. Roth IRAs not only allow for tax deferred interest but also allow for withdrawals to be made tax free, subject to qualifications. This is generally the opposite of traditional IRAs; however, there are income restrictions to be able to invest in a Roth IRA. Finally, **Keogh** accounts are similar but are designed for self-employed individuals so that they can take advantage of the same benefits that others can.

Payment Systems

Payment systems are an important part of the banking system and are an important discussion as part of the overall deposits of a bank. **Payment systems** are means (vehicles) for transacting business. Like transaction accounts, payment systems are used to pay bills, pay for purchases, and satisfy obligations that may occur on a day-to-day basis. These systems evolved out of need and convenience as a means of exchanging value. In this section there are two traditional forms of payment systems in use that require understanding. Although newer systems have evolved and are evolving, which will be discussed later in this section, these lay the foundation for the core payment systems in existence.

Traditional Payment Systems

Traditional payments systems are those that have been in use for some time. These systems are physical in nature and flow through the hands of individuals and other organizations. There are two types of traditional payment systems:

- cash (currency)
- checks

Cash

Cash, also called **currency**, has been in existence for hundreds of years. Cash (currency) is the substitute for the value it represents, based upon denomination. In the United States, these are dollars (U.S. currency) and they are generally in denominations of $1, $5, $10, $20, $50, and $100 bills (see Figure 3.5).

FIGURE 3.5 $1 Bill

Earlier in the history of the United States, the actual bill itself was backed by a physical metal, such as gold or silver. Since these precious metals were deemed valuable in society, rather than carry gold or silver around, a specific bill could represent the equivalent value of the precious metal. In other words, the bill was backed by the denomination amount shown on the face of the bill. This means it is redeemable for that amount in gold or silver. These gold certificates or silver certificates (see Figure 3.6) were plentiful until the United States went off the gold standard in the 1970s.

FIGURE 3.6 Silver Certificate

Today, currency is no longer backed by precious metals; instead, they are "federal reserve notes" (see top of Figure 3.5). Notes are a form of debt, and these bills are backed by the credit worthiness of the United States government. These notes are payable by the government and carry value because of the strong credit rating of the United States. Since the United States has the power to tax, these bills have value in the world marketplace. Nevertheless, currency is a major form of payment. Coin is also part of the payment system and comes in many denominations, ranging from a penny (one cent) to a silver dollar. Currency and coin are part of the overall **money supply**, which is a critical economic indicator and influenced by the Federal Reserve in their monetary policy.

Currency is in circulation in the United States, but where does it come from, and how is it replaced if it is torn or worn out? Because currency flows through many hands, it is heavily used and can rip and become so frayed that it is difficult to use. For this reason, there is a **cash distribution system** that is employed to address this concern (see Figure 3.7). There are three primary entities engaged in this system regularly: commercial banks, the Federal Reserve bank, and the U.S. Treasury. Within this system, as illustrated, cash is moved to and from these entities in a routine flow. Commercial banks receive cash from the Federal Reserve, via armored car, so that they have sufficient cash available for teller drawers and based upon demand from customers and others. Banks maintain this cash in their vaults; however, they do not maintain vast amounts, because cash sitting in the vault does not earn a return (i.e., no interest is paid). During the day, cash is flowing to and from the bank (cash inflows and outflows). The net result of this movement of cash is known as **liquidity**. Banks must always be liquid in anticipation of demand. At the end of the day, any excess cash is returned to the Federal Reserve again via armored car.

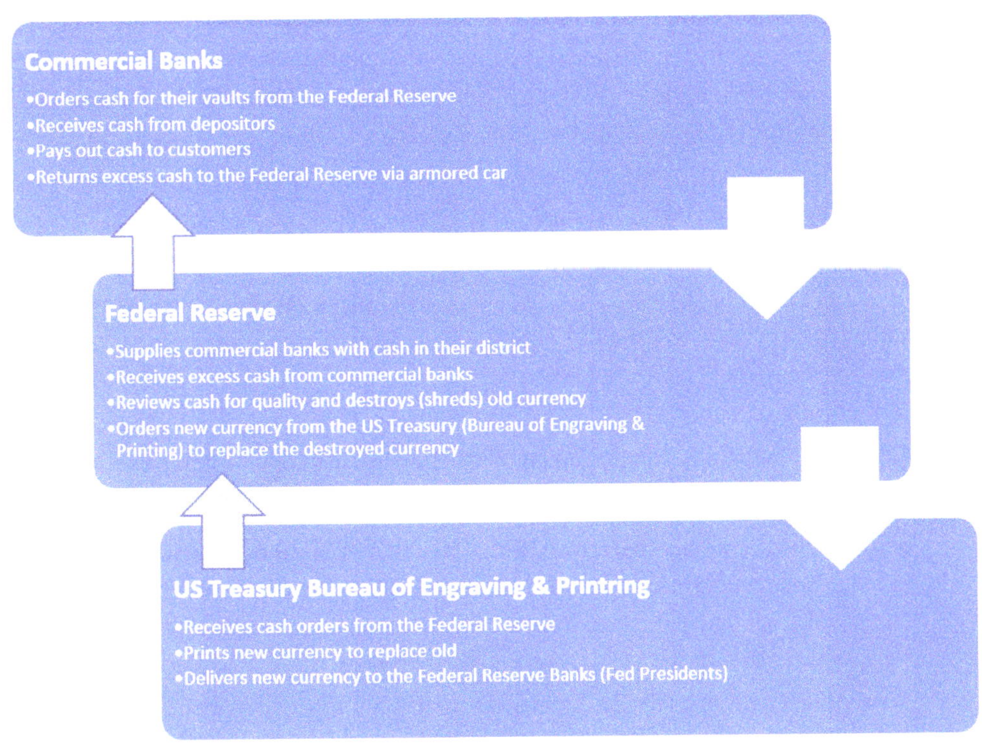

FIGURE 3.7 Cash Distribution System

The Federal Reserve scrutinizes all cash coming from banks within its district and evaluates it to find counterfeit money and check the quality of the physical currency. If the currency is significantly worn, the Fed will destroy the bill by shredding it. Each of the Federal Reserve banks does this. The amount of cash destroyed is then counted, and an order for new currency is placed with the U.S. Treasury Bureau of Engraving and Printing for replacement.

Finally, the U.S. Treasury receives these orders and prints new cash in the denominations indicated. This new cash is sent back to the Federal Reserve banks and put into circulation once the Federal Reserve disburses it to the commercial banks. In this regard, the money supply, or M1, remains constant.

Checks

The second, more traditional, form of payment system is checks, or checking accounts. **Checks** are considered negotiable instruments, a substitute for money, and are used to pay for purchases and satisfy other obligations. They were developed as a means of providing value in return for goods and services without the need for using cash. Checks are documents that are completed by the owner specifying the instructions for payment. They emanate from checking accounts, or demand deposit accounts (DDA), which were previously discussed in this section. Checking accounts are transaction accounts and are used very frequently as a security measure and convenience so that the issuer does not have to send cash through the mail and risk loss. Checks, unlike cash, can be stopped if lost or stolen, preventing the issuer from losing money. However, when cash is used and is lost or stolen, there is little recourse to the owner for recovery or prevention of use. In this regard, checks have been a stalwart in the industry for years. Only recently have checks been declining in volume from the significant levels used a few decades ago. Checks are also part of the money supply and between this and cash make up most of the money supply. An example of a typical check is shown in Figure 3.8.

Parts of a Check

As shown in the illustration, checks are standardized and are made up of three parts:

- drawer: This is the individual who writes out the check (the owner of the account). The drawer will execute the check by writing the dollar amount of the transaction in both numeric and handwritten language. The written portion of the dollar amount is a check on the dollar amount indicated to ensure that the proper amount is paid. The drawer will sign each check on the face of the check for it to be valid.
- payee: When a check is written, it is paid to someone. This is the payee and can be an individual or an organization. It is the destination of where the money will be directed or paid and is written on the first line of the check starting with "pay to the order of."

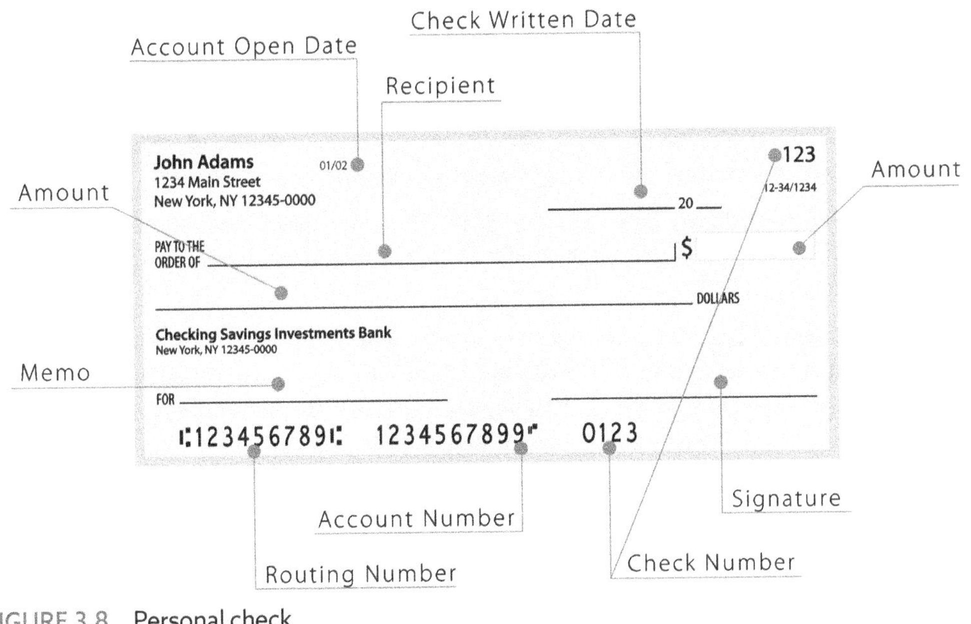

FIGURE 3.8 Personal check

- drawee: The final part is the drawee, or the entity from which the check is drawn upon. This will be the bank that holds the account and from where ultimate payment will be made. The bank name is prominently displayed on the check.

Beyond the key parts of a check, other important information is contained on the face of the check at the bottom. Two sets of numbers are included, MICR encoded on each check. The first number is called the **routing and transit number**, or just simply "routing number." This number identifies the drawee bank or the bank that the check is drawn upon. All U.S. banks have a routing number and is MICR encoded for easy machine reading and identification once the check flows through the check clearing process. The second number, immediately to the right of the routing number, is the checking account number. This number is also MICR encoded and identifies the account number of the checking account from which the funds are going to be drawn. Computers will identify, categorize, and tally information from these two numbers.

Elements of Negotiability

The predominant elements of negotiability for a check are very specific and involve five requirements:

- payable to the order of bearer: Checks can be written to "cash" or "bearer." This means that whoever holds the check can cash the check as if this were cash in hand. An alternative to this is a check made payable to an individual who has endorsed it (i.e., signed their name on the back of the check). In this case, the check now can be cashed by whomever holds the check with that endorsement, regardless if it is made out to them or not.

- unconditional order to pay: This means that there are no conditions of payment. The check must be paid as written without any form of specific conditions to be met.
- fixed amount of money: The amount to be paid must be specific (dollar and cents) and not a range or nonspecific amount. Both the written and numeric amounts must be the same as well.
- payable on demand or at a definite time: Checks require a date that the amount indicated can be paid. In most cases checks are dated as of the date written, which means funds are available to be paid at any time. If no date is indicated, then the check is considered payable on demand. Sometimes individuals may issue a postdated check. This is a check that has a future date indicated. This means that the check cannot be cashed until the date has occurred. Postdated checks are used sometimes to demonstrate good faith that the obligation is intended to be satisfied, but not at this time. Banks will not honor a check postdated until the date has occurred.
- written and signed: Finally, the check must be signed by the drawer or owner of the account. If the check is not signed, it cannot be cashed.

Clearing Process

The process for clearing checks can be somewhat complex; however, it is changing due to the advent of acceptable electronic processes. It is important for the student of banking to understand, nevertheless, how this process works, as it continues to this day. As stated earlier, the amount of personal checks is, and has been, declining in volume. As a result of this, many commercial banks no longer have check or "item" processing departments as they once did, simply because the volume is not there to support the cost of the equipment and staff needed to process these checks. Because of this, item processing has been relegated to third-party providers. These organizations have been able to consolidate the volume of checks, making it worthwhile for them to offer the business for a cost to the banks. Regardless of who provides the service, the clearing process is the same and follows the sequence indicated.

1. A check is written by the drawer of the check for the purchase of goods or services.
2. The check is given to the payee as payment for the goods or services.
3. The payee delivers the check, generally at the end of the day, to their depository bank for deposit to their account.
4. The depository bank receives this check and hundreds of others throughout the day. These checks are bundled into a *cash letter* and sent to their third-party item processor, via courier. A cash letter is a deposit slip that accounts for every check in the bundle.

5. The item processor then sorts all the checks received, from a variety of banks, by the banks drawn upon. This is determined by the high-speed sorters and scanners reading the routing and transit number that is MICR encoded on each check. This tells the processor what bank they are drawn upon and which Federal Reserve district they belong to.
6. All the checks, for a bank, are captured electronically, and the amounts are transmitted to the bank for updating the bank's systems.
7. The item processor groups all checks and again prepares a cash letter. These checks are then bundled and delivered to a clearing agent. This is generally the Federal Reserve, although there are other banks offering this service as well. Nevertheless, the checks get presented to the Federal Reserve.
8. Clearing agents offer different levels of availability of the funds, depending upon when they receive the cash letter. This can be same-day or next-day availability. This means that if the cash letter is received, say, by midnight, all the checks in the cash letter will receive immediate availability or usage of the funds.
9. Availability, ultimately, involves the Fed's handling of the checks. Once received, the Fed will charge the drawer's bank's reserve account for the amount. Checks may be drawn upon banks in other Fed districts, which will be notified. The payee's bank will be credited with the amount as well. In short, the Fed simply debits and credits the accounts of their member bank's reserve accounts to handle the transactions. The checks are then delivered to the drawer's bank.
10. The drawer's bank charges the customer's personal checking account for the amount and then truncates the check. In the past, checks were returned to the customer, physically, for their records. This no longer occurs, as electronic means are available that replace this need.

Today, with the dawn of the Check 21, this process has been streamlined considerably. Check 21 is the Check Clearing for the 21st Century Act of 2004. This law paved the way for the usage of substitutes for paper checks, utilizing electronic images. This was an attempt to move towards the checkless society. Checks seldom must be bundled in cash letters, as bank are now able to electronically capture checks at the teller line. This is called **branch capture**, whereby checks are scanned and transmitted electronically to the item processor. The process flow is still the same, but it is much more efficient today.

Other Types of Checks

Beyond personal checks, there are a variety of other types of checks that are used for specific purposes. These checks are issued by banks or other entities and are designed to provide greater certainty that the money is available to be paid. Unfortunately, not everyone will accept a personal check as payment. Many times, one might see signs in a local store that say, "No personal checks accepted." The reason for this is the store takes the risk of accepting the personal check, not knowing whether the issuer has the funds in their account to obtain payment. Unfortunately, people sometimes write personal checks knowing full well that the funds are not in their account, and when presented for payment, the check will be returned, or *bounce*, meaning it will be sent back to the merchant unpaid.

Since store owners do not want to turn away sales but also do not want to take a lot of risk in payment, or there is an obligation that is very significant, such as a large dollar amount (e.g., for a deposit on a home), that it is too big of a risk, they may require more assurance of payment. To accomplish this and avoid the risk, the payee may require the payer to obtain one of the following type of checks, which will be backed by, or guarantee, that funds are available in the account. These special checks are not personal checks but drastically reduce the risk to the payee.

- cashier's checks: These are often called "official" checks, as they are issued by the bank itself. These are the bank's own checks and are drawn on the bank's checking account. Customers requiring these checks must purchase them for a fee and provide them with the actual funds in the amount for which the check is written. When an official check is used, the payee can count on the funds being there because the bank has the actual funds, and it is drawn on the strength of the bank itself. The check, in this regard, is not going to be returned unpaid, as there is very little risk that the payee will not get the money.
- teller's checks: These are very similar to cashier's checks in that they are bank checks. In this case, however, the bank will issue the check, but it will be drawn upon another bank. Since it is still drawn on a bank, it carries little risk that it will be unpaid and would still be considered an official check. Banks sometimes partner with third-party banks that offer this service, whereby the customer still must purchase the check from the issuing bank and then provide the amount to the bank for the check. The benefit to the bank that it is drawn on is that the funds deposited for the check amount will be held by the bank it is drawn upon. The bank drawn upon will earn interest on the funds received and held until the check is collected in the check processing process. Since float occurs until the check is presented for payment, the drawee bank can earn interest for the days it is holding the funds prior to payment. Banks that do this are offering the service whereby they will receive a considerable amount of funds (in volume), which will produce income to the bank and can be very profitable. An example of this are checks used for controlled disbursement, which relies on float due to the geography of the drawee bank, thereby earning interest for a longer period before the check is presented for payment.
- certified check: This is, again, a guaranteed check and good for the payee, as it virtually eliminates the risk. Unlike the prior two types of checks, however, this is not a check drawn on the bank's own account. In this case the customer writes out a personal check and takes it to a bank and asks for it to be "certified." After paying a fee for this, the bank will verify that the funds are available and will place a stamp on the back of the check and sign it, indicating that the funds are available in the payer's account. Should there be a problem with this,

the bank that certified the check carries the liability and must cover the check. So, in this regard, the bank is still guaranteeing payment but is now using the payer's personal check.

- money order: Money orders are issued by third parties. These are not banks but could be a currency exchange, a supermarket, or another entity. The check operates similarly to that of an official check in that the money order is issued from the entity itself, which usually is a known entity and one deemed solvent to cover the check. The customer purchases the money order for a fee and provides the funds to the entity to cover the amount of the check. Money orders are used to send payment through the mail rather than using cash or a personal check. This is typically by request of the entity where the purchase is being made. Cashier's checks are probably more preferable due to the backing of the bank; nevertheless, money orders are frequently used.
- traveler's checks: These instruments are somewhat a thing of the past, but are still available. Traveler's checks are generally purchased for usage on trip, in many cases a foreign trip. These were used mostly when credit and debit cards and ATMs were not available or not as plentiful in the world as they are today. It gave travelers peace of mind when travelling far from home. The checks eliminated the need to carry a large amount of cash with them on the trip and risk losing it along the way. Traveler's checks are purchased at a bank for a fee. Additionally, the traveler paid the bank the amount of money for which they want the checks. For example, if a traveler planned to take $1,000 on a trip with them, they would pay the bank $1,000, plus a fee, to purchase the checks. The traveler would specify what denominations that want the checks in (e.g., $10, $20, $50, $100). Each check would have the specified amount preprinted on the check. As the traveler purchased items during their trip, they would present a check for, say, $50 to cover the item. The merchant would accept the check and pay any remaining amounts in cash to the traveler. The appeal of these checks was (a) they were recognized and accepted worldwide (for the most part); (b) if you lost the checks while in transit, you did not lose your money (the traveler would merely find a bank or organization that supports these checks and the lost checks would be replaced); and (c) the checks, if lost or stolen, could not be used by anyone, as they require the traveler to sign the check, in their presence, and the signature must match that of the signature signed on the check when purchased. Large organizations, such as American Express, offered these, and still do. Therefore, traveler's checks were a significant benefit to travelers and reduced the risk of loss of funds. So how does the issuing bank or organization benefit? Float. Recall that the customer must pay the face amount of each check when purchased. This may be a week or even several weeks before travelling. Once on the trip, checks are cashed over time during the trip, and dependent upon where they are cashed, it takes times to get back to the bank for payment. This represents a significant amount of float for these checks and allows the issuing entity to invest the amount of the funds provided for a significant amount of time before they must pay the checks. Float can range anywhere from 7–14 days and, in some cases, even 30 days before presented for payment. That can be a long time to invest the volume of funds received for this business. The other benefit is that travelers often come home from their trips with uncashed traveler's checks. By the

time they get back to the bank to redeem these, it adds even more float to the issuer. With the widespread deployment of ATMs, debit cards, and credit cards, travelers seldom needs these checks any longer. With cards, the traveler need not carry much cash but would have immediate access to needed funds through ATMs. However, since there are still places where there is not a large network of ATMs, traveler's checks can still provide a significant level of security and, for that reason, still exist today.

Alternative Payment Systems

Although traditional payment systems continue to be used today, several other payment systems have evolved over the years as alternatives to cash and checks. Many of these have been in use for quite a while, whereas some are quite new. Students of commercial banking should be aware of these payment systems, how they operate, and their future potential. These alternative payment systems will continue to evolve, and there is no doubt that others will follow in the years to come due to technological advancements. For now, however, we will focus on the primary ones in operation today.

Alternative payments systems are those that relay on something other than cash or checks to pay for goods and services. As such the form of payment is quite different, but nevertheless accomplishes the same end. Five alternative payments systems in use today include:

- automatic teller machine (ATM) cards
- credit cards
- debit cards
- stored-value cards
- crypto currencies

Automatic Teller Machine Cards

ATMs have been in existence since the 1980s. Over these past four decades, they have evolved into core payment systems, a necessary service for all banks to participate in to be considered a full-service bank. The primary reason for their existence was to be able to withdraw cash without having to go into a bank and withdraw funds at a teller window. The objective was to reduce the traffic at the teller lines in lieu of self-activated withdrawals. Banks would deploy ATMs on the outside of their bank lobbies, at their drive-ups, and in more remote areas, eventually being placed in gas stations, retail stores, supermarkets, and so son. This made it convenient for customers to withdraw cash. Using a card, like a credit or debit card, issued by the bank, the customer would slide the card into the machine, enter a PIN number, and receive the necessary cash. These machines are fully online, so they read and update the customer's account for all transactions made. Today, ATMs can do more than withdraw cash and include the following services:

- cash withdrawal
- make a deposit
- transfer funds between accounts
- obtain a status (balance) on one's account
- make loan payments
- complete applications
- interactive communications

The last two bullets are among the newer features. Some banks have deployed very sophisticated ATMs even in their lobbies, at the teller line. When customers log in with their card, they can speak, in real time, with a banker in video mode. In this way they can literally converse with a live representative without the need for the banker to be physically present. Obviously, this creates many opportunities for the banks to ease staffing levels. Bank representatives could literally be anywhere.

ATMs were revolutionary at the time and are still very viable today, providing much convenience to the customer by allowing 24/7/365 access to these devices. Although they do produce cash, one of the two traditional payment systems, they can be used as a substitute for cash by transferring funds electronically, making payments, and conducting other financial transactions without using a check or cash.

Credit Cards

Although credit cards are considered a debt instrument (a revolving loan), which will be discussed in the loan section of this chapter, they are also, very much, payment systems. Many people today seldom carry much, if any, cash with them, yet they can easily be comfortable throughout the day for any needs they might have if they have a credit card. Credit cards are a substitute for both cash and checks. They are used to purchase goods and services on credit, or for payment later. Whenever a credit card is used, the charge to it is added to the balance on the account. The customer has the option at the end of the month to either pay the balance in full or to make a minimum payment, as specified on the statement. The latter option affords the customer a considerable boon in their purchasing power. They now can purchase up to the designated credit limit on their account without having to have the cash at that point in time. In most cases, cardholders usually make minimum payments and carry the rest on their balance. As a payment system, however, they are a tremendous tool and negate the need to carry cash throughout the day. Nevertheless, the balance must be paid back at some point. These can be very effective tools if used prudently.

Debit Cards

Debit cards are very similar to credit cards and are often combined with ATM cards. They are a substitute for cash and checks, hence an alternative payment system. They are used similarly to credit cards as payment for goods and services, using plastic. However, where they differ from credit cards is that the transaction that is made is deducted from their checking account immediately (based upon the network transmission). This is the equivalent of writing out a check, but less flexible, as checks carry some float, whereas debit cards do not. Because of this the user must always be conscious of the amount of funds in their checking account to make sure they are not overdrawn. In this regard, debit cards require prudence out of necessity rather than out of will power, as with credit cards.

Stored-Value Cards

This payment system is also card based, like the others. The big difference is that the usage of the card is dependent upon the amount of money designated in the chip in the card. This is a finite amount and limits the user to that amount for purchases of goods and services. Today, gift cards are plentiful and are excellent examples of stored-value cards. They are definitely substitutes for cash and checks and are not tied to any account or credit. Once the card is fully utilized, it can be discarded. Stored-value cards are purchased for the denomination desired. The purchaser pays the merchant this amount, and the card is active. Today, many retail organizations, such as Starbucks, Amazon, various restaurants, and a wide variety of organizations, offer these for purchase. These are the most limited of the cards already discussed.

Crypto Currencies

Crypto currencies have been evolving over the last decade or so. The most popular form of crypto currency is **Bitcoin**. Bitcoin evolved following the financial crisis of 2008 as a means of not having to rely on banks, governments, or other entities in the control of their money and without the need for fees and other issues. They are considered a digital form of currency that is decentralized. For Bitcoin and other crypto currencies, there are no intermediaries, such as banks, and transactions are made directly from one member to another, based upon *block chain*, which is a ledger of participating individuals that are known to one another and considered secure and trustworthy. Bitcoin, and others, are a form of currency, but not in a physical sense. They have value and they fluctuate considerably in the marketplace. This volatility has caused these to be an acquired taste. The downside is that they are not regulated or federally insured by the FDIC or SIPC. Crypto currencies are a definite work in process and can be extremely volatile. There is much discussion of crypto currencies and news about these instruments, which is beyond the scope of this book. Nevertheless, they are in existence as an alternative payments system and are evolving.

Recap

Overall, the aforementioned deposits are generally regarded as **core deposits**. These are also called **stable funds**, as they are generally available and can be counted upon for funding for the bank. Commercial banks are very protective of core deposits, as this is the primary source for loanable funds. Banks advertise frequently to attract these desirous deposits, and the acceptance of these deposits is one of the key elements that defines a bank.

Loans

The second part of the definition of a bank is the ability to make loans. Loans produce the predominant source of revenue for a commercial bank. Banks charge an interest rate for loans, which is the pricing for the product. This produces interest income, which is generally higher than the interest expense paid to depositors for the funds to make the loans, which produces net interest income, or the profit from making loans. Unlike deposits, loans are assets for the bank or uses of funds. They are like accounts receivable for a corporation in that they become monies owed to the bank from the customers. Loans arise out of need. The primary reasons that loans occur is due to the following (Vermaak, 2018):

- cash flow: Businesses and consumers, from time to time, find themselves short of cash to meet current obligations.
- capital expenditures: Capital expenditures are significant long-term investments, generally that have lives beyond one year, usually longer. Most corporations plan for capital expenditures in their budgeting process, year by year. These purchases must be "funded"—that is, a source of funds must be obtained to purchase these. Funding can take the form of a loan or could be from other sources but nevertheless must be funded.
- timing/opportunity: For both corporations and consumers, time sensitivity can create an advantage if acted upon. This could be an investment opportunity or something else that could produce a significant benefit to the recipient. These are generally ad-hoc events.
- short-term needs: These represent more immediate demands that an individual or business may have. This could be as acute as staying in business or the ability to pay rent. These are critical needs where there is little choice but can only be solved with an infusion of money.

Loans for a commercial bank, generally, fall into two broad categories: commercial loans and consumer loans. These categories, which will be expanded upon shortly, relate to business loans versus loans to individuals. For the most part, commercial, or business, loans are the older of the two. Regardless, these loans are the primary source of revenue for a bank.

Commercial Loans

As stated, commercial loans are business loans. These are loans made to small and large businesses for a variety of needs. Banks arose as a source for funds when the business fell short. Since businesses began within the community (the town), banks arose in the same community or town to aid these enterprises. For businesses, loans are not a negative mark against the firm: Even though they are debt to the company, this is part of growing the business. Therefore, within the community, businesses would go to the community bank to seek a loan. The community bank prospers by making the loan, and businesses prosper by obtaining funds that are turned into revenues for the business. Since the early days of banking, banks became the source of funds for these businesses because they had the funds obtained from deposits made by people in the community. Loans of this nature are called **senior debt**. The reason for this is that it has priority, for payback, over other types of debt the business may have.

For the purposes of this chapter, and in this section, we will refer to business loans as commercial loans. Although there is a myriad of different types of commercial loans, they typically can be categorized into five primary areas:

- bank loans
- wholesale Loans
- commercial and industrial loans (C&I)
- real estate construction loans
- information, communication, and telecommunication loans

Within these categories, the actual types of loans made will vary based upon the circumstances.

Interbank Loans

Bank loans, or **interbank loans**, are loans made to other commercial banks that have a relationship with the bank making the loan. These are assets to the bank. As will be explained fully in subsequent chapters, banks must always be liquid. Liquidity thresholds, in fact, are mandated by regulation. As a result of this, to maintain these levels of liquidity banks that conduct business with other banks, also called *correspondent banks*, may be falling short of liquidity levels and therefore need to replenish this quickly. One source is another bank. When a bank makes a loan to another bank, it usually is of a short-term nature and may have less risk. The lending bank will then generate revenue from this loan on the interest rate they will receive. This rate is generally less than is typically charged to corporations. Making bank loans not only earns the lending bank revenue but also builds a favorable relationship with the bank so that, if the need exists, the lending bank may require a loan themselves. Therefore, they have a ready source of liquidity should the need arise. In this case, they would borrow from the bank, which would become a liability to them, or an **interbank deposit**.

Wholesale Loans

Wholesale lending is a form of lending whereby the bank that funds the loan is different from the organization who "originates" the loan. In this regard, the wholesale lender is indirectly related to the transaction, providing the funds and the credit decision, whereas the originator provides the contact and the relationship. The bank, in this regard, is behind the scenes. In contrast, *retail lending* is where the provider of the loan is also the originator. Wholesale banks offer their loans through third-party brokers. They sell these services to large clients, which could include other banks, government agencies, and the like. The keyword for understanding this category is "indirect." That is, they do not make these loans directly to the customer. Most banks provide wholesale lending, and this provides another avenue of revenue generation, through brokers who are not on staff at the bank, while at the same time making loans directly to customers using their own staff.

Commercial and Industrial Loans (C&I)

One of the largest areas of lending is **commercial and industrial loans**. In general, these represent manufacturing- and production-related loans as well as loans to other businesses. Loans in this category are generally relatively short term and are made for capital expenditures, working capital, and other cash flow needs. These loans are typically secured by collateral. C&I loans are competitive, and prices are negotiated based upon LIBOR (London Interbank Offered Rate) or other prime lending rates. Lenders in this category are skilled in analyzing businesses both structurally and financially.

Real Estate Construction Loans

Business loans related to real estate construction involve the financing of the construction of plants, apartment complexes, housing developments, and other major building initiatives. Construction loans are used to provide the funding while a project is being built. These funds are used by an enterprise to pay the general contractor and subcontractors while the building is being constructed. Since real estate is a very specific discipline, a specific lending department is typically developed to focus on this category. These lenders have knowledge and expertise in the real estate industry, in addition to financial and lending skills. Construction loans are not permanent loans but rather temporary funding to pay contractors. Once the building is constructed, the loan is rolled into a permanent loan, such as a mortgage loan.

Information, Communications, and Telecommunication Loans

The needs of the technical industries are another area of lending for commercial banks. These loans typically involve infrastructure funding that can relate to cabling, wiring, towers, transponders, and so forth. In some cases the terms for these loans may be relatively short, given the changes in technology that continue to occur regularly, or may be longer if for foundation or infrastructure technology that does not change frequently. The types of loans within this category may be like that of C&I loans. Given the longer nature of the technology, these tend to be term-type loans.

These are broad categories of loans; some banks may have different segments as categories. The purpose for these categories is to define the focus and expertise of business lending for the bank. Other categories can include health care, agribusiness, small business, and others. These categories are by design and are based on the strategy of the bank, the expertise of their lenders, and the geographic area they cover.

Loan Types

There are various loan types that occur within the loan categories. Loan types are referred to as **facilities**. Facilities denote the specific need for the loan and the way in which it is funded and operates. Some loan facilities are more specific to the category of the loan, such as real estate construction; however, others can be used within all categories. There are, broadly, five types of facilities that will be used when lending money to businesses:

- lines of credit (LOC)
- term loans
- mortgage loans
- construction loans
- bridge loans

Lines of Credit (LOC)

Lines of credit are not loans, at least not yet. This type of loan is designed to provide the borrower with an approved amount of money that they can draw upon when needed. Lines of credit are required by businesses facing a cash flow shortage due to seasonality or other short-term needs. This is like a credit card in that the borrower is granted a preapproved amount of money that cannot be exceeded. The customer then can draw on that limit for the immediate needs they have. This does not have to be the full amount but could be only a partial amount. Once the draw is made, this becomes a loan, as the amount is borrowed. Borrowers are required to service the debt by either paying interest or paying it back based upon a specified requirement. In many cases, corporations request lines of credit for funding **working capital** needs, which are funds needed to satisfy current obligations. Lines of credit, just like any other loan, must be analyzed based upon the full amount of the line. In most cases, however, lines of credit are generally short term and are very popular and a necessary part of running a business. Ultimately, however, there is a term, or maturity, where the loan must be paid back fully.

Term Loans

In contrast to LOCs, **term loans** are actual loans made, and disbursed, and have a specified maturity (term) in which the loan must be paid back. The cost of the loan is typically a fixed interest rate for the specified term. Term loans are generally made to fund capital expenditures or major projects of a long-term nature. This could include major equipment purchases, technology purchases, trucks, and other machinery. Where LOCs are short-term loans, term loans are long term and are typically needed for the purpose of expansion and growth. Most corporations seldom have the cash to self-fund major purchases. For this reason, term loans are very popular and frequently used. These types of loans carry significant interest rate risk for the bank. If the loan is made at a fixed rate of interest for a longer term and interest rates increase, the bank is at risk of earning less than would be possible in the current environment, which would remain until the loan is paid. This would be favorable to the client but would reverse if rates decline.

Construction Loans

For businesses, **construction loans** are made to fund the building of physical plants, apartment complexes, housing developments, and other structures. Construction loans are temporary in that they are initiated to provide funding to the business to pay contractors and subcontractors as the physical structures are built. These would be like consumer residential construction. Construction loans are evaluated and funded based upon the full cost to build the structure. They operate, in a sense, like a line of credit. The borrower will draw on the construction loan when the subcontractor bills the business for their services. Once drawn, the amount is part of the loan. The borrower will be required to make interest payments on the amounts funded until the project is completed. As each subcontractor is paid, the amount of the loan funded will grow until it equals the original amount approved. Once the project is complete, the construction loan will either be paid back, or it will be rolled into a mortgage loan, which is the permanent loan and will carry a term of multiple years, anywhere from 10–30 years. Construction loans, therefore, are very short term, usually within the span of one year, but could be more, based upon the size of the project.

Mortgage Loans

As indicated above, construction loans can evolve into a mortgage loan. However, mortgage loans, for businesses, can occur for the purchase of physical properties already in existence. A **mortgage loan** is a long-term loan made to fund the purchase of property, including physical structures. The loan is usually for a significant amount, and the asset that is purchased has a life that will exceed multiple years (10–30 years). The loan is typically secured by the value of the property that is purchased. In this regard, if they loan is not repaid, the bank has the right to take ownership of the property in lieu of nonpayment. These types of loans will generally fall within the real estate category of loans.

Bridge Loans

The final type of facility discussed in this chapter is a bridge loan. **Bridge loans** can be relatively short term, but are more specifically event-specific, which might be longer. Typically, a bridge loan arises when a specific event triggers some form of windfall for the business. However, to either take advantage of the windfall or to fund operations during the interim, a business may require a bridge loan. The amount borrowed is reflective of the amount to be obtained once the event occurs, and that is when the loan is paid in full. In this regard, during the interim, interest payments may be made on the loan and then the full principal is repaid upon the occurrence of the event. Lenders make their evaluation on the likelihood of the event, as well as the probability of the amount to be received when the event takes place. Obviously, the goal is to make the loan based upon the certainty of the event, and therein lies the risk to the lender.

Consumer Loans

Consumer loans fall within the retail banking environment. These are loans that are made directly to individual consumers, not businesses. Consumer loans are relatively newer products on the scene for commercial banks. Nevertheless, like commercial loans, consumer loans are assets of the bank, money owed to the bank. They are made to fund a variety of purchases that are relatively significant to the consumer, where funds are not available to purchase the item. In several ways, they operate the same as commercial loans in that they have terms, are priced based upon an interest rate and fees, and have a defined amount borrowed. Consumer loans tend to be among the riskiest due primarily to the reasons for the borrowing and the resources of the consumer. Unlike businesses, consumers do not always have the resources that businesses may have access to for repayment. In addition, education and income levels play a large role in the use of credit for consumers, defining both the need for credit as well as the source of funds for repayment.

There are four basic categories of consumer loans that represent the bulk of the consumer loans made. For each, there are a variety of types or specific needs for the loans and very broadly can fall into similar types as commercial loans, but are somewhat different, as explained below.

- personal loans
- residential mortgage loans
- home equity loans
- credit cards

Personal Loans

Personal loans are loans made to individuals. These loans are generally made to finance the purchase of a particular asset needed by the individual. Personal loans can consist of automobile loans, boat loans, equipment and appliance loans, educational loans, debt consolidation loans, and others. These loans arise out of need and may occur because of unplanned events. For example, a refrigerator in a home may be old and one day simply stop working. Refrigerators are considered big-ticket items and likely will cost more than $1,000. When consumers do not have the cash to pay for a critical item, such as a refrigerator, they can borrow money to pay for it. This is called *financing.*

In general, personal loans like this can be obtained directly at a bank by visiting the branch and talking to a personal banker. As an alternative, many retail stores that sell appliances have arrangements with banks in the background and allow consumers to apply for financing directly with the retailer, although the bank may be the ultimate provider of the funds. These are considered indirect loans but nevertheless are personal loans. Automobile dealers typically operate in this fashion.

Personal loans may be either installment or noninstallment loans. **Installment loans** are what the name implies, loans that are repaid over time in installments. The amount of money borrowed, the term, and the interest rate are amortized over time to produce interest and principal payments. These payments are fixed, based upon the rate of interest charged, and paid over the term of the loan (usually three to five years). Since most personal loans have an underlying asset as the purpose for the funding, the asset (like a car) remains the property of the bank until the loan is paid off.

The other type of personal loans is a **noninstallment loan**. These are for shorter terms than installment loans and for smaller amounts of money. In this regard, there are no periodic payments to be made, only a single lump-sum payment at the defined maturity of the loan. Typically, loans of this nature are for periods of less than six months and are for the immediate cash flow needs of the consumer. These loans are charged interest over the term which is paid back with the principal in a single amount at maturity.

Regardless, personal loans are a significant need of consumers and a key part of the lending process for a bank. Although individual loans may not be as large as commercial loans, since there are many that are made, the collective balances of these can be a considerable amount on the balance sheet of a bank.

Residential Mortgage Loans

One of the most popular and well-used consumer loans is the residential mortgage (real estate) loan. Mortgage loans are made to families to finance the purchase the largest single asset that families typically have, the home. Whether a home is built (new construction) or purchased from an existing owner, few consumers have the cash to pay for the home outright. Home prices can range from as low as $200,000 to well into millions of dollars. Many commercial banks make these loans, but not all. Mortgage loans can be among the riskiest of loans made to consumers, considering the amount and the fluctuating value of properties in the marketplace. Since a purchase price for a home is fixed at a point in time, it can either appreciate or depreciate in time. The bank will always seek to obtain the full amount of the loan principal back, plus interest, regardless of whether it is worth that much in the marketplace. This was seen during the financial crisis of 2008 where consumers obtained loans to purchase homes and the values plummeted in the marketplace. It was not unusual to see the value of a home be less than the amount of money owed to the bank. For this reason, the banks accept considerable risk for these loans, which can be sizeable in dollar amounts.

Another reason for risk is the term. Mortgages are long term, anywhere from 15–30 years. The longer the term, the more risk the bank faces, due to fluctuating interest rates as well as changing market values. The mortgage business is somewhat unique among the other types of loans. For this reason, banks typically have clearly defined departments for handling mortgage loans. Although they are part of retail banking, personal bankers do not generally make mortgage loans. A special group of trained mortgage originators is the sales force that solicits and takes applications for mortgage loans. Mortgage underwriters analyze the loans and make the credit decision, and mortgage services handle payment processing, customer service, and other back-office needs.

Home Equity Loans

Another retail loan available to consumers is the home equity loan. **Home equity loans** are available to consumers who own property, usually a home. In this regard, the consumer may have taken out a residential mortgage loan at some point in time. Whether they still owe a balance or not with the bank, home equity loans are based upon the equity in the home itself. Equity is the difference between what the home is worth (fair market value) and how much is owed on the home. For example, if an individual bought a home for $400,000 and took out a mortgage to pay for it in the same amount, at Day 1, they would have zero equity ($400,000 value – $400,000 loan = $0 equity). As time progresses, homes usually appreciate while, at the same time, the amount owed is declining. This increases the equity value in the home. Assume within three to five years the home increases in value to $600,000. If the amount owed on the mortgage is now $350,000, then the home has $250,000 equity ($600,000 – $350,000 = $250,000). This means that if the consumer could sell the home for $600,000, they would earn a profit of $250,000 after paying off the mortgage loan. Rather than having to sell the property to obtain the profit, home equity loans were developed to obtain the usage of the equity through a loan, based upon the home's increased value as collateral. Many consumers use the equity in their homes to obtain funds to remodel the home, add a pool, purchase a boat, take a big trip, or fill other more discretionary needs. Home equity loans allow this, leveraging the value of the home to obtain immediate funds. Obviously, the loan is an add-on to the existing mortgage and must be paid back, but the fact that positive equity exists creates the opportunity for the consumer that they might not otherwise have.

The downside of home equity loans is that if the property values decline suddenly, as they did during the financial crisis of 2008, a consumer may owe more than the home is worth (this is called being "underwater"). In this regard, even if the home could be sold, the amount of proceeds they would obtain would not be enough to pay off the original mortgage, plus any home equity loans. Therefore, consumers must be careful, and prudent, in how they consider home equity loans. Overall, home equity loans, like mortgage loans, are secured by the home itself. During the crisis, when many consumers were underwater, they literally walked away from the homes, and the banks took ownership of the collateral—an extreme situation, but nevertheless one to be cautious of.

Credit Cards

By far, one of the most popular forms of consumer credit are credit cards. Banks that offer credit cards often do so as part of an arrangement with an external party, and do so to obtain fee and interest income, or a share of it. Seldom are they direct issuers, as this requires a complete infrastructure to manage all aspects of the portfolio, requiring a strategic decisions, which is the province of larger banks. Credit cards are an extension of credit (i.e., a loan), very similar to a commercial line of credit. Once approved, the bank will establish a credit limit, based upon evaluative criteria, to be discussed later in this text. This flexible instrument allows the consumer to use the credit card to make purchases up to the defined credit limit established. For younger card holders, credit limits are often established at the $300–$500 range, to begin and build a credit history. All purchases made will be added to the ongoing balance owed, and a minimum payment will be charged to repay. Since this is also called *revolving credit*, as payments are made the amount of "available" credit (up to the credit limit) will be available to the cardholder and will continue over time.

Credit cards are one of the most flexible consumer loans available, as they put the borrowing amounts in the hands of the consumer. At the same time, credit cards are among the riskiest consumer loans. The reason for this is that they are fully unsecured, requiring no collateral. If the borrower does not repay the balance, there is no collateral for the bank to take ownership of. Given this and the flexible usage of the loan, interest rates are quite high on credit cards—much higher than installment loans or others. This compensates the bank for the lack of collateral and the highly risky nature of repayment. Because the interest rates are high (also called "usury rates"), it behooves the cardholder to repay the balance due each month to avoid paying excessive interest charges. However, most consumers do not do that and typically carry a balance, making minimum payments instead of paying off the full balance. This is acceptable to both bank and consumer and creates the appeal for this product. Today, after establishing solid credit repayment histories, credit limits can range upward of over $50,000. In this regard, significant purchases can be made for a small business or for large ticket items, such as a boat, major appliances, or major mechanicals (e.g., furnaces and air conditioning units). This is very valuable to consumers.

Recap

There is a wide variety of loans that can be made by a bank. These loans, particularly in the commercial area, can be further broken down into small business, middle market, and large cap organizations. Lenders are assigned based upon their experience and success in these areas. Loans generate interest income, which is the largest revenue source for the bank. It is important to understand the most common products offered to customers and how these contribute to the economy and the local communities.

Wealth Management

"Wealth management" is a newer term for "trust departments," which many banks had but now have expanded into a broader range of financial and investment services. As a result of this expansion of investment services, the concept of a trust department itself was somewhat limiting and therefore evolved into wealth management. Wealth management areas capitalize on the concept as the keepers or guardians of money, in a **fiduciary capacity**, which means that they act in the sole interest of the beneficiary's interests, not their own.

Interest income has been and continues to be the predominant source of income for a commercial bank. However, as banks have expanded their services and focused more on the financial needs of clients, the opportunity arose to develop a broader range of services to help meet the longer term needs of clients rather than the shorter term from loans and deposits. Wealth management combines the products and services that clients need to accumulate, grow, distribute, and transfer wealth. These products and services are needed throughout the life of clients, at various stages, and are used to produce net worth.

Wealth departments today are comprised of two primary areas, wealth and trust services. Both departments sell products and services for a fee, which is noninterest income for the bank. The products and services under each are outlined in the next several pages.

Wealth Services

Wealth services today are much more expansive and will be based upon the size and expertise of the bank. This is a strategic business and is competitive. In the past, individuals did not often consider commercial banks for their investment management needs; rather, they went to third parties offering these services individually or collectively. In many cases, investment banking was an area where individuals would go to have someone manage their investments. As banks began consolidating and offering these services, the concept grew in popularity based upon the financial strength of commercial banks and due to the other financial services banks already have managed. Today, wealth services consist of four primary areas:

- personal financial planning
- investment management
- retirement planning
- tax planning

As can be seen, these services collectively provide overall planning for the long term for a given client and are designed to grow and protect wealth for the future.

Personal Financial Planning

Personal financial planning is a holistic concept that focuses on the financial needs of a client throughout their life. There are professionals in practice today that offer these services independently, including certified financial planners (CFPs), chartered financial consultants (ChFcs) and personal financial planners (PFPs). Although many are in private practice, commercial banks have employed them as well for the delivery of these services.

Personal financial planning is a process and involves several areas of financial needs, including:

- insurance or risk management planning
- investment planning
- retirement planning
- tax planning
- estate planning

These are deemed the basic needs of a client, and the assessment of each dictates the plan. The process that is conducted for clients is orderly and follows a routine set of steps that financial planners will complete with the client. Although this is part of the traditional personal financial planning process, many of these functions are provided independently within wealth services. However, personal financial planning, as a discipline, involves several steps that will be utilized by the planner.

- information gathering: When working with the client, the first step is to obtain information about the client. Planners will gather information about the client's income, budget (if any), expenses, age, children and ages, plans to grow the family, insurance coverages, tax returns, trusts and/or wills, and other pertinent information to begin the process. This information will be studied, and a personal financial statement will be prepared. This will be a balance sheet and income statement for the individual (family) that identifies the overall net worth of the individual.
- identifying client's financial objectives: This is one of the most important parts of the process, and one individuals often overlook. This is a process to uncover what the current and future financial objectives are for the client. Planners will probe to determine what these items may be, but these goals and the time frame in which they are desired to occur is critical to the decisions that will ultimately be made. Client objectives will center around the following:
  - property ownership: future purchase of a home, second home, or larger home and when
  - college planning: ages of children (and future children), whether attending state or private schools, and when, to determine what the future financial needs will be
  - insurance protection: Proper coverage for insurance includes home, auto, disability, life, long-term care, and health insurance. Ultimately, all will be needed at some point in time. Many clients may not be aware of some of these needs, which is the job of the planner to remedy. Insurance is designed to protect hard-earned assets.
  - emergency funds: As part of the analysis, it should be determined how much money is needed in the event of a job loss to be able to sustain bill payment and quality of life until a new job is found. This can also be used for catastrophic medical needs.
  - capital expenditures: Define goals for a larger home, second home, boat, major travel, and other discretionary objectives that are desired. These must be defined, as the means to attain them must be planned for. This may define when they can make such purchases, if at all, and what one must do to be able to afford these in the future.
  - investment objectives: Define the goals for savings and investing, over time. It is important to define this to determine whether the expenditure goals above can occur or not. This may indicate how much risk the client must take to achieve this.
  - tax management and planning: As wealth increases, the tax burden will also increase. Taxes always must be considered in the process as well as strategies that can improve

or reduce a tax burden in the future. This may require involving a CPA or other tax specialist in the wealth department.

- » retirement planning: When would the client like to retire? At normal retirement age, sooner, or later? Will they be able to live as they have before once they retire? Both the time of retirement and the amount of funds needed in retirement must be defined in the plan.
- » estate planning: What are the overall objectives for transferring wealth after death? Who does the client wish assets to go to, or which charities, or other options? These objectives must be defined; otherwise, these can go into probate.

- analysis of the present position: The planner compiles all the information gathered, evaluates the objectives, and evaluates the present position of the client in conjunction with these. At this stage, the planner will consider alternatives to address deficiencies and define ways to meet the objectives, if possible.
- development and implementation of the plan: Based upon the alternatives determined and discussed, the planner will take all prior information and develop it into a comprehensive plan for the client to meet the defined and feasible objectives.
- periodic review and revision: Obviously, circumstances can change and can impact the execution of the plan. For this reason, a period review of the plan (semiannual or annual) is the final step. The reason for this is to ensure that the plan is being followed and events are occurring as planned. Depending on the extent of circumstances, the plan can be modified. The goal is to have a functioning plan that can be used all throughout the client's life.

Investment Management

The bank will employ investment advisors that are educated in the skills to make investments, manage a portfolio, and allocate assets in the most effective way. Clients seek experts who are well versed in the markets and are dedicated to managing one's portfolio to achieve the highest return possible while maintaining the safety of the principal.

Retirement Planning

Planning for retirement is challenging at times due to the span of time between the current age and planned retirement. The wealth services staff can estimate, based upon client input, the desired postretirement income needs to sustain one's lifestyle. Once determined, the planner will evaluate current and future income and contributions to savings accounts, 401(k) plans, IRAs, and others that can be used in retirement. In addition, a determination will be made of whether pensions exist or not and how much in social security can be expected in the future. All of which will contribute to the amount of income available at retirement. If the amounts are not sufficient, it may dictate working longer or paring back on living costs in retirement.

Tax Planning

It is necessary, as part of this department, to offer tax planning strategies to retain income. The tax law changes frequently, and as people age, their incomes tend to go up, putting them in higher tax brackets. To protect income earned, tax strategies should be considered and planned for to optimize income for savings to accomplish objectives and to save for retirement.

Trust Services

Trust services are the traditional trust management function that have been performed historically through the banks. Now, with the advent of wealth services, trust services are an excellent complement to the financial decisions being made in overall financial planning. These become additional products and services needed. Trust services can grow into sizeable operations for a bank with millions of dollars under management. This is predominantly due to wealth that has been created over a lifetime and that now must be administered for the benefit of others. Trust, like wealth services, generates fee income (noninterest income) for the bank. Most trust departments will offer the following range of services to clients:

- trust administration
- guardianships
- estate planning and management
- personal agency services

Trust Administration

There are literally hundreds of types of trusts that can be employed to provide instructions for the future beneficiaries of the client. Many trust administrators are lawyers, and this is needed when setting up complex trusts. The purpose of a **trust** is to manage estate assets. These trusts are managed by the bank on behalf of the beneficiaries and expected to act in this fiduciary capacity. Although there a myriad of trusts, too numerous to mention in this text, some of the more common include living trusts, charitable trusts, testamentary trusts, bypass trusts, and many more. They are used predominantly for the following reasons:

- to build assets for specific needs
- to receive insurance proceeds for distribution to minors or others
- to provide money to charities
- to manage the funds on behalf of beneficiaries too young or not capable of managing the assets effectively (to protect it)

To understand the nature of trusts, it is important to know the language of trusts. These include four parts:

- trust: This is the "corpus" of the trust; it represents the assets (e.g., cash, investment securities, real estate, etc.) that are contributed to form the trust.
- trustor: This is the person who creates the trust.
- trustee: person or entity that administers the trust or controls it. This would be the trust officer of the bank typically.
- beneficiary: This is the individual for whose benefit the trust is created.

Guardianships

These are established if a parent or guardian has died and the beneficiary is underage and not capable of managing the funds. Guardianships provide oversight of the funds, providing income to the beneficiary, but making all the financial decisions. This will include discretionary spending requested by the beneficiary. Often, these are established to provide income for the minor until they reach a certain age or to provide management and income if the trustor has felt that the beneficiary was incapable of managing the money effectively.

Estate Planning and Management

Estate planning is the process of passing on wealth to family and others by direction of the owner. Unfortunately, not everyone plans for this effectively, and when this occurs, assets may be distributed to unintended beneficiaries. For this reason, if an individual has developed a fair amount of wealth in life, it behooves them to plan and clearly define where the assets should go upon their demise. Part of the planning process includes a few terms that are important for understanding and planning:

- probate: *Probate* is a legal process whereby one's assets, after passing, are brought to probate court where an administrator may be appointed to manage the disposition of the assets. This can take quite some time and can be costly and is best avoided if possible. There are several ways to avoid probate, and these would be discussed with the client utilizing these services.
- wills: *Wills* are the final testament of the deceased and direct an executor to administer the will to the beneficiaries as intended. It is always best to have a will, as this puts the control into the maker of the will as to the disposition of their assets. Otherwise, the probate court will determine this.
- intestate: This results when an individual dies without having executed a will. In this case, the probate court will assign an administrator, and they will determine how assets will be distributed. This usually will be along the lines of surviving relatives, beginning with the spouse, if any. Although assets will be distributed eventually, this may not be how the deceased may have wished these assets to be distributed.

- estate taxation: Finally, estate taxation is the process by which the government evaluates the assets of a deceased and determines the amount of estate tax due the government. Estate taxation thresholds change and therefore must continually be evaluated. If someone accumulates enough wealth (this includes the value of property, stocks, bonds, savings accounts, etc.) beyond the threshold, they are subject to estate taxation. This can be considerable and will limit the amount of assets available to heirs; therefore, careful planning is required. Again, this can be complex and will require an estate expert or lawyer to guide the individual.

Personal Agency Services

The last area within the trust purview is personal agency services. These entail the safekeeping and custody of physical assets. Stock certificates and bonds as well as deeds and other important documents can be held by the agent on behalf of the client. This provides not only safety and security but also the ability to more easily perform other services related to the assets held.

Recap

Wealth management products and services, as outlined, are different than the core products of loans and deposits. Nevertheless, each of these services builds upon the entire financial relationship that the client may have with the bank. Wealth management, then, helps to solidify the entire relationship and retain the client for the long term, which is a goal of the bank. These services and products provide the final snapshot of what a bank offers in the marketplace, all financially driven. As banks build these holistic relationships, they enhance the loyalty of the customer and provide themselves with the greatest opportunity for revenue generation. Although wealth management services are noninterest (fee only), they contribute to the bank's overall income and are not generally subject to interest rate risk; therefore, they can be a welcome revenue base when interest rates are dropping.

CHAPTER SUMMARY

Often, the casual observer of commercial banks is not aware of the depth of products and services a bank might offer. As presented in this chapter, these products and services are financial and can be considered somewhat abstract instruments, as opposed to the tangible products of a retail store. Nevertheless, these are the products and services that are sold to generate revenue for the bank. New instruments continue to evolve and can be very creative for banks to compete with nonbank entities offering similar services. Crypto currencies, investment firms, mortgage companies, and fintechs all are competing to obtain clients needing these services.

It is important to understand the workings of the products offered for future planning. Banks start with a sales plan in their budget, which includes all the assets discussed (loans) and estimate the expenses generated from the deposits. This is a major part of the forecasting process in addition to the fluctuation of interest rates, which will be discussed in a later chapter.

END OF CHAPTER QUESTIONS

1. What is the difference between transaction and nontransaction accounts?
2. What accounts are considered "core" deposits?
3. What are the two traditional types of payment systems?
4. Identify at least two of the alternative payment systems.
5. What is the definition of "crypto currencies"?
6. What entity prints new currency?
7. What are the three parts of a check?
8. Name at least three reasons for loans to occur.
9. What, generally, is the purpose for a term loan?
10. What is the most important part of the financial planning process?
11. What two types of services are found in a wealth management department?
12. Identify at least three of the financial needs in the financial planning process.
13. What is the purpose of trust?
14. What is the purpose of a home equity loan?
15. What is another name for a loan?

Figure Credits

Fig. 3.1: Copyright © 2014 Depositphotos/VIPDesignUSA.

Fig. 3.2: Copyright © by Sergio Ortega (CC BY-SA 3.0) at https://commons.wikimedia.org/wiki/File:SampleBankbook.png.

Fig. 3.3: Copyright © by Sergio Ortega (CC BY-SA 3.0) at https://commons.wikimedia.org/wiki/File:BankStatementChequing.png.

Fig. 3.4: Source: https://www.dol.gov/olms/regs/compliance/smunion/smunions.htm.

Fig. 3.5: Source: https://commons.wikimedia.org/wiki/File:US_one_dollar_bill,_obverse,_series_2009.jpg.

Fig. 3.6: Source: https://commons.wikimedia.org/wiki/File:US-$1-SC-1935-A-Fr.2300.jpg.

Fig. 3.8: Copyright © 2012 Depositphotos/cteconsulting.

CHAPTER 4

Central Bank

Throughout the world, banks have proliferated and are integral to the ongoing economies of the communities they serve. Although not a prerequisite to the growth of commercial banking, many countries have developed a central bank for their country. *Central banks* are the banks for the commercial banks within the country. They provide a wide variety of functions and services, which varies based upon the type of government in the country. Nevertheless, as the world becomes a smaller place, financially and economically, the need for central banks has become an important ingredient in the stabilization of the financial system. The United States is no different. The central bank of the United States is the Federal Reserve, headquartered in Washington, DC.

This chapter will orient the reader to the role the central bank plays in the economy and how and why decisions are made. In the United States, the Federal Reserve is an independent body that works toward controlling any volatility in the economy to ensure its smooth operation, minimizing crises. Although not perfect, the Federal Reserve has been successful in its efforts during some of the most recent financial crises faced in the recent period in this country, and the world, for that matter. The following pages will provide the reader with a strong overview of what the Federal Reserve is all about.

Key Terms

Federal Reserve Board of Governors	Contractionary policy
Consumer price index (CPI)	Discount rate
Contractionary	Reserve requirement
Gross domestic product (GDP)	Moral suasion
Monetary policy	Federal Financial Institutions Examining Council (FFIEC)
Open market operations	CAMELS
Federal Open Market Committee (FOMC)	Discount window
Federal funds rate	Capital
Expansionary policy	Surpluses and deficits
	Entitlements
	National debt

Learning Objectives

By the end of this chapter, the student will:

- Understand the primary functions of the Federal Reserve in the United States.
- Know predominant goals of the Federal Reserve.
- Understand how the Federal Reserve is organized, how members are appointed, and terms.
- Learn about the role of the key committee of the Fed, the Federal Open Market Committee.
- Know the services that the Fed offers to its member banks.
- Learn about monetary and fiscal policies, how they are used, and their impacts.
- Understand and define the key Fed policy tools.
- Know the components and importance of the Fed's balance sheet.

Quick Overview of Central Banking in the United States

The United States did not always have a central bank. Alexander Hamilton, a confidant of George Washington, became the first treasury secretary of the United States, following its independence from England. Mr. Hamilton was an advocate of having a bank for the United States and, as a result, formed the first U.S. central bank in 1791. Although he maintained the need for this central entity, it did not function as well as intended. Unfortunately, Alexander Hamilton was killed in a duel and was not able to emphasize and support the need for a central bank, and it was formally closed in 1811.

For the next 100 years, the United States had no central bank. As the country grew and prospered, banks did evolve within the colonies and in the states that grew from expansion. Unfortunately, with no central federal oversight of these banks, there were many perils they faced, which impacted the smooth functioning of the economy. The much-heralded bank robberies of the Wild West of the late 19th century as well as numerous financial upheavals wreaking havoc on the marketplace provided the critical need for central oversight and stabilization. If the country was going to continue to grow and flourish, this was a necessity.

In 1913, Woodrow Wilson saw this need and resurrected the central bank through the Federal Reserve Act of the same year. Finally, after over 100 years, a central bank was developed, with the most immediate charge being to promote economic stability. The primary job of the Fed, from its inception, was to:

- Control the growth of money and credit.
- Ensure the supply and cost of money, and ensure credit from banks.
- Contribute to the nation's economic goals.
- Operate independently of the U.S. government for funding and policy.

Although much can be written about these early days, it is beyond the scope of this text.

Central Banking Around the World

Briefly, central banks exist throughout the world. The reason there is any mention of foreign central banks is to draw a comparison to them and the Federal Reserve in the United States. Additionally, as a result of globalization, financial markets operate across national boundaries and have been for some time. It has been learned all too well during the financial crisis of 2008 how much the world economy affects the United States—and how the United States affects the rest of the world. Central banks, albeit different internationally, play a key role in the stabilization of the world economy. As will be seen in Chapter 5, international agreements play a significant role in the functioning of banks within all countries.

Some of the primary central banks in the world are outlined here, along with their differences from the U.S. Fed (Rose & Hudgins, 2013).

European Central Bank (ECB)

Formed in 1998, this entity is headquartered in Frankfurt, Germany, and provides financial services to the European Union. The ECB is owned by member central banks throughout Europe, which is close to the Fed districts of the United States. This entity is relatively free to operate independently, similar to the Federal Reserve. Because they service sovereign nations, it would be necessary for them to operate independently of any country's control. In addition, this fosters greater economic stability of Europe, which aids stability in the world overall.

Bank of Japan

Although the Bank of Japan (BOJ) dates back to 1882, it was reorganized in 1942 and again in 1949, post–World War II. The Bank of Japan is owned by the Japanese government (55%) but carries 100% voting interests. Therefore, there is considerable government interest in the decision making of the BOJ, which would suggest less independence.

People's Bank of China

Headquartered in Beijing, China, this is the central bank of the People's Republic of China. The People's Bank of China (PBOC) is fully owned by the State Council of the People's Republic of China, established in 1948. Of the central banks outlined, this remains the least independent of government control.

Comparison

The purpose of this comparison is to establish some differences with the United States Federal Reserve. In addition, it is interesting to note that central banks, at least those discussed here, have not been in existence for hundreds of years, but are relatively newer phenomena; this is due, in part, to the growing industrialization of the economies and the growing global economy overall.

Independence is a much discussed topic in Washington, DC. Many argue that the Federal Reserve has too much power and that this should be under greater central control and oversight by the government. Although there are pros and cons to this and lessons that can be learned around the world, the reality is that the greater the independence of the central bank, the more likely they are to achieve the nation's economic goals. The following pages will outline how the Fed in the United States accomplishes these objectives and why they should or should not remain independent.

Organization of the Federal Reserve

In order to understand how the Fed operates, it is important to know its structure in the United States and why it is organized in such a way. The Federal Reserve is headquartered in Washington, DC. There are four primary components to the Fed's structure:

- Federal Reserve districts
- Federal Reserve chairman and vice-chairman
- Federal Reserve Board of Governors
- Federal Reserve presidents

Federal Reserve Districts

The Federal Reserve is organized into 12 Fed Districts throughout the United States. These districts are located throughout the United States in major cities. Each district services a geographic area (i.e., states and portions of states), providing services to all member banks within that district. The districts and cities are identified as follows (the number corresponds to the Fed district they support):

Table 4.1 **The 12 Federal Districts of the Federal Reserve**

Fed District	City	Geographic Area
1st	Boston	Maine, Vermont, New Hampshire, Massachusetts, Connecticut, Rhode Island
2nd	New York City	New York, northern New Jersey, southwestern Connecticut
3rd	Philadelphia	eastern Pennsylvania, southern New Jersey, Delaware
4th	Cleveland	Ohio, western Pennsylvania, eastern Kentucky
5th	Richmond	West Virginia, Virginia, Maryland, North Carolina, South Carolina
6th	Atlanta	Georgia, eastern Tennessee, Alabama, Florida, southern Mississippi, southern Louisiana
7th	Chicago	northern Illinois, Iowa, southern Wisconsin, northern Indiana, eastern Michigan
8th	St. Louis	eastern Missouri, southern Illinois, southern Indiana, western Kentucky, western Tennessee, northern Mississippi, Arkansas
9th	Minneapolis	Minnesota, northern Wisconsin, western Michigan (UP), North Dakota, South Dakota, Montana

(Continued)

Table 4.1 *(Continued)*

Fed District	City	Geographic Area
10th	Kansas City	Kansas, Nebraska, Oklahoma, northern New Mexico, Colorado, Wyoming
11th	Dallas	Texas, southern New Mexico, northern Louisiana
12th	San Francisco	California, Washington, Oregon, Idaho, Nevada, Utah, Arizona, Alaska, Hawaii

Board Chairman and Vice-Chairman

The Federal Reserve is led by a chairman and vice-chairman. The specifics of their appointments are:

- appointed by the U.S. president from the current board
- must be confirmed by the U.S. Senate
- appointed for renewable four-year terms

The past five chairman (over 40 years):

Chairman	Period in office
Jerome Powell	2018-present
Janet Yellen	2014-2018
Ben Bernanke	2006-2014
Alan Greenspan	1987-2006
Paul Volcker	1979-1987

Board of Governors

The **Federal Reserve Board of Governors** meets regularly with the chairman and vice-chairman in Washington, DC. These represent the voting members of the Federal Reserve system. Like the chairman and vice-chairman, they must be appointed.

- comprised of seven persons
- selected by the president of the United States
- confirmed by the U.S. Senate
- appointed for 14-year terms
- provide oversight of the Federal Reserve banks

Governors are appointed for lengthy terms of 14 years for two primary reasons: so that they are not influenced by any one administration since presidents will be in office for no more than eight years and to gain experience in witnessing economic cycles in order to be able to respond to the job of stabilizing the economy.

Federal Reserve Bank Presidents

Each of the 12 banks (districts) has a president of the Federal Reserve in that city. These individuals provide oversight of those Federal Reserve banks. Federal Reserve bank presidents are selected in accordance with the following:

- in accordance with the Federal Reserve Act
- identified and evaluated by the by the directors of the Federal Reserve bank
- approved by the Federal Reserve Board of Governors
- have terms of five years

Federal Reserve presidents are the chief executives of the Federal Reserve bank in that region and are responsible for, among other things, communicating monetary policy, ensuring a strong system of supervision to member banks, obtaining economic data and providing analysis and communication to member banks, and providing feedback to the Federal Open Market Committee.

Goals of the Federal Reserve System

As previously indicated, the Federal Reserve System functions independently of government intervention, with the exception of appointments. This is by design: to remain above the politics and remain focused on their primary mandate. This provides the chairman and the Board of Governors with tremendous power, as is outlined in further sections. The mandate of the Fed revolves around four primary goals:

- Keep inflation in check.
- Maintain full employment.
- Moderate the business cycle.
- Contribute toward achieving long-term growth (Rose & Hudgins, 2013).

These goals are focused predominantly on the economy, regardless of the administration and the politics of the time. One might ask, "How can a federal agency control each of these significant items, which seemingly are beyond the scope of most politicians, let alone the Fed?" The answer to this is through a variety of tools that, as will be seen, are powerful and can have immediate impact on the economy. Before explaining the impact of each of these and how the Fed has influence, the student should consider the financial crisis of 2008 and even the impact of the more recent COVID-19 pandemic and how these upheavals affected each of these four items and what was done about it. It is highly recommended that students pay close attention to the indicators of these areas and watch the Fed's actions over time to gain a strong understanding of these important focuses.

Keep Inflation in Check

Inflation is a measure of the increase in cost of goods and services measured by the change that occurs from period to period in percentage terms. This emanates from the change in the **consumer price index (CPI)** as the primary economic indicator that indicates the presence of inflation. The challenge with inflation is that as costs increase rapidly, it erodes the stability of the economy by reducing demand and depleting consumer funds, making large purchases unreachable and having a negative effect on consumer sentiment, relative to growth and prosperity. The impact is a slowing of commerce and therefore less profits. As this occurs, businesses will have to reduce their costs and conserve elsewhere, which will likely involve salaries, or employment. The bottom line is that inflation is very detrimental to the economy and that the Fed strives to maintain this at optimal levels. Generally, the Fed has applied a 2% threshold for inflation as the point in which action to raise interest rates would occur. Recently (August 2020), however, the Fed has moved to an "average inflation targeting" approach, which allows inflation to creep above 2% to a reasonable level and for a longer period of time before action is taken.

As will be seen later in the chapter, the Fed has many tools in order to affect inflation. One of those tools is to raise interest rates by making the cost of money more expensive. As the Fed increases rates, banks must do the same. By doing so, this will slow down demand, as it will cost more to borrow money and therefore slow the economy. Inflation occurs when there is more demand than supply or products; therefore, costs go up. By raising rates the Fed can slow this, as it will cost businesses more money to produce more to keep up with demand, and thus, as demand diminishes, costs will diminish. This is what is called a **contractionary** move by the Fed. In short, the economy is overheating and cannot continue at that pace.

Maintain Full Employment

By now most students are familiar with the unemployment rate, which is published periodically. The lower the rate, the better state the economy is in, as most people are employed. The Department of Labor publishes the unemployment rate regularly, and this is considered a key economic indicator. Although the unemployment rate is unlikely to ever hit a zero percentage rate, full employment is considered when the rate is in the 3%–4% range.

Unemployment is carefully watched, and again, one might ask how the Fed can have this as their goal if they do not control hiring people in businesses. The way the Fed does this is through the economic cycle, as discussed in Chapter 1. Employment is a function of business prosperity. As businesses grow and are profitable, they will grow through investing in new products, plants, technology, and other capital expenditures. As they do this, they will expand their workforce through hiring more people. Therefore, the Fed must influence businesses to grow and hire more people, thus reducing unemployment. If this maintained at 3%–6% ranges, the Fed is doing its job.

Moderate the Business Cycle

Moderating the business cycle is maintaining the stability of commerce. The reason the Fed exists is to ensure that frequent financial crises and panics do not exist or are kept at an absolute minimum. Prior to 1913 and in the 100 years after the original central bank failed, the United States experienced multiple financial and economic crises. This created significant hardships for burgeoning companies, especially during the early industrial period. In order to stabilize the business cycle, the Fed closely monitors many factors and the impacts these have on stability. Interest rates, money supply, loans, inflation, and jobs are all part of ensuring the stability of the business cycle. As illustrated in the economic cycle in Chapter 1, the Fed accomplishes this by monitoring closely these indicators and then taking action, using the tools it has available to moderate the cycle, if necessary. This is a proactive approach, allowing the Fed to monitor key economic indicators and data and to take action prior to it becoming a crisis and then reactively dealing with it after the damage has been done. An excellent example of this is the work the Fed did following the financial crisis in 2008. Although one might say this was reactive on their part, which it was to a degree, the further actions they took to prevent a worse situation were truly proactive and even nimble. Governments without this oversight can find themselves in frequent economic turmoil due to this instability, similarly to what has happened in Argentina over the years and now with Venezuela.

Contribute Toward Achieving Long-Term Growth

Although the Fed is independent of U.S. government control, like corporations, the prosperity of the United States and its ability to perpetuate the benefits that all U.S. citizens share is based upon growth. Growth for the United States economy is not measured in share price or net profit, but rather **gross domestic product (GDP)**. Gross domestic product is the sum of all goods and service sold in the United States. Growth is measured on a quarterly basis as to the percentage change in GDP from quarter to quarter. The reason GDP and long-term growth are so important is because they indicate production. As production grows, revenues increase, and as revenues increase, jobs proliferate, which is an indicator of prosperity. This growth also indicates that businesses are growing, requiring funding (loans), which facilitates this growth. It literally expands the opportunity for growth and lending. The Fed, therefore, contributes toward long-term growth by manipulating the money supply, manipulating interest rates, and stimulating the opportunity for growth to occur. Obviously, the Fed will act to prevent crises, which may slow the economy, but they are there to fuel the economy once they are certain that stabilization has returned, thereby contributing to the long-term growth of the country.

Functions of the Federal Reserve

Now that the goals of the Federal Reserve are known, let's now explore what functions they actually perform to achieve those goals. This is a very important section of this chapter, as this will define not only what functions the Fed performs but also what tools they have available to them to use. To begin, the Fed has three primary, broad functions. These include:

- monetary policy
- bank supervision
- financial services

Each of these functions is deep and provides the Fed with exceptional abilities, as will be explained.

Monetary Policy

Monetary policy is often talked about with regularity in the news. When the Fed acts, within this context, it has immediate impact. **Monetary policy** refers to the implementation of money and credit policies to achieve the Fed's primary goals of contributing to long-term growth and avoidance of high levels of inflation. Only the Fed has the ability to execute on monetary policy, and this is the most significant function they perform. Monetary policy is different than fiscal policy, which is the province of the executive branch and will be explained more fully later in this chapter. This is the primary function that affects the economy, influencing the legal reserves of banks, interest rates charged on loans, and currency values.

To understand monetary policy, one must understand the primary tools that are used to affect behavior. The four primary tools of the Fed include:

- open market operations
- discount rate

- reserve requirements
- moral suasion

These tools are significant and have immediate impact on the economy.

Open Market Operations

Before understanding this tool, it is necessary to understand the primary vehicle from which open market operations are orchestrated. This is accomplished by a committee, called the **Federal Open Market Committee (FOMC)**. The FOMC has as its primary function the implementation of monetary policy. Before delving into the actual tools utilized through this committee, it is important to understand its structure (Lehmann, 2005).

Meeting frequency

- approximately eight times per year, or every six weeks or so

Composition

- 12 members total
- Seven members of the Board of Governors plus five of the 12 Federal Reserve bank presidents, all voting members
- The Federal Reserve bank presidents serve on a rotational basis for terms of one year.
- Only the president of the New York Federal Reserve is a permanent member of the FOMC.

This committee is a policy-setting committee for the purposes of executing open market operations, which involves two primary tools.

- buy/sell government securities: The securities bought and sold in open market operations are U.S. Treasury securities (T-bills), T-notes, and T-bonds. These securities are assets on the Fed's balance sheet (discussed later in the chapter). Dependent upon the current state of the economy, the Fed will either purchase or sell securities in the marketplace. The reason for this is to either increase or decrease the money supply. Treasury securities are issued by the U.S. Treasury and are debt instruments of the United States government. These are issued to fund budget deficits in the fiscal budget. Once issued they are sold in the primary market by the Federal Reserve and are owned by investors. If the Fed, through open market operations, wishes to pursue a more expansionary policy (i.e., easy money), they will purchase securities from investors. As this occurs, these funds will be deposited in banks and therefore will increase the overall reserves at the Fed. As banks have more deposits, they will lend more, thereby helping businesses to grow, create jobs, and produce. This will stimulate or jump start the economy during times of slow growth or even recessions. This has a direct impact on the money supply and is how the Fed can directly impact the availability of money to stimulate or slow down the economy. To illustrate how this works, envision a bucket (see Figure 4.1). In the bucket is the money supply, predominantly M1 (checking accounts and cash), but also M2 (savings and time deposits). The bucket is finite in that the amount in the bucket does not exceed the size of the bucket. As the Fed sells securities, the money supply will decrease in the bucket and flow to the Fed's balance sheet. Less money will be available in the bucket because investors have purchased these securities, so less money is now available in bank reserves, which means less deposits in banks, which leads to less money to lend, and so forth. When the Fed buys securities, they are shrinking their balance sheet by ingesting money into the bucket (putting it back). Now, bank reserves go up because the bucket has now filled up again, which translates into more bank deposits and thusly more money for banks to lend. In short, the amount of water (M1) in and out of the bucket is the same water; it is simply poured back and forth between the Fed and the money supply.

Money Supply Example

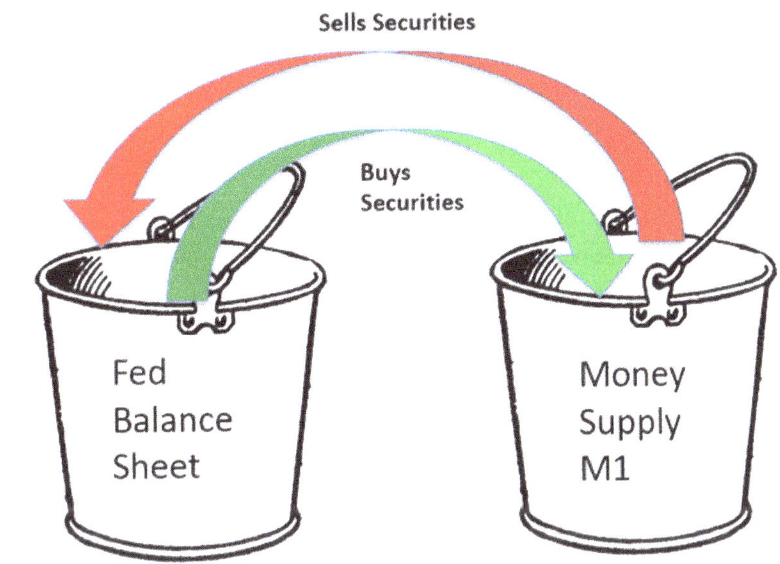

FIGURE 4.1 Money Supply Increase and Decrease

- changes to the federal funds rate: The second tool, which may coincide with buying and selling securities (but does not have to), is the manipulation of the **federal funds rate**. This rate is the rate that banks will charge one another when making loans to one another. When the Fed changes this rate, through the FOMC, it has an immediate impact on the lending rates of the banks. If the Fed raises this rate, lending rates (prime, LIBOR) will increase, very quickly, and the same when rates are lowered. The purpose for this is similar to purchases and sales of securities. In slower economic times, the Fed wants to stimulate the economy; therefore, they will likely lower the federal funds rate to make obtaining loans easier and cheaper. As this occurs businesses are more apt to borrow since their borrowing costs will be decreased. Again, this would be considered an **expansionary policy** whereby interest rates, which is the cost of money, are lowered. The reverse occurs when the economy is accelerating too rapidly. In this case the Fed would increase the federal funds rate to slow down the economy by making it more expensive to borrow. This is considered a **contractionary policy**. The federal funds rate is a powerful tool and has an almost immediate impact on the economy. It is considered a key economic indicator and is watched very closely as an indicator of how the Fed views the current state of the economy. Not only does this affect borrowing but it also affects the market (positive or negative), as it provide a glimpse of where the economy may be heading. The Fed will make changes in increments of 25 basis points, or more, although that has been the norm in the most recent period. Finally, it is this tool that is the driver for all interest rates and is a very good example of the Fed's ability to engage directly with the economy.

By far, this is the most important role that the Federal Reserve plays. The actions of the Fed translate into two policy actions, based upon what is occurring in the economy. The following is a handy chart for understanding the impact of either an expansionary or contractionary policy.

Discount Rate

Another rate that is controlled by the Fed is the **discount rate**. The discount rate is the rate that the Federal Reserve charges banks to borrow money from the Federal Reserve. The discount rate is set by the Federal Reserve bank's board of directors and is approved by the Federal Reserve Board. This occurs every 14 days for each Federal Reserve bank. Generally speaking, the borrowing of money from the Fed is not positively viewed and therefore is considered the "lender of last resort." This implies negative circumstances and that the bank has immediate or more urgent funding needs and may not be able to raise these funds through other sources, such as other banks. Borrowing from the Fed could also be called "central bank advances." Regardless of the terminology, the raising and lowering of the rate functions similarly to that of the federal funds rate: It will either stimulate or slow down borrowings. During the financial crisis of 2008, the discount rate was lowered significantly to near zero. Obviously, more banks took advantage of borrowing from the Fed than usual during this time. The goal of the Fed was to make sure banks had sufficient liquidity and funding sources so that they could continue to lend. In this regard, the nature of this action was viewed less negatively than previously.

Reserve Requirement

The **reserve requirement** is the amount of money that member banks of the Fed must maintain on deposit at the Fed. A formula exists that is applied for the determination of this amount, as well as its timing, which is based upon two items: the percentage rate charged and the total dollar threshold for determining what rate is applied. This system

Table 4.2 **Monetary Policy Impact**

Fed policy	Symptom	Fed action	Effects	Impact
Expansionary (easy money)	Periods of recession; economy at the bottom of the cycle	Buys treasury securities Puts money into the economy Grows the balance sheet	Bank reserves	Increase: deposits in bank expand
			Interest rates	Decrease: stimulates growth through cheaper credit
			Bank lending	Increase: Banks have more money to lend.
			Money supply	Increase: MI (DDA+Currency) increases.
			Demand	Increase: Fed incents people to borrow, cost of money goes down.
Contractionary (tight money)	Economy at its peak	Sells treasury securities Takes money out of the economy Restrains growth to prevent inflation Slows the economy	Bank reserves	Decrease: Deposits go down due to payment for securities
			Interest rates	Increase: Fed funds goes up, money harder to get
			Bank lending	Decrease: Banks lend less, more costly to borrow money
			Money supply	Decrease: MI (DDA+currency) decreases due to money leaving the system
			Demand	Decrease: Money more costly, demand for money goes down

is based upon a tiered amount of deposits on file at the bank. Only transaction deposits are taken into account when this calculation is made; however, vault cash can be a part of the total requirement. Once the calculation is made, this becomes the amount of money that must be maintained at the Fed. Although these funds earn a nominal rate of interest, they cannot be used by the bank for the specified two-week period. As banks grow their deposits, their reserves will grow, expanding the money supply. Since bank deposits can change daily, the Fed uses a two-week interval to make the calculation and determine the dollar amount to be maintained. The Fed seldom changes the rates; however, the thresholds of dollar deposits changes more frequently. The reserve requirement came about after the Great Depression and the stock market crash of 1929. During that time there was no reserve requirement, and many banks failed as a result. More specifics will be revisited during the liquidity chapter.

Moral Suasion

The last tool of monetary policy is **moral suasion**. Although this tool is not financially based, it is nevertheless very powerful. The Federal Reserve is the central bank of the United States, and since most banks are members of the Fed, they are influenced by the Fed. The Federal Reserve exerts tremendous influence over banks through the three tools already mentioned. As a regulator as well, the Fed can exert intense psychological pressure by the fact of their power. This is done to ensure conformity with its policies. Banks will seek approval from the Fed prior to actions they are considering taking. This is preferred, as opposed to being criticized by the Fed, which can result in monetary penalties or restrictive covenants. Therefore, this tool is very real for banks.

Bank Supervision

The Federal Reserve, in addition to being the nation's central bank, is also a bank regulator. Although there are several bank regulators, which will be identified in the next chapter, the Fed also performs examinations of banks. In general, the Fed will work in tandem with state regulators for state chartered banks. The Federal Reserve is also part of the **Federal Financial Institutions Examining Council (FFIEC)**. This council is made up of the Federal Reserve, the Office of the Comptroller of the Currency, the Consumer Financial Protection Bureau, the National Credit Union Administration, and the Federal Deposit Insurance Company. These regulators work in concert to develop and ensure that principles and standards are uniformly applied to the examination of financial institutions.

The primary exam performed by the Fed is annual safety and soundness exams of financial institutions that are regulated by them. The Fed trains and employs a group of examiners whose job it is to perform these examinations. A typical examination is conducted each year and will last at least two weeks, if not more. The Fed, as with other regulators, will evaluate the bank on the basis of a standardized rating system, entitled **CAMELS**. CAMELS is an acronym for capital, asset quality, management, earnings, liquidity, and market (interest) sensitivity. This is the scope of a typical exam of a bank from which the Fed will render a score on a five-point scale.

In addition to analyzing the bank's performance in these areas, they also evaluate and ensure that the bank is compliant with current laws. These will include the many key regulations that will be discussed in the next chapter but also social responsibility laws relative to the Truth in Savings, Truth in Lending, Equal Credit Opportunity, and Credit Responsibility Acts.

The results of these examinations can have a tremendous impact on the bank, dependent upon the ratings received. If the bank is deemed less than satisfactory or below (a score of 3, 4, or 5 in CAMELS), the Federal Reserve can levy penalties and/or restrictions or other covenants that can restrict the bank from a variety of activities until improvement is made to their satisfaction. In this regard, the Federal Reserve has tremendous power and can take very draconian actions, as deemed necessary, which are best avoided. The examination role is intense; few organizations are examined with such detail as commercial banks. This primary function of the Fed provides the public with confidence that they are managing the hard-earned assets of the public in an accurate and legal manner and in the true capacity of a fiduciary. This is also a source of significant career opportunities for students seeking a governmental role and deep understandings of the workings of banks.

Financial Services

The Federal Reserve is, after all, the bank's bank. In this regard, they render financial services to member banks. This final function of the Fed is more operational than economic or regulatory, as discussed previously. Commercial banks are encouraged, and desire, to be members of the Federal Reserve. They do this not only for the confidence of the public but also to avail themselves of the many services the Fed provides to banks—many of which are not available elsewhere. First, commercial banks must purchase stock in the Federal Reserve to become members. This can be up to 3% of paid-in capital and surplus. Banks, then, can utilize the following primary services that are offered by the Fed:

- wire transfer: The Fed provides the Fedwire system to member banks to enable making wire transfers for customers of the bank. This is the secure, electronic movement of funds from the bank to the entity requiring it.
- safekeeping: The Fed provides the safekeeping and custody services for securities that are owned by the bank.

- coin and currency: The Fed supplies the cash and currency needed by commercial banks within their district via armored car. This is the cash needed for banks to operate on a day-to-day basis. This cash is maintained in the Fed's vaults, and they destroy old cash and order new currency from the U.S. Treasury.
- loans to banks (discount window): As mentioned previously, the discount window allows commercial banks to borrow money from the Fed, if needed. The Fed charges the discount rate as the rate of interest paid by the commercial bank. This, typically, will be at a premium above the base federal funds rate.
- clearing checks: The Federal Reserve is a clearing agent in the check collection process. Checks are still used in the financial environment and ultimately have to be collected. This collection process culminates with credits and debits to the reserve accounts maintained by banks at the Fed.
- new security issues: The Federal Reserve issues new Treasury securities received from the U.S. Treasury. These are new securities issued to fund federal spending and deficits. The U.S. Treasury issues the securities, and the Federal Reserve, through the Federal Reserve Bank of New York, issues these to the public through auction. Once sold, they are then traded in the secondary market.
- bank information: The Federal Reserve regularly performs economic research as well as compiles and analyzes information about banks and makes these available to the public. This is a very valuable service and contributes to the transparency and oversight function of the central bank.

Federal Reserve Balance Sheet

Similar to banks and other corporations, the Federal Reserve has a balance sheet. The balance sheet provides a point-in-time view of the assets and liabilities of the Federal Reserve. As part of monetary policy, the news media often refers to the Fed's balance sheet and whether they are reducing or increasing their balance sheet. What this predominantly refers to is the buying and selling of Treasury securities, an open market operation. Treasury securities are assets; they are instruments held by the Fed. However, the balance sheet of the Fed has other accounts that relate to the many functions of the Federal Reserve. It is for this reason that it is important to understand what is contained, at a high level, on the balance sheet so that the student will have a deeper understanding of how this is a snapshot of the various actions the Fed takes.

Figure 4.2 provides a picture of what this balance sheet may look like. This is denominated in billions of dollars. Each of the components will be explained following this statement.

Federal Reserve Balance Sheet
(In Billions)

ASSETS		LIABILITIES	
Gold, Foreign Exc.	$ 18.17	Fed. Reserve Notes	$ 1,656.47
US Govt. Securities	4,378.63	Bank Deposits	2,278.46
Loans to Banks	.34	Other	8.92
Other	53.09		
		Capital	
		Total Capital	56.38
Total Assets	$4,450.23	**Total Liabilities & Capital**	$4,450.23

FIGURE 4.2 Federal Reserve Balance Sheet

Assets

The assets of the Fed's balance sheet are divided amongst the largest categories of assets, including gold, Treasury securities, loans to banks, and others.

Gold

Looking at the balance sheet, the first primary line item is gold and foreign exchange. This represents the approximate current value of these instruments, which is most closely related to cash or cash equivalents. Although the United States is no longer on the gold standard (since the 1970s), it has maintained gold bullion as a foundation for representing its wealth and prosperity and provides tangible substance of this wealth, albeit not as important as it once was. Many people believe all the gold that is maintained is held in Fort Knox, Kentucky. This is only partly true. The rest of the gold is held in the New York Federal Reserve Bank; the West Point, New York, mint; and the Denver mint. Gold is held by the Federal Reserve via certificates issued by the U.S. Treasury as a custody service that is performed. Obviously, gold value will fluctuate with the market, but this is the derivation of the amounts reflected in the balance sheet.

U.S. Government Securities (Treasuries)

These represent the U.S. Treasury securities that the Fed has. These are assets and represent the amount of securities the Fed has purchased, and held, over time. When the Fed is shrinking or growing its balance sheet, it is here where this occurs. The Fed uses the purchase or sale of Treasury securities to either increase or decrease the supply of money in the market. As can be seen in the balance sheet, this is a large portion of the total assets; therefore, it is a significant tool of influence in the Fed's arsenal.

Loans to Banks

Again, this is an asset to the Fed, and relatively small in proportion. The reason for this is that, as has been learned, the Fed makes loans to banks. This is done via the **discount window**, as the "lender of last resort." It is for this reason that the balance in this account is relatively low. Banks do not go to the Fed for money regularly—only when it is an emergency, or the last resort.

Other assets

The remainder of the total assets for the Fed would be vested in equipment, property, and other tangible assets that are not significant in the Fed's economic role. For this reason, these will not be discussed in depth.

Liabilities

As with other corporate balance sheets, the Fed has liabilities, or money owed to others. These are obligations of the Fed and, in part, cause the balance sheet to balance (short of capital). As will be seen, the primary accounts illustrated here have a bearing on some of the assets discussed. This is an important learning opportunity, as it may clarify the derivation of some of these accounts and create further understanding how the Fed operates. Only the most significant of the liabilities are outlined here: Federal Reserve notes, bank deposits, and other.

Federal Reserve Notes

As noted, this is a significant portion of the liabilities on the balance sheet. Federal Reserve notes are obligations of the government and, in short, cash or currency. If one would look at a typical bill, of any denomination, and look at the top of the bill, the words "Federal Reserve Note" will appear. As discussed in Chapter 3, this is the United States' currency and are now "notes," or obligations of the government through the Federal Reserve. In the distant past, currency was not Federal Reserve notes but, rather, certificates redeemable in gold or silver. Silver certificates can still be found today, but mostly in auction houses or through collectors. Since these no longer exist, generally, Federal Reserve notes have replaced them and therefore must be reflected as obligations (debt) on the Fed's balance sheet. This means that they are redeemable for the face amount indicated in the denomination, and it is the government's obligation to back that. Since the U.S. government has a strong credit rating, these notes have value. Federal Reserve notes are currency and, as such, represent a portion of M1, cash. When the Fed sells Treasury securities, M1 will decline because money is flowing out of the system. The next account is also affected by the Fed's monetary policy actions.

Bank Deposits

This account represents the reserves that member banks hold at the Federal Reserve. Since these are deposits made to the Fed, the Fed owes these funds to the banks. This, also, carries a significant balance on the balance sheet. The main reason for this is that through the buying and selling of securities (open market operations), this amount will go up when the Fed buys securities and down when it sells securities. When more money flows into the money supply through purchases of securities, it will be deposited at banks. As bank deposits increase, reserves at the Fed will increase. Therefore, the act of buying and selling securities from the Fed's balance sheet will impact Federal Reserve notes and checking accounts (M1) and the amount of reserves held at the Fed. Reserves, however, are only a portion of the total deposits, consisting of transaction deposits and the percentage that must be maintained, 3%–10% of these amounts. That is what is represented in bank deposits.

Other

This is a relatively immaterial amount and is beyond the scope of this discussion. These would represent other, miscellaneous obligations that the Fed might have.

Capital

The final part of the Fed's balance sheet is **capital**. Capital, generally, represents ownership. Since this amount is not significantly material, no real depth will be provided. However, one aspect of this account would represent the ownership that member banks have. As one will recall, member banks must purchase shares in the Federal Reserve to enjoy these services. This amount is fixed as a percentage of the capital the banks have and is reflected here as capital.

Recap

Although the balance sheet shown in Figure 4.2 is dated (past five years or so), it is shown to highlight the key aspects of what the Fed's balance sheet entails. Understanding the nature of these accounts helps to understand how the Fed uses these accounts to achieve its goals defined earlier in this chapter. The next section, the fiscal budget, is not controlled by the Fed and is not one of their tools; however, it is important to discuss because the actions of the federal budget have a bearing on the Fed's balance sheet and should be understood.

Fiscal Policy (Budget) of the United States

Fiscal policy is not a tool of the Fed, but rather that of the executive branch, and approved by the legislative branches of the government. So why include it in a chapter on the central bank? The answer to this question is the economy. As outlined, the Fed is responsible for stabilizing the economy and supporting long-term growth. Fiscal policy, on the other hand, is the government's plan for the fiscal year in terms of receipts and disbursements. Each year, the executive branch (the president) works with their staff to develop a budget for the next fiscal year. This is the equivalent of an income statement. As this is completed, it must be presented and approved by congress before it can be put into operation. For the U.S. government, the fiscal year-end is September 30th; therefore, the budget process must be started early to have the time for development, changes, and final approvals. Since the U.S. government is a nonprofit entity, the job of the executive branch is to set forth the plan for the coming fiscal year in terms of the receipts expected and how these will be spent. As with other nonprofits or government entities, receipts should equal disbursements (i.e., only spend up to what is earned). In reality, we all know that does not always occur, and when it does not is when **surpluses and deficits** occur, and therein lies the relationship to the Fed.

An example of an abbreviated fiscal budget is presented in Figure 4.3. Similar to the Fed's balance sheet, this is a dated budget (last several years), but that is not important. What is most important is understanding the key items that make up receipts and disbursements and what the net result is. For the purposes of simplicity, these items are reflected in trillions of dollars.

Receipts

Receipts represent funds flowing into the government, or revenues. Although the U.S. government has many forms of revenue sources, the most significant and the drivers of the fiscal budget are the items shown in Figure 4.3. Some of these are well known, whereas others may have been heard about many times in the news but may not be well understood in regard to where they come from or what impact they have overall.

Fiscal Budget and Policy (Trillions of Dollars)

Category		Last Year	Proposed Year	% Increase (Decrease)
Receipts				
- Income Tax		$1.38	$1.48	7.25%
- Social Security		1.02	1.06	3.92%
- Corporate Tax		.33	.41	24.24%
- Indirect/Other		.26	.29	11.54%
	TOTAL	**$3.00**	**$3.24**	**8.00%**
Disbursements				
- Social Security/Welfare		$2.23	$2.42	8.52%
- Goods & Services/Defense		1.18	1.16	(1.69%)
- Debt Interest		.22	.24	9.09%
	TOTAL	**$3.63**	**$3.82**	**5.23%**
Surplus (Deficit)		($.63)	($ .58)	(7.94%)
Total Debt (approx.)		$17.9	$18.5	**3.31%**

FIGURE 4.3 Fiscal Policy (Budget) of the United States

Income Tax

The largest of the key drivers of revenue is personal income tax. This is the income taxes all citizens pay to the federal government in our paychecks and through other sources of income. Each year, the Internal Revenue Service requires everyone with earned income (beyond a certain amount) to file a tax return. This is the accounting of all earnings and payments of tax made throughout the calendar year. As taxes are collected through payroll withholdings or payments made by April 15th, this is a very significant portion of the total receipts of the U.S. government—roughly 45% of all receipts. This ability or authority to tax provides the U.S. government with the high credit rating they enjoy.

Personal taxation becomes a very political topic for individuals seeking the presidency. The population tends to not favor tax increases or unfair tax assessments, so using this as a vehicle to increase receipts can be precarious. Nevertheless, it is the law, and this is a significant portion of all receipts, which are used to fund the disbursements.

Social Security

Social Security is an entitlement. It ultimately provides retirement and disability benefits to the population. However, these funds, although paid by the government, come from individual paychecks. All citizens who are working have withholdings beyond income tax that the government receives. In this segment, this is called **FICA** (Federal Insurance Contributions Act). This is a percentage of each paycheck that is withheld and paid to the government. In a sense, it is like a retirement savings account, as some of this will be returned when one retires. Unfortunately, this is not on a dollar-for-dollar basis, as the funds are used for other purposes, which will be explained in the Disbursements section. In addition to FICA, Medicare is another area of contribution. Withholdings for Medicare fund this social insurance program that is available to everyone when they reach the age of 65.

As illustrated, Social Security and Medicare account for at least another 35%–40% of total receipts, such that together with income tax this is 80% of the total receipts. Both are quite significant sources of revenue, and generally can be counted on, as it is based on the law.

Corporate Tax

Similar to individuals, businesses are also taxed. Corporations and other business forms must file tax returns and pay taxes based upon their revenue earned. For businesses this has been as high as 40% and is now in the 20% range. Although very large corporations can produce a high amount of revenue, and therefore a sizeable amount of taxes, corporate taxes represent about 12% of the total receipts.

Indirect/Other

The last area is made up of a variety of sources of revenue. These are lumped into this category whereby they, individually, may be less material. For this reason, the focus, for emphasis, is on the sources that represent over 90% of the receipts indicated.

Disbursements

Disbursements represent what the government plans to do with the money that is received from its citizens. Since the majority of revenue is generated from taxation, all of the disbursement categories are paid for from mostly taxpayer dollars. It is for this reason that a concern is always raised when significant expenditures are made. As with receipts, the focus for disbursements will be on the three broad areas where money is spent. Although there is much more detail going into those accounts, they clearly define where money is going.

Social Security/Welfare

These are called **entitlements** because they are guaranteed payments to individuals who qualify for these programs. As disbursements, the U.S. government will make Social Security payments to individuals who have reached retirement age, are on disability, or who do not have income sources and need to receive welfare payments. The challenge with this disbursement area is that it does not match the source of funds received to fund it since welfare recipients may not have paid into the program (or paid very little) and individuals who qualify for disability can obtain payments without contributions. When compared to receipts in this category, the disbursements are over 100% of receipts. Therefore, more money is being spent than what is received. It is for this reason that the sentiment of younger people is that there will not be enough funds available when they retire to receive payments. Whether this is true or not, it clearly is an area that requires attention, given the receipts. Other social programs proposed, such as free college education and Medicare for everyone, would become additional entitlements and therefore increase disbursements.

Goods and Services and Defense

Approximately 30% of disbursements are directed to the defense of the country and other goods and services. The largest of the two would be defense, which includes all branches of service, supplying the military with equipment and arms and maintaining troops around the world. This is another very political and controversial area of disbursements. The defense of all citizens is constitutional but will fluctuate based upon the current administration's plans. Goods and services include other items the government is involved in offers. These would include the various agency staff expenses, equipment, salaries, and others.

Debt Interest

The last area of disbursements is not subject to discretion. Although this is only about 6%–7% of total disbursements, its derivation is an important consideration. The U.S. government is obligated to "service" its debt. What that means is that they have to make interest payments on borrowings, which is a contractual obligation. For the most part, this represents the interest payments that must be paid on Treasury securities in existence. Treasuries are either T-bills, T-notes, or T-bonds. Investors purchase these because they are virtually risk-free and they pay interest. This is a good place to invest in times of uncertainty because they are backed by the full faith of the U.S. government, predominantly because the government has the power to tax and raise funds to make these payments. Nevertheless, they represent a growing obligation of the government that evolves from the fiscal budget. This will be explained fully in the next two sections.

Surplus or Deficit

When looking at the fiscal budget, as described previously, receipts should equal disbursements. However, in reality, this seldom occurs with the U.S. government. If more money is spent than what is received, it is call a *deficit* or *deficit spending*. When this occurs for an individual, they either have to earn more money, reduce their expenditures, or borrow money to pay for the deficit. That is exactly what the federal government does, but on a regular basis. As shown in the fiscal budget for the "proposed year," a deficit of ($.58 trillion), or approximately $58 billion, exists. This shortfall must be funded; otherwise, the government would have to reduce their expenditures or increase their revenues, neither of which are easy to do. Therefore, the government borrows money to fund the deficit. To do this, the U.S. Treasury issues new Treasury securities, which are sold in the primary market by the Federal Reserve. As investors buy these securities, the government has the funds to pay the deficit. This is where there is overlap with the Federal Reserve and creates the existence of Treasury securities, which are a significant part of the Fed's role in affecting the economy.

Securities are purchased by a wide variety of investors, including foreign governments, like China and others. Ultimately, when they mature, the principal must be repaid. Obviously, the goal is to spend within one's means. If this occurs, where receipts match disbursements, this is called a *balanced budget*. When this occurs, there is no need to issue new securities. If the opposite occurs—a surplus—more money was received than paid out. This is fiscally the best scenario, for the reasons indicated in the next section.

Total Debt

This is the bottom line for the U.S. government. When budget deficits exist and the shortage must be funded by issuing debt (Treasury securities), the amount issued is added to the **national debt** of the country. As deficit spending continues, the total debt continues to grow. Today, this is approximately $25 trillion (and growing). If the fiscal budget were to generate a surplus, this would be used to reduce the national debt. The question becomes, how much is too much in regards to the national debt? As major programs are advanced, requiring more deficit spending, who pays the debt in the future? Many indicate this will be passed on to future generations. Regardless, the national debt is growing and will only get larger unless new revenue sources are opened or taxes are increased.

Recap

The fiscal budget is a very telling document and helps to shed light on how the economy functions and how the work of the Federal Reserve is intertwined with the executive branch of government through the fiscal budget and the Department of the Treasury. The Treasury Department is responsible for collecting the taxes through the Internal Revenue

Service (revenue) and issuing Treasury securities to fund deficits, which are sold through the Federal Reserve.

CHAPTER SUMMARY

The central bank is an important role in any country. For the United States, the Federal Reserve is a critical ingredient for the stability of the economy, and the reason it exists. This chapter is a crucial ingredient in understanding commercial banks: how they operate, why, and how they are regulated and controlled. Commercial banks are integral to the economy and are instruments of growth and prosperity for commerce and the populace. The Federal Reserve is the bank for commercial banks as well as the government's bank. For this reason, understanding how the Fed manages and controls the economy is paramount to success of the country and the prosperity of its citizens. Understanding this economic role, the integration of commercial banks and the government's role, provides the foundation for truly understanding the important discipline of commercial banking.

END OF CHAPTER QUESTIONS

1. Identify the four goals of the Federal Reserve.
2. When was the Federal Reserve formed?
3. What are the key tools of monetary policy?
4. Identify the three primary functions of the Federal Reserve.
5. What is the term limit for the Federal Reserve governors?
6. How many governors are on the Fed board?
7. If the Fed is pursuing an expansionary policy, are they purchasing or selling securities?
8. What is the difference between monetary and fiscal policy?
9. What is the discount window of the Federal Reserve?
10. How many Fed districts are there in the country?

CHAPTER 5

The Regulatory Environment

One of the major differences between commercial banks and other organizations is regulation. *Regulation* refers to supervision for compliance with laws. Commercial banks manage close to 25% of the financial resources in the country. As such, trust and confidence as well as accuracy of reporting are vital to ensure the public trust. Because of the importance of commercial banks to the economy, regulations are a critical ingredient in the protection of hard-earned client assets. As learned in the last chapter, the Federal Reserve is a major part of the regulatory environment, and the reason for its existence. Economic and financial stability are an absolute necessity for a well-functioning country, and therefore, some level of oversight is needed.

Regulations tend to be reactive in nature and for this reason evolve around economic upheaval or periods of financial instability. The goal is to prevent reoccurrence. As such, regulations can also become too restrictive, such that they impede growth and prosperity. A happy medium, therefore, is in order, and with well-thought-out regulations and oversight, economic stability will prevail. Of course, this is a big job. This chapter is not only about outlining the myriad of key regulations in existence today and laying the structural groundwork for how they banks are supervised and evaluated but is also about how to understand what regulations create and to critically review the necessity for timely and prudent development for the future.

Key Terms

- Dual banking system
- Federal Financial Institutions Advisory Council (FFIEC)
- Community Reinvestment Act (CRA)
- Annual percentage yield (APY)
- Personally identifiable information (PII)
- Suspicious activity report (SAR)
- Public Company Accounting Oversight Board (PCAOB)
- Toxic assets
- Troubled Asset Relief Program (TARP)
- Consumer Financial Protection Bureau (CFPB)
- Volker Rule
- Systemically important financial institutions (SIFI)
- FinREG
- Basel Accords
- Basel Committee on Banking Supervision (BCBS)
- CAMELS
- Uniform Financial Institutions Rating System (UFIRS)
- Component and composite ratings

Learning Objectives

By the end of this chapter, the student will:

- Understand the reasons for bank regulation.
- Become familiar with the principal regulators.
- Know the foundation regulations that paved the way for the future.
- Learn the complexities of the more recent regulations affecting banks.
- Understand how banks are supervised and rated by the regulators.

Why Are Banks So Heavily Regulated?

Commercial banks are among the most intensely regulated industries today. These regulations have emerged over time but following financial upheavals, such as the Great Depression of the 1930s and the financial crisis of 2008. Regulations are born of necessity but, more importantly, are in place to protect consumers (Rose & Hudgins, 2013).

Regulation Rationale

The rationale for regulations centers around three principal needs. These needs form the basis for the creation of regulations for the industry. Regulations can be most effective if designed with these needs in mind. There can be no argument that they are needed, especially considering the financial crises that have occurred over the years. The challenge is to design these in ways that are not significantly restrictive or that work against the stability of the bank.

Safeguard the Public's Savings

Clients must have a place to safely store their funds. Trust, as a result, is an absolute necessity. Clients must be comfortable to deposit funds in the bank and expect that it is protected and will not be lost. During the Great Depression, many people lost their money when runs occurred on the banks. At that time there was no insurance to protect savings from loss. What resulted from this crisis was the FDIC Act, creating the Federal Deposit Insurance Company, which now insures deposits up to $250,000. Without this protection, customers would be reluctant to put their money in banks, and if banks do not get the deposits they need, then they cannot lend money to businesses for them to grow. The economic cycle stops, and the banking system would be in peril. Safeguarding the public's savings, therefore, is a major reason for regulation.

Bring Stability to the Financial System

As indicated above, if savings (deposits) cannot effectively be protected, the overall financial system (commercial banks) would be jeopardized. The financial system in the United States is central to the economic cycle. Banks function as intermediaries between consumers and businesses to stabilize and cause the financial system to prosper, resulting in a strong economy. This stabilization is a goal of the Federal Reserve, and this is aided by the establishment of the rules (regulations) for oversight.

Prevent Abuse of Financial Service Customers

The last focus of regulation is to prevent abuse. Although commercial banks are critical components of a functioning economy, they are independent corporations. As corporations, they have shareholders who invest in the bank to earn a return and grow their investment. In pursuit of these goals, profitability and growth become major incentives for the bank and create the possibility that riskier actions might be taken in pursuit of this or that inappropriate usage of customer funds may occur. To prevent these possibilities, regulations are designed to monitor activities and provide rules for proper behavior, which is examined by the regulators to ensure compliance. Although regulations generally prevent most of these improper activities, issues do occur. Examples of this include Wells Fargo's fraudulent account openings and the passing of the Volcker Rule to prevent banks from making risky investments using client funds. Nevertheless, preventing abuses is a major emphasis. The Consumer Financial Protection Bureau (CFPB) exists for this reason.

Impact to Commercial Banks

One of the challenges to commercial banks is that regulations can be burdensome. They are costly, in that the implementation of the regulation may require an increase in staff, significantly, to perform the actions required of the regulations. A good example of this is the Bank Secrecy Act (BSA), which has required the creation of whole departments to meet the requirements. The risk management function is another example of significant increases in staff required over the last several years as a result of regulations. So, in a sense, regulations have in some ways reduced the profitability of banks by increasing their expenses and/or limited their ability for discretionary spending due to capital requirements. As costs increase, banks' efficiency ratios will increase unless they can find other ways to generate revenue or decrease costs. For these reasons much of the response from the banking community has been less favorable toward regulations, with the general sentiment being that they impede their ability to innovate and grow. In some cases, regulations have been so draconian as to place smaller community banks at risk of failure.

Regulation implementation and regulatory exams are very time consuming and deter from a bank's primary role of providing products and services to clients. This battle between meeting the regulatory demands and the demands of the bank (i.e., satisfying the CEO and shareholders or satisfying the government) is a constant challenge. In both cases, they are "must do" situations and continually raise the need for responsible regulation.

Today, commercial banks are under a dual mandate of federal and state oversight. This **dual banking system** provides both governing bodies significant regulatory authority. Dependent upon the bank's charter, examinations may be carried out by both a federal agency (Federal Reserve or FDIC) and the state in which the bank is domiciled. If a bank is chartered by the state, the state has oversight authority for regulating that bank. Although state chartered, the Federal Reserve (for Fed member banks) or the FDIC (for non–Fed member banks) both have authority as well to conduct oversight exams. The Office of the Comptroller of the Currency (OCC) only has authority over nationally chartered banks, which are among some of the largest banks in the country.

Principal Regulators and Responsibilities

There are a myriad of regulators in the United States today that provide oversight of the financial sector. Although there are a handful of primary regulators for commercial banks, there are several others that are important to know, as they handle more specific needs of banks and other organizations. In addition to the individual regulators, a consortium of some of these regulators comes together as the **Federal Financial Institutions Advisory Council (FFIEC)**. The FFIEC is made up of the Federal Reserve, OCC, FDIC, and the Consumer Financial Protection Bureau (CFPB). The purpose for this council is to ensure that the regulatory guidance and examination procedures are regularly updated, and in concert with one another, as to how banks will be guided and examined. In this way, each separate regulatory body is not developing independent guidance, which would serve to cause confusion among banks. Nevertheless, it is important to clarify exactly what each does and the role they play in the regulatory environment (Rose & Hudgins, 2013).

Eight primary regulatory agencies exist that provide oversight to the financial sector. These include:

- Federal Reserve System
- Office of the Comptroller of the Currency (OCC)
- Federal Deposit Insurance Corporation (FDIC)
- state boards and commissions
- Department of Justice (DOJ)
- Securities and Exchange Commission (SEC)
- Commodities Futures Trading Commission
- Consumer Financial Protection Bureau (CFPB)

Federal Reserve System

The Federal Reserve is the central bank of the United States. As discussed in Chapter 4, the Fed has many functions and tools that it uses that relate to the oversight of the economy in the United States. From a regulatory standpoint, one of the primary functions of the Federal Reserve is supervision of banks and bank holding companies. The Fed's role of a regulatory body involves the following responsibilities:

- <u>supervises and examines all state-chartered banks</u>: It provides safety and soundness exams of state-chartered member banks of the Federal Reserve. These are conducted annually, utilizing the CAMELS rating system. This supervision is conducted in conjunction with state commissions as part of the dual banking mandate.

- supervises holding companies and financial holding companies in the United States: It provides supervision of these entities that now may offer broader services that are placed at the holding company rather than the bank level.
- reserve requirement: All member banks are required to maintain, on reserve at the Fed, a percentage of their deposit accounts. This reserve requirement is mandated by regulation. The Fed has the authority to manipulate the reserve requirement as it deems necessary in pursuit of economic stability.
- merger and acquisition activity: The Fed has the authority to approve all M&A requests by member banks as well as new branch openings and sales. The latter is important to ensure that banks have exposure within certain geographic distances for the fair delivery of products and services in the communities they serve. All such requests must be approved in advance by the Federal Reserve.
- chartering international banks: The Fed provides charters for foreign banks operating in the United States as well as U.S. banks operating in foreign lands.

Office of the Comptroller of the Currency

The OCC is the regulator for the largest banks in the United States. This is the oldest of the bank regulators, being formed with the passage of the National Currency and Bank Act of 1864. The primary responsibilities of this agency are included below.

- charters all national banks: The OCC issues charters for all new national banks. This allows them to open and conduct business as a national bank.
- merger and acquisition and branch approval: The OCC is responsible for approving all M&A activity for nationally chartered banks in addition to approving branch applications for the same banks.
- supervises nationally chartered banks: The OCC is responsible for supervising and examining all nationally chartered banks. This represents the largest banks in the United States, including the systemically important financial institutions (SIFIs). For these banks, only the OCC provides supervision; there is no dual regulation.

Federal Deposit Insurance Corporation

The FDIC is a government agency that was created from the Federal Deposit Insurance Corporation Act of 1933. This evolved from the Great Depression of the 1930s and was designed as an insurance corporation to provide coverage for customer deposits in the event the bank fails. In addition to this most important function, the FDIC has additional responsibilities as a regulator:

- supervises state-chartered financial institutions: The FDIC provides supervision of state-chartered banks that are not members banks of the Federal Reserve, thrifts, as well as the alternate regulator of the remaining state-chartered FDIC-insured institutions. As a regulator, they examine most banks in the United States.

- insurance provider of deposits: The FDIC provides insurance protection for customer deposits for banks and thrifts electing to do this. Institutions insured by the FDIC must pay insurance premiums for this protection, which is considerable. Nevertheless, most institutions seek this protection as a necessity to attract deposits.
- merger and acquisition and branch approval: The FDIC provides approval authority for all insured institutions for M&A activity and branch expansion.
- financial report submission: The FDIC requires all insured institutions to submit an annual report of their financial condition, labeled the "Call Report," on a quarterly basis.

State Boards and Commissions

All the states in the United States have the authority to charter banks. In addition to that, as part of the dual mandate, they provide supervision of these banks in conjunction with the Federal Reserve. Their primary responsibilities include:

- chartering state banks: They provide charters for new institutions desiring to operate within the state.
- supervising state-chartered banks and thrifts: They provide regulatory supervision of all banks and thrifts that receive charters from the state. These institutions would also be jointly supervised by either the Federal Reserve or the FDIC, dependent upon whether they are member banks of the Federal Reserve.

Department of Justice

The Department of Justice is part of the executive branch of the United States and is not an agency of the federal government enacted by law; rather, it is part of the Attorney General's office. Regulatory agencies do not have prosecutorial powers, so certain violations of law that may be identified by the agencies are referred to the DOJ for further action. The DOJ plays a role for financial institutions in a limited sense. Their responsibilities are focused on the following:

- approves merger and acquisition activities: The antitrust division of the DOJ, in conjunction with the Federal Trade Commission (FTC), reviews all M&A activities for impact on competition and provides approvals if these are satisfied. This includes taking appropriate legal action in the event competition would be unjustly impaired by the M&A activity.

Securities and Exchange Commission

The Securities and Exchange Commission is predominantly focused on investment securities, and organizations offering these. So, in this sense, their scope is broader in nature. However, since financial institutions generate securities, the SEC has oversight, with the following responsibilities:

- approval of public offering of securities: For banks and thrifts, any debt (bonds) and equity (common and preferred stock) issues offered to the public must be approved by the SEC.

Commodities Futures Trading Commission

Like the SEC, the Commodities Futures Trading Commission also has a very focused role with regard to financial institutions. This involves reviews of activities in this arena by financial institutions that may be deemed at risk.

- review of derivative instruments: It provides monitoring of all futures, options, and swaps that may be issued by financial institutions to ensure that it does not expose the institution to undue risk that may jeopardize their stability.

Consumer Financial Protection Bureau (CFPB)

The CFPB is not considered a regulator, per se, but is included in the Federal Financial Institutions Examining Council (FFIEC). This is comprised of the Federal Reserve, the FDIC, and the OCC as the major participants. The CFPB is an agency that is designed as a watchdog for abuses in the financial services industry. They tend to be reactive in nature and will focus on violations or complaints that are brought to their attention. They have broad powers to levy fines and carry out other punitive actions on violators brought to their attention. This agency originated from the Dodd-Frank Act.

Overall, as can be seen, commercial banks have a significant amount of oversight for the reasons previously indicated. Being the purveyors of the nation's financial resources, the need for regulation, and the regulators involved, to protect against the disruption to the economy is imperative. Unfortunately, the difficulty involves the requirements and the costs of regulations. As regulators perform exams and provide guidance on regulation, these become very time-consuming activities that deter efforts from the primary goal of banking corporations of creating shareholder value.

For most corporations (nonbanks), this level of oversight does not exist. Banks, on the other hand, cannot arbitrarily take discretionary action without oversight and approval. Therefore, building effective relationships with the primary and secondary regulators helps to make the process less disruptive and more collaborative, and therefore more effective.

Bank Regulations

Bank regulations have been in existence for many years in the United States. For the student of commercial banking, knowledge of some of the history of these laws and regulations, as well as more recent major regulations, are a must. For this reason, this section will provide an overview of the most important regulations, what they created, and what the major provisions of the law entail. From a foundation standpoint, with no central bank until 1913, most of the regulations have occurred within the last 100 years. Many of the landmark regulation occurred as a reaction to the Great Depression (Rose & Hudgins, 2013).

Banking regulation can be divided into four primary categories:

- landmark foundation regulations
- social responsibility laws
- transformational regulation
- global accords

Landmark Foundation Regulations

Although these regulations occurred, for the most part, approximately 85 to slightly over 100 years ago, one regulation occurred over 150 years ago. These are landmark regulations because they are very much debated and relevant today, as they were when they were enacted. All bankers must be aware of their importance and how they impact the operation of banking even today.

- National Currency and Bank Act (1863–1864)
- Federal Reserve Act (1913)
- Banking Act of 1933, Glass-Stegall (1933)

National Currency and Bank Act (1863–1864)

This was one of the first major federal government laws. It was passed during the Civil War. The primary purposes of this act were twofold: to create a national currency primarily to finance the Civil War and to create a national banking system, allowing for the chartering of national banks. Although there was no central bank in existence, banks began to proliferate, and the need to have some level of oversight for this activity was needed. Rather than allow banks to open arbitrarily, this new law established guidelines for oversight and assessing the need for the chartering of a bank. In addition, like many regulations, it created a new entity, the Office of the Comptroller of the Currency (OCC), which was housed under the Department of the Treasury. In addition to approving charters for national banks, the OCC was responsible for supervising the chartered banks. This created the first, and oldest, of the regulators, the OCC. For bankers, the OCC continues to this day to supervise all nationally chartered banks, which constitutes the largest of the banks in the country. To summarize, the impact of this act to commercial banks was:

- agency created
  - » Office of the Comptroller of the Currency (oldest regulator)
- key provisions
  - » chartering structure for new national banks
  - » first and oldest of the regulators, the OCC
  - » supervision of all nationally chartered banks by the OCC

Federal Reserve Act (1913)

As indicated in Chapter 4, due to the frequency and magnitude of the financial crises occurring over the years, the need for a central bank to provide guidance and direction for the economy became an absolute necessity. With the establishment of this act, the Federal Reserve system was born. The primary reason for this creation was to stabilize the economy and the financial markets, which were problematic at the time, as well as to function as the lender of last resort, or the bank for banks. Although the Federal Reserve has several tools available to them today, in pursuit of this mandate, promoting economic stability has been the driver of this independent agency since inception. The importance and power of the Fed has evolved over the past 107 years to become the most powerful entity today. The Federal Reserve is also the federal government's bank, as it was in the initial attempt at a central bank in the late 18th century. To summarize, the impact of this act to commercial banks was:

- agency created
  - » Federal Reserve System
- key provisions
  - » central bank of the United States government
  - » independent agency
  - » supervision of commercial banks
  - » lender of last resort (bankers' bank)
  - » responsible for economic stability

Banking Act of 1933 (Glass-Stegall)

This law was enacted during the Great Depression. The reason for its existence was because of the bank closures and the loss of deposits that customers experienced during this time. Banks were not safe during the period prior to this. In other words, there was no means of guaranteeing the safety of the public's funds in banks. Obviously, this created quite a problem for banks, as the lack of trust would deter the public from making deposits in banks, which is the key source of funds needed to make loans. If deposits do not occur, lending will decline, or cease.

During this period, many banks failed for lack of liquidity. As people panicked, they raced to the bank to withdraw their funds, causing a "run" on the bank. When the funds were depleted, the bank failed, and customers lost their money. There was no recourse for them. As a result, Glass-Stegall was passed. The primary focus of this act was to protect consumers; therefore, the act focused on two key items: (a) restricting banks from taking inordinate amounts of risk through risky investments of customer funds by separating commercial banks from investment banks and (b) providing insurance to cover customer losses (to a specified amount) in the event a bank fails by creating the Federal Deposit Insurance Company (FDIC). The majority of this act was repealed with the passage of the Gramm-Leach-Bliley Act in 1999.

- agency created
  - » Federal Deposit Insurance Corporation (FDIC) through the Federal Deposit Insurance Company Act of the same year
- key provisions
  - » insures bank deposits in the event of failure
  - » provides coverage to each depositor up to $250,000 today (originally began at $2,500)
  - » regulates insured state-chartered banks

Social Responsibility Regulation

Several laws were passed within the last few decades that focus on protecting bank consumers. These differ from the general regulations discussed previously. The prior regulations were enacted to stabilize banking and the economic environment, whereas the next few important laws resulted from abuses and provide for more transparency in bank practices and the information supplied to customers. The following synopses are important to the student for understanding the breath of these laws.

- Consumer Credit Protection Act (Truth in Lending)
- Community Reinvestment Act (CRA)
- Competitive Equality in Bank Act (Truth in Savings)
- Equal Credit Opportunity Act

Consumer Credit Protection Act of 1968 (Truth in Lending)

The purpose of Truth in Lending was to make as transparent as possible the customer's rights and responsibilities as it pertains to loans. This involves outlining and clarifying information that is contained in loan agreements, which become contracts. Although the detail is now explained, customers seldom read the fine print and, in some cases, may not understand the financial terminology involved.

- agency created
    - no agency created
- key provisions
    - applies to mortgage and auto loans, as well as credit cards, among other consumer loans
    - requires the type of information that must be disclosed to customers obtaining a loan
    - Credit cards cannot charge unreasonable penalty fees for late payments.
    - Bankers cannot guide customers to certain types of loans that improve their compensation, unless beneficial to the client.
    - Mortgage loans with adjustable rates (ARMs) must clearly outline how payments can increase and decrease with interest rate fluctuations.

Community Reinvestment Act (CRA) of 1977

The focus of the **Community Reinvestment Act (CRA)** was lending, both consumer and commercial. The objective of the law was to ensure that banks provide credit equitably to meet the needs of low to moderate income customers, not just certain areas within their market area. Banks cannot avoid making loans to customers based upon the neighborhoods they live in for fear that they may present much more risk of repayment. This law has been in existence for over 40 years. During that period, technology has changed considerably. This has formed the basis for recent changes due to the expansion of services through the internet. Since banks now offer services through their websites, their trade markets have greatly expanded, which impacts how they provide lending services.

- agency created
    - no agency created
- key provisions
    - Bank regulators will review bank's lending patterns to ensure compliance.
    - This will occur regularly, and the results will determine whether the bank is successful in meeting the credit needs of low to moderate income levels.
    - Recent changes are designed to provide more clarity in the interpretation and evaluation of banks, which was most welcome for banks, considering the technological advances over the past 43 years.

Equal Credit Opportunity Act of 1974

Originally, at inception, the focus of this act was to prevent bias and discrimination in extending credit to women or based on marital status. In 1977 Congress expanded the scope to prevent discrimination in credit issuance based on race, religion, color, national origin, age, and receipt of public assistance income. Like the previous two laws, this is again a credit-extension law and is an important addition to regulations. The reason for this is risk. Making loans always involves risk; therefore, banks were reluctant to extend credit to different groups of individuals based upon their perceived ability to repay or their track record, rather than an unbiased individual assessment. The law does not stipulate that banks cannot turn down loans but demands that banks must do so based on individual credit worthiness of the individual.

- agency created
  - no agency created
- key provisions
  - must notify applicants on actions taken and decisions in a timely manner
  - supply applicants with copies of appraisal reports involved in the decision-making process
  - cannot provide different information or services to individuals during the process
  - cannot use different standards in making the credit decision for some applicants
  - The same issue applies to collateral offered in the process.
  - In short, standards must be equally applied to all applicants, without exception, in the extension of credit.

Truth in Savings Act of 1991

Originally, this was a part of the FDIC Improvement Act and ultimately became mandatory as Regulation DD with the Fed's finalization of this. The objective of this act is like that of Truth in Lending and focuses on transparency and full disclosure to consumers on savings accounts related to advertising, timely statement communications, and interest calculation. The law is designed to prevent misleading information about savings products to attract customers and to ensure clarity in interest calculation. The **APY (annual percentage yield)** must be stated in the disclosure. With this rate, consumers must be made aware of whether it will change or not, penalties for early withdrawals, and all other fees attendant to the accounts. This law is designed to provide accurate information to consumers in their disclosures.

- agency created
  - no agency created
- key provisions
  - requires banks to provide APY in disclosure statements
  - Banks must use the average daily balance method in calculating APY.

  - required to disclose ONLY amounts available for consumer's immediate use when viewing balance

Transformational Regulations

Transformational regulations are those that have evolved more recently, triggered by significant events, changing technology, or other reactive impetus. Many of the key regulations identified here have had significant impact on the banking industry and are, hence, transformational in nature. Although there are many regulations that have been enacted, only the most significant are identified here, which the student of banking should be aware of. In some cases, these regulations are currently evolving and will continue to, based upon the needs of the economy and the industry. The key regulations that fall within this category are outlined as follows:

- Riegel-Neal Interstate Banking Law (1994)
- Financial Services Modernization Act/Gramm-Leach-Bliley Act (1999)
- USA Patriot Act
- Sarbanes-Oxley Accounting Standards Act (2002)
- Check 21/Check Clearing for the 21st Century (2004)
- Emergency Economic Stabilization Act (2008)
- Dodd-Frank Wall Street Reform and Consumer Protection Act/FINREG (2009)

Riegel-Neal Interstate Banking Law of 1994

This law was truly transformational. Prior to its existence, banks were not permitted to open branches of their bank across state lines. Branching laws were the domain of the state. Many states did not allow branching of banks even within the state, for several years. Illinois is a good example of this and the reason that there were many banks in the state, since it was a unit-bank state. Nevertheless, this transformational legislation opened the door for large banks to establish branches in the major cities throughout the country. Today, as a result, the largest of the commercial banks have a presence in the major cities in the United States, creating greater competition and growth among banks.

- agency created
  - no agency created
- key provisions
  - Holding companies that are well-capitalized were permitted to acquire banks in any state in the Unites States.
  - Bank holding companies could merge banks in different states into a single network of branches in 1997.

  - Holding companies could not control more than 30% of the total deposits within a given state, subject to a given state's change in threshold, and 10% of the total deposits within the nation.
  - States were given the option to either participate or not allow holding companies to enter their state, by mid-1997. At the time only Montana and Texas did not opt to participate but have since changed their posture.

Financial Services Modernization Act (Gramm-Leach-Bliley) of 1999

Gramm-Leach-Bliley is a very broad and sweeping legislation affecting banks. This is a multifaceted act and affects many aspects of banking, including privacy, insurance, Glass-Stegall, ATM fee disclosures, and others. The most notable and well-recognized aspects of this act was the repeal of Glass-Stegall and privacy notices for safeguarding client information, or **PII (personally identifiable information)**. The repeal of Glass-Stegall allowed banks to offer security services and sell insurance. Glass-Stegall originally separated commercial and investment banks and the offering of these services. This change paved the way for banks and holding companies to offer a much wider variety of services, which created greater diversification.

- agency created
  - no agency created
- key provisions
  - overturned Glass-Stegall
  - allowed banks to offer securities and sell insurance
  - regulates the disclosure and collection of private financial information of customers
  - greater powers for bank holding companies to consolidate with other financial service providers

Bank Secrecy Act (BSA) of 1970

This act was originally passed to focus on fighting the war on drugs. Banks were required to report information learned to the federal government that may involve or appear to involve criminal activities. In 1992 the Anti-Money Laundering Act was passed. Banks were required to monitor suspicious activities that may have led to money laundering. Again, in 2001, following 9/11, another important act was included, called the "USA Patriot Act," which added several requirements for reporting for banks. Banks are required, under FinCEN (Financial Crimes Enforcement Network), to file **suspicious activity reports (SARs)** when activities of a suspicious nature are noted.

- agency created
  - Financial Crimes Enforcement Network (FinCEN)

- key provisions
  - » report transactions over $10,000
  - » dedicated BSA officer required at the bank to manage compliance with BSA
  - » issuance of suspicious activity reports (SARs) to the federal government
  - » requires annual bank training of all bank employees for BSA awareness

Sarbanes-Oxley Accounting Standards Act of 2002

This act, also called "SOX," was reactively passed following the activities of two major organizations, Enron and Worldcom. Additionally, the largest accounting firm, Arthur Anderson, became deeply involved as the external auditor of Enron. The focus of the act was corporate governance and emanated from the monitoring and reporting of inaccurate and misleading information to the public. Furthermore, the oversight of external auditor practices was challenged due to Anderson's inability to determine and report these inaccuracies. The result was significant requirements imposed on all corporations that are publicly traded, including banks. In addition to enhanced governance requirements of corporations, a new agency was created to monitor the practices and activities of accounting firms. The **Public Company Accounting Oversight Board (PCAOB)** was created to act as the accounting "police" to perform this monitoring of auditing of the auditors.

- agency created
  - » Public Company Accounting Oversight Board (PCAOB)
- key provisions
  - » requires the CEO and CFO of corporations (and banks) to attest the accuracy of financial statements contained in 10Q and 10K reports, under penalty of fines and incarceration
  - » requires more objective audits of financial statements and reports by external auditors
  - » Securities cannot be sold by insiders during defined blackout periods.

Check Clearing for the 21st Century Act (Check 21) of 2004

As a result of improving technology and the need to decrease float in the banking industry, Check 21 was passed to permit banks to process checks more quickly and efficiently, electronically. Physical checks must be cleared through the check clearing system, which was accomplished by physically moving checks to the drawer's bank. This could take anywhere from two to five days. During this period, the drawer had the usage of the funds until it was physically presented for collection. This act, for the first time, allowed the presentment of an electronic image of a check as a "substitute check," the legal equivalent of the original check. This allowed for much faster processing of checks and therefore the reduction of float in the industry, which has been an elusive concept for years. During this period, checks were beginning to decline with the advent of more automated tools for moving money. This act paved the way for greater efficiencies for this transformation in the industry.

- agency created
  - no agency created
- key provisions
  - creation of the electronic substitute check
  - allows banks to "truncate" checks, which is the elimination of returning physical, cleared checks to the customers, reducing costs and creating further efficiencies

Emergency Economic Stabilization Act of 2008

This was a reactive measure taken at the onset of the financial crisis of 2008. At this time, with the decline in home values and subprime lending, banks were faced with significant amounts of real estate loans as assets on their balance sheets, declining in value and with little prospect of repayment. The loans were captioned **toxic assets**, as the only way they would be removed would be through write off. To avoid heavy losses to the banks and subsequent failure, congress authorized the U.S. Treasury to purchase these toxic assets to stabilize the banks. Although the U.S. Treasury was authorized to purchase these toxic assets, instead they created the **Troubled Asset Relief Program (TARP)**, which was designed to infuse capital into the banks by purchasing preferred stock in the bank. This created additional sources of capital to the bank to cover the toxic assets that were destabilizing the banks for shortage of capital. Banks were required to make dividend payments, contractually, to the federal government and ultimately paid back TARP to the government. This act also raised the insurance coverage limit of the FDIC to $250,000 per depositor, up from $100,000. This was designed to be a temporary increase. Although designed as a temporary measure, the reason this act is important is that the U.S. government actually became an investor in commercial banks and because the preferred shares were convertible to common shares, to actually become owners of the bank in the event they converted their shares. Although a considerable amount was injected into the banking system, via TARP, literally all of TARP was paid back, and the government generated a considerable amount of interest income (5%).

- agency created
  - Troubled Asset Relief Program (TARP)
- key provisions
  - purchase of capital in banks through TARP
  - temporary increase of FDIC insurance limits to $250,000

Dodd-Frank Wall Street Reform and Consumer Protection Act (FinREG) of 2009

Also a response to the financial crisis, this was a major, sweeping legislation that incorporated many provisions in response to the crisis and focused on many issues related to Wall Street and the banking industry. Among the most significant was the creation of the **Consumer Financial Protection Bureau (CFPB)**, which was designed as an independent organization to oversee abuses to consumers in the financial services industry. This agency had no oversight and was left to act at the discretion of the director. The Financial Stability Oversight Council (FSOC) was also created under Dodd-Frank. This council was empowered to monitor and respond to the risks facing the financial system in the United States. Another significant feature was the imposition of the **Volcker Rule**, which prohibited banks from making risky investments (derivatives) for their own behalf using customer funds. "Too big to fail" became the moniker of the largest banks that became **systemically important financial institutions (SIFIs)**. Under the act, banks were not protected from abusive practices, because the fact they deemed too big to fail prohibited the regulators. Maintenance of specific capital levels were also mandated by the act. In short, the act, nicknamed **FinREG,** has become the largest single piece of legislation affecting the banking industry and is the subject of much discussion and modification today.

- agency created
  - Consumer Financial Protection Bureau (CFPB)
  - Volcker Rule
- key provisions
  - defined SIFI banks
  - moved thrift organizations under the oversight of the OCC
  - raised FDIC insurance coverage for depositors to $250,000 per deposit
  - prohibited banks from investing in risky securities for their own benefit
  - established an independent agency for the protection of consumers from abusive practices (CFPB)
  - mandated capital requirement maintenance of banks in conjunction with Basel

Global Agreements

The last area that relates to the prior regulations is the broader worldwide financial guidelines. These guidelines, although not regulations or laws of the United States, are part of a global set of agreements with select countries to provide guidance to the financial services industry. As was learned in the financial crisis, economic disturbances can create impacts felt throughout the world. Banks, being at the center of these economies, can impact the worldwide economy. To provide more uniform control and standardization in the global economy, the **Basel Accords** were established in 1974 by a group of 10 countries' regulators.

Basel Accords

The Basel Accords were focused on establishing global standards for maintaining adequate amounts of capital to absorb losses and being able to continue to lend money. There is a series of three regulations that have been established by the **Basel Committee on Banking Supervision (BCBS)**. The Basel Committee is made up of 27 members (countries) today, including Argentina, Australia, Belgium, Brazil, Canada, China, France, Germany, Hong Kong, India, Indonesia, Italy, Japan, Korea, Luxembourg, Mexico, Netherlands, Russia, Saudi Arabia, Singapore, South Africa, Spain, Sweden, Switzerland, Turkey, the United Kingdom, and the United States. Basel I, II, and III have been in existence since 1988 and each have defined specific areas of focus, in addition to capital, as well as defining other aspects of capital management. The Basel standards have been adopted by the member countries, establishing more uniform protection for the major economies in the world. Although Basel will be defined more fully in a later chapter, its importance is significant in stabilizing the global economy.

- agency created
  - » Basel Committee on Banking Supervision (BCBS)
- key provisions
  - » Basel I (1988): focused on capital standards and market risk
  - » Basel II (2004): focused on above, plus credit risk
  - » Basel III (2010): focused on the prior two Basel standards, plus liquidity risk

Regulatory Examinations

Regulations are only as good as the level at which they are adhered to. In the United States, regulatory agencies have been established as the supervisory vehicle to ensure that the law is being followed by banks. As discussed earlier in the chapter, there are several regulators that have been empowered to perform these responsibilities. They accomplish this through examinations of banks that are performed on a regular basis. Among the variety of exams conducted (i.e., Compliance, CRA, and Information Technology exams), one of the more important of these exams is the Safety and Soundness Exam. This is performed on an annual basis. The purpose of this exam is to focus on specific risks and aspects of the bank that will enable it to rate the bank in terms of overall safety and soundness.

All regulators examine banks using a uniform set of guidance, which is approved and endorsed by the Federal Financial Examinations Council (FFIEC). This council is made up of the major regulators in the United States and provides for the uniformity of standards regardless of the size of the bank. For the purposes of this section, the Safety and Soundness Exam is the focus, and the specific rating system used for this is called **CAMELS**.

Examinations

Examinations are mandated and occur at least annually, but could be more frequently. These are significant exams for the bank and require at least two weeks to complete. Examiners render a requirements list to the bank in advance of the exam for the bank to compile the required files, policies, and information for review. The specific regulator (OCC, Federal Reserve, or FDIC) will bring a team of examiners to perform the audit. These are generally experts in the segment of the exam on which they will focus. In the case of Safety and Soundness, CAMELS is used and will result in a "component" and "composite" rating of the bank. These ratings are not made available to the public but only to bank management and the board of directors, in addition to leadership within their own organizations. Banks will generally have 30 days or so to respond to comments in the exams.

CAMELS

CAMELS is an acronym for capital, asset quality, management, earnings, liquidity, and market sensitivity. This is the basis and scope of the exam. CAMELS refers to the financial strength of the bank as well as the key financial risks the bank faces, as follows:

- capital: Regulators focus on capital adequacy, based upon the capital adequacy ratios defined within the Basel standards. Examiners determine whether the bank is undercapitalized, adequately capitalized, or well capitalized.
- asset quality: Asset quality is a major risk of the bank. This refers to the amount of loan losses and nonperforming (nonpaying) loans the bank has in relation to its total loans. Asset quality is very important to the health of the bank. Higher ratios of asset quality will create more risk for capital adequacy, which, if too many loans become losses, must absorb these losses, and still allow the bank to operate.
- management: Management is more functional and relates to the bank's management structure, organization, span of control, expertise, and experience of the management team of the bank. Examiners review the structure, résumés, and conduct interviews and meetings with key management to obtain an assessment of the quality of management and their ability and experience to currently manage the bank as well as to do so in a crisis.
- earnings: Regulators are concerned that the bank is profitable, that it is vibrant and a "going concern." The degree of profitability is not their concern, but their objective here is to establish that the bank has the revenue necessary to produce the bottom-line net income to

support the needs of the bank. Obviously, banks having a loss, or continued losses, in their net income will be at risk of erosion of capital and may challenge their existence.

- liquidity: Liquidity is another major risk facing banks. This component of CAMELS is vital to the success of the existence of the bank. Banks must be liquid, always, due to the demands made of the bank. Liquidity also provides "funding" for loans. If funding is not adequate, the bank will not be able to make as many loans and may shrink in assets (size), which is a major reason banks exist. Additionally, banks must be able to meet their cash demands every day. When banks cannot meet such demands, it can create a run on the bank, which could force them to close their doors.
- sensitivity: "Sensitivity" refers to market sensitivity, understanding the market within which the bank operates, as well as interest rate sensitivity. Interest rate risk is, again, another major financial risk the bank faces. This is the risk that is created because of fluctuations in interest rates, driven by the Federal Reserve. The critical elements to profitability, for a bank, are interest income and interest expense. The net of the two provides the direction of interest rates since it has so much impact on the bank's profitability.

Uniform Financial Institutions Rating System (UFIRS)

The **Uniform Financial Institutions Rating System (UFIRS)** was adopted by the FFIEC and is the rating system the examiners use to rate each component of CAMELS and render an opinion, as well as rate each on a 5-point scale. In addition to this, examiners will define findings that would require attention and/or immediate attention. Each component of CAMELS will receive a score (rating), called the **component rating**, and based upon the six ratings, a **composite rating** will be rendered for the bank as well. The rating system used is as follows:

- Strong (1): top rating. The bank demonstrates strong oversight and management of the component, or overall. Also, the risk is managed very well and has few, if any, findings.
- Satisfactory (2): Although banks aspire to be rated "strong," this usually requires more cost to ensure that absolutely everything is addressed at a high level. As such, achieving a "satisfactory" rating is very good and is very acceptable to the bank, and regulators. There may be a few findings, but nothing is putting the bank at significant risk in the component area or overall. Banks always seek to be rated 1 or 2.
- Less than Satisfactory (3): The rating name indicates what is occurring. The bank is performing at a level that is not satisfactory but not at such a level as to de considered deficient or critically deficient. This rating results from several findings indicated that are likely to require more immediate attention. Components with this rating put the bank on notice, requiring prompt resolution. Ratings at this level will likely require more frequent follow up by examiners.
- Deficient (4): The next two ratings are to be avoided. A "deficient" rating indicates severe and significant issues that must be addressed immediately. These issues, if not addressed

quickly, can result in limiting the viability of the bank. Regulators will define time frames for resolution and frequent follow-ups will occur.

- Critically Deficient (5): The last rating is the most severe. This rating presents a direct threat to the bank, with negative impact likely. In this regard regulators will be very closely involved with bank management to monitor any possibility of improvement and/or take action to terminate the charter of the bank (closure), especially in the case of a composite rating of 5.

CHAPTER SUMMARY

Navigating the complexity of bank regulations can be a challenge. For the student of commercial banking, a healthy understanding of the need for and rationale for regulations is of paramount importance. Banks are integral to the economy, and their proper functioning contributes to a stable economy. Therefore, regulations are imperative to ensure that the public's trust is not breached and that individuals will have confidence in the industry to manage their financial resources. Although a necessity, prudent regulations are of most importance to ensure both stability and growth. There is a fine line between compliance and operational performance, which is the reason for well-balanced regulations that are well thought out and achieve the goals intended.

This chapter has identified the most important of the regulations, although there are many more. Future regulations will continue to evolve and usually as a reaction to some negative event. Ideally, proactive development is the goal, but this is unlikely given the political challenges involved. However, awareness and understanding of the origin and rationale for the regulations and regulatory environment is a major step toward effective reform.

END OF CHAPTER QUESTIONS

1. How many iterations of the Basel Accord have occurred over the years? Name them and the major focus.
2. Which regulator is responsible for examining nationally chartered banks?
3. Which regulator supervises most banks?
4. Which law created the PCAOB?
5. What do the components in the acronym CAMELS stand for?
6. What is the purpose and function of the Federal Deposit Insurance Company (FDIC)?
7. What is the rating scale used by the examiners in a Safety and Soundness exam?
8. What is the oldest regulatory agency, and what law created it?
9. What is another name for the Dodd-Frank Wall Street Reform Act?
10. What does CFPB stand for, and which law created it?

CHAPTER 6

Understanding a Bank's Financial Statements

Key Terms

- Primary reserves
- Correspondent, or respondent, banks
- Float
- Secondary reserves
- Treasury bills
- Repurchase agreements (REPOs)
- Reverse repurchase agreements
- Gross loans
- Allowance for loan losses
- Nonperforming loans
- Net loans
- Provision for loan losses
- Servicing
- Retail loans
- OREO (other real estate loans)
- Core deposits, stable funds
- Discount window
- Shareholder equity
- Undivided profits
- Internal funding
- Net interest income
- Margin, or spread
- Net interest margin
- Fractional reserve banking

Learning Objectives

By the end of this chapter, the student will:

- Understand the components and differences in a bank's balance sheet.
- Identify and understand the meaning of "off-balance sheet" items.
- Understand the components and differences in a bank's income statement.
- Understand how banks create money through the money multiplier.

Financial statements are the lifeblood for understanding the financial activities and performance of all corporations. For banks, financial statements are the same, but more importantly, they form the basis for the future planning and forecasting of the revenue for the bank. The major importance, and the reason for this chapter, is that bank financial statements have some differences from traditional corporate financial statements. Although the three primary financial statements are used, just as with any other corporation, the accounts in the financial statements are different and require some explanation.

In addition, banks are financially driven institutions: They deal in money and financial products and services. In this regard, they do not sell manufactured products that require raw materials or cost of goods sold, but rather have interest as the predominant driver of revenue. A bank's financial statements reflect that. This chapter is designed to focus on the primary accounts of a bank's financial statements, relatively simplistically, to understand the purpose and nature of the accounts. Although bank financial statements can be quite complex, the core accounts discussed will provide a firm foundation for understanding.

The Bank's Balance Sheet

The balance sheet is the bank's statement of condition. This is a point-in-time snapshot of the assets, liabilities,

ASSETS			
Cash	3,622	3,465	3,583
Derivative Assets (IRS)	0	0	0
ST Gov Securities	4,973	3,489	2,311
Loans to banks	20,000	17,500	25,000
Reverse Repos	0	0	0
LT Gov Securities	19,546	19,689	20,228
Loans to Customers	146,607	142,787	148,980
Other Assets	8,645	8,560	8,475
TOTAL ASSETS	**203,393**	**195,490**	**208,577**
LIABILITIES			
Derivative Liabilities (IRS)	0	0	0
Dep. from banks	30,000	26,250	36,471
Savings Deposits	67,210	69,378	72,182
Current Accounts	41,700	43,224	45,110
Cert. of Deposit	35,950	26,013	26,030
Floating Rate Notes	11,500	11,248	11,643
Repos	0	0	0
Centr Bank Advance	781	2,537	0
Taxation	125	175	119
Subordinated Debt	5,000	5,014	5,014
Shareholder's Equity	11,126	11,652	12,008
Total Capital	16,126	16,666	17,022
TOTAL LIABILITIES & SH's EQUITY	**203,393**	**195,490**	**208,577**
OFF-BALANCE SHEET			
Commitments	0	0	0
Interest Rate Swaps	0	0	0

Assets	Latest B/S	Projected	New Business	Forecast
Cash	3,622	3,146	5	3,151
Derivative Assets (IRS)	0	0	0	0
Loans and advances to banks	20,000	0	17,500	17,500
Local Currency	20,000	0	17,500	17,500
Reverse Repos	0	0	0	0
Government Securities				
Treasury Bills	4,973	3,487	2	3,489
Treasury Bonds	19,546	19,506	2	19,508
Treasury Bonds AFT	7,895	7,855	1	7,856
Treasury Bonds HTM	11,652	11,652	1	11,653
Commercial Loans	84,815	80,196	2,002	82,198
Wholesale Enterprises	14,938	13,920	347	14,267
Manufacturing	22,788	21,221	530	21,751
ICT	18,002	16,748	418	17,166
Construction & R/Estate	29,087	28,307	707	29,014
Drawdowns			0	
Retail Loans	61,792	59,961	1,502	61,463
Personal Loans	10,547	9,055	232	9,287
Credits Cards	11,980	11,650	290	11,940
Mortgages Variable	39,265	39,255	980	40,235
Other Assets	8,645	8,558	0	8,558
TOTAL	203,393	174,853	21,013	195,866

Liabilities	Latest B/S	Projected	New Business	Forecast
Derivative Liabilities (IRS)	0	0	0	0
Deposits from banks	30,000	0	750	750
Local Currency	30,000	0	750	750
Savings Deposits	67,210	67,210	16,800	84,010
Savings Deposits	67,210	67,210	16,800	84,010
Current Accounts	41,700	41,700	10,400	52,100
Certificates of Deposits	35,950	16,950	9,063	26,013
3 Month	15,000	0	4,000	4,000
1 Year	11,200	8,200	3,063	11,263
2 Year	9,750	8,750	2,000	10,750
Floating Rate Notes	11,500	8,500	8,500	17,000
5 year	11,500	8,500	8,500	17,000
Repos	0	0	0	0
Central Bank Advance	781	24,563	−24,563	0
Taxation	125	−49	49	0
Subordinated Debt	5,000	5,000	14	5,014
Shareholder's Equity	11,126	10,979	0	10,979
Ordinary Shares	6,000	6,000	0	6,000
Reserves	5,126	4,979	0	4,979
TOTAL	203,393	174,853	21,013	195,866

Off-Balance Sheet Items	Projected	New Business	Forecast
Commitments	0	0	0
Interest Rate Swaps	0	0	0
IRS : Receive Floating - Pay Fixed	0	0	0
IRS : Receive Fixed - Pay Floating	0	0	0

FIGURE 6.1 Balance Sheet

and shareholder equity of the bank, no different than for other industries (Vermaak, 2017). In this section, the core accounts contained in the balance sheet will be identified and explained. To be able to manage a bank, it is important to have a firm understand of these accounts, what they mean and what they do for the bank. The three parts of the balance sheet will be explained, consisting of assets, liabilities, and shareholder equity. An example of a typical, abbreviated balance sheet for a bank is shown in Figure 6.1.

Assets

As in any balance sheet, assets are the "uses" of funds obtained. They are the tools that are used by a corporation to produce revenue. For a bank, the core assets identified in this section are the most integral to the bank's performance and include the following accounts:

- cash and due from banks

- loans and advances to banks (interbank loans)
- marketable securities (Treasury securities)
- reverse repurchase agreements (REPOs)
- loans
- other assets

Cash and Due from Banks

Cash is required to meet current obligations. This is extremely important for a bank and is part of the liquidity requirement of a bank to satisfy such obligations. As will be discussed in detail in a later chapter, there are many events that trigger cash inflows and cash outflows for a bank. These transactions occur every day, every hour, and must be managed closely to ensure that the bank can meet these needs and avoid a run on the bank. Within this broad category, there are many parts, which result in the total. This asset is sometimes called the **primary reserves** of the bank for the liquidity reasons indicated. This is made up of the following areas of cash:

- vault cash: Banks maintain a certain amount of cash in the vault for day-to-day purposes. This will include cash for the teller drawers, check cashing and other needs, replenishing ATMs, and to meet the general needs of the day. Banks receive cash from the Federal Reserve in their district via armored car. Banks do not stockpile cash. Although it is important to not have "cash-out" situations, since cash is a "nonearning" asset, they maintain only an optimal amount of cash, on average, and return any excess to the Fed to be credited to their account for reinvestment purposes. The goal is to maintain only what is needed and ensure the remainder is earning interest.
- deposits with other banks: Banks have relationships with other banks. These are called **correspondent**, or **respondent, banks** and are established for many reasons. Excess cash can be maintained at other banks in interest-earning accounts, like a deposit a consumer would make with a bank. In this way, the bank puts their idle cash in production so that interest income is earned.
- reserve account at the Federal Reserve: All member banks of the Federal Reserve system must maintain a portion of their transaction deposits on deposit at the Fed. These funds are required and do earn a nominal rate of interest, but the bank cannot use these funds. Although they are considered earning assets, the origin of this requirement is the lessons learned from the Great Depression. To avoid not having the liquidity that occurred during this crisis, the reserve account mandates that amounts be set aside for this purpose and, hopefully, to avoid such drastic results.
- cash in the process of collection: Checks are received every day at the bank. Physical checks are used to make deposit additions at the bank. These check deposits are credited to accounts at the bank, although the physical funds have not been received yet and are in the process

of being collected. These are included in the cash account, as the total amount in cash. The delay in the collection of these is called **float** and while in this process is a nonearning asset.

Loans and Advances to Banks (Interbank Loans)

As previously discussed, banks maintain relationships with other banks. In addition to depositing funds at other banks, banks make loans to other banks. The reason for this is that banks need funds to to meet appropriate liquidity levels on a short-term basis, usually overnight. Therefore, if the bank has excess funds (cash), lending to other banks allows them to earn interest on the loan, making these an earning asset. The amount of money lent to other banks is called *Fed funds* and comes from excess reserves a bank has on deposit with the Fed and loaned at the going federal funds rate of interest plus a small premium. In addition to earning interest income, the bank deepens its relationship with these banks in the event they themselves need short-term funding in the future.

Marketable Securities (Treasury Securities)

Like other organizations, banks invest in marketable securities as a means of generating interest income and develop portfolios of investment securities. These are generally designed as highly liquid assets that can be turned into cash quickly, if necessary, and therefore satisfy the liquidity requirements of the bank. For banks, their securities portfolios are made up of three categories of investments: liquid portion, trading account, and investment portfolio (held to maturity).

- liquid portion: The objective of this portion of the portfolio is liquidity. The ability to sell the securities quickly and turn them into cash, if needed, is very important. But the ability to generate earnings via interest income is also important. Therefore, within this portfolio are relatively risk-free, highly marketable securities. Since they are highly marketable, they are also known as **secondary reserves**. Among the securities in this portfolio are U.S. government securities (Treasury securities), the primary one of which is **Treasury bills**. Treasury bills are very short-term investments with less than one-year terms. Since cash is a nonearning asset, Treasury securities are an excellent investment since they are guaranteed by the U.S. government, will earn interest income, and are highly marketable. Treasury securities, therefore, become an important part of the liquid portion of the portfolio. In addition to Treasury bills, other short-term investments are invested in the liquid portion of the portfolio. These include investments in the money market (short-term market), including commercial paper, interest-bearing time deposits, and other short-term securities.
- trading portion: This portion of the portfolio is designed for trading, the goal of which is short-term profits. Banks invest in securities not only to earn interest income but also to trade, buy, and sell and produce gains for the bank. These gains can increase the net income of the bank in times when net interest income is lower and therefore can be very

instrumental to the bank's profitability picture. One of the primary investment instruments for this portion of the portfolio is, again, U.S. Treasury securities. Rather than using the very short-term Treasury bills, banks invest in both Treasury notes (terms greater than one year and less than 10 years) and Treasury bonds (terms beyond 10 years). Although these have longer terms, they are still highly marketable and can easily be bought and sold in the secondary market and are "risk-free." Banks also invest in other securities for this section of the portfolio. Since the goal is to generate securities gains for the bank, the greatest return for some of these investments is desired, which has caused banks to invest in more risky investments. Unfortunately, investment instruments, such as derivatives, can be extremely risky and can result in losses to the bank, impacting both their profitability and liquidity. Since investments are made from funds received from customer deposits, these investments can risk client funds. As a result, during the financial crisis of 2008, and as part of the Dodd-Frank Wall Street Reform Act, the Volcker Rule prohibited banks from investing in these risky investments. Although this limited the risk in the portfolio, which created part of the concerns during the crisis, it eliminated an avenue that banks had relied upon to generate gains in their portfolios and therefore impacted profitability.

- investment portion (held to maturity): The final segment of the securities portfolio is the long-term portion. These investments were made to hold these to their maturity. The goal of this portion is capital appreciation, to produce growth in the assets and capital gains upon maturity. The instruments used in this section can be long-term bonds, municipal bonds, and U.S. Treasury bonds. Treasury bonds are the least risky and therefore have definite appeal for the bank. During the term of the investment, the bank will earn interest income, with a return of principal at maturity.

Reverse Repurchase Agreements (REPOs)

Repurchase agreements (REPOs) relate to Treasury securities. REPOs involve the buying and selling of securities on a short-term basis, with the underlying asset as the collateral in the transaction. In this regard, they are considered relatively risk-free. To add to the lesser risk of these investments, U.S. Treasury securities are often the instrument used in the transaction. In the case of **reverse repurchase agreements**, the bank purchases Treasury securities from another bank, or seller, for a short-term period, under agreement to sell them back to the seller at the end of term. During the time the bank has possession of the securities, the securities themselves are collateral in the event they are not re-purchased in the timeframe indicated.

The reason a bank engages in these transactions is another means of using excess cash to earn interest income. If the bank holds the securities, they will earn interest on these, adding to their income. These also remain very liquid for the bank as marketable securities.

Loans

Loans are the primary assets banks use to generate interest income. In addition, making loans is the major economic role banks play, and defines them as a bank. Of all the assets, this is the most important and is the largest dollar amount in the asset section of the balance sheet, representing over 70% of the total assets. Loans are the equivalent of accounts receivable for a corporate balance sheet, representing money owed to the bank. The economic role loans play is stimulative. As corporations borrow money to grow, they create jobs and more products, which consumers purchase. The additional jobs and increased salaries translate into more consumption and therefore economic vitality. Although many banks have a wide range of lending products and specialty loans, this section of the chapter will focus on the two broad categories of loans that banks make to provide a firm foundation of the nature of this important asset.

Loans, in general, may be reflected as **gross loans**, which is the total amount of loan proceeds disbursed, net of principal payments made. However, bank financial statements for loans have a "contra-account" for loans called **allowance for loan losses**. This account reflects the amount of potential loan losses anticipated by the bank, which is being reserved. These are loans where repayment is in question, and they would be considered **non-performing loans**. This amount is then subtracted from gross loans on the books to arrive at **net loans**. In other words, the balances are written down to account for these potential losses. Net loans are the amount used in calculating the total assets of a bank. For this reason, the student should be cautious when reading bank financial statements and know whether the amount of loans reflected is gross or net. The allowance for loan losses is calculated using the formula in Figure 6.2. As illustrated, another item of this equation is similar, entitled **provision for loan losses**. This should not be confused with allowance for loan losses, which appears on the balance sheet, as provision for loan losses is an income statement item and functions as an "expense" to the bank, reducing their net income. Nevertheless, it is part of the equation. Therefore, the allowance for loan losses equation takes the provision for loan losses into account, as well as the actual amount of loans written off. These are loans fully taken off the books as losses and must be removed from the calculation of allowance for loan losses to arrive at the new amount. Finally, recoveries of previously written off loans are added back to offset the losses in the equation. Most recently a new accounting methodology has been advanced, which all banks are required to use. The method is called **CECL (current expected credit losses)**. This was issued by the Financial Accounting Standards Board (FASB) and is a new method for estimating credit losses. In the past credit losses were estimated based upon history. With the new methodology banks must now look forward and be more predictive of potential losses, utilizing predicative analytics. This now requires assessing risk profiles of business relationships and reporting utilizing predictive tools anticipating risks. Ultimately, allowances for loan losses and provision for loan losses are still a part of the financial statement, but the method used to estimate the amounts will be different.

Beginning Allowance for Loan Losses
+ This Year's Provision for Loan Loss
= Adjusted Allowance for Loan Losses
− Actual Charge-Offs of Worthless Loans
+ Recoveries from Previous Charge-Offs
= Ending Allowance for Loan Losses

FIGURE 6.2 Allowance for Loan Loss Calculation

Banks make loans in two broad categories, commercial and consumer loans. In addition to this, banks also offer leases; however, the focus, for the sake of simplicity, will be on the two categories indicated.

- commercial loans: Commercial loans are business loans. These are loans made to small businesses, midsize businesses, and large corporations to fund growth, working capital, and major investments. These loans, once made, are recorded in the financial statement at the amount of the loan proceeds disbursed. Loans charge an interest rate, representing the price of the loan that the borrower pays over time. This is known as **servicing** the debt on the part of the borrower. The payments made will consist of two parts, repayment of principal and payment of interest. On the balance sheet, the loan balance, the asset, will reduce as payments are made based upon the principal portion of the payment. The remainder of the payment made will go toward interest income, which is a major part of the revenue of a bank, given the dollar amount of total loans. Commercial loans consist of several categories to meet the needs of the communities they serve and where other markets are evolving. A few of the primary categories of commercial loans are outlined below to emphasize the breadth of this key area.
    - commercial and industrial (C&I): This is one of the major areas of commercial loans, which includes manufacturers, corporations, small businesses, and a broad array of businesses.
    - construction and real estate (CRE): These are major construction loans to build plants, apartment complexes, hospitals, and other major buildings. Included is land purchases. Construction loans permit funding throughout the construction process to pay subcontractors and, when complete, funded amounts are rolled into a commercial mortgage loan.
    - agribusiness: These are loans made to the farming community to fund major equipment purchases, working capital, and other needs related to the farming industry.

- consumer loans: Consumer loans represent loans to individuals, rather than businesses. Nevertheless, these are loans and are assets of the bank. The amount of the loan proceeds issued is recorded on the financial statements. These are also called **retail loans** to indicate the individual consumer nature of the loans made. Loan balances will decrease based upon the principal payment portion made throughout the year. Consumer loans consist of several primary categories, which are familiar to most people:
    - installment loans: These are loans made to purchase automobiles, boats, major appliances, and other needs, such as debt consolidation loans. These are generally term loans where there is a specific term of two to five years to repay the loan fully.
    - mortgage loans: Consumers purchase homes by taking out a mortgage loan. These are long term in nature, from 15–30 years, and are amortized over time. The home itself is the collateral for the loan.
    - credit cards: Banks offering credit cards is a form of revolving loan to individuals. Although these balances fluctuate considerably, they are assets of the bank and earn significant interest income.

Other Assets

This last category of assets involves the remainder of the assets. These, generally, are physical assets, and although they do not earn interest income, they can be instrumental in the production of revenue. Again, rather than complicate this section, a few broad categories are discussed to provide understanding and a foundation for this remaining asset section, including bank premises, fixed assets, other real estate owned, and goodwill and intangibles.

- bank premises: These represent the value of bank branches, headquarters, operating centers, and other physical locations where bank business is conducted. Buildings are expensive, and the market value of these assets is recorded in this category. As banks buy, build, and dispose of properties, this balance will be adjusted. Bank properties, particularly branches, are deployed geographically to attract deposits and customers who have financial needs for loans and other services. So, in this sense, the strategic deployment of branches has the potential to produce revenue for the bank by generating deposits, which, in turn, are loaned to customers and earn interest income.
- fixed assets: In contrast to branches, fixed assets accounts for the wide variety of other equipment a bank owns. This may consist of computers, file servers, network routers, safe deposit vaults, printers, ATMs, cash dispensers, furniture, and any other equipment that has value. These are recorded at their cost and are depreciated in value over their useful life in the bank's fixed asset system.
- other real estate owned: Bank real estate loans are typically secured by the underlying asset (e.g., homes, building, etc.) as collateral. The purpose of collateral is for the bank to take possession of the asset if the loan is not paid back and then to sell it to recover some of the

amount loaned. When banks do this, it is called "**repossession,**" and these then become assets of the bank. These assets are called **OREO (other real estate owned**) properties. OREO properties are held until they can be sold to recover some of their costs, which may take some time. During the time when these properties are held, the bank will incur expenses to maintain the assets. For this reason, the bank's goal is to sell these as quickly as possible. Nevertheless, until they do, they remain assets on the books of the bank and are nonearning assets.

- goodwill and other intangibles: Banks will hold other assets that could be of an intangible nature and have value. These could include patents, contracts, or other items not of a physical nature. In addition, goodwill may be recorded on M&A transactions or other deals that require recording. These would also be considered nonearning assets.

Liabilities

The liabilities of a bank represent the accounts that provide a "source" of funding to support the bank's liquidity and lending efforts. Liabilities are certainly monies owed to others, and these can be both short and long term. Liabilities also produce *interest expense*, which is the cost of borrowed funds. In general, liabilities are divided broadly between deposits and nondeposits. Within these broad categories, several subcategories are typically defined within this section of the balance sheet. As with assets, only the major categories of liabilities will be discussed to establish a foundation of understanding, including:

- deposits
  - » savings deposits
  - » checking accounts
  - » time deposits
- nondeposits
  - » interbank
  - » repurchase agreements
  - » subordinated debt
  - » floating rate notes
  - » central bank and other advances

Deposits

Deposits, like loans to assets, are the largest dollar section of the liabilities. These deposits are tied closely to the amount of loans on the balance sheet and are, for the most part, the source for funding loans. Because of this, these deposits are deemed **core deposits**, or **stable funds**, to reflect the significant role these deposits play for the bank and for the fact that they more stable and can be counted on by the bank, as opposed to other investment-related deposits. As indicated, deposits produce interest expense to the bank, for the use of the funds. Banks regularly advertise for deposits for this reason. They also deploy branches and build other channels, such as the internet, to attract deposits. In addition to making loans with these funds, they also are part of the liquidity needs of the bank. The deposits in this section originate from both commercial and retail (consumer) customers.

- savings deposits: Savings accounts are deposits that are made by consumers to earn interest and grow the balance. This is accomplished through compounding. The interest paid on savings deposits is interest expense to the bank and is generally less than the amount of interest earned on loans. Savings are valuable to a bank, as they tend to be held longer than other deposits and are therefore a good funding source. To consumers, unfortunately, the interest paid is not large, so balances in savings tends to be smaller.
- checking accounts: Checking accounts are transaction accounts. As such, they fluctuate in balance frequently, as they are used by consumers and businesses to pay bills and other transaction needs. These are significant to banks for two reasons: They generally do not pay interest, and most consumers and businesses need checking accounts as a key payment mechanism. Included in this group is other interest-bearing accounts, such as money markets and NOW accounts.
- time deposits: Time deposits are savings deposits that are contractual in nature, paying a specified interest rate, fixed for a specified term. This allows the bank to count on these funds in their loan and liquidity needs. Certificates of deposits, IRAs, and other deposits of a contractual nature are included. The interest expense incurred by the bank is generally higher for these types of accounts to compensate for the length of the term.

Nondeposits

Nondeposits are also liabilities, money owed to others, and a "source" of funding. Unlike core deposits, these are not marketed by the bank using heavy advertising to attract individuals to the bank. For the most part, nondeposits represent other avenues for the bank to obtain funding. These instruments will produce interest expense for the bank, as with deposits. The purpose of these instruments is to establish relationships where the bank can readily obtain funding, if needed. The accounts typically included under nondeposits are identified below:

- interbank: This is the opposite of the asset. This account is a funding source for the bank, which is accomplished by borrowing money from other banks. The bank will incur interest expenses as its cost, at the federal funds rate plus a small premium. By lending money to banks on a short-term basis, the relationships established allow banks to borrow funds from these banks when needed.

- repurchase agreements (REPOs): Another source of funding that is readily available is selling Treasury securities on a temporary basis under agreement to buy them back. This is the opposite of a reverse REPO (asset) and is an excellent source of funds. This requires that the bank have enough Treasury securities to use for this purpose. The bank will pay interest (interest expense) on this to the bank they sold them to.
- subordinated debt: Subordinated debt is typically corporate debt issued to raise funds. In most cases, this would be corporate bonds, or "debt." These issues are for a fixed period, with interest fixed by contract. Terms for subordinated debt could be anywhere between 10 and 30 years and are designed to fund long-term expenditures. This is a good source of funds and will obligate the bank for a longer period, which can create risk to the bank based upon interest fluctuations.
- floating rate notes: Notes are contractual obligations and pay a rate of interest that is adjustable, or floats with changes in interest rates. This is also debt to the bank, but for a limited period and with less interest rate fluctuation risk.
- central bank and other advances: These are loans that the bank takes out from the Federal Reserve, using the **discount window**, when the bank is desperate for immediate funds. These loans should be more of a last resort because the interest rate paid is high and very costly to the bank. Nevertheless, this is another source of funding to the bank. Other short-term advances can come from the Federal Home Loan Bank or other sources.

Shareholder Equity

Like other corporations, banks also have a typical **shareholder equity** portion of the balance sheet. This includes the typical accounts that one might find as part of the overall capital structure. Recall, also, that banks are corporations and raise capital through common shares issued. Accounts in this section are "sources" of funds to the bank from both external and internal sources, with the trade-off being ownership to shareholders. For simplicity, only the core accounts in this section of the balance sheet are identified: preferred stock, common shares (capital), and retained earnings. Banks may identify other items, but the items below will provide an adequate foundation for understanding.

Preferred Stock

Preferred stock issued is like subordinated debt and is called "quasi-debt." Preferred stock is a funding source and is issued to investors to raise money. Banks are one of the largest issuers of preferred stock, for the fact that it avoids ownership issues with common shareholders and can positively impact a bank's ability to satisfy capital requirements, particularly Tier 1 capital. These are contractual obligations and require the bank to pay a dividend (interest) regularly (quarterly, semiannually, or annually). The rate is fixed, by contract, and will not change. Some preferred share issues are convertible into common shares at a point in time.

Common Stock

Common stock is ownership in the corporation. These shares carry voting privileges. This is another funding source whereby the bank raises funds for major growth opportunities. After initial offerings, the issuance of more common stock can be dilutive to other shareholders and therefore is deemed low on the priority list as an additional funding source. Other avenues would likely be pursued prior to this source of funds. As a benefit, however, dividends are not fixed by contract and are not required to be paid. The board of directors can decide whether dividends are paid or not, so from an expense standpoint, they may be a less costly source.

Retained Earnings

For a bank, retained earnings are referred to as **undivided profits**. This is the term that will be seen in a bank's balance sheet. Nevertheless, the meaning is the same. Retained earnings are derived from operations, the net income, of the bank. The amounts retained, after payment of dividends, is **internal funding** for the bank and contributes to shareholder value.

Off-Balance Sheet (OBS)

Off-balance sheet describes, perfectly, the meaning of this section. All items contained here are not recorded on the books of the financial statements, the balance sheet. These are accounts and transactions that are separate contracts, agreements, or commitments made that do not appear on the balance sheet and are not counted as assets, liabilities, or shareholder equity. Typically, these would be included in the notes to the financial statements, which describe the nature of the items and are important to understand other obligations that the bank may have and that may affect the financial picture or performance of the bank at some point in time.

Over the years, these items have grown considerably for banks and can represent a fair amount of risk to the bank based upon the obligations they represent. As with other categories, this section will focus only on basic OBS items. Although these can be extensive, the primary accounts represent some of the more typical that are included: commitments, standby credit agreements, interest rate and other swap agreements, and other derivative contracts.

Commitments

Commitments involve obligations to perform certain functions and tasks that the bank must do when the situation arises that triggers these. Since they are commitments, only, they have not occurred yet and therefore have not manifest into an actual financial event. When they do occur, these will be recorded in the bank's financial statements, but for now appear only as notes. While analyzing a bank's financials, these are important considerations because the amounts may be material once the triggering event occurs. In this regard, they do represent risk to the bank. Commitments can involve contracts or other legal obligations that have not occurred yet and therefore would be important considerations in analyzing a proformance statement for the bank.

Standby Credit Agreements

These are credit obligations made to a borrower in which the financial event, or payment of loan proceeds, does not occur until it is needed, if ever, and therefore can be a way to minimize interest rate risk for the bank. These would not become assets (loans) until the needed funds are disbursed. Other than that, they remain in the notes, but need to be considered when analyzing a bank's financials. These are analyzed the same as any other loan for the customer. Once approved, a specified dollar amount will be targeted as the dollar range that is approved to be disbursed.

Interest Rate and Other Swap Agreements

Swaps are contractual agreements between two parties to perform specific activities. These are designed as interest rate risk mitigation techniques, affecting the income statement. In the case of interest rate swaps, which will be discussed in a later chapter, one party agrees to pay a fixed rate amount of interest, and the other pays a floating rate of interest. The concept is to adjust for interest expense by either receiving more interest or paying less than what is accrued on the balance sheet. By completing a swap, the monies paid and received from the contract will be recorded in the income statement and improve the risk from the balance sheet. Nothing is changed on the balance sheet; the transaction occurs fully outside of this but does get recorded on the income statement. The same would occur with other credit type swap agreements as well.

Other Derivative Contracts

This can consist of other contracts related to investment instruments that are future-oriented and relate to actions or options that exist but do not financially exist until execution. Obviously, these can carry more risk based upon their nature and should be closely monitored to understand the bank's total exposure.

Balance Sheet Recap

Overall, understanding the nature of the accounts in a bank's balance sheet is very important to understanding how a bank operates, obtains its revenues, manages its liquidity and funding, and its financial risks. Understanding these accounts, and their differences, will aid the reader in understanding how to manage a bank.

Income Statement

A bank's income statement is quite different from that of a corporation. It remains a report of income, over a period, like all corporations, but the nature of income and expenses is different and is derived from the accounts in the balance sheet. The income statement itself is structured to focus on the primary items that define a bank: loans, deposits, and interest. An example of a bank's income statement is shown in Figure 6.3. These are broken down into three major categories and the subcategories, as depicted below.

- income
  - interest income
  - noninterest income
- provision for loan loss
- expense
  - interest expense
  - noninterest expense

Income

A bank's income is derived, primarily, from making loans and charging interest. In addition, the bank utilizes other assets to generate interest income and services to produce fee income, which is not derived from interest. This is how a bank generates revenue, unlike other corporations who produce a physical product for sale. As a result of this, other traditional income statement accounts are missing, such as cost of goods sold.

Interest Income

Banks earn interest from various instruments. These are all included as assets in the balance sheet. For the most part, most of the interest income is derived from making loans, the bank's primary product. However, as financial institutions, banks manage money and therefore strive to be certain that all available assets are generating interest income. This becomes the total revenue produced by the bank's assets. Fortunately, or unfortunately, interest rates fluctuate based upon activities by the Federal Reserve, which will affect the total revenue the bank earns. The primary interest-generating sources for a bank included in this category include the primary assets discussed on the balance sheet. These are identified below and will be found on a typical bank income statement.

- interest on loans: All loans are charged either a fixed or floating rate of interest, based upon the term of the loan. Interest is included in the loan payment, along with a principal

INCOME			
Interest Income	**2,010.6**	**1,988.7**	**1,483.2**
Treasury Bills	26.0	14.2	12.3
Treasury Bonds	189.0	189.0	189.1
Loans to banks	96.3	84.2	39.1
Reverse Repo	0.0	0.0	0.0
Commercial Loans	869.4	830.4	554.4
Consumer Loans			
Personal Loans	183.8	157.7	131.7
Credit Cards	293.5	351.0	304.1
Mortgages Variable	352.7	362.1	252.5
Interest Expense	**–814.2**	**–322.8**	**–812.4**
Dep. from banks	–168.8	–177.2	–269.0
Deposits			
Savings Deposits	–109.2	–182.1	0.0
Current Accounts	–5.2	–5.4	0.0
Cert. of Deposit	–311.4	–286.8	–277.5
FRN	–151.8	–181.3	–204.8
Repo	0.0	0.0	0.0
Subordinated Debt	–60.9	–61.1	–61.1
C/Bank Advance	–6.9	–28.9	0.0
Net Interest Income	**1,136.4**	**1,065.9**	**670.8**
Other Income	**721.7**	**620.5**	**303.6**
Fees	180.2	102.8	184.6
Insurance Comm.	34.0	8.3	25.5
Private Banking	368.8	297.6	145.8
Investment Banking	331.6	71.8	21.4
Fin. Transactions	–192.9	140.0	526.3
IRS (Net Result)	0.0	0.0	0.0
TOTAL INCOME	**1,918.2**	**1,686.4**	**1,574.3**
EXPENSES	**–1,416.3**	**–385.6**	**88888**
Operating expenses	–1155.4	–737.0	–760.5
Loan Losses	–260.9	–248.7	–338.9
INCOME BEFORE TAX	**501.9**	**700.8**	**475.0**
Taxation	–125.5	–175.2	–118.7
INCOME AFTER TAX	**376.4**	**525.6**	**356.2**
PROFIT APPROPRIATION			
Dividend - Ord Shares	0.0	0.0	0.0
Addition to Reserves	376.4	525.6	356.2
Dividend/ord share*	0.0	0.0	0.0

*Cent/Share

FIGURE 6.3 Income Statement

portion to the customer. Interest rates are based upon federal funds rate and indices, such as prime rate or LIBOR. Loans are amortized over time, which defines how much interest is included in the total payment. In most cases, interest represents the largest portion of the loan payment in the early years of the loan term and then reduces later in the term. Therefore, most of the interest on the loan is recovered first.

- income from investment in securities: Banks earn interest income from their investment in Treasury securities and other investments. Much of this is invested in risk-free instruments, such as treasury securities, to ensure that idle cash is producing income. Although these are subject to interest rate fluctuations, they are "earning" assets.
- reverse repurchase agreements (REPOs): Banks purchase Treasury securities from other banks, under agreement to sell them back to them at the end of a specified term, usually short term. Banks do this to utilize idle, or excess, cash to earn interest income. The bank charges the seller of the securities a rate of interest for the securities, therefore increasing their interest income. This is a quick way to earn interest income without having to purchase more securities and incurring interest rate risk.
- interest from bank loans (interbank): Loans made to other banks are loans, and an interest rate is charged. This is lower than other loans, such as for commercial loans, but produces interest income nevertheless.
- other interest income: There may be other interest-earning instruments that a bank may use. Although the major categories are defined above, banks may find opportunity areas for producing more interest income to increase their revenues.

Noninterest Income

The other sources of revenue are those generated from other sources that do not involve interest. Banks produce other products or services that generate revenue related to fees charged based upon balances maintained or per item. These are titled "noninterest income" and are an important part of the revenue-generating efforts of the bank. This revenue is less risky, as it is not subject to the fluctuations in interest that occurs. Some of the primary accounts seen in the income statement are outlined below.

- fees earned from wealth management services: The primary products and services offered by wealth management include trust services and investment services. Both services are based upon the amount of assets under management and are charged a percentage of those balances on an annual basis. Although not as large as interest income on loans, these fees can be considerable and are part of the strategic plan of the bank.
- fees earned on cash management services: Cash or treasury management services are services rendered to businesses. These are services that include lockbox, ACH, positive pay, wire transfers, controlled disbursement, merchant services, and others. All these items are priced as specific fees, based upon volumes, frequency, or other metrics of usage.
- service charges on accounts (deposits): These are specific service charges for various items that relate to customer deposit accounts. Fees relate to minimum balance fees, ATM fees, overdraft fees, insufficient funds fees, stop payment fees, penalties, and others that relate to checking, savings, and time deposit accounts. Many of these service fees only occur when violations in account agreements occur, such as an early withdrawals on a CD, not meeting a minimum balance, or submitting a check for which funds are not available, while others are

transaction based, such as ATM usage fees, debit card transaction fees, and others. Again, these are not the most significant dollar amounts; however, given the volume of deposit accounts, service charges can grow.

- securities held to maturity: Securities held to maturity as well as other trading securities produce gains or losses to the bank. These represent income, hopefully, to the bank from the "gain on sale" of the instrument. These, alone, can be significant if the trading activities are managed effectively.
- other noninterest income: Banks today are involved in a variety of services and products that have grown in popularity, and have been enabled through regulation, over the years. These include insurance services, travel services, credit cards, and a variety of others. All of these produces other fee income for the bank and contribute to its overall profitability.

Expense

Expenses to the bank relate mostly to expenses derived from paying interest of deposits. These are significant because they are the funding source for loans, the largest of the assets. Therefore, the total dollar amount of deposits is large, hence the significant interest expense. Interest expense occurs from other funding instruments as well. In addition, there are the usual noninterest expense accounts that one would see on a typical income statement, which are general and administrative in nature. However, for banks, these are categorized under "noninterest expense."

Interest Expense

Like interest income, interest expense is the largest of the bank expenses appearing on the income statement of a bank. Interest expense is also affected by fluctuations in interest rates due to Fed actions. However, for deposits, interest rate changes tend to lag more than loan interest rates after a Fed adjustment to federal funds rates. When rates change, though, it creates risk for the bank if rates go up, in which case the bank will pay more interest expense. Beyond deposits, some interest expense may be fixed, such as for subordinated debt. Although this creates a risk if interest rates go down, one can see that interest rate volatility plays a major role in the overall profitability of the bank. Interest expense is incurred for the key liabilities outlined in the bank's balance sheet, as described below:

- deposits: This would be divided among checking, savings, and time deposit accounts. However, some of these accounts are noninterest bearing, such as demand deposit (checking) accounts. Also, time deposits are, by far, the largest of the interest expense.
- interbank deposits: These are loan proceeds received from other banks as a funding source. Banks will pay the federal funds rate plus a small premium in interest for these funds.
- repurchase agreements (REPOs): This is the interest expense incurred by temporarily selling Treasury securities to obtain funding. This rate is determined at the time of the sale and as part of the transaction but is short term in nature.

- subordinated debt: This is a debt instrument, and the interest rate paid is set by bond indenture and fixed for the term of the instrument.
- central bank advances: Loans from the Federal Reserve bank, via the discount window, are priced in accordance with the discount rate defined by the Federal Reserve. This rate is higher than others and will incur a significant amount of interest expense and for this reason should be used very prudently.

Noninterest Expense

Noninterest expenses, literally, are all other expenses the bank incurs that do not relate to interest rates. These are the operational expenses incurred to run the business. Although these include general and administrative expenses, they are titled "noninterest expenses." These expenses will be more familiar to the reader and include the following.

- wages, salaries, and employee benefits: These are the actual expenses incurred for the workforce employed by the bank. Included in these are regular salaries, insurance benefits, and retirement benefits of former employees. Wages, salaries, and benefits generally amounts to approximately 60% of the total noninterest expense and is often the one most focused upon when attempting to reduce costs.
- premises and equipment: As an expense, this includes the maintenance costs related to all bank branches for upkeep, rental of physical properties, insurance, and other related expenses incurred for the bank's physical locations. In addition, repossessed properties (OREOs) must also be maintained, like the bank's branches, until the properties are sold. Finally, the other large amount included is equipment and technology expenses for maintenance.

Provision for Loan Losses

Another unique line item on the bank's income statement is provision for loan loss. This account is an expense for the bank and represents the amounts that have been identified for loss. This item appears on the income statement and has a relationship to the contra account on the balance sheet (allowance for loan losses) as part of the calculation in arriving at the ending allowance for loan losses. As an expense, this will reduce the net income derived from loans based upon the quality of the loan portfolio. This amount is determined as anticipated loan losses from nonperforming loans where it is relatively certain they will not recover. Since this is an expense, the bottom-line net income will decline as a result. Once the actual amount of charge-offs occur, this amount is adjusted from the provision for loan losses in arriving at the ending allowance for loan losses.

Net Interest Income

Another account shown on a bank's income statement is **net interest income**. This is the difference between interest income and interest expense. The reason this is highlighted is that this is somewhat the equivalent of "gross profit" on corporation's income statement. The "net" amount remaining represents the **margin,** or **spread,** highlighting the profit derived from the lending process. Banks rely on a ratio called **net interest margin** to determine how effective the bank is at the lending process. Most of the funds used to make loans originate from deposits, which the bank pays interest to customers on. Since the bank earns interest from making loans, the difference between this interest income and interest expense is an important line item to monitor in the income statement.

Income Statement Sequence

Because of the differences in a bank's income statement, it is important for the student of banking to understand the sequence of accounts and the flow of the income statement to see how to evaluate the document. Several line items have been discussed in this section of Chapter 6. Understanding the sequence puts these items in their proper order for proper analysis. A snapshot of this order is contained in Figure 6.4.

Income Statement Sequence

- interest income
  - » assets: interbank, securities, reverse repos, loans
- minus: interest expense
  - » liabilities: deposits, interbank, debt, central bank advances
- equals: net interest income
- minus: provision for loan loss
- plus: noninterest income
  - » income: fees, service charges, other
- minus: noninterest expense
  - » expenses: wages, benefits, property, equipment, technology, marketing
- net profit loss

FIGURE 6.4 Income Statement Order of Accounts

Money Creation

The final section in this chapter is somewhat an outlier. However, it is an important one to understand the uniqueness of banking and its impact on the economy. The receipt of deposits, a liability on the balance sheet and a major funding source, is a critical function in more ways than those discussed. As banks receive deposits, particularly transaction deposits (checking accounts), a unique phenomenon occurs. This phenomenon is known as "money creation" or **fractional reserve banking**. Fractional reserve banking allows banks to create money and expand the money supply, M1. This occurs because of the reserve requirement that member banks are responsible to maintain at the Federal Reserve. In general, the reserve requirement mandates a 10% reserve withholding, above certain thresholds of transaction deposits. This partial withholding allows the creation of money, as the following process explains.

Process

Money creation occurs through the deposit process. This focus is on transaction accounts since those are the ones that are included in the reserve requirement. The sequence is outlined as follows:

1. Customers open transaction accounts (checking accounts) at banks by depositing funds.
2. Banks are required, above a specific threshold, to withhold 10% of the amount deposited.
3. This leaves 90% of the deposit available for the bank to use. Banks then lend the 90% to other customers in need of a loan. This is how loans are funded and what banks need to make these loans.
4. When a loan is made to a customer, the recipient of the loan will receive the funds and will deposit those funds in their banking account (checking account) so that they can use the funds for the purposes intended.
5. When funds are deposited from the loan made, the bank that receives the deposit will have its transaction deposits grow. When this occurs, they must withhold 10% of this again in their reserve account.
6. The remaining 90% is available to the bank to lend to someone else, which they do. When the loan is made, the process begins again.
7. This results in a 10-fold increase from the original deposit.

Formula and Example

The entire process can be reduced to a formula, which can be used to determine the amount of "new" money is created in the money supply based upon the original deposit. The formula is included in Figure 6.5. Utilizing this formula and using an initial deposit of $1,000, the amount of new money created is $9,000, as shown below:

- ((1 / 10% reserve requirement) × $1,000 deposit) – $1,000 original deposits = $9,000

$$\left(\left(\frac{1}{\textit{Reserve requirement }\%}\right) \times \textit{Deposit}\right) - \textit{Original deposits} = \textit{New Money Created}$$

FIGURE 6.5 Money Creation Formula

A further, expanded example is contained in Figure 6.6 using an Excel spreadsheet.

MONEY MULTIPLIER CONCEPT					
Reserve Reqmt.	10.00%				
Deposit	5,000.00				
New Money	48,000.00	NOTE:	Each new deposit creates increases in Money Supply		
Deposit	**Reserve Requimt.**	**Loan**	**New Money Added**	**Accum. Money Supply**	
5,000.00	500.00	4,500.00	0	0	$5,000 is not new,
4,500.00	450.00	4,050.00	4,500	4,500	already in $ supply
4,050.00	405.00	3,645.00	4,050	8,550	
3,645.00	364.50	3,280.50	3,645	12,195	
3,280.50	328.05	2,952.45	3,281	15,476	
2,952.45	295.25	2,657.21	2,952	18,428	
2,657.21	265.72	2,391.48	2,657	21,085	
2,391.48	239.15	2,152.34	2,391	23,477	
2,152.34	215.23	1,937.10	2,152	25,629	
1,937.10	193.71	1,743.39	1,937	27,566	
1,743.39	174.34	1,569.05	1,743	29,309	
1,569.05	156.91	1,412.15	1,569	30,879	
1,412.15	141.21	1,270.93	1,412	32,291	
1,270.93	127.09	1,143.84	1,271	33,562	
1,143.84	114.38	1,029.46	1,144	34,705	
1,029.46	102.95	926.51	1,029	35,735	
926.51	92.65	833.86	927	36,661	
833.86	83.39	750.47	834	37,495	
750.47	75.05	675.13	750	38,246	
675.43	67.54	607.88	675	38,921	
607.88	60.79	547.09	608	39,529	

FIGURE 6.6 Example Money Creation

Overall, this process outlines the importance of the deposit function to banks and how banks can affect the money supply, an important ingredient in the prosperity of the economy.

CHAPTER SUMMARY

A bank's financial statements are truly unique. Understanding the differences in the balance sheet and income statement is a critical learning outcome for any student of commercial banking. The accounts contained within these financial statements are very descriptive and define clearly where the revenue and the expenses occur for a bank and how interest rates are a significant ingredient in the profitability of a bank. A clear understanding of these statements and accounts is a prerequisite to calculating and interpreting the performance metrics of the bank. These performance metrics are vital to the management of the bank.

Planning begins with the balance sheet, beginning with the assets as the source of revenue. These produce interest income, which is enabled from deposits from customers that create interest expense for the bank. The difference between the two defines the bulk of the profitability that the bank earns. Other sources of income, not related to interest, contribute to revenues as well and are important to the bank. Finally, expenses related to the operations of the bank, again not related to interest, complete the financial picture. Having a strong mental picture of the flows between the balance sheet and the income statement and the order in which they occur is a critical success factor for management and the resulting performance of the bank.

END OF CHAPTER QUESTIONS

1. What is the difference between interest income and interest expense called?
2. Which financial statement should the allowance for loan losses appear in?
3. Identify two nondeposit sources of funds for a bank.
4. What is the name of the system that affects the money supply through money creation?
5. What is the key ingredient in the money creation formula that enables the creation process?
6. Of the nondeposit sources of funds, which is considered a choice of last resort?
7. What is the difference between a REPO and a Reverse REPO?
8. What impact does provision for loan losses have for a bank?
9. Identify and explain two off-balance sheet accounts.
10. What is another name for "retained earnings" that is used in a bank's financial statement?

Forecasting the Balance Sheet

The balance sheet of a commercial bank is the starting point for planning the future profitability of the bank. Although it is the income statement that reports the income and expenses incurred, the sources that create this income and expense are defined within the balance sheet. In order to understand how to manage a bank, understanding the balance sheet and its components forms the basis for future growth and profitability.

This chapter outlines the steps involved in developing an effective forecast for the next year and beyond, along with how this is accomplished. Establishing forecasts is an essential part of the planning process. Typically, the forecast is based upon the establishment of financial objectives in particular, asset growth. Once determined, the balance sheet forecast is established to support and achieve those goals. This chapter provides the rudiments for this and how it is determined.

Key Terms

Share of wallet	Loan segment
Organic growth	Earnings per share (EPS)
Correspondent/respondent bank	Other real estate owned (OREO)
Reverse REPOs	Discount window
Interest expense	Net interest margin
Net interest income	Subordinated debt
Sales forecast	

Learning Objectives

By the end of this chapter, the student will:

- Understand the sources of interest income and interest expense.
- Know how the forecast relates to the results in the income statement.
- Know the mechanics for creating the forecasts.
- Understand the key components of assets and liabilities, which form the basis for decision making.
- Know how to develop a bank budget.

How Banks Make Money

The foundation and, in fact, the definition of a bank is based upon their ability to take deposits, subject to withdrawal, and to make loans to businesses, in particular. Loans are the largest of the bank's assets, and deposits are the largest of the bank's liabilities. Since assets generate interest income, loans create the largest portion of this, by nature of their size. The same is true for liabilities, with deposits incurring the largest portion of interest expense. The net amount between the two indicates a good portion of the profitability of the bank. As a result, the importance of forecasting the balance sheet is paramount in the creation of profitability and growth for the bank.

Although the balance sheet is the topic of this chapter, the work that is done in forecasting the balance sheet has a direct relation to the income statement of the bank, and profitability. To truly understand the importance of this, one must understand the importance of competition.

Competition

Strategic planning and competition go together. The reason for strategic planning and establishing growth and performance objectives is that banks are corporations and are in business to generate a profit and increase shareholder value. To do so, the bank must understand the competition. Because there are over 6,000 banks in the United States and the Riegle-Neale Act has permitted interstate branch banking, there is considerable competition for products and services. Since bank pricing is governed by the actions of the Federal Reserve (federal funds rate), all banks are affected by this, creating margins that are similar. In short, banks must differentiate themselves from the competition to attract more business. For this reason, a clear mission statement is imperative.

Another reason that competition has intensified for banks is a direct result from deregulation. Banks must now compete, not only with other banks but also with nonbanks offering financial services. Deregulation opened the door for nonbank mortgage companies, credit unions, investment companies, and a wide range of other financial service businesses to take a percentage of the assets previously managed by banks.

Commercial banks remain the largest holder of financial assets and resources in the country, at approximately 25%. However, the remaining 75% is distributed among the competition. This is precisely the reason that planning is imperative. Banks want to obtain **share of wallet**, which is the percentage of financial needs a typical household has, that is managed by the bank. As this percentage expands, banks will generate more revenue and, hopefully, greater profitability. For this reason, pricing is important as well as service and other differentiating factors to increase the share of wallet.

Although there are many organizations competing with banks for financial products and services, banks are unique in that they are the only ones accepting deposits subject to withdrawal. Since this is the funding source for loans, banks compete with one another for deposit dollars, and then with the loans they intend to make. To do this effectively, banks must know what the other banks are charging. This is often accomplished by "shopping" other banks to find out what they are charging. With today's access to the internet, this is easier, as many depository products and some loans are published on websites (e.g., bankrate.com). Commercial banks must know what their strategy is going to be, then, to be competitive. Are they going to be the low-price provider, competitive provider, or high-price provider? This is determined by strategy, and it should be defined in the plan.

Overall, success in competition does not happen by chance; it occurs by developing specific objectives and defining the pricing strategy that will achieve that goal. Pricing for commercial loans is more unique than other products and services. In many cases, commercial loan pricing is tied to an index, such as prime or LIBOR (changing to SOFR). As a result, when the federal funds rate is changed, the overall rate that the customer is charged will fluctuate (i.e., floating rate). Details of how this is accomplished are outlined in the pricing chapter of this book. Nevertheless, one must understand what the competition is doing and have a strategy to be successful. Gone are the days where bankers waited for customers to walk into the bank and purchase their services. They now must go out and get them.

Growth Plans

As part of the planning process, developing specific objectives for asset, loan, and deposit growth are necessities in this highly competitive environment. The establishment of growth objectives sets the bar for what level is to be achieved. This aids the bank in meeting the overall general objectives established. The three principal growth goals for commercial banks are:

- loan growth
- asset growth
- deposit growth

Loan Growth

Making loans is one of the primary activities that defines a commercial bank. In addition, making business loans generates the greatest amount of interest income, a major part of the overall revenue for the bank. Loan growth, therefore, must have a target goal so that the staff has an objective to work toward. Loan growth objectives are generally a percentage target growth, on an annual basis. This might range from 3%–5%, or higher. Without this objective, revenues would likely decline. Like a corporation, annual budgets always begin with the sales budget because this drives all other expenses related to achieving it. This is the same for commercial banks, although sales will generally be loans, which generate interest income.

Loan growth will be tied to pricing as well to forecast what amount of revenue will be derived. This type of growth is called **organic growth** and is generated from making sales (generating new loans). Because this is the sales budget, banks typically determine how much they want to earn in the coming year. This will drive other key metrics, such as earnings per share and net profit margin, important for the market makers of the bank's stock. As it is understood how much the desired sales revenue is, and given pricing strategies, the amount of new loans necessary to be made can be obtained. A comparison, then, to the amount of loans from last year will indicate the percentage of new loans that must be made—hence the loan growth objective.

Once the percentage of growth is determined, this is the "total" loan growth required (both commercial and consumer). Since loans will be broken down by the two broad groups of "commercial" and "consumer," they will also be identified by subcategories, or segments of loans. Therefore, the growth goals must be distributed among these segments effectively so that the sales force is aware of their goals.

Loan growth is a core result in banking, very similar to achieving sales growth in a corporation. In addition, this should be synchronized with the mission statement and overall general objectives. Regardless, loan growth is critical for banks. Not only does it contribute significantly to the size of the bank but it also accounts for the largest amount of revenue produced. Additionally, since this is the largest of the assets, this is an important consideration in conjunction with the next topic, asset growth.

Asset Growth

Bank size is measured by the amount of assets they have (dollars). This defines the bank in terms of size categories and activities previously discussed: community, regional, and money center banks. With loans being the largest of the assets, starting with loan growth objectives accounts for a considerable portion of the bank size. Nevertheless, asset growth objectives for other components in the balance sheet are also important.

When considering general asset growth, beyond loan growth, it must be remembered that assets are the producers of interest income. As a result, by establishing overall asset growth objectives, this defines the vehicles to produce revenue, interest income. Investments in Treasury securities, reverse repurchase agreements, interbank loans, and other investments will expand the opportunity for revenue production and therefore the overall profitability of the bank. Since these assets are not the primary source of revenue, significant growth is not warranted. In most cases, growth in securities or interbank loans will be based upon need and opportunity, as well as on history.

For planning purposes, cash should be considered first and forecast based upon the requirements of the bank, which include the Federal Reserve requirement and needed vault cash to ensure that the bank does not experience cash outs. Reserve requirements should be determined based upon the bank's size and the established thresholds. For rough planning estimates, 10% of the total amount of transaction deposits should be used. Transaction deposits predominantly consists of checking accounts. Vault cash is part of the overall reserve requirement calculation; however, the bank will have an established level of cash that is desired to be maintained, which is based upon need (history).

Deposit Growth

Assets represent "uses" of funds; therefore, this indicates that a source of funds is needed. For this reason, deposits must be planned to support the planned asset growth. Deposits are the source for loans. As part of the planning efforts, deposits must be forecast to support the asset growth. Therefore, establishing objectives for deposit growth is an important part of the planning effort.

Balance Sheet Importance

The balance sheet is made up of assets, liabilities, and equity, like most corporations. However, the components of the balance sheet differ, as outlined previously. These differences clearly define the nature of the business of banking, as outlined below.

Assets

Assets are "uses" of funds and, as such, are employed to create revenue. In all aspects, the primary assets of a bank are designed for this purpose. Understanding how this occurs is important in the planning process for identifying how these accounts will grow. For the purposes of this chapter, only the primary accounts will be discussed, although this will vary significantly by bank and by the size of the bank.

The primary assets of a bank include the following:

- cash and due from banks
- interbank loans
- Treasury securities
- reverse repurchase agreements (REPOs)
- loans
- other assets

Each of the assets indicated has the opportunity to produce interest income, which is the major source of revenue for a bank. When planning the next year, or the near future, growth in these accounts creates greater opportunities for increased interest income, each of which is explained below.

Cash and Due from Banks

Banks maintain cash by way of a vault cash and in the process of collection. Cash, in itself, does not generate interest income. However, banks place deposits on reserve at the Federal Reserve, which does earn interest income, albeit slightly above the federal funds rate. In addition, excess cash is deposited at other banks in accounts that generate interest income, the goal of which is to put the most amount of cash in interest-producing accounts as possible.

Interbank Loans

These are short-term loans extended to other banks. These are designed for funding needs. The loans are generally made to banks in which the lending bank has a relationship as a **correspondent** or **respondent bank**. Banks will earn interest income similar to that of a typical loan, although these rates are typically at the federal funds rate, plus a slight premium. It is good practice to establish these lending relationships, as this creates the opportunity for your bank to borrow, on a short-term basis, as required.

Treasury Securities

Banks have investment portfolios. Within the portfolio, banks will invest in United States government securities, due to the risk-free nature of these instruments. Nevertheless, Treasury securities do pay interest based upon coupon rates. This yield will generate interest income to the bank from their portfolios. This will be from the liquid, trading, and held-to-maturity portfolios. The yield on these securities is not as high as other assets but provides significantly less risk than others and affords the bank a place to put excess cash and earn interest income at the same time.

Reverse Repurchase Agreements (REPOs)

Reverse REPOs are securities purchased from other banks or entities under agreement to sell them back to the bank from where they were purchased. These are short-term sales and are purchased from other banks to generate interest income from the selling institution for the period of time held. Again, this produces interest income for the bank. If the selling bank does not repurchase the securities, the bank purchasing these will take ownership.

Loans

All loans, commercial and consumer, will earn interest income. This is based upon the rate charged by the bank. Since loans are the largest of the assets, these will produce the greatest amount of interest income and is therefore where growth is typically forecast.

Other Assets

Other assets will include physical assets, such as branches, OREO properties, equipment, and others. Although these are not directly interest income producing, they create the possibility of generating growth in some of the other asset accounts, which, in turn, will generate interest income.

Liabilities

Liabilities are "sources" of funds. They provide the funding necessary to support the assets on the balance sheet, particularly loans. Therefore, when forecasting growth in assets, they must be funded by liabilities and must balance with the total assets. Liabilities incur **interest expense,** which is the cost of obtaining funds. Interest expense, in the aggregate, would be less than interest income (revenue), which would produce **net interest income**, which provides a significant amount of the overall profitability for a bank. Liabilities, therefore, must be forecast to not only "fund" the growth of assets but also identify interest expense to determine profitability.

The typical liabilities that a bank would have would fall into the following items:

- interbank deposits
- deposits (checking, savings, time deposits)
- repurchase agreements (REPOs)
- central bank advances (Federal Reserve)
- subordinated debt
- other funding sources

Each of the above items, although not exhaustive, are the primary producers of interest expense and funding for the bank. The following explains how they generate interest expense.

Interbank Deposits

These represent borrowings from other banks, on a temporary basis, for the funding needs of the bank. The bank would pay interest expense for these funds at the federal funds rate, plus a slight premium. These are lower rate borrowings but are nevertheless important funds that are used to support asset growth.

Deposits

The primary source of funds used to support loans emanates from customer deposits. These consist of checking, savings, and time deposit accounts. Each of these accounts produce interest expense, as the cost of obtaining these funds. These rates are "priced" by the bank, generally, less than the rates charged for loans to obtain the appropriate spread or margin to create profitability.

Repurchase Agreements (REPOs)

This is another source of funds. Banks that have invested in Treasury securities have the ability to sell those temporarily to obtain needed funding. The bank would sell these to other banks and entities under an agreement to repurchase these in a specified time frame. Banks will pay an interest rate (interest expense) for the money borrowed.

Central Bank Advances (Federal Reserve)

Borrowing from the Federal Reserve, through the discount window, is a source of funding, albeit as a last resort. If the bank is having difficulty raising consumer deposits to support its asset growth and other sources do not exist, the bank can obtain funds from the Fed. Unfortunately, this borrowing will require a higher rate of interest (interest expense) and can be costly and have other negative connotations.

Subordinated Debt

Subordinated debt, generally, is raising funding through the issuance of corporate bonds. This will incur a fixed rate of interest through a coupon rate that the bank will be obligated to pay, through maturity. This incurs increased expense, as have the others.

Other Funding Sources

Banks establish relationships with other organizations, such as the Federal Home Loan Bank, and a variety of other sources to obtain necessary funding when it is needed. Each of these additional sources will incur interest expense. If relationships are built early and cultivated, banks can keep interest expense at a minimum; however, without having a previously established relationship, the bank will incur higher interest expense.

Equity

Issuing common or preferred stock as a means of raising needed funding can be done, but this is generally employed after other avenues are exhausted. This can create dilutive effects to existing shareholders. This can create interest expense from the issuance of preferred stock and dividends for common stock. Dividends are not interest expense but a return of capital, so it does not impact net interest income.

Summary

The balance sheet, in summary, involves interest income from assets and interest expense from liabilities, the "net" of which is the major source of bank profitability. This is net interest income, which is interest income minus interest expense. Therefore, the importance of effective planning and forecasting this important financial statement will define the bank's ultimate success.

Income Statement Importance

Thus far there has been very little focus on the bank's income statement. In fact, only the balance sheet is forecast. The reason for this is that the assets and liabilities produce the primary income statement accounts, including interest income and interest expense. Pricing of assets and liabilities are the primary planning drivers that will ultimately indicate the degree of interest income or interest expense. Therefore, the income statement is a "result" of the work that is done to forecast the balance sheet, at the onset.

In addition, the bank does produce other sources of income that do not relate to interest. These are fee income items and are included on the income statement under "noninterest expense." Ultimately, the income statement identifies the bottom-line profitability of the bank. This is a direct result of the importance of the balance sheet forecast.

Forecasting the Balance Sheet

Now that the importance of the balance sheet has been established, the actual sequence and steps necessary to forecast the balance sheet, and the resulting net interest income, must commence. Forecasting first involves how it is accomplished. This can be achieved either from growth and performance objectives and/or based upon history. Once this is determined, the actual sequence of forecasting can occur.

Determine the Forecasting Approach

One must always ask the question, "Why does the bank need to grow its loans and assets?" In most cases the answer is not merely just to grow but rather what it will produce for the bank. Loans and assets produce interest income, which is the revenue for a bank. Therefore, as assets grow, increased revenue grows, and thus profitability for the bank, which, in turn, will create shareholder value for the investors. During the strategic and tactical planning process, banks establish goals and objectives that they plan to achieve at the end of the planning period, usually the end of the year. These objectives set the tone for controlling where the bank should be at the end of the period. Forecasting on this basis is proactive in that management is establishing what must happen in order to achieve these goals. Once this is established, these very specific objectives are communicated within the organization, and specifically to the departments who can control these. In this way the activities and behaviors that will follow will ensure their attainment.

On the other hand, and in conjunction with this, some forecasts are accomplished more reactively, based upon historical patterns. In this approach, which is more indirect, the forecast is accomplished based upon the historical distribution of the assets or loans, and these patterns are repeated in the forecast. Since growth objectives are the foundation of a plan, this is also a "hybrid" approach, which applies the overall percentage growth to the total loans and deposits and then distributes the amounts according to the distribution patterns.

Regardless of the approach, the forecast will be produced. Planning also must take into account the end result of this, which is revenue and profitability. For this reason, considerations must be made for the desired performance goal or the actual return objective desired. Return on assets is an excellent metric to assess in relation to this. The general flow is as follows:

- asset growth
- loan growth
- return on assets

Asset Growth

Asset growth is the total amount of assets that the bank plans to grow. This establishes the threshold, or boundary, goal for growth. Since banks are measured by asset size, establishing the asset growth objective identifies the change in size of the bank. Asset growth can be determined using the same methodologies as for loan growth, using the direct or indirect approach. The primary difference is that all assets are included rather than just loans. Asset growth is important because these are literally all of the sources of interest income, which is the primary revenue of the bank. Other key assets under consideration in this category would include cash, interbank loans, Treasure securities, and reverse repurchase agreements.

Although either the direct or indirect approach can be used, the bank will likely determine the growth in these accounts on the basis of their plan, proactively. Generally, although other assets will generate interest income, it will not be the amount that loans generate. However, in many cases there is less risk associated with the other accounts (standard ones mentioned). As a result, forecasting these items will relate to how much risk they entail and the amount of interest income they generate. For example, Treasury securities are literally risk-free since they are backed by the United States government. This will become important in planning the actual total capital adequacy ratio the bank has, another important consideration when forecasting.

Loan Growth

Loan growth may be planned based upon a percentage increase from the prior year. For example, suppose the bank has planned that loans will grow at a rate of 8% for the year. Forecasting this, then, is relatively simple: The prior year's ending loan dollar balance is the starting point. From this an estimate of the amount of payments made on the loans will be subtracted, and then the net loans will be projected from this amount based upon the percentage increase. However, loans are divided between commercial and consumer, broadly, and then by segments within. If the example 8% increase is for total loans, then this must be distributed among all segments and result in the total 8%. There are two ways to accomplish this, a direct and indirect approach.

Direct Approach

The bank derives its plan based upon how they price loans and the opportunities within each loan segment in the marketplace. In this approach, a growth goal is established for each loan segment (within commercial and consumer), the aggregate of which may result in the 8% loan growth, more or less. This is a more proactive "push" approach based upon detailed planning. Therefore, the aggregate of all segments will indicate the total loan growth planned.

Indirect Approach

Another way to accomplish this is to do it indirectly. The indirect approach requires the bank to begin with a specified goal percentage (e.g., an 8% growth rate). In addition, the bank will review the historical distribution of loans and assets. This is more reactive, or "pulling" of the information. In this approach, one must first look at the current portfolio of all loans (commercial and consumer), sum all of the loans, and then determine a percentage of the total that each segment represents. This is their percentage of the total, which would then be applied by calculating the total dollar amount of loans and applying the growth percentage to determine the dollar amount growth. From this result, multiply each segment's share of the total (percentage) times this amount to determine its individual dollar growth amount and, hence, the forecast. Table 7.1 provides the actual steps for each approach.

Return on Assets

Banks will have established a return on assets (ROA) goal for the bank as part of their planning efforts. The ratio is calculated as (net income / total assets). As part of forecasting, once the bank has established the asset growth objective, one can back into how much net income is necessary to achieve the ROA objective. For example, if the total forecast, with growth, is planned to be \$350 million and the ROA objective is to be 2.0%, then solve for net income as follows: \$350 million × 2.0% = \$7 million. If net income is, historically, say, 23% of interest income, then the bank will need to produce interest income of \$30.3 million (\$7 million net income / 23%).

This is valuable information. Now, from a forecasting standpoint, assets must produce \$30.3 million dollars. Therefore, in forecasting, an assessment of each asset and loan segment can be done to determine how much interest income they will generate, based upon

Table 7.1 **Direct and Indirect Approaches to Forecasting Loans and Assets**

Direct approach

1. Identify dollar loan balance by segment:
   - commercial
     - » commercial and industrial
     - » wholesale
     - » information, technology, and communications
     - » real estate
   - consumer
     - » installment loans
     - » credit cards
     - » mortgage loans
     - » home equity loans
2. Estimate anticipated payments and maturities for each segment and subtract from the beginning amount.
3. Identify the percentage growth objective for each segment, and apply it to determine the forecast.
   - (Last year amount − Estimated payments and maturities) × (1 + Growth rate goal) = Forecast
4. Sum the segment forecasts for each and divide by the beginning total dollar amount to determine the overall loan growth rate goal.
   - (Sum of segment dollar forecasts − Beginning sum of segment dollars) / Beginning sum of segment dollars = Total Loan Growth Rate (%)

Indirect approach

1. Determine the existing distribution of loan segments to the total loans.
   - (Beginning balance of each segment / Total dollar of all segments) = % of total by each segment
2. Calculate the total dollar loan growth forecast (both commercial and consumer).
   - (Sum of total loan segments × Planned loan growth %) = Total dollar growth forecast
3. Calculate the individual segment dollar forecast.
   - (Total dollar growth forecast × Individual segment % of total loans) = Individual segment dollar forecast

current and forecasted rates for the year. In many ways, this should be the first activity completed, as this would be the **sales forecast** for the bank. Most organizations begin their planning processes with the desired sales forecast, from which the necessary activities (assets and liabilities) are determined to meet this. Nevertheless, it must be considered to control the end result goal.

Forecasting Sequence

Although the actual loan and asset forecasts are known, there is a specific sequence that must be followed in order to complete the budget. This sequence must be followed for the reasons identified in each section, as defined below.

1. Total asset growth forecast
2. Loan growth forecast
3. Distribution of loan portfolio
4. Deposit growth forecast
5. Remaining assets growth forecast
6. Central bank advance disposition
7. Remaining liabilities growth forecast
8. Balance the balance sheet
9. Reserve requirement compliance

Capital Requirement Compliance

Total Asset Growth Forecast

Since assets produce the majority of the revenue, or interest income, for the bank, they must be forecast first. This is the equivalent of a sales forecast. In a sense, by forecasting the assets, the majority of the revenue sources that appear on the income statement will be identified. As a result, the asset forecast will provide the basis for forecasting a portion of the income statement.

Both assets and liabilities have a general sequence when forecasting. This will become clear as each of the primary parts of the balance sheet are discussed. Nevertheless, the total asset forecast is determined by the desired growth of the bank's total assets. Generally, this is determined as part of the planning process and, although the majority of the growth will be in loans, loan growth must fit within the total growth in assets (less than total asset growth). Similar to loans, asset growth will be based upon the prior period, applying a growth percentage to this original amount (e.g., prior period × [1 + growth rate]). This will become the next period forecast for assets. However, before other accounts can be forecast, the dollar growth amount is needed (i.e., prior period amount × growth %). This will form the basis for forecasting the remainder of the assets, beginning with loans.

Loan Growth Forecast

Since loans produce the largest amount of revenue (interest income) and are primary to the bank's purpose, this forecast should be developed next. This includes both commercial and consumer loans. The objective of this forecast is to project the size of the loan portfolio at the end of the next period. The first consideration is the goal or objective that has been determined as the growth percentage. Banks, in general, will use the direct approach (previously discussed) to increase the size of the portfolio by **loan segment** (individual types within commercial and consumer loans). The departments or loan divisions that are responsible for the specific loan segment will usually define this objective. Regardless, the base amount used in determining the forecast must be the dollar amount of the existing portfolio (prior period), although it is expected that the portfolio amount will decrease, naturally, during the quarter due to loan payments, payoffs, and maturities. It is best that the growth be based off of the prior period portfolio, not including payments, payoffs, or maturities; otherwise, basing growth on the reduced portfolio balance may not show an overall growth. From the prior period portfolio amount, the growth percentage would be applied to produce the forecast (e.g., prior period portfolio dollar amount × (1 + the growth %)).

Once this is accomplished, the actual forecast multiplied by the anticipated rate charged will indicate the amount of interest income that could be generated. This is a key ingredient in determining the profitability of the bank, net income, which will be important in determining an important market ratio, **earnings per share (EPS)**. If a quarterly budget is being established, the annual growth objective must be divided by four to achieve a quarterly budget.

Distribution of Loan Portfolio

When an overall loan growth rate is determined for the entire portfolio, it must be allocated among the various loan segments in both commercial and consumer loans. The loan growth percentage is for the total portfolio, all segments, so each segment must develop its own growth forecast. To do this, one must determine the distribution percentage each loan segment (within commercial and consumer) represents to the total loan portfolio amount. This is easily done by dividing each loan segment amount by the total loan portfolio amount to obtain the percentage it represents. Once determined, the percentage for each segment is multiplied by the dollar amount of the total loan growth to produce the forecast for that segment (e.g., commercial and industrial amount % × total loan growth amount). Loan segments will include the following general items within commercial and consumer loans.

- commercial
    - commercial and industrial
    - wholesale loans
    - real estate loans (construction and mortgage)
    - agribusiness
    - asset-based loans
- consumer
    - installment loans (personal loans)
    - residential mortgage loans
    - home equity loans
    - credit cards

This will provide a forecast for each.

Deposits Growth Forecast

Deposits emanate from consumers and consist of transaction, savings, and time deposits accounts. These are considered "core" to the bank and a major part of the definition of a bank. Since deposits represent the largest amount of liabilities and the largest source of interest expense, they are very important to the forecasting process. Banks must advertise to obtain these funds. In order to forecast these, one must consider the types of deposits individually, as rates will vary with each. The primary accounts include:

- transaction accounts
    - checking accounts
    - NOW accounts
    - money market accounts
- savings accounts (passbook savings)
- time deposits
    - certificates of deposit
    - individual retirement accounts

The first consideration is interest expense. Since regular checking accounts do not pay interest, this is a considerable source of free funds. However, checking accounts can be closed at any time, so there is nothing holding them to the bank. NOW and money market accounts pay interest and carry some restrictions, so they are less likely to move. However, consumers shop rates, so some runoff can be anticipated. Savings accounts pay interest, but at a low level, so they have less interest expense but do not move much. Finally, time deposits will pay the most interest, and they are established by contract. Therefore, since they generate the most interest expense, the bank should plan this carefully. The advantage of these are that they will not move readily; otherwise, they will incur a penalty.

The reason that deposits are forecast next in the sequence is due to the determination of the reserve requirement. Deposits will fund loans, predominantly, but it is necessary to know what the forecast will be because the Federal Reserve reserve amount is based upon a percentage of the transaction deposits. In order to ensure that the reserve requirement is satisfied, which will be part of "cash" in the balance sheet, the deposit forecast must be determined. Once determined, the bank can check to make sure that enough funds are in the cash account to satisfy this.

When forecasting deposits, the following steps should be observed:

1. First, determine the historical loans-to-deposit ratio. This can be determined by calculating this from the prior period and is simply total loans divided by total deposits. This is a percentage, which will be used next.
2. Obtain the new loan forecast (total loans) for the next period (prior period loans + loan growth forecast), and divide this by the loan-to-deposit ratio (determined above). This will produce the total deposit forecast for the next period. Subtract from this amount the total deposits from the prior period. The result will be the dollar amount of deposit growth.
3. Determine the distribution percentage of each of the deposit types (savings, checking, and CDs) based upon the prior period deposit total.
4. Multiply each percentage by the dollar amount of deposit growth previously determined. This is the growth forecast for each deposit type.

Although this will achieve a realistic look at the required deposits, the bank will also consider any specific campaigns planned for increasing deposits that may increase these. In addition to this, considerations for the direction of interest rates in the economy is also important. If rates are increasing, campaigning for CDs will increase interest expense. In this sense, an eye on the net interest margin is an important consideration when planning and making adjustments to the forecast. Remember, deposits must be marketed; therefore, there is a cost of obtaining these funds, which, although an noninterest expense, will have an impact on bottom-line net income.

Forecast the Remaining Assets

Cash and due from banks: The next most important area to forecast is the cash account. The reason this is so important is due to the bank's liquidity position. Banks must be liquid, and when forecasting, one wants to make sure there is enough funds available for the following:

- satisfy current obligations
  - » withdrawals from deposit accounts, disbursing loan proceeds, teller cash drawers, and other current needs

- reserve account
  - » ensuring that the bank meets the specific percentage requirement defined (3–10% of transaction accounts)

When building the forecast, the above items form the basis for the amount to be projected. Although the bank will earn some interest income, from the reserve account, the rest does not. The goal of the cash account is to make sure that an adequate level is maintained, with a cushion, but not significantly much more than this. In order to estimate this, determine the required reserve amount first, based upon the size of the transaction deposit portfolio (checking, NOW, and money market accounts). The rest should be estimated from the historical amount from the past quarter. In this regard, determine the cash amount from the last quarter, subtract the reserve requirement amount from that quarter, and then add this amount to the current reserve requirement. Remember this will change once the liabilities (deposits) are forecast for the current quarter; therefore, your cash account may have to be adjusted again to arrive at the final forecast, once this is done.

To assess compliance with the reserve requirement, multiply the new, forecasted transaction deposits by the reserve requirement (3–10%). If the cash account meets or exceeds this amount, the bank will meet its reserve requirement. If the cash account is below the reserve requirement, forecast growth in the cash account until this is satisfied (add to the cash account). In most cases, the bank will want to satisfy this and have a cushion to cover fluctuations or demand that is not accounted for. This is absolutely important because the reserve requirement will be met, regardless. If the bank is short and they have no other avenue for funding this, the last resort is the Federal Reserve discount window, or central bank advance. This is not desired, as the interest rate is not favorable and interest expense will climb, eroding net interest income.

It is also important to remember that liquidity and funding will come from the amount of deposits and other nondeposit sources obtained. This number will change during the quarter and may or may not mirror the forecast, so the bank must be prepared to deal with this.

Interbank loans: These are loans to other banks and help establish relationships with other financial institutions for reciprocal activities. As an asset, the bank is lending money, temporarily, to banks using the federal funds rate (plus a premium). This creates interest income (revenue) as well, but not at the level of the loan portfolio. However, this is a way for the bank to utilize excess cash, earn interest income, and establish relationships where the bank may be able to borrow, if needed. Therefore, when forecasting, view the historical amount from prior quarters and develop a forecast. As with cash, this may be adjusted, dependent upon the capital adequacy ratio and the amount of risk-weighted assets included in that calculation. Interbank loans, generally, would be less risky than business and consumer loans.

Treasury securities: The bank will maintain an investment portfolio. Within this portfolio, U.S. Treasury securities will be bought and sold based upon economy and the marketplace. To account for this in the forecast, history will play a role. One must first consider the detailed investment portfolio to account for maturities that will reduce the portfolio as well as sale of securities from trading. From this, the bank would determine the amount that are planned to be purchased, and this will be instrumental in determining the forecast. Treasury securities are desired because they are risk-free assets, therefore having a positive impact on the capital adequacy ratio, and they earn interest income. In addition, owning Treasury securities allows the bank to participate in the REPO market should they need to generate nondeposit funding. Decisions about Treasury securities (buy/sell) are based upon the direction of the economy, coupon rates, term, and so forth. Since Treasury security yields are economic indicators themselves, they should be considered when determining whether to buy or sell and at what level.

Reverse repurchase agreements (reverse REPOs): This is another source of interest income. Based upon additional cash, the bank can purchase Treasury securities from other banks, temporarily, under agreement that the borrower will buy them back. During the time held, the bank will earn interest income. Similar to loans to other banks, building a relationship for these transactions is helpful to expand the bank's funding sources, if needed. The forecast for these can be determined based upon history, recognizing that reverse REPOs would likely be paid down relatively quickly (within the quarter) as a result of their temporary nature. Therefore, the forecast would be part of the bank's strategy to remain active in this marketplace. The bank would also receive fee income from the seller. These instruments are essentially short-term loans, backed by the security itself as collateral. If the seller fails to buy these back, the bank would retain the security as their recourse.

Other assets: Other assets will include physical assets, such as the bank branches, **other real estate owned (OREO)** property, physical equipment, and other tangible assets that the bank possesses. The reason this is considered in this sequence is that the bank will be budgeting for capital expenditures as part of their budget planning. These purchases will require funding from the liabilities, but may produce increases in the account. Other assets on the balance sheet will diminish in value due to depreciation and other disposition of the assets, so this must be planned. After this consideration, new assets planned can then be added. These do not directly produce interest income; however, in the case of new branches, these become platforms from which clients will be attracted, which could generate more deposits and ultimately loans, which will produce interest income. Nevertheless, growth in this category would be the utilization of cash to purchase assets, so this will reduce cash, which must be monitored closely to ensure compliance with reserve requirements and overall liquidity.

Central Bank Advance Disposition

Although the **discount window** is considered a last resort source, this is an important consideration early in the process. When forecasting, the bank should consider any past borrowings from the Fed that may still be outstanding. Because interest expense tends to be higher for the discount window, it is desirable to pay this off as soon as possible. Because there may be a balance and the bank is trying to optimize its interest expense to obtain the highest **net interest margin** possible, reducing this amount should be part of the plan. In addition, when planning for this, if the balance is paid off, it will further reduce the total liabilities and increase the overall gap between assets and liabilities, increasing the funding need. For this reason, it is considered first.

It is best to account for this early. In most cases, advances from the central bank would be short term in nature, as these loans are, more or less, last resort type loans to shore up funding needs.

Remaining Liabilities Growth Forecast

At this juncture, there are more assets projected than liabilities on the balance sheet. This difference must be funded further. Since deposits (checking, savings, and CDs) already has a preliminary forecast, the bank must consider other funding sources to close the gap. This may require increasing deposit forecasts. However, expanding deposits beyond the historical or normal levels may be challenging. This would require more effective pricing, more marketing, and sales to generate more deposits, which is not guaranteed. Therefore, banks must consider other sources of funds that can be utilized. These appear as liabilities and can be considered, as indicated below.

<u>Interbank deposits</u>: Interbank deposits are excellent sources of funds, if needed. For the reasons mentioned in interbank loans (an asset), relationships are built with other banks that permit the bank to utilize these relationships to raise temporary funds, if necessary. The forecast should begin with the amount of remaining funding needed, after the deposit forecast. This amount indicates what amount must come from other sources. These are generally lower rate loans (less interest expense) and should be considered on that basis. The forecast should be based upon historical borrowings and in conjunction with changing interest rates and concentrations in other nondeposit sources, where the bank may be locked into lower rates when rates may be rising.

<u>Repurchase agreements (REPOs)</u>: This is the opposite of reverse REPOs. Banks utilizing this source are selling existing Treasury securities to other institutions, short term, under agreement to repurchase them at a specified time. The bank must own Treasury securities in their portfolio to take advantage of this source of funds. Interest expense will be incurred during the time the bank uses the funds. The bank that purchases the securities holds them in the event that the borrowing bank does not repurchase them

as collateral and will keep them in the event of a default. Therefore, they carry less risk and are more available for short-term funds. Similar to other nondeposit sources, the forecast will be based upon how big of a gap remains to fund and in relation to historical utilization.

Subordinated debt: Another source of nondeposit funding is **subordinated debt** or fixed-income type instruments, usually corporate bonds. Since these are generally of a long-term nature, the bank must consider the market rate of interest and the direction of interest rates in the future in planning. Because of this, the bank will be obligated to pay a fixed rate of interest for a long period of time. This must be considered when planning to further raise funds in this regard.

Other nondeposit sources: There are a variety of other sources of funds that may be utilized to fund the assets. These can include the Federal Home Loan Bank and others. It is important for the bank to plan and build relationships with a variety of sources in advance. If the bank were to need funding, quickly, predetermined sources will be easy to obtain the necessary funding and at a good rate. If, however, these have not been predetermined, the bank runs the risk of not being able to get the funds when needed, or they will pay a premium for these. Again, this will be based upon need, so history does not necessarily dictate the forecast. It becomes a matter of how the bank wants to distribute the funding sources and the amount of interest expense charged.

Preferred stock is another form of funding that can be utilized. Preferred stock is quasi-debt and is part of the overall capital structure of a bank. Banks take advantage of this frequently, as it provides benefits for increasing both total capital and Tier 1 capital ratios. Preferred stock is a type of ownership in the bank but usually does not have voting ability, as common shareholders do. However, they not only earn dividends, fixed by contract, but they also have priority claim on dividends over common shareholders.

Equity: Finally, the issuance of common stock is a source of funding as well. This is last on the list in the sequence because the issuance of more shares may be dilutive to existing shareholders. This will also have some impact on the price of the stock. Although this does not produce interest expense, contractually, dividends may be paid, which will impact net income. This is truly a strategic consideration and must be considered with care. The goal is to provide the funding from the prior sources indicated first and then to consider this last in the pecking order.

Balance the Balance Sheet

As previously indicated, liabilities are used to fund assets. This step compares the asset growth to the liability growth to ensure that this and the next period forecast are in balance. In short, assets must equal liabilities plus equity. If this is not the case and there are more assets than liabilities, the bank must make a decision to either decrease the asset growth planned to equal the liabilities or increase the funding (liabilities) to balance. At this stage, the bank can increase the growth rate of the major source of funds, deposits, first. Since these are the primary sources of funds and are usually sizeable, the first step is to determine whether it is feasible to increase the deposit growth originally determined. If so, this should be done to close the gap in balancing. If this is not feasible, then the bank should take another look at the other sources of funding previously mentioned and increase the growth amount to balance the balance sheet. This, of course, is an oversimplification. Care must be taken to determine the right instruments, the right level, interest rates, and the economic forecast when considering other instruments to make the most prudent financial decision for the future.

Reserve Requirement Compliance

Banks have reserve requirements that they must meet at the Federal Reserve. As mentioned previously, this is not optional and must be met. After the balance sheet forecast has been balanced, it is necessary to ensure that there are enough funds in the cash account (asset) to cover the percentage of transaction deposits necessary to meet the reserve requirement. With the deposits forecast, this is a simple calculation of multiplying the reserve requirement by the total transaction deposits. For example, if the reserve requirement is 10% for the size of bank and transaction accounts totaling $1,000,000, then $100,000 is the reserve requirement. (Note: this is oversimplified for illustrative purposes. In reality, a portion of the reserve requirement is 3% up to a specified threshold and then 10% thereafter. In addition, an average over a two-week period is taken before the calculation is made.) The reserve requirement is compared against the forecasted cash balance in the asset section to determine if enough is available to satisfy this, with a cushion. If this is not the case, the growth forecast for cash must increase while not changing the overall asset forecast. This means that the increase in cash will have to be taken away from the growth factor of another asset, such as loans, Treasury securities, reverse REPOs, interbank loans, or other assets. When enough has been allocated, recheck to ensure that the balance sheet is still in balance.

Capital Requirement Compliance

The final step is to ensure that the bank meets the capital requirement threshold for both total capital and Tier 1 capital. Generally, these formulas are relatively simple, with the denominator in both cases as "risk-weighted" assets. Therefore, knowing the risk rate percentage for each of the assets is imperative. For example, business loans tend to be of the riskiest and usually carry a risk rate of 100%. This means that every dollar is fully a risk and is not reduced. Interbank loans may be less risky and carry a risk factor of, say, 50%. If that is the case and the total forecast for interbank loans is \$100,000, then only \$50,000 will be included in the denominator of the capital equations (\$100,000 × 50%). The numerator for the capital ratios relates to the capital structure of the bank (i.e., common stock, preferred stock, retained earnings, subordinated debt, etc.).

Therefore, make the calculations using the capital ratios provided in this text, and compare them to the compliance thresholds. If they meet or exceed the threshold, nothing further needs to be done. If, however, the bank is below the threshold on either capital ratio, changes must be made to the forecast to ensure that the thresholds are met. There are two methods of accomplishing this, in general: Increase the numerator by increasing amounts in the capital structure, as this will raise the capital ratios, and/or decrease the amount of risk-weighted assets in the denominator. In both cases, by making changes of this nature, it will likely put the balance sheet out of balance and changes will need to be made to both assets and liabilities to rebalance. In all cases, the goal is to keep the asset forecast as planned but manipulate the forecasts of loans to reduce risk-weighted assets and increase other less risky assets. The same would be done with liabilities as funding sources, the numerator, to increase this.

Once the capital ratios are in compliance, recheck to make sure (a) the asset forecast has not changed, (b) the balance sheet balances, and (c) the reserve requirement is satisfied. If so, this is the final forecast.

Summary of Liability and Equity Forecasting

Liabilities are less established by planned growth objectives than are assets. Funding is a process of identifying sources that will support the planned growth indicated in the asset section of the balance sheet. The forecasting of this will require somewhat a trial-and-error approach until the balance sheet is balanced. In some cases, it may be that the amount of funds needed to support the asset growth may not be feasible. In this regard, the bank may have to reconsider their growth plans and potentially scale this back to ensure attainability. Practice will help to make this process more effective. A bank's forecast does not end with balancing the balance sheet. As indicated, both the cash reserve requirement and capital ratios must be met during the process. In addition, one other consideration is important as well, interest sensitivity. During the forecasting process, the bank must consider how sensitive the assets and funding sources are to interest rate fluctuations. The bank should monitor whether they are asset or liability sensitive and how this does or does not change with the forecast. This, in conjunction with a solid understanding of the direction of interest rates, will aid in the forecast process. Like the reserve requirement and the capital ratios, this should be monitored throughout the forecast process to manage the bank's liquidity position.

CHAPTER SUMMARY

The balance sheet forecast is the most important part of the forecasting process. When planning revenue and profitability, most would look toward the income statement as the starting point. To some degree, this is true. Banks, like other corporations, usually begin the process with a sales forecast. For a bank, this is interest income (revenue, or sales), so this is an important consideration. However, understanding which assets will produce the maximum amount of revenue places the emphasis on the balance sheet forecast. From this, the necessary growth or forecast of assets can be determined that will achieve that revenue level and, then, the funding necessary to achieve that growth.

In all cases, it is a balancing act to produce the forecast. This is a very fluid process. The bankers must know the economy and the direction of interest rates, manage compliance with capital, understand their sensitivity to interest, forecast assets that produce the most interest income, fund their growth with the least amount of interest expense, and manage their reserve requirement. This is all a part of the balance sheet forecast.

END OF CHAPTER QUESTIONS

1. Which asset produces the greatest amount of interest income?
2. How is the total amount of funding needs determined?
3. What is the difference between the direct and indirect approaches to forecasting assets?
4. Which asset should be the first to consider when developing a forecast?
5. What is the purpose of a REPO? A reverse REPO?
6. Why is ROA important in the development of a balance sheet forecast?
7. Which liability produces the greatest amount of interest expense?
8. What is the relationship of the income statement to the balance sheet forecast?
9. What role does net interest income play in the forecasting process?
10. What is the purpose of interbank loans in the forecasting process?

CHAPTER 8

Reading and Understanding Economic Indicators

Commercial banks are an integral part of the economy. Their functions and products all relate to an aspect of the economy that is not readily intuitive to the general populace. Not only do the efforts of banks help to strengthen the economy through loans and deposits but they are also affected by the results of the economy. Most organizations will be affected by what occurs in the economy, but banks are particularly so, given their financial nature and their specific role in the economy. Banks make loans not only to generate revenue but also to invest in businesses, which can stimulate the economy through growth, creating new jobs, and increasing salaries to households. As identified very early in this text, banks are an integral part of the economic cycle, and when banks do not function well, the economy is negatively affected. This understanding of the role that the economy plays and the indicators that measure prosperity or decline are the elements of understanding that can aid the bank in planning and developing strategies for success.

The economy must be interpreted, and this occurs through results that generate changes to key economic indicators that can guide banks in their actions. These indicators must be understood to plan effectively. Although banks are financial entities, they perform a very important economic function, and for this reason, this chapter identifies these economic aspects and indicators. Readers and students of banking must have a strong understanding of the economy to be effective as bankers. Although there are many economic indicators,

Key Terms

Economic indicators
Federal funds rate
Federal Open Market Committee (FOMC)
Yield to maturity
Repurchase agreements (REPOs)
Reverse repurchase agreements (Reverse REPOs)
Gross domestic product (GDP)
Consumer price index (CPI)
M1
M2
Quantitative easing
Reorganization

Learning Objectives

By the end of this chapter, the student will:

- Understand the importance of the economy and its impact on commercial banking.
- Know what an economic indicator is and what it does.
- Learn the primary economic indicators that ultimately impact the bank and its activities.
- Understand the underlying drivers that cause changes to economic indicators.
- Know how to interpret the economic indicators for action.

this chapter will highlight the most important economic indicators that banks should monitor, understand, and ultimately embrace for action.

Overview of Economic Indicators

Economic indicators are exactly what they purport to do: They provide a direction, an indication of a result. **Economic indicators** consist of data that is tracked over time and reported periodically and compared to prior periods. This data aids in the understanding of recent events based upon the results they show and can help to interpret what the future may hold or provide a sense of the current environment. Since they are "economic" indicators, they provide data about the current state of the economy and a potential direction of where it may be going. Obviously, this can be very important to a bank since the customers they serve are affected by what is occurring in the economy. Businesses are most acutely affected, which will translate to affecting the individuals who work for the company. In this regard, the key stakeholders of economic indicators are banks, businesses, and individuals. Whether one believes that these indicators do or do not have a bearing on their life, one need only look to the most recent examples that have occurred within the last decade, the financial crisis of 2008 and the pandemic of 2020.

Economic indicators can be almost anything that the reader chooses, to provide a snapshot of the economy or future prospects. This is more than interpreting the tea leaves, although indicators can be developed that have historical accuracy that can guide performance for the future. Nevertheless, indicators are applied to action or guidance to action, and economic indicators do that effectively for the economy, which can be most instrumental in a bank's planning efforts (Ritter, Silber, & Udell, 2009).

This chapter will identify the key economic indicators that are most important to banks.

Understanding and Interpreting Economic Indicators

Although there are many economic indicators, the scope of this chapter is on the top 10 economic indicators that can guide or affect a bank's behavior. Each of these originates from a variety of sources, which are important to understand and will be outlined in detail. In addition, each of the indicators relates to specific outcomes. These indicators and outcomes are outlined in Table 8.1 below (Baumohl, 2008).

Table 8.1 **Primary Economic Indicators and Outcomes**

Economic indicator	Outcome
1. Federal funds rate	Interest rate fluctuations
2. Treasury security rates	Term structure; direction of rates, economy
3. Gross domestic product (GDP)	Growth and prosperity; production
4. Inflation rate	Cost of goods and services
5. Money supply	Expansion or decline of M1 (money supply)
6. Housing starts	Number of permits, indicates optimism of not
7. Stock market index	Optimism, earnings, and prosperity
8. Property price index	Property appreciation
9. Unemployment rate	Jobs, prosperity, economic growth
10. Bankruptcies	Poor earnings, slow economy

This is a handy chart to gain a general sense of the impact of these indicators. However, a more detailed understanding of each is important to be able to use them effectively for interpretation and action. Economic indicators should be viewed in conjunction with other indicators, like how financial ratios for a company are viewed. One economic indicator may provide an explanation for the performance of another, as can be seen in the following pages.

Federal Funds Rate

Overview

One of the more pervasive indicators and tools of monetary policy is the **federal funds rate.** As outlined in the central bank chapter, the Federal Reserve bank of the United States manipulates this rate based upon other economic indicators—namely, inflation—to slow down or energize the economy. Changes to this rate not only affect all other rates but can also have immediate impact, therefore making it a very affect tool of the Federal Reserve. The Fed, through its **Federal Open Market Committee (FOMC)**, will evaluate this rate each time it meets, usually eight times per year, if not sooner.

Impact to Banks and the Economy

Once a change is made by the Fed, commercial bank rates that are tied to indices, such as prime rate, LIBOR, or SOFR, will change in conjunction with the incremental change made, up or down. When this occurs, if the federal funds rate is increasing, banks can earn more revenue (interest income) on their loans where they are tied to an index. The reverse will occur if they drop. In this regard, a change can have an immediate impact on the bank's income statement, and therefore, banks will quickly respond with management efforts to protect their interest rate margins. When the federal funds rate is held very low for long period of time, as during the financial crisis of 2008, it is cheaper to obtain a loan. Monitoring the trends in federal fund rate changes will provide an indication of the economy and how the Fed is trying to manage it. If rates continue to go down, the economy is anemic, and they are trying to stimulate growth. When the economy is moving in this direction, the gross domestic product is likely declining as well.

Reasons for Change

The Federal Reserve usually will change this rate to either stimulate the economy or slow it down. When rates are dropped and held low for a long period of time, as in the financial crisis of 2008, the Fed is making credit cheaper to stimulate borrowing and to hopefully fuel the economy with growth, jobs, and, ultimately, prosperity. However, when the economy is depressed, banks earn less on the loans they make, and they will seek other means of income to make up for the lost revenue. Loans during these periods are not only cheaper but also may be riskier to the bank, given the depressed nature of the economy. The Fed uses the inflation rate to guide them when to raise or lower the federal funds rate. In general, the Fed has relied upon a 2% inflation rate threshold, above which rates would be raised and below which they would be lowered. Changes to the rate are usually in increments of 25 basis points, unless more aggressive action is required. When there is no change, that is a statement unto itself and indicates that the economy is stable and is being monitored. Nevertheless, the primary driver of change is the direction of the economy.

Access

The federal funds rate gets immediate press whenever the FOMC meets, whether a change is made or not. These are published regularly in newspapers but can be found by going to the Federal Reserve website (www.federalreserve.com). This can also highlight the detail of the FOMC meeting. Other applications, such as Bloomberg, are good sources for accessing this information.

Treasury Security Rates

Overview

Treasury securities are debt issued by the United States government to fund spending deficits in the fiscal budget. These securities are issued in three general maturity categories:

short term, intermediate term, and long term. The securities pay a coupon rate to the holder as compensation for purchasing the security. The securities are considered **risk-free** because they are backed by the full faith and credit of the U.S. government, with the power to tax for servicing and payback of the debt. The types of Treasury securities include:

- Treasury bills: These are short-term notes that have terms of 3, 6, and 9 months. These are issued at a discount with the full-face value paid at maturity.
- Treasury notes: These are intermediate-term notes that have terms of 15, 18, and 21 months. These will pay a coupon rate of interest.
- Treasury bonds: These are long-term bonds that have terms of 2, 5, 10, and 15 years. These also pay a coupon rate of interest.

Because of the varying levels of maturities for these securities and their safe and reliable nature, they are used frequently for yield curves to understand the direction of interest rates. One of the Treasury securities that is particularly useful for understanding the market and the direction of the economy is the yield on 10-year treasuries. This security is indicative of investor confidence: As 10-year Treasury yields go up, the bond price will decline, and investor confidence will go up because they are optimistic about the future and feel they can get better returns elsewhere and do not have as much need for safety. The opposite occurs if 10-year Treasury yields go down. For a full understanding of Treasury yield performance under various scenarios, see Table 8.2.

Table 8.2 **Treasury Security Response to Events**

Impact on	Federal funds UP (interest rates)	Federal funds DOWN (interest rates)
Yield to maturity	UP	DOWN
Price	DOWN (sells at discount)	UP (sells at premium)
Coupon rate	BELOW market	ABOVE market
Demand for treasuries	DOWN, sell treasuries	UP, buy treasuries
Investor confidence	HIGH, can find higher returning investments elsewhere	LOW, cannot get better rates, safer to invest in treasuries to avoid loss of principal
Result	If priced below par, yield goes up because receive par value at maturity, which is more than what was paid.	If priced below par, yield goes up because receive par value at maturity, which is more than what was paid.

It must be remembered that Treasury securities are not the highest paying instruments (coupon rates) available. When investor confidence is low, the demand for these securities will go up, especially during turbulent economic times, for the primary reason of safety of principal. Even though the interest payments are lower, they will still generate a return, and the investor will not lose principal. Treasury rates represent their yields, which is the **yield to maturity**. As shown in Table 8.2, as these yields go down, the price of the security goes up because there is significant demand for the security, due to declining investor confidence. Therefore, the yield to maturity will decline because the security will be sold at a premium (above par value), but at maturity the investor will receive only par value, less than the amount paid.

Treasury securities fulfill many needs as economic indicators and provide bankers, and others, with a glimpse of the current and future state of the economy.

Impact to Banks and the Economy

Banks use Treasury securities for many reasons—first, as an indicator of the marketplace and signals of investor confidence in the economy. This can be very helpful to a bank, especially in monitoring yield curves. As yields are up, interest rates are going up, which will expand the bank's interest margin, and is a positive outlook for the economy. This would be more indicative of the longer term rates, or yields. This would cause banks to be more aggressive on growth plans.

Another reason for usage is that banks continually seek to generate interest income (revenue) from their asset portfolios. Of course, this comes mostly from making loans, but it also comes from investments in securities. Since banks must be liquid, they do not want to have in inordinate amount of cash in their vaults that are nonearning. Therefore, investing in Treasury securities allows them to earn interest income while at the same time protecting them from loss of principal on these risk-free instruments.

A further reason they are important to banks is as a funding instrument. When banks own Treasury securities, they can sell them temporarily to raise needed funds, for liquidity purposes, under an agreement to purchase them back in a short period of time. These are called **repurchase agreements (REPOs)** and are included in the liability section of the balance sheet. During the time held, the bank will pay interest on these. The bank can also purchase Treasury securities from other banks, under the same agreement to have the seller repurchase them after a short period of time. This is a means of raising additional interest income, as the seller will pay interest to the bank. These are called **reverse repurchase agreements, or Reverse REPOs**.

Reason for Change

Treasury yields will change, increasing or decreasing, in response to events in the economy. Following the chart in Table 8.2, this will provide a key for understanding the reasons for these changes. In general, U.S. treasuries are important to assess as indicators of the economy. As Treasury yields are going up, this is an indicator that investor confidence is growing in strength. Interest rates are going up, precipitated by federal funds increasing, indicating signs of prosperity. Therefore, U.S. treasuries are excellent indicators to watch for signs of the future. The Fed raises rates to curb inflation and to settle down a raging economy. The demand for U.S. treasuries will decline; therefore, prices will drop for these securities, which will increase their yields. The bottom line is that the direction of these securities are very telling about the economy.

Access

Information about United States Treasury securities can be found easily by visiting the U.S Treasury website (www.treasury.gov or www.treasurydirect.gov) for a wealth of information regarding these securities. These would typically be tracked regularly by the treasury department of the bank (finance department).

Gross Domestic Product (GDP)

Overview

Gross domestic product is one of the most-watched indicators of the economy. **Gross domestic product (GDP)** is a measure of the sum of the value of all goods and services produced by the United States (or other economies). It is an indicator of growth of the economy and is measured as the percentage change from quarter to quarter. An upwardly increasing percentage is a positive indicator, noting improvement in the economy. Economies are also measured by the size of their GDPs. The degree of the increase, or decrease, indicates how robust the change was, and that can provide a sense of impact as well as an indicator.

Understand GDP is an assessment of growth. As the GDP increases, it indicates that businesses are producing more products and services and are growing, which is indicative of a positive economic climate (cycle) where jobs are available, companies are producing, and households are consuming—all positive to the economy.

Impact to Banks and Economy

To understand the impact of GDP for banks, one must look back to the economic cycle. When companies are growing and producing, their revenue are increasing (from operations). This growth produces the need for more jobs. As more jobs exist, households have more disposable income, which they use to consume more products and services, and they invest. More deposits are put into banks, which provides more funding for banks to make loans. Banks will now make more loans, and the positive cycle continues. The impact to the banks, then, is that increasing GDP expands the opportunity for loan growth. Businesses have a more optimistic outlook and wish to continue to grow, which will require funding, causing them to borrow. Growth to the economy is imperative for the outlook to the economy and production.

Reasons for Change

The primary reason GDP changes is a function of the businesses and organizations that produce products and services. The actual percentage emanates from the degree of change in GDP from one quarter to the next. The percentage typically ranges from 1%–4%, although this can be considerably more or less during an economic upheaval, such as those in the 2008 financial crisis and the 2020 pandemic.

The result that causes the change is "production," which, in a free enterprise capitalistic society, is the primary driver.

Access

GDP can be found easily in newspapers, applications (e.g., Bloomberg), and other sources. The major source for this in the United States is accessing the Bureau of Economic Analysis, which can be found online (www.bea.gov).

Inflation

Overview

Inflation represents the escalation of prices for goods and services in the economy. Prices increase through demand: As the economy strengthens, with more disposable income available, the demand for goods and services increases. This indicates that the economy is heating up, and the Federal Reserve is watching. Too much inflation is not positive, as it will result in a reduction of purchasing power through increased prices; therefore, a threshold is monitored that provides a gauge for determining the timing of action. The Federal Reserve has relied upon 2%, historically, as that threshold. Once inflation climbs to that level and increases beyond this, the Fed will utilize its tools in monetary policy to slow this growth. Their goal is to stabilize and "even out" the economy. In this regard, inflation is a major economic indicator.

The inflation rate is determined by the change in the **consumer price index (CPI)**, which is released monthly, expressed as a percentage change. Although released monthly, the change in CPI is more effectively measured by reviewing the annualized 3, 6, 9, and 12 month changes (quarterly changes). Observing trends is important in understanding whether this is a sustained change or monthly anomaly.

Impact to Banks and the Economy

One of the major impacts to the banks is the action that the Federal Reserve will take. When inflation is rising, above the 2% threshold, the Fed will act by increasing interest rates through the federal funds rate. By raising rates, the cost of credit increases, making money more difficult to obtain. When this occurs, the economy will respond and slow down. Although interest rate increases will positively affect interest income for the bank, increasing their interest margins, the demand for loans will decline. Ultimately, the Fed wants to slow the economy, and by raising rates, they can accomplish this. So, although the federal funds rate itself is an economic indicator, it generally is raised or lowered by the growth or decline in inflation. If inflation is stable or if it is declining too much, the Fed will lower rates to stimulate the economy. In this scenario, the cost of credit and, therefore, money is cheaper, which should stimulate action on the part of households and businesses.

Reasons for Change

As indicated, the consumer price index is the vehicle used to monitor change in prices. These include an assessment of retail prices. However, the major reasons for increases or decreases result from demand. In this regard, when the demand from consumers and businesses increases, challenging the supply of these products and services, prices will increase and will continue to increase unless something is done to stop this before it becomes truly negative. Increased prices decrease the purchasing power of consumers, sapping them of funds for the same products and services they purchased previously, demanding more of their incomes and savings. When this occurs, greater uncertainty and instability of the economy will occur, which will be most negative for consumer confidence.

Access

Access to consumer price index data is obtained from the Bureau of Labor Statistics. You can visit the website for the Bureau of Labor Statistics (www.bls.gov/); however, there is a more direct site to go to for actual, up-to-date inflation results (www.bls.gov/cpi/).

Money Supply

Overview

The money supply in the United States is measured by M1 and M2. **M1** is the total amount of currency plus in checking accounts in the United States. This is the most liquid of funds. **M2** includes M1 but adds the less liquid savings accounts and certificates of deposit. The combination of the two is the money supply. The money supply is an important indicator, as it is one of the elements that is manipulated by the Federal Reserve, which provides an indicator of the availability of money. The money supply is a finite amount of funds that exist in the economy. As more money is available in the economy, per the economic cycle, households have more discretionary funds for investments in savings accounts, CDs, and other instruments.

The money supply is viewed as all the money that is in use in the economy and changes hands throughout the normal course of living. Money does not disappear, nor is it spontaneously created. It simply exists. The greater the money supply, the greater the availability of funds, and vice versa.

Impact to Banks and the Economy

When the money supply is plentiful, households and businesses are growing, consuming, and saving. This is a positive indicator for the economy and banks, as households and businesses expand their deposit accounts (savings and checking accounts). As deposits increase, banks have more funding from which to manage their liquidity positions and more have more money to make loans, increasing their ability to raise interest income (revenue). In this regard, it is viewed positively by banks as a sign of prosperity and growth. When the supply of money diminishes, less disposable income is available. Therefore, there are fewer deposits less potential for making loans. This tends to slow down the economy.

Reasons for Change

The money supply does not arbitrarily change. It is affected by the Federal Reserve through monetary policy. The Fed uses its open market operations to manipulate the money supply. Like inflation as an indicator of either a raging economy or decline, the money supply is a part of this. To slow down an economy that may be heating up too fast, causing inflation, the Fed will most immediately adjust interest rates to begin this process. However, another tool they have available to them is buying and selling U.S. Treasury securities. Recall that the money supply is a finite amount of money, as in a filled bucket of water. When the Fed wants to slow down the economy, they may begin a process of selling Treasury securities. Since the Fed owns securities on its balance sheet, if they begin a process of selling these in the secondary market, investors will purchase these securities, taking money out of the money supply. Bank deposits and bank reserves will decline. As in the "bucket of water" example, some of that water (money) is poured into the Fed's bucket through these sales and taken out of the economy. As less money is now available, there is less disposable income to save money, and these funds may be needed to pay for day-to-day living expenses.

When the opposite occurs, during times of recession or in a crisis (e.g., the financial crisis of 2008), the Fed would "buy" Treasury securities in the secondary market. In this case, they are increasing their balance sheet with securities and ingesting the economy with more money, pouring more of the water from their bucket back into the economy's bucket. This is known as **quantitative easing** and effectively expands the money supply to stimulate the economy. Since the overall supply of money is finite, it is either in the Fed's hands on their balance sheet or in the economy's hands in the form of M1 and M2. Because the overall supply is finite, the Fed can be effective in manipulating the economy. Finally, it is the change in money supply that provides the economic indicator of the strength of the economy.

Access

The Federal Reserve tracks the amount of money in M1 and M2. This may be accessed by going to the Fed's website (www.federalreserve.gov) and searching under "money supply" and/or "M1and M2." This is reported monthly. The indicator can be reflected as a percentage change over a trending period, such as over a quarter. Like many indicators, this should be viewed in conjunction with changes to the federal funds rate, as well as inflation.

Housing Starts

Overview

Housing starts, as an economic indicator of the economy, is an advance measure of the number of new homes being constructed. As an indicator, when residential building is growing, it signals optimism in the economy, as households are not likely to embark on the construction of a new home in times of recession. Therefore, when more construction is occurring, the indication is not only an optimistic outlook but also a signal of declining interest rates, which is the cost of mortgage borrowing. For example, in the months leading up to the financial crisis of 2008, residential construction was booming. Consumer confidence was high, and more individuals were making the plunge into home ownership and new construction.

Impact to Banks and the Economy

Obviously, this is a positive indicator, showing signs of strength and the willingness of households to take on more risk. For banks, this is an opportunity for mortgage lending, as new construction will require both construction loans and the more permanent mortgage loans thereafter. This is quite positive for banks, mainly because mortgage loans not only generate interest income but generally are also of lesser risk, so they are very positive for banks.

On the downside, when housing starts decline, households are risk-averse and will not take on large loans like these until there is a more optimistic outlook. This is because, in times of recession, there is uncertainty as to whether an individual will have a job or not and will be able to pay back the loan.

Reasons for Change

As indicated, housing starts provide an advance indicator of economic prosperity or the reverse, based upon risk. Housing starts are measured based on the number of building permits purchased. Historically, this has been a very successful advance indicator of the economy. Because the purchase of residential homes is driven by interest rates, as interest begin to decline, more people will look to build and own homes to take advantage of lower rates. This growth of building permits signals a continued low-rate environment where credit is cheaper. Although this will be a time when the Fed is looking to stimulate the economy, as housing permits increase and building begins to grow, this will bode well for other business who provide the supplies to builders. These will include building materials and will increase the demand for skilled subcontractors, improving the labor market.

In short, housing starts denotes optimism and provide an indicator of the direction of interest rates.

Access

Housing start information is provided from the United States Census Bureau, Department of Commerce. Housing starts are released monthly and are measured in thousands of units (permits). These monthly figures are compared to the prior month, and a percentage change is determined to indicate growth or decline. This can also be determined over longer periods of time for trends, such as quarterly or year-over-year.

Stock Market Index

Overview

The stock market index has been one of the major sources of economic outlooks for some time. Indices such as the Dow Jones Industrials or the Standard and Poor's 500 (S&P) have provided investors with glimpses of the future and the direction of the economy. Stock market indices are collections of stocks that collectively measure the movement of these stocks in terms of overall market price and volume of transactions. As economic indicators, they are very fluid, immediately available, and provide a sense of confidence in the marketplace. As indicated, the stocks that make up the indices that are tracked are very responsive to conditions in the economy, the marketplace, and world and local events; therefore, they must be viewed a bit differently as indicators. Since they can be quite volatile, as an indicator they should be viewed based upon trends, as opposed to immediate movements. As a trend, if the market prices of these "blue-chip" stocks is declining, there is less optimism in the future and more risk in investments. Stocks tend to move in opposition to interest rates. When interest rates are increasing, to slow the economy and increase the cost of money, stock prices tend to fall because the cost of credit is higher, preventing companies from borrowing to grow and produce. Therefore, their value is diminished. When interest rates go down, stock prices are up since it is now cheaper for businesses to borrow and grow. In addition, the stock market is future oriented in the sense that investors are looking ahead and investing in stocks, raising its prices, when the future, longer term is optimistic or progrowth. This type of outlook will raise the value of the firms, overall, and therefore their stock prices.

The stock market is reflecting "market prices" or current sales prices, not the book value of a company's stock. Book value is the underlying liquidation value of a company, and on a per share basis, the payment of a premium for the stock above book value denotes optimism and a brighter future. In that sense, they provide an indication of prosperity.

Impact to Banks and the Economy

Obviously, banks are corporations and issue stock to shareholders. As an economic indicator, depending upon which direction the index is moving, they will provide a sense of direction for the bank as well. If the stock market indices are growing, a lower interest rate environment is the likely direction. This can be challenging for banks, as their interest margins will likely decline, although the opportunity for more loans is higher due to lower rates. So banks must be cautious on how they use this information. As the market declines, interest rates will likely increase, expanding the opportunity for more interest income and better interest margins, but this will make lending more competitive due to the increasing cost of credit. Therefore, given the relationship with interest rates, the stock market can be an indicator of the direction for these. During the 2020 pandemic, interest rates were reduced near zero by the Fed, with prospects of remaining at or near zero. However, the stock market indices climbed substantially with optimism of a robust recovery. With low interest rates, businesses can obtain the needed funding to grow, and with cheaper funds, the future value of the stocks themselves will increase with the prospect of increased earnings. This is signaling a more positive future, so banks can plan accordingly.

Reasons for Change

As indicated, the market can change dramatically, very quickly. However, it is the sustained direction that is more meaningful. The underlying reason for sustained changes in the stock market result from the marketplace and how investors are viewing the future. If investors are pessimistic about the future and do not see an upturn, the demand for stocks will decline, indicating more risk to their investments. If investors see optimism in the future, the demand for stocks will increase, with more optimism toward increased shareholder value due to perceived prosperity and opportunity in the future.

Political decisions and directions from new administrations can signal changes that can impact businesses, such as increased taxes or more regulations. When this happens, the outlook for the future would see decline in earnings and therefore shareholder value, and greater investor risk. As this occurs, the indices would decline, forecasting this sentiment.

Access

There are many sources for access to the stock market. Local and national newspapers report on changes to stock market indices every day. With the current technology, these indices can be monitored every minute, every hour, throughout the day. Other applications, such as Bloomberg, are good sources of this up-to-date information, as are a wealth of smartphone applications that can be downloaded. The comparison is always how much change has occurred from time to time, which is measured by dollar and percentage.

Property Price Index

Overview

Again, this is another index, one which identifies the change in property prices from period to period. Like stocks, when the value of property is increasing such that businesses and households will pay a higher price, there is optimism that demand is strong and that value is increasing, a sign of prosperity. When the outlook for the economy is optimistic, people will take more risk and purchasing will expand. As this occurs, demand will increase the prices paid for homes and other properties. As an indicator, this supports other economic indicators, such as the stock market index and possibly even inflation. Everyone desires that the largest asset they own, their home, grows in value. This creates wealth and potential prosperity once sold. These are all positive signs for the economy and the marketplace.

Impact to Banks and the Economy

As home prices and other properties increase in value, banks would view this as a positive indicator for the future, as with "housing starts" and opportunity for more mortgage lending. With increasing demand and less potential risk, this would create an opportunity for expanded volume of mortgage loans, at higher values, and therefore higher dollar borrowings and increased revenue from interest income.

Reason for Change

Like the stock market, this is an advance indicator of confidence and sentiment about the future. People are willing to pay more for their investments when the economy is improving, as they will take less risk with their investment and likely obtain a strong return upon sale. So, this is a sign of optimism for the future.

Access

Property price indices may be obtained from a variety of sources. Sites such as Green Street's Commercial property index (https://greenstreet.com/insights/CPPI) will reflect changes in commercial property prices. In addition, a source for the residential home prices can be found through the Federal Housing Finance Agency website (www.fhfa.gov), which produces a housing price index (HPI). These are measured as percentage change quarter-over-quarter and year-over-year for specific areas and cities in the country.

Unemployment Rate

Overview

Unemployment is another of the most important economic indicators in the country. This is a measure of the percentage of working age individuals that are unemployed. This is an emotional indicator, as when it grows it can indicate an environment of layoffs, lack of earnings, and downturn. Ensuring full employment is one of the primary goals of the Federal Reserve. Although this rate will never be at zero, the closer the percentage is in proximity to zero is considered full employment.

When the economy is declining, from an economic cycle standpoint, businesses are not generating the revenue they seek, which causes them to reduce staff. As staff are reduced, the overall economic cycle slows down: Households do not save money; therefore, they make fewer deposits, and there is less lending. When lending declines, companies do not grow, so their profitability is strained and they must find ways to reduce costs, the biggest of which is staffing.

Declining employment is a negative trend and will create concern for most households. This can trigger a pullback in spending, which will impact the earnings of businesses, and even though this is reactionary in anticipation of the risk of job loss, it may create job loss if households do not consume, a self-fulfilling prophecy.

Impact to Banks and the Economy

The largest concern for banks when unemployment rises is concern for payback of outstanding loans. As unemployment rises, household income will decline, putting pressure on loan payments and defaults. Furthermore, business clients of the bank are likely under earnings pressure as unemployment increases. This is a double concern of banks, with the possibility of nonpayment of loans. This can create a need for the banks to increase their provisions for loan losses, which will decrease their overall income. Therefore, the unemployment rate is one to be watched closely.

Reason for Changes

One of the most prevalent reasons for a change in unemployment is lack of earnings, or an increase of earnings. Both relate to what is occurring in the economy: As economies decline, earnings will decline and therefore create pressure to reduce costs. When the percentage grows, it provides an outlook that is generally negative to the economy.

Access

Unemployment rates are released monthly. These are produced from the Bureau of Labor Statistics (http://stats.bls.gov). A more direct source of changes in the unemployment rate can be obtained by accessing one part of the website (http://statis.bls.gov/news.release/empsit.toc.htm). These statistics will also be available in major newspapers and other media sources.

Bankruptcies

Overview

Bankruptcies are another major indicator of the economy. Bankruptcies have negative connotations, certainly, but it does not totally mean the end. There are a few levels of bankruptcy. Nevertheless, the more bankruptcies that occur, the more negative the indications are for the economy. For the purposes of this chapter, this represents a combination of all small- to medium-sized enterprises (SMEs). Unfortunately, when bankruptcies increase, businesses cannot pay their bills and must eliminate their debts. This is accomplished in one of three forms:

- Chapter 7: This form of bankruptcy is total liquidation. This can be used by businesses and individuals. When used by businesses, the company is going out of business and is liquidating all its assets to pay off any outstanding debt to the extent possible. This is the most severe form of bankruptcy.
- Chapter 11: This form of bankruptcy is called **reorganization** and is only available to businesses. When this occurs, the business is not going out of business, but reorganizing, meaning downsizing, selling off unneeded properties, cutting costs, cutting product lines, and taking other actions. By reorganizing, the business can continue and will have an ability to pay off their debts, albeit on altered schedules.
- Chapter 13: Similar to Chapter 11, this bankruptcy is for individuals and permits them to repay their debts at lower payments and over a longer period. This allows the individual to improve their credit standing and integrity among their creditors—a much more positive outcome than Chapter 7.

Regardless, the presence of bankruptcies as an economic indicator identifies the challenges that businesses are facing to pay their bills, due to reduced earnings and a declining economic environment.

Impact to Banks and the Economy

Banks are creditors. They loan money to businesses. When businesses file bankruptcies, the bank will likely take a considerable loss from the loan. When it is full liquidation, creditors are paid back after all the assets are liquidated. If there are many creditors or if the assets are not worth much, there will be only a small amount of value remaining, indicating that the bank will take the loss on the remaining balance due. This will impact the bank's earnings and capital. This directly relates to credit risk, nonpayment of loans. When companies reorganize under Chapter 11, the bank may be able to restructure the loan and, ultimately, get paid back.

When the number of bankruptcies (SMEs) increases, this signals a declining economy, and bankers must review existing loans and communicate to hopefully avoid these negative situations. This is not a positive sign for the economy and signals a continuing downturn.

Reason for Change

The major reason for increasing numbers of bankruptcies is declining earnings of SMEs. These can occur from a slowdown in the economic cycle, caused by significant events in the economy, such as a financial crisis or pandemic affecting corporate earnings.

Access

Access to bankruptcy statistics can be obtained from the American Bankruptcy Institute (ABI). Although there are likely other sources, statistics can be obtained by accessing their website (www.abi.org/newsroom/bankruptcy-statistics).

CHAPTER SUMMARY

Economic indicators can paint a very informative picture of the current economic environment and the prospects for the future. These indicators should be compared to one another for a more thorough examination and to deepen the understanding for the future. For the student of banking, understanding these key indicators, at the very least, will help to understand how to make decisions for the future. These indicators are not always discussed enough when a bank is planning its future, but literally all bankers should understand the meaning of these. Specifically, lenders need to focus on their clients and how they are being affected by the economy. This helps the monitoring process and may help to prevent a loan loss in the future.

Additionally, the type of investments a bank will make, how they price products, and whether they will be aggressive in lending will be part of their analysis based upon the direction of these economic indicators. For these reasons, following these indicators as they are produced is an important routine that bankers want to adopt. Bankers more than other business are affected by the changes in the economy simply for the fact that they are part of it as well, as in the economic cycle. Banks are an integral part of the economy, thus making them both an economic as well as a financial entity. A deeper understanding of the economy is a critical ingredient in the management of commercial banks.

END OF CHAPTER QUESTIONS

1. Identify five of the 10 most important economic indicators, and identify the outcome/impact of each.
2. What are the different types of U.S. Treasury securities, and what do they represent?
3. How is the 10-year Treasury yield used as a proxy for the economic outlook?
4. Which economic indicator relies on the consumer price index for its measurement?
5. Explain the differences between a Chapter 7 and Chapter 11 bankruptcy, for a business.
6. What is included in M1 and M2 in the money supply?
7. How is the gross domestic product measured as an economic indicator?
8. When Treasury yields decline, what relationship does this have to interest rates and investor confidence?
9. What organization produces the unemployment rate?
10. When corporate stock indices decline, what is the impact to interest rates?

CHAPTER 9

Pricing Loan and Deposit Products

One of the greatest challenges in any business is to determine how products and services will be charged and what amount will produce the optimal amount of revenue needed to sustain the business. By far the easiest part of this is to arbitrarily set the amount, without analysis. This is fraught with issues and can immediately change behaviors in ways not intended. Lowering prices extremely low may attract customers but sacrifices overall revenue, whereas raising prices higher may produce more revenue, but the volume of clients will likely decline. Without effective planning and a strategy, this will create tremendous risk for any organization.

Although commercial bank products and services are different than for other corporations, they are highly competitive. Banks have their primary products, loans, and deposits regularly displayed in places like bankrate.com for all to see and compare. In this regard, it is imperative for banks to understand their competition and ensure that they price competitively to maintain and grow their base. This chapter focuses on what pricing is and how it is done for commercial banks, and how this relates to bottom-line income.

Key Terms

Basis points (bps)
Fixed Rate
Adjustable Rate
Prime rate
LIBOR
SOFR
Cost plus pricing
Default risk
Maturity risk
Spread
Price leadership pricing
Customer profitability analysis
Earnings credits
Annual percentage rate (APR)
Adjustable rate mortgages (ARMs)
Mortgage points
Annual percentage yield (APY)
Marginal cost pricing

Learning Objectives

By the end of this chapter, the student will:

- Understand the meaning and impact of pricing for a bank.
- Know how pricing impacts the elements of the income statement.
- Understand how loans and deposits are priced and what methodologies are employed to do so.
- Know how relationship and lifeline banking play a role in pricing.
- Understand key indices used in pricing commercial loans.

Introduction

Products that are sold by commercial banks are found in three primary areas: loans, deposits, and fee-based products and services. As was discussed in Chapter 6, understanding a bank's financial statements, the income statement is made up of four primary areas: interest income, interest expense, noninterest income, and noninterest expense. In this chapter, the focus will be on interest income and interest expense. The reason for the dedication of the chapter to only these two categories in the income statement is that this represents the primary area of profitability for a bank, which is "net" interest income (interest income minus interest expense). By far this is the major focus for bank revenue generation and profitability.

As discussed in the last chapter, interest income and interest expense result from the decisions made in the balance sheet. Profitability begins with forecasting new business for the next period and actively pursuing a plan to attain the organic growth anticipated. Assets ultimately produce interest income, and liabilities produce interest expense. Loans are the largest of the assets and are therefore responsible for most of the revenue (interest income). Deposits, on the other hand, are the largest of the liabilities and produce the greatest amount of interest expense, resulting from the funding necessary to support the growth of loans. Interest rates are often discussed in **basis points (bps)**. Basis points are a decimal of the percentage point. For example, 25 bps is the equivalent of .25%, or 100 basis points is 1.0%, and so on.

In this chapter, with the emphasis on interest income and expense, pricing will be concentrated on the following areas:

- commercial loan pricing
- consumer loan pricing
- deposit pricing

Pricing for these products is the interest rate that is charged to the client for a loan, or the interest rate that is paid for deposits. In this regard, there is no dollar charge but rather the rate of interest that will be applied to the balances involved to produce the interest income or expense. Since all rates are affected by changes that the Federal Reserve makes to the federal funds rate, these rates carry interest rate sensitivity, indicating that they may be lowered or raised based upon decisions made outside of the organization. For this reason, banks must manage their interest rate sensitivity to plan effectively for the performance of the bank.

Commercial Loan Pricing

Commercial loans represent the largest amounts of loans for a bank given that they are made to small, medium, and large corporations. The cost of these loans, or credit, is interest. Commercial loans are divided into segments, which target specific categories of loans that may be priced differently based upon the nature of the category. For example, commercial and industrial (C&I) loans are generally business loans for a variety of needs in the business community, whereas real estate construction loans, albeit made to businesses, are focused on the construction and purchase of commercial property. These will be priced differently based upon term length, risk, collateral, and other considerations. In short, each loan will be different, and pricing will be uniquely tailored to the loan. Unlike other areas or in the retail world, commercial loan pricing is not standardized. In fact, the only common denominators, in general, for pricing these products is the federal funds rate and other indices used to define the price.

Because of this variability, pricing can be risky as well as challenging to be effective. On one hand, the goal is to attract the client but at the same time earn an effective return, or margin. Nevertheless, most commercial loans, as a result, are considered adjustable since they will float based upon the federal funds rate and the indices they employ.

Indices for Pricing

Commercial loans are generally priced based upon an index. While commercial loans can also be priced based upon a **fixed rate**, a rate that does not fluctuate, many are priced on the basis of an **adjustable rate**, or one that will change based upon changes to the federal funds rate. Today, the primary pricing indices used for commercial loans include prime rate, LIBOR, and now SOFR.

- prime rate: **Prime rate** is an index and represents the rate banks charge to their very best customers. It is often quoted as prime, or prime plus or minus a certain amount of basis points. Prime rate is adjustable in that it can vary. Prime is affected by changes in the federal funds rate. When the federal funds rate goes up or down, the prime rate will go up or down, generally, by that amount. In addition, this will happen very quickly after a federal funds rate change. Nevertheless, as this is adjustable when the rate changes, customer interest payments will increase, and therefore, the total payment will go up or down with these changes during the term of the loan.
- LIBOR: **LIBOR** is the London Interbank Offered Rate. This is another index and readjusts for changes in federal funds, as with Prime. LIBOR is also an index. Many bankers favor this rate, and although there are various frequencies of update, the most popular is the three-month rate.
- SOFR: This is the latest index, which is a potential replacement for LIBOR, entitled **secured overnight financing rate (SOFR)**. Although this is beginning to be used, there are other indices evolving that bankers may be more comfortable with for the future.

Pricing Methodologies

Although, in most cases, commercial loans tend to be tied to an index and are floating, fixed rate loans do occur. This is part of the structuring of the loan deal, as outlined in Chapter 13. The primary objectives in determining the rate is to select one that:

- covers the internal costs required in the underwriting process
- compensates for any risk in default or term (maturity)
- covers the cost of raising the funds to make the loan
- provides a profit margin to produce revenue for the bank (Rose & Hudgins, 2013)

To accommodate these objectives, there are several methodologies employed in "pricing" the loan that can be considered. For the purposes of this chapter, we will focus on three of these methods:

- cost plus pricing
- price leadership
- customer profitability analysis

Cost Plus Pricing

Cost plus pricing is exactly what the name implies. This method is used to arrive at a specified interest rate to charge a customer based upon covering the costs attendant to the production of the loan. As indicated previously, this will address many of the objectives needed in pricing a loan. The theory behind cost plus is that the optimal price is one that covers all the costs involved in the production of that loan, plus a profit margin. The primary elements involved to make this determination is illustrated in Table 9.1.

Table 9.1 **Cost Plus Pricing**

Cost of raising funds	1.0
+ Operating costs to produce the loan	.60
+ Premium to compensate for risk (default or term)	.15
Subtotal	1.75
+ Profit margin (10% desired × subtotal)	.18
= Loan interest rate	1.93%

Each of the elements illustrated in Table 9.1 is expresses as basis points (bps) or as a percentage, the sum of which will indicate the rate to be used. Obviously, once determined, this is subject to negotiation with the customer and may change from the original proposed. Nevertheless, this becomes somewhat an art when negotiating and mathematically straightforward when determining.

- cost of raising funds: Banks make loans from funds they receive from customers by way of deposits. Although this is the largest of the sources, it is by no means the only source. Banks do have many sources of funds to draw upon, and this is where this first component can be tricky. The goal is to cover the cost. To raise funds, banks must pay an interest rate (interest expense) to attract and retain deposits or to obtain funding from nondeposits (e.g., REPOs, subordinated debt, etc.). Therefore, when a lender is applying this, they should determine this from the average costs incurred for all types of sources, likely on a weighted average basis. Consideration should be given for the current rates paid as well since these rates can and will change.

- operating costs to produce the loan: To make commercial loans, there are several costs that are incurred. Among them are salaries of the officers making the loans, cost of staff in the support roles to book and service the loan, attorneys to prepare documents, office supplies, occupancy costs, and utilities. If done effectively, the bank will capture all these costs and reduce it to a percentage (basis points) on average to compensate for all the costs incurred. This is sometimes referred to as *overhead*. This is determined by summing all these costs over a given period and dividing them by the total loans handled during that period to arrive at a per unit (loan) share. Again, it is important to capture this as accurately as possible to ensure that the loan is properly priced to cover these.
- premiums to compensate for risk: Commercial loans are risky. For the bank to compensate for this, premiums can be added. The greater the risk, the higher the percentage, and vice versa. Generally, two major areas of risk may be involved, default risk and maturity risk. **Default risk** is the risk that the customer will not repay the loan. If the customer has had prior loans with the bank and paid them effectively, then there is less default risk, and a premium may not be needed. If the loan term is for a longer duration, perhaps five to 10 years, a premium can be added to compensate for the unknowns in the future, such as a changing economic climate, future upheavals in the industry, and other threats that will only increase when the term is extended. This is called **maturity risk**. Both are expressed as basis point additions.
- profit margin: Finally, once the prior elements are determined, they should be summed to produce a subtotal. Then the subtotal is multiplied by a specified or desired profit margin, such as 5% or 10%. This result is then added to the subtotal to produce the final interest rate.

Essentially, the cost of raising funds is a given; the other components represent the **spread**, expressed as basis points to add to the cost of funds. Using the example in Table 9.1, the cost of raising funds is 100 basis points (bps), or 1.0%. To arrive at the final quoted price, 93 bps is added as the spread. This spread can be adjusted upwards or downwards based upon the competition and negotiation.

Price Leadership Pricing

The prior method, cost plus, "derives" an interest rate based upon the various components. **Price leadership pricing**, in contrast, defines the rates based upon indices used in the marketplace. These indices are defined by the marketplace using prime rate (the reference rate), LIBOR, or SOFR. These rates are adjustable based upon changes in the marketplace driven by changes in the federal funds rate by the Federal Reserve. The reliance on a "reference rate" is used instead of some of the other components in the cost plus model as the rate that is reserved for the best customers of the bank. Although the reference rates are used, this model is still comprised of various components, some of which are like the cost plus model.

Cost plus assumes the rate is defined by components related to risk, profit, and cost. Price leadership focuses on risk and the federal funds rate. Therefore, there is a reliance on the reference rate to cover costs as well as profit. The primary components involved in this model are included in Table 9.2.

Table 9.2 **Price Leadership Pricing Components**

Prime rate (reference rate)	3.25
+ Federal funds rate	.25
+ Risk premiums (default and/or term)	.25
= Loan interest rate	3.75%

Although there is no specific profit margin, or cost of obtaining funds included, this rate will adjust with changes to the federal funds rate. Furthermore, the prime rate is defined as the rate charged to the bank's best customers. As such, this rate is a proxy for cost and profit margin. Since this rate will adjust, a prime rate of 325 bps will increase or decrease by the incremental change in the federal funds rate, maintaining the profit margin. From that rate the bank will then charge a premium based upon the default or maturity risk that the borrower has. Therefore, the total rate is federal funds rate + prime + premiums, as explained below.

- prime rate: The prime rate, as mentioned, is the rate that banks charge their best borrowers, or those that represent the least amount of risk. In addition to prime, bankers also use other reference rates, such as LIBOR or SOFR, as their base rate. These are indices used by bankers and published regularly.
- federal funds rate: The federal funds rate, the rate that banks charge one another for borrowings among them, is the driver of all rates. This is defined by the Federal Reserve through the Federal Open Market Committee (FOMC) when they meet, approximately eight times per year. When the Federal Reserve either raises or lowers the rates, prime and other reference rates will change based upon the incremental change. For this reason, they are added or subtracted from the base rate utilized.
- premiums to compensate for risk: As with cost plus, risk is still a concern and is compensated for by assessing premiums. The greater the risk, the higher the percentage, and vice versa. Generally, two major areas of risk may be involved, default risk and maturity risk. Default risk is the risk that the customer will not repay the loan. If the customer has had prior loans with the bank and paid them effectively, then there is less default risk, and a

premium may not be needed. If the loan term is for a longer duration, perhaps five to 10 years, a premium can be added to compensate for the unknowns in the future, such as a changing economic climate, future upheavals in the industry, and other threats that will only increase when the term is extended. This is called maturity risk. Both are expressed as basis point additions.

The sum of the basis points defined for these components is the rate to be assessed. Although this calculation is straightforward, negotiation with the customer must occur to arrive at an agreed-upon deal.

Summary

Although all these types of methods are employed to price commercial loans, the bottom-line will be what the market will bear. Banks face heavy competition from other banks in their market area, and to obtain the business, the banker may have to price it competitively. Banks are in business to make loans; therefore, it is understood that risks will be taken to obtain the business. In this regard, the rates determined from the various methods can be increased or decreased, via basis points, as a means of attracting and maintaining new business.

Customer Profitability Analysis

The final method employed for commercial loans, **customer profitability analysis**, is somewhat a hybrid. This method not only considers the various components, as in the cost plus method, it now considers the overall relationship that the customer has with the bank. The reason for this is that the more business a client brings to the bank, the more the bank will earn revenue and earn a specific return, which should be taken into account when pricing the loan. This is determined by calculations focusing on revenues and expenses earned. The formula for calculating the return is shown in Table 9.3.

Table 9.3 **Customer Profitability Analysis Return Calculation**

$ Revenue from loans and other services	$10,500
Less: Expenses from loans and other services	$9,500
/ (Loan amount - Customer deposits)	($100,000 - $20,000)
= Return on the relationship	1.25%

The resulting return provides the lender with an idea of whether the loan that is proposed and other services are priced acceptably. Once the return is determined, a positive number would indicate that the loan, and its pricing, are acceptable. A negative return indicates that the loans and services are not properly priced, and these need to be reconsidered.

In short, customer profitability analysis is an effective way to look at the total relationship and understand how risk is being compensated for. As an example, if the return is higher and positive, the greater the perceived risk. In other words, the bank is requiring a higher return to compensate for the risk in the loan. Components and explanations of the calculation are below (Rose & Hudgins, 2013).

- revenue from loans and other services: When looking at the total relationship, the first part of the calculation is to determine the annual revenue generated from the loan and other services. This would include the loan multiplied by the interest rate that would be charged to produce interest income. This would be done for all loans if there are more. In addition, the client may pay fee income (noninterest income) for treasury management services, or other bank services that they may be using. In addition, the CEO may personally have a wealth management account and is paying a fee for this. The goal is to obtain the total revenue that is generated from the relationship. For this reason, banks tend to cross-sell services to build the relationship and therefore revenue.
- expenses from providing loans and services: Similar to the cost plus method, the overall cost to the bank (expenses) incurred because of the loans and services made to the relationship are determined. This would include the cost of raising funds used to make the loan. Therefore, if a loan is made for $100,000, what does it cost the bank to raise these funds from deposits or nondeposits to fund this? This would be considered noninterest expense. In addition, salary expense, supplies, facility, and other overhead expenses must be determined to obtain a true picture. This can be relatively difficult because the bank must have systems to accomplish this, which also requires standards for unit and product pricing. Regardless, all attendant costs must be determined to be accurate.
- net loanable amount: This amount is the difference between the loan amount and the total dollar amount of customer deposits. This is the "net" loan amount that is being extended to the customer. So this represents the bank's exposure (net of deposits).

The concept of relationship banking is highly desired by banks since commercial clients have a variety of financial needs beyond borrowings. This can include depository accounts, trust relationships with key officers, treasury management services, and more. By learning what level of return the bank is obtaining (income minus expenses) divided by the net loanable amount, the bank will know the effectiveness of the relationship. It will also tell the committee whether the loan is properly priced. If the return is positive, the loan would likely be approved. If the return is negative, the loan would likely be denied.

Earnings Credits

Another tool used by bankers is to provide customers with **earnings credits**, which are credits for the earnings banks generate from the monies held on deposit at their bank. This would be a credit toward other fees related to the overall relationship. This is an incentive to the customer to maintain sizeable deposits at the bank—the larger, the higher the credit. This, like customer profitability analysis, requires systems to provide these calculations and to produce statements to customers that reflect these credits. This is generally called "analysis." Although not all banks offer this, it is desirable for large customers who consolidate their banking relationships with a single bank.

The calculation for the earnings credit is based upon several components (see Table 9.4).

Table 9.4 **Earnings Credit Calculation**

Customer average deposit balance	$100,000
Less: Average dollar float in the balance	$10,000
= Net amount of "collected" funds	$90,000
Less: Required legal reserve % (i.e., 10%)	$9,000
= Net investable funds	$81,000
× Rate used (selected rate by the bank)	2.0%
× 1/12 (percentage equivalent of one month)	.083
= Dollar earnings credit	$135
= Dollar amount of monthly credit to be applied	

Obviously, bank systems are designed to automatically provide these calculations and results, for ease in communications. The net result will be to provide incentive to the customer to maintain more deposits so they obtain these credits. The components of the calculation are explained below:

- customer average deposit balance: This is the average balance maintained by the customer or relationship. For a business, this can be significant, and associating other deposits balances to the relationship can make it even larger. By determining the average balance for a given period (e.g., a month), this will consider fluctuations throughout the period.
- average dollar float: Float represents the amount of funds that are deemed "uncollected." This means the amount of money that is in the process of being collected. This refers to checks written to deposit in accounts. Since checks must be cleared and ultimately be presented to the bank to be withdrawn, this takes time. During this period, the money is not available to the bank from which to earn revenue. Therefore, the float amount must be subtracted to arrive at the "collected" balance.
- net amount of collected funds: This is the average balance minus float in the balance, or amounts in the process of collection, to arrive at the collected balance. This amount is available to the bank to use toward generating earnings.
- required reserves: Since banks are required to maintain legal reserves at the Federal Reserve bank, these amounts are not available to the bank and therefore must be subtracted.

Although reserve requirements are defined by the size of the transaction deposits, customers most will likely be required to maintain a reserve requirement of 10%. This is calculated on the net amount of collected funds.

- net investable funds: The reserve requirement dollar amount is subtracted from collected funds. This results in the amount of the balance that is truly available to the bank to invest.
- rate applied: A percentage rate is applied to the net investable funds as the amount the client can earn. The rate used will vary by bank but could consist of a short-term investable rate that is available in the marketplace, such as for short-term Treasury securities.
- monthly amount: Finally, after the rate is applied, it is divided by 12 months to produce the monthly earning credit.
- dollar earnings credit: This is the final dollar amount that is available to the customer's account to offset other charges and/or result in a discount based upon the size of deposits maintained.

Ultimately, earnings credits can be very beneficial to a bank and desirable by customers. This can be a reason for customers to be attracted to a specific bank and further fosters the client relationship concept.

Summary

As can be seen in this chapter, the concept of commercial loan pricing can truly be called an art. Although there are a variety of components that go into pricing loans, these are standards, or guidelines. The ultimate result will be based upon negotiation and the competition in the marketplace. The concept of relationship pricing is newer but highly desirable. Banks are continually seeking "share of wallet" based upon all the financial needs individuals and businesses have. By understanding relationships and the value in these, banks can not only ensure that their returns are acceptable but also provide further incentives to attract more business.

Consumer Loan Pricing

Consumer loans are typically produced in the retail bank. These are loans to individuals rather than businesses and consist of installment loans, residential loans (mortgages), and credit cards. In concept, pricing is like commercial, but less variable and less subject to negotiation. In most cases, banks publish consumer loan rates, and although these rates will be affected by changes in the federal funds rate, they are nevertheless more fixed rather than tied to indices (Rose & Hudgins, 2013)

Banks determine the rates they will charge for a variety of consumer loans. These will be based upon the competition as well as earnings. For the purposes of this chapter, consumer loan pricing will be based upon the traditional types of pricing most familiar and most used. In this regard, the focus of this section of the chapter will be on the following pricing:

- cost plus pricing
- annual percentage rate (APR)
- fixed rate
- adjustable rate

Cost Plus Pricing

Like commercial loan pricing, cost plus is utilized as well to determine the interest rate to charge. Cost plus, as previously discussed, is made up of all the components attendant to a consumer loan. This is a matter of factoring in profit, risk, operating costs, and cost of raising funds. This process ensures that the rate charged will cover its costs and produce an acceptable return to the bank. Overall, this provides a base price to charge, which is the prerogative of the bank to apply. However, banks shop rates in the marketplace to determine how competitive they want to be in offering specific rates. In this regard, rates can change based upon changes in the economy, demand, and other circumstances.

Cost plus is calculated very similarly to that of commercial loans, as shown in Table 9.5.

Table 9.5 **Cost Plus Consumer Pricing**

Cost of raising funds	1.0
+ Operating costs to produce the loan	.60
+ Premium to compensate for risk (default or term)	.15
Subtotal	1.75
+ Profit margin (10% desired × subtotal)	.18
= Loan interest rate	1.93%

Each of the elements indicated in Table 9.5 is expressed as basis points (bps) or as a percentage, the sum of which will indicate the rate to be used. Cost-plus pricing for consumer loans utilizes the same basic components as in business loans, cost of raising funds, operating costs to produce the loan, premiums to compensate for risk, and profit margin. These explanations were outlined previously in the chapter.

The cost of raising funds is a given. The other components represent the spread, expressed as basis points to add to the cost of funds. The spread would account for the competition and what the marketplace is offering. In this regard it is based less on negotiation and more on the marketplace and is usually defined through the asset liability process.

Annual Percentage Rate (APR)

Once the loan rates are determined, they must be communicated, or disclosed, to the customers. This usually involves a mailing as well as publishing of rates via sites such as

Bankrate.com. The **annual percentage rate (APR)** is the nominal, or stated, rate. This rate is applied to the loan balance to produce the loan payment, which is comprised of both interest and principal portions. This amount is determined in the loan amortization process, which is the process of paying interest and principal back, resulting in a zero balance at the end of the term.

Once a specific rate that the bank will charge on consumer loans (personal installment loans) is determined, this will become the annual percentage rate used to determine the principal and interest payment required.

Fixed Rate Loans

Most consumer loans are fixed rate. That indicates that the rate assessed is "fixed" throughout the term of the loan and does not vary. This would be the case for automobile loans, furniture loans, appliance loans, and other types of personal loans. Another example of a fixed rate consumer loan is mortgage loans. Mortgage loans are loans incurred to purchase a home. Typically, mortgage loan rates are quoted as 15- or 30-year fixed rate loans. These are longer term loans and are amortized over the defined period to zero.

Mortgage loan rates are influenced by changes in the federal funds rate and the longer term bond market. The amount of the rate influences home purchases as well as refinances. Refinancing occurs when mortgage loan rates fall, and an individual may be locked into a high rate. This affords them the opportunity to change the rate by refinancing the overall loan.

Adjustable Rate Loans

Adjustable rate loans are most popular for mortgage lending. These types of rates are called **adjustable rate mortgages (ARMs)**. With ARMs, the interest rate is fixed for a period and then it will float, with a lifetime cap, for the remaining period. So when rates go up based upon the changes made by the Federal Reserve, the overall payment will go up. These are popular when one does not plan to stay in a home for 30 years, but much less. In this way the amount of interest can be lower for the fixed period of time (e.g., five or seven years), and if one does not stay in the home, they will have paid less interest than they would with a 30-year fixed rate loan. The downside is that if one remains in the home beyond the fixed rate period, rates can fluctuate, to a cap, which can raise or lower the payment. One must be prepared for this possibility and make sure they can afford it to the lifetime cap. Since rates are fixed in the early period and are lower than a 30-year fixed rate loan, this creates an opportunity for the borrower to purchase a home of greater value, making it more affordable. The major risk with ARMs is that when interest rates go up and the borrower remains in the home, the overall mortgage payment will go up. When this occurs, this could put strain on the borrower and make it difficult for them to make payments.

During the financial crisis of 2008, many individuals took advantage of ARMs and purchased more expensive homes, with the anticipation of continued home appreciation. The feeling was that since homes were appreciating, the borrower would not remain in the home and sell it at the appreciated price and earn a large gain, allowing them to purchase another, potentially bigger, home. Unfortunately, as the economy declined, the demand for homes also declined, and prices fell. Those who purchased more expensive homes were left with a significant loan amount, but with declining home values, in some cases below the loan amount. Since home prices dropped, many people would not sell to get out, as they would lose money. This resulted in homeowners walking away from their homes.

Today, ARMs are better regulated because of the lessons learned from the crisis. Tighter caps are included so that changing rates would not create a major disadvantage to the borrower. Nevertheless, ARMs continue as a viable mortgage pricing alternative. The rates themselves are determined as others would be for consumers, based upon components of the cost plus methodology, as well as the performance of the Fed and other instruments. ARMs, then, have discounted rates in the fixed rate period, since the period is shorter, much less than 30 years, but will float after that period.

Mortgage Points

Another pricing tool for mortgage loans is a concept called **mortgage points**. Mortgage points are additional fees that must be paid at the time of closing the mortgage loan. These are additional fees that may be charged to compensate for lower FICO scores (default risk) or lower down payments. They are expressed as points but are, in fact, interest percentages. For example, 2 points would be the equivalent of a 2.0% fee. This percent is multiplied by the amount of the mortgage loan and is paid at closing. These are one-time fees and do not reoccur.

Summary

Consumer loan pricing is much less complex than commercial loan pricing. In many cases, these become static rates and are regularly published for borrowers to shop from. Although many different types of interest rate calculations, such as add-on interest or others, have been used in the past, the primary ones indicated in this section are the types most often used. These loans will amortize over time, like commercial loans, but are evaluated much differently than commercial loans.

Deposit Pricing

The last area of pricing to be considered is the interest expense side of the balance sheet, or deposit pricing. The prior discussion of loan pricing (commercial and consumer) is focused on interest income. Now the emphasis shifts to the deposit side as the source of funds to make the loans. This is the last element in the production of net interest income (Rose & Hudgins, 2013).

Like all rates, these rates can and will change with changes made by the Federal Reserve to the federal funds rate. As the Fed raises rates, loan rates will respond quickly, and deposit rates will ultimately follow. In this way, the margin will remain relatively the same but may not change that quickly. People put money into deposit accounts to save money, to use for making transactions, and to save for longer term retirement goals. These three reasons relate to the three primary types of deposits that banks offer: savings accounts, checking accounts, and time deposits. The objective of the bank is always to attract consumer deposits, and to do so, they must offer a competitive rate that will retain the customer's deposit while at the same time allow enough of a margin to meet the bank's profit margin objectives. Unfortunately, the marketplace has a tremendous impact on the rates that banks pay. This results from competition, the wide variety of other banks offering similar depository accounts. In fact, this has become much more acute due to the internet. Bank deposit rates are published regularly online. Customers have the opportunity of easily shopping rates to get the best gain for the dollars they put away for savings. This is particularly true with longer term deposits, such as certificates of deposit (CDs). Although other instruments, such as interest-bearing checking and savings accounts, are often very competitive, they do not vary significantly enough to merit moving to a different bank. However, CDs are different. First, these are contractual, in which case the rate paid is fixed for the period of the term. Second, they pay a higher rate of interest because the goal is that customers keep money on deposit for a longer period, therefore the value proposition.

Before discussing pricing methodologies, it is important to understand that deposits are based upon an annual percentage rate (APR), which is the stated or nominal rate of interest, much like consumer loan APRs. The APR indicates how much interest will be paid on the account to the client. The dollar amount of interest is determined by the following formula:

- average deposit balance × APR

Although this used to be the only disclosed rate, with the advent of the Truth in Savings Act of 1991, banks are required to disclose the **annual percentage yield (APY)** that the account pays. APY is used to reflect the true rate of earnings, which is based upon compounding. As part of the disclosure process, banks will indicate what the compounding period is, whether annual, semiannual, quarterly, monthly, daily, or continuous. The more frequent the compounding period, the more interest that is earned. The value of compounding is that the interest earned is added to the prior balance and then multiplied by the APR. As the compounding period is more frequent, the balance grows more frequently from the interest added, and is then compounded. The APY accounts for the compounding and reflects the true rate that is earned, or available from the bank. The formula for APY is shown in Table 9.6.

Table 9.6 **Annual Percentage Yield**

$100 \times ((1 + \text{interest earned} / \text{average account balance})^{365/\#\text{ days in period}} - 1)$

Pricing Methods

For deposits, determining the interest rate that the bank will pay for the deposit will be based upon the competition. As interest rates change, banks must pay different rates to account for the change in rates. Simplistically, the bank can price their products based upon several strategies, as follow:

- to attract more deposits
- to maintain core deposits
- to obtain a certain type of deposit

The pricing strategy is important because the bank will want to be able to plan for deposits they will obtain. In this regard, banks would add basis points to their existing rates based upon the strategies, as indicated below:

- to attract more deposits: In this case, banks may wish to increase the rates paid by a specific amount of basis points, considering the competition. If they price higher, clients can earn more, and presumably, they would attract more deposits. However, the bank must also advertise, notifying the public about the premium rates they are paying. This will certainly add to interest expense; however, if the bank needs deposits for loan growth, they may be able to make more loans and ultimately increase their revenue. Of course, there is no guarantee that this will happen, which is why it is so important for a bank to understand the competition and how much they plan to raise rates.
- to maintain core deposits: This strategy is designed to retain clients and make sure there is no attrition. In this case the bank must understand the competition and the marketplace and make sure they price the deposits so that customers will not leave the bank.
- to obtain a certain type of deposit: Another strategy is to focus on specific types of deposits desired to obtain. In this strategy the bank may take a maintenance pricing strategy with other deposits and then aggressively price a specific type of deposit to capture a greater share of the market.

All these strategies are important to consider, as having no strategy can likely result in a loss of clients. Deposits are the lifeblood of the bank and provide the largest source of funds for making loans and are therefore of vital importance.

Having identified these strategies, the bank can focus more on marginal cost to establish the interest rate paid rather than historical pricing.

Marginal Cost Pricing

Determining the interest rate that the bank will pay on deposits is an important task. As indicated before, this is partly competition and partly obtaining funding. One way to accomplish this is the usage of **marginal cost pricing**. Marginal cost pricing attempts to establish the optimal rate to pay on deposits by defining which of the marginal costs of new funds provides the greatest earnings level.

In this regard, the rate determined is not arbitrary but more calculated, focused on profits earned. There are three key parts of this approach, as outlined below:

- Determine the marginal cost.
    - » (New interest rate × Funds raised at the new rate) – (Old interest rate × Funds raised at the old rate)
- Determine the marginal cost as a percentage of new funds attracted.
    - » Marginal cost / Additional funds raised
- Determine the difference between marginal cost % and the marginal revenue %.
    - » Marginal revenue % – Marginal cost %
- Identify the total profit earned for each incremental amount added.
    - » (Total accumulated deposits × Marginal revenue %) – (Total accumulated deposits × Average interest rate charged)
- Determine the optimal rate to pay.
    - » Select the interest rate that produces the highest profit earned.

As illustrated, determining the rate to pay using this approach is focused on determining the rate that produces the most profit. Clearly, this is important; otherwise, the profit margin could be eroded if a planned approach is not considered. By looking at various rates of interest, producing an incremental increase of deposits at each change in rate, the optimal level of profit is determined. The interest rate that produces the highest amount of profit would be the selected rate to pay.

Understand the overall profit that will be determined is key to the bank's profitability. If the bank must lower rates to compete, they should be aware what this will do to profits so that other initiatives can be taken to compensate for the loss of revenue. Without effective planning, the bank's earnings could decline.

Summary

Deposit pricing is quite different than that of loan pricing. Nevertheless, it is the largest expense that a bank faces and is a key element in the profitability of the bank. In addition, deposits are a major funding source for the bank. Determining the optimal rate, then, should not be taken lightly and requires the appropriate systems to model profitability levels.

CHAPTER SUMMARY

Interest is the predominant tool used in the pricing process to produce income. Interest generates both income and expense to the bank, which are the largest sources of revenue and expense. As a result, pricing becomes a critical activity in this process. As illustrated in this chapter, there are several components that need to be considered in determining these rates. Internal costs, cost of raising funds, risk, profit margins, marginal costs, and others all play a role. In addition, other external factors, such as competition and the activities of the Federal Reserve, are part of the mix as well.

Most people are unaware of the complexities of the pricing process for banks. This chapter is designed to help the student of commercial banking appreciate the intricacies associated with this major function and understand the challenges banks face in a world of fluctuating interest rates.

END OF CHAPTER QUESTIONS

1. Define the purposes of interest rate pricing in a commercial bank.
2. What is the difference between prime rate and LIBOR/SOFR in the pricing process?
3. How does the Federal Reserve influence pricing products to the customers?
4. What is the purpose for annual percentage yield (APY), and how is it used?
5. What are the key components of the cost plus pricing method for commercial loans?
6. What is the purpose for points in mortgage lending, and how are they applied?
7. Describe the differences between adjustable rate mortgages (ARMs) and fixed rate mortgages.
8. What is the meaning of "marginal costs" when determining optimal deposit pricing?

9. Describe what earnings credits are and how they are determined in the commercial lending process.
10. Describe the purpose for assigning a default premium in arriving at the optimal loan price.

CHAPTER 10

Managing Fee Income and Discretionary Expenses

Throughout this text the topics have centered on how banks make most of their money. It goes without saying that the lending process produces the interest income, which drives the profitability of the bank. That is a true statement. However, banks also have multiple sources of revenue that they target in addition to interest income. Fee income, or noninterest income, plays an important role. Many banks cultivate other areas or opportunities for generating revenue, which would complement the primary source of revenue, interest income. Another reason for this is diversification. Services that are fee-driven are not subject to interest rate fluctuations and therefore have less risk, or interest sensitivity.

In addition to noninterest income (revenue), discretionary expenses and operational expenses are part of noninterest expense and impact the overall profitability of the bank. Although this might be the case, discretionary expenses, such as technology, marketing, training, and branch network, are investments that are designed to create potential for revenue generation. Understanding how discretionary expenses contribute to the overall revenue-generation process of a bank is a critical ingredient in the overall success of a bank.

The purpose for this chapter is to highlight often overlooked areas in order to understand their role and contributions to the profitability of the bank.

Key Terms

- Cost plus profit margin pricing
- Conditional pricing
- Relational pricing
- Households/expanded households
- Share of wallet
- Unbanked/underbanked
- Payday loans
- Lifeline banking
- Nonsufficient funds (NSF)
- Overdraft fees
- Stop payments
- ATM surcharges
- Debit card interchange fees
- ATM interchange fees
- Automatic bill payment
- Official checks
- Lockbox services
- Remote deposit capture (RDC)
- Automated clearing house (ACH)
- Cash vault services
- Account reconciliation
- Positive pay
- Controlled disbursement
- Direct deposit
- Merchant card services
- Wire transfer
- Discretionary expenses

Learning Objectives

By the end of this chapter, the student will:

- Understand the definition and components of noninterest income.
- Know the difference between operational and discretionary expenses.
- Define the purpose of cash management in the bank.
- Know the primary services offered through cash management.
- Identify the primary depository service charges that are incurred by deposit account holders.
- Understand the purpose for and importance of lifeline and relationship banking.
- Identify key noninterest expenses that are important to banks.
- Know how to use discretionary expenses and fee income to expand the competitiveness of the bank.

Noninterest Income

For a bank, noninterest income entails revenue that is produced from sources other than interest. Although interest income is, by far, the largest source of bank revenue, banks must actively plan to have alternative sources. Given the volatility of interest rates, if rates fall, net interest margin will narrow, and earnings will decline. As a result, banks develop other services that can expand revenues. Revenues produced from noninterest income are derived from fees charged, based upon conditions, volume, or balances under management. This section outlines these standard areas of fee income, but it is not exhaustive. There can be many areas that banks and holding companies engage in to generate additional revenue, but this will vary by size of bank and opportunity. Nevertheless, the primary areas that will be seen on the income statement and how they are derived are outlined below.

Deposit Fee Pricing

Deposits are the major funding source for banks. These provide most funds for lending to businesses and individuals. Although the bank pays interest to depositors, which is an expense to the bank (interest expense), there are more costs involved in handling deposits. Since interest rates on deposits are highly competitive, the bank may not have as much control over this expense, because they do not control overall interest rate fluctuations. Therefore, in order to compensate the bank for the costs attendant to managing deposits, service charges (fees) are assessed based upon a variety reasons. These fees are part of the noninterest income the bank earns and contribute to offsetting the operational costs associated with deposits.

To understand the nature of these fees, why they exist, and how they are calculated, it is important to understand the methods that are used to determine these fees. Beyond that, a breakdown of the service charges assessed are identified.

Methods and Types of Pricing

The methods employed to "price" deposit service charges are designed to cover the costs associated with administering deposits, as previously mentioned. This approach focuses on cost recovery based upon key components. In addition to the determination of service charge pricing, other broader concepts relative to pricing merit discussion. The following are important concepts for understanding the nature of noninterest deposit pricing, including:

- cost plus profit margin pricing
- conditional pricing
- relationship pricing
- lifeline pricing

Cost Plus Profit Margin Pricing

Very similar to cost plus pricing for loans, **cost plus profit margin pricing** considers the costs involved in the administration of the deposits, in addition to a profit margin. These components can be uniquely defined based upon the specific aspect of the service provided. In this regard cost plus is designed to "cost out" what is involved in delivering each service. This is accomplished on a unit-cost basis. What this means is that the actual costs are accumulated in each area and divided by the amount of deposit or services delivered.

The three components of cost plus profit margin pricing include operating expenses, overhead expenses, and profit margin:

- operating expenses: Operating expenses are those costs incurred to deliver the product or services. Since the bank would have these captured in their general ledger system, the bank can relatively easily obtain the raw data. Dependent upon the service, these expenses would include software and information technology costs, staff salary and benefit costs, supplies, postage, advertising and marketing, and training, to identify a few of the key items. The formula for pricing this aspect of the service charge is outlined in Table 10.1.

Essentially, the administration of deposits involves many things, and these represent a considerable cost to the bank. However, although these costs are significant, they are not the only ones, as overhead plays a key role as well.

- overhead: Overhead is different than operating expenses, in that these are not specifically tied to the administration of the deposits, but rather the "common" elements involved in running a business. Common elements may include the cost of building maintenance, utilities (e.g., lighting, heating, etc.), parking lot maintenance, snow plowing, landscaping, and so on—literally all the costs attendant to the physical confines where business is conducted. The goal here is to determine a per-unit cost for overhead, much the same as was accomplished previously with operating expenses. An example of this is offered in Table 10.2.

Table 10.1 **Operating Expense Unit Cost**

Sum of the following (annual costs):
• salaries and benefits of retail staff (including tellers) costs involved in deposit handling
• related supplies, postage, and materials cost
• training costs (ongoing)
• advertising costs associated with marketing deposits (e.g., billboards, tv, radio, newspapers, internet, etc.)
• amount of transaction per account and cost
Divided by:
• total number of deposit accounts (checking, savings, time)
= Annual unit cost per deposit account
Divided by:
• number of months in a year (12)
= Monthly cost per deposit account

Table 10.2 **Overhead Costs**

Sum of the following (annual costs):
• utility expenses
• landscaping, snow plowing
• repairs and maintenance costs
• parking lot maintenance
• date networking expenses, internet access
• telephone service expenses
• administration costs (salaries and benefits of senior officers, board, etc.)
Divided by:
• total number of deposit accounts (checking, savings, time)
= Annual unit cost per deposit account
Divided by:
• number of months in a year (12)
= Monthly cost per deposit account

Obviously, the challenge is to capture all these costs and to break them down between overhead expenses, broadly, and operating expenses, specifically, to the deposit function.

These can be determined from the bank's systems: The more detailed they can get, the more accurate the unit costs.

- profit margin: The last portion of this determination is to factor in a profit margin. The profit margin represents the percentage, over and above coverage of costs, that the bank hopes to obtain. In most cases this should be the desired return that the bank would like to obtain, net of costs. To determine this, the bank could focus on the overall net interest margin percentage. Since this represents the amount the bank earns in profit (interest income minus interest expense), in relation to total assets, this percentage could also be used as the desired profit margin. This is only a suggestion to put it into perspective, but the bank could affix any profit margin they desire without pricing themselves out of the market. Once this percentage is determined, the final cost can be determined to be assessed to the customer, as shown in Table 10.3.

Table 10.3 **Total Cost Plus Amount**

• Total annual per unit operating expense
+ Total annual per-unit overhead expense
= **Total annual per-unit cost**
× (1 + Profit margin %)
= **Grand total annual per unit cost**

At this juncture, the bank now has what it costs to administer deposits (noninterest costs) and, after building in a profit margin, can use this as a basis for pricing deposit products. As with other pricing areas, competition and the marketplace must be considered, as customers will shop other banks if they feel costs are too high. In addition, banks also must account for under what circumstances these charges are applied.

This establishes the basis for determining unit costs. Now comes the determination of how these will be assessed.

Conditional Pricing

Banks must advertise to obtain and retain deposits. Since deposits are the fuel for making loans, the major revenue source, banks must be aggressive in garnering deposits. In part, the interest paid on deposits to the client is a major factor in determining the success of obtaining deposits. But beyond that, banks must cover their costs. A good portion of bank deposits do not pay interest to the client; these are noninterest-bearing transaction accounts, or regular checking accounts (demand deposit accounts [DDA]). Banks frequently advertise these as "free checking," meaning the customer will not have to pay a monthly fee for administering the account. This is an incentive to deposit with that bank. However, in most cases, banks will rely on a concept called **conditional pricing** when determining how to cover its costs (Rose & Hudgins, 2013).

Conditional pricing is based upon the average balance a customer maintains in the account at the bank. Put simply, if a customer's balance falls below a certain level, they are charged a monthly fee. If the balance remains above a certain threshold, then there is no charge (see example in Table 10.4). The threshold that is determined for the account is technically the break-even point, the point at which the bank's cost is absorbed. The break-even point is determined based upon what the deposit produces for the bank. To determine this, the bank must know how much it costs to administer the deposit (previously determined) using the cost plus pricing and then determine the balance at which these costs are absorbed. The formula itself also considers the bank's earnings rates and the reserve requirement.

Table 10.4 **Conditional Pricing Example**

Regular Checking Account	
• Average balance maintained	
» $0 to $400	$6.00 per month
» $400 to $1,000	$3.00 per month
» Greater than $1,000	Free

The formula for determining the break-even balance is as follows:

$$\left(\frac{\text{Per unit operating cost} + \text{Per unit overhead cost}}{\text{Bank earning rate}}\right) \div (1 - \text{Reserve requirement})$$

Using the above formula, the bank earning rate is the percentage the bank earns from the activities that produce revenue. For the most part, this is going to be at least the current federal funds rate or the rate that the bank earns from the deposit. This could be the average loan interest pricing minus the average deposit interest expense. Since the federal funds rate is embodied in both, the difference becomes the net earnings rate. Finally, the number of deposits able to be utilized, net of reserve requirements, must be considered for transaction accounts. This will produce a dollar amount that is the threshold above which the bank is profitable on the deposit balance and below which the bank is not profitable. Therefore, any balances falling below this threshold should receive the monthly fee to compensate for the lost profitability. An example of this is shown in Table 10.5.

Table 10.5 **Break-Even Example**

- Annual operating per unit cost = $75
- Annual overhead per unit cost = $50
- Bank earnings rate = 2.0%
- Reserve requirement = 10.0%%

$$\left(\frac{\$75+\$50}{.02}\right) \div (1-.10) = \$6{,}944 \text{ Break-even balance}$$

Generally, many of the products offered by banks are not profitable until a certain balance level is obtained. For this reason, it is important to understand what that balance threshold is for the individual bank. Once this is understood, it will tell the bank where they should establish the conditional pricing level. Once again, however, the marketplace must be taken into consideration. Competitive surveys of what other banks are charging is very important if the bank intends to remain competitive and obtain needed deposits, but armed with the break-even balance point, the bank can truly evaluate what they can do to make this more favorable to the bank. For instance, if the bank were able to lower their operating and/or overhead per-unit costs, the break-even threshold would reduce. By reducing this balance, the bank may be more attractive to new deposits and can compete more effectively. The same is true if they were to expand their earnings rate. Regardless of the earnings rate used, the rest is simply math and will pinpoint the balance threshold.

Relational Pricing

Banks have been striving toward the ability to effectively price products, based upon the total relationship for some time. **Relational pricing** occurs when the bank can attract the customer to use as many of the services and products that the bank offers, and in turn, the bank will reduce the fees charged to the customer based upon the overall profitability of the relationship.

For relationship pricing to be effective, one of its major challenges is to determine the definition of a "relationship." In theory, a relationship is the aggregate of all products and services used by a customer. This understanding has expanded to include the influence the customer has on other family members and businesses that may start doing business with the bank. In short, the more expansive the number of products and services used by the relationship, the greater the profitability. In this regard, banks would lower or waive fees once they understand the overall profitability of the relationship. However, back to the definition of the relationship. Banks now use the term **household** and/or **expanded household** to understand the relationship. In terms of "household," this is anyone within the immediate family of the customer. As more household members use the bank, the greater the expansion of the relationship. In addition, there is another concept, called **share of wallet**, which defines the universe of financial needs of an individual and determines what percentage of these services are met by the bank. Obviously, the goal of most banks is to get all a client's financial business for business loans, personal loans, deposits, investments, credit cards, and all their financial needs. Customers tend to spread their financial needs around with other institutions, leaving a somewhat meager percentage with the bank. Therefore, if the bank were to only capture another "x" basis points increase in share of wallet for every customer, it could be huge for the bank. Couple this with the expanded household and accomplishing the same goal, the bank's profitability would dramatically increase, a worthy goal.

To attract this type of business, banks have offered preferred pricing of their products and services based upon the total relationship. In this regard, a standard conditional pricing model with specified threshold balances and fees would still be published and utilized for the standard customer, but would not apply to a relationship, which would have its own thresholds and requirements. The more the relationship expands, the more the bank would lower or eliminate fees for a variety of services, some of which will be discussed in the next section. Now, considering the household or expanded households, banks can do much more that would be of interest to the relationship and use this as an enticement for more services to be utilized.

Expanded households can grow to include business relationships and other areas where the primary customer has influence. The major challenge is to be able to define these relationships clearly and effectively and to have the systems that can compile the total relationship and price it accordingly (Rose & Hudgins, 2013).

Lifeline Banking

One area that is an important social issue is whether everyone has access to, or utilize, banking services. This is a topic of much discussion at the federal level. Although difficult to believe, currently, there are individuals in the country that do not utilize banks at all, or very little utilization. These are termed **unbanked** or **underbanked** individuals or households (Rose & Hudgins, 2013).

- unbanked: This segment of the populace does not have any loans, deposits, or other services (i.e., credit/debit cards, ATMs, etc.) with banks. They rely predominantly on cash. They are paid in cash and use the currency to pay for food, bills, living expenses, and other costs of living. If a check is needed, they can obtain money orders from various places by paying cash for these. If money is needed, normally loans, they obtain this through pawn shops, or payday loans. **Payday loans** are a lot like a bridge loan in that money is borrowed when cash is short, but the loan will be paid in one payment at the next payday. Individuals are charged a very high interest rate for this type of loan due to the risk involved. These are extremely short term, within one or two weeks, with the lender having options to attach the paycheck if not repaid. This is just an example of how the unbanked population addresses their financial needs, fully, without a bank.

- underbanked: This segment has very limited utilization of the financial services of a bank. They still rely on many of the avenues for their financial needs, but they may use some bank services that are critical to them. This could be a loan or other need that they would be able to obtain, but their use of this is very limited.

In both cases, part of the reason for their existence relates to overall "financial literacy." This deficiency, although relatively prevalent in the society, is concentrated more in low socioeconomic groups. These groups may not understand the financial concepts, disclosures, loan terms, and other aspects of the banking products available and therefore are subject to decisions they may not understand and can be detrimental to them in terms of exorbitant interest rates or other penalties not well understood.

Early on in this text, an article was quoted that talked about "modern banking is the greatest contributors to human progress" (Trennart, 2015, p. 178). As you reread that quote and the detail behind it, it becomes clear that banking has been instrumental in improving quality of life and reducing poverty in our society. Therefore, it is important that there is a focus on these unbanked and underbanked individuals so they can obtain these benefits and help improve the quality of their lives, and not be subject to predatory banking practices. This benefits the entire society, educating the populace and contributing to a stronger economy—all worthy causes.

To accomplish this, **lifeline banking** is designed for these groups to provide services that provide needed loans, as well as earning interest on savings rather than simply holding cash, which earns nothing. This requires a focus on the part of the bankers to price services in such a way as to meet the needs of these groups. This has benefits to commercial banks as well. As products and services are made available to these groups and they continue to use these services, they eventually become loyal bank customers and expands the number of households' banks desire. Banks that have programs for this will price the products and services such that the lower income customers can afford them. This will be through lower minimum balance accounts (conditional pricing) and lower overall fees or service charges. Again, this benefits both the society and the financial institutions—a win-win scenario.

Service Charges on Deposits

We have been discussing methods for pricing deposits and services. Another aspect of pricing fees relates to service charges that occur because of the utilization of the deposit accounts. These service charges generally do not relate to the size of the balance on an account but are mostly ad hoc and occur because of an event, or based upon the volume of usage.

Service charges are priced based upon the costs attendant to the service that is performed, like cost plus. However, another component is the competition. Banks typically shop service charge pricing at other banks to make sure they are in line with the market. Since service charge fees must be disclosed to all depository clients, customers will see the costs, and significantly higher service charges may get attention and can impact the client's loyalty, causing them to leave the bank.

Nevertheless, service charges on deposits are a part of the noninterest income that a bank earns, some of which can be significant. Bank service charges fall into three categories and are important to understand. As indicated, these are required to be disclosed to the customers, by law, whenever a change is made. Most clients do not read these thoroughly, and even though they are disclosed, they may still not be aware of a price change. This is typically because customers do not incur these charges frequently, so the cost may be less of an issue. The three categories of these charges are service charges, transaction account fees, and other service fees.

Service Charges

These fees are directly related to the depository accounts and occur only in relation to usage of the deposit account. These are the primary types of service charges that a client would see and should be aware of. These only occur based upon usage or out of need; they do not occur on a regular basis unless there is activity. These fees are required to be disclosed to clients in advance, by mail, and allow at least 30 days before the actual change is made. This, presumably, allows for any client comments or dissention before charges take affect or allow them to transition to another bank if they are not comfortable with the changes.

Although this list is not exhaustive, it does encompass the most common service charges, including:

- nonsufficient funds
- overdraft fees
- stop payments
- ATM surcharge fees
- debit card interchange fees
- ATM interchange fees
- bill payment

Nonsufficient funds (NSF): This service charge pertains to transaction deposit accounts, particularly checking (demand deposit accounts), and results when a check is presented to the bank against the account and there are not enough funds to cover this check. In the more common vernacular, this is referred to as a "bounced" check. This occurs because of the time the check takes to get back to the bank on which it is drawn. This may occur by accident or when writing out checks with the hope that by the time it reaches the bank, funds will be available. When this occurs, the bank will not pay the check and will return it to the payee as insufficient or NSF. In addition to this, the bank will assess a service charge for the event. This is a one-time charge and can range from $25–$50 per occurrence. The fee is then charged automatically to the checking account.

Overdraft fees: Overdraft fees occur because of nonsufficient funds. An overdraft is a check presented against an account balance that is more than what is available, or nonsufficient funds. The difference is that rather than the bank returning the check to the payee, unpaid, the bank pays the check and accepts the difference. Like NSF, there is a charge for this, and it is assessed upon occurrence and, in some cases, daily if the account remains in an overdraft state. Although this service is available to consumer accounts as well, businesses typically use this as a matter of doing business. In other words, businesses build this into their process of payments, and the banks permit this, for the most part. It is understood that shortages may exist from time to time, and rather than disrupt the business transaction by not paying it, the bank pays it and charges a fee. This becomes an "unsecured" temporary loan, as the bank is covering the shortage by making up the difference. This shortage, of course, must be made up, but checks are not returned. The same holds true for consumer accounts, but customers must open an overdraft protection account, which is a revolving credit account. In this case, no checks are returned, and there is no individual charge. The customer pays a one-time fee for the overdraft protection account, and any overage is applied to this revolving credit account. Once there, if not paid off immediately, it will function like a credit card, and the customer will pay a monthly interest charge for the outstanding balance. Regardless, this is a decided convenience for the customer, and many people use these accounts for this reason.

Finally, overdraft fees or fee income for this can be significant for a bank, particularly on the business side, and banks plan for this as an ongoing revenue source.

Stop payments: Stop payments are ad hoc; they do not occur frequently. A stop payment, or "stop," is placed on a specific check from a checking account. This may occur when a check has been written and sent to a payee, and either an error has occurred, a change of mind, or a payee indicates they never received the check. In these circumstances the drawer of the check would contact the bank to stop payment of the check and potentially reissue a new one. Stop payments can be costly: These can reach as much as $50 per occurrence. Therefore, people do not do this cavalierly. This is designed as protection to the drawer of the check but is costly.

ATM surcharges: ATMs, or automatic teller machines, are devices for making transactions without going to the bank. ATM surcharges are charges that were permitted after several years from deployment. The charge is a per-transaction fee. For example, when a customer wishes to withdraw funds from their account, they will be charged a surcharge of \$1.50–\$3.00, or higher, dependent upon the bank. Prior to the advent of surcharges, ATMs were extremely costly to the bank, made up of hardware costs, network costs, staff costs to replenish the machine, and maintenance costs. All these costs were absorbed by the bank, and the service was provided as a convenience to the customer. Today, ATMs are an essential service, and customers demand this of the bank they are using regardless of the surcharge. Charges are based upon whether the ATM is considered foreign or not. This means whether the ATM is owned by the bank in which you have your account. In this case there may be no surcharge to the customer.

Debit card interchange fees: Today, debit cards are a very popular payment mechanism. This is a card used to transact business, like a credit card, but not resulting in credit, rather a direct reduction to the checking account balance. Since these cards utilize network transmissions of the transaction back to the checking account, fees exist, which are called interchange fees. These fees are volume based—that is, they occur based upon the transaction or the volume of transactions. Businesses, or merchants, pay the interchange fee to the bank issuing the debit card. Although this is a cost to the business, it is acceptable because this allows them to make it more convenient for customers to purchase goods from them. In short, the benefits outweigh the costs. Costs typically are found to be approximately .3% of the transaction. The fees help to absorb the risks and handling of these transactions by the bank, as well as absorption of processing costs.

ATM interchange fees: These are fees established by the credit card networks, which occur when transactions are conducted at an ATM. Different than debit card interchange fees, these fees are paid by the card-issuing bank to the bank who owns the ATM where the transaction is taking place. This provides income to offset the various costs related to managing and maintaining the ATM. Therefore, the ATM owner will receive both the surcharge and the interchange fee as noninterest income. These typically amount to about 2% of the transaction value.

Automatic bill payment: Automatic bill payment is a service that many banks offer, which allows customers to pay bills, automatically, through the bank by way of an ACH transaction or a physical check. This is a highly desired service and one that is not charged to the customer. Like the advent of ATMs, where a service innovation has become a necessary service required by customers, no fees were assessed, initially. Whether this will become a service charge or not will be determined over time, primarily due to the cost of providing this service. However, banks tend to view this as a "glue" in that it a valued service, but takes some time to set up. Therefore, customers are less likely to leave the bank due to the work required to set it up again elsewhere. Therefore, it forces a sort of loyalty to the bank, which is a true benefit to the bank.

Transaction Account Fees

Transaction account fees, in part, were discussed earlier in the chapter. These are fees that are assessed not by volume or transaction, but by events. As with other fees, the foundation for these is absorption of costs. The two items for discussion include monthly account fees and early withdrawal fees.

Monthly account fees: Previously, conditional pricing was discussed. The fees assessed from conditional pricing emanate from the amount of money on deposit and maintained at the bank. These occur when balances fall below a certain threshold or to a different tier. As explained previously, the determination of minimum balance levels is based upon break-even analysis and is designed to cover the costs attendant to maintaining the accounts. These are monthly fees and are charged directly to the account. Customers must be aware when balances drop below certain levels to avoid these charges. Mobile banking has helped in this regard by providing the ability for alerts when events such as these occur. As an attraction for deposits, banks may offer free checking or other types of accounts. When they do this, they are not charging, at least at this point, any fees for the transaction account.

Early withdrawal fees: Another fee triggered by an event is an early withdrawal fee. These fees are typically assessed when a contractual requirement on the account has been violated. Certificates of deposit are contracts. They specify a fixed interest rate that is paid to the customer if they maintain the original amount deposited for the specified term, usually one to three years. In this situation, if the customer withdraws any amount from the principal, a penalty is assessed. The penalty will be based upon the amount of interest that is paid for the contractual balance. When the balance changes, the customer will be penalized an amount equivalent to the preferred rate they were receiving on the required balance. These, generally, are infrequent. They are punitive in nature because the bank was relying on a specific balance to be maintained.

Other Service Fees

The last area of service fees are miscellaneous products that the bank offers to customers by nature of their depository relationship. These products are used to fulfill other financial needs. The fees are assessed based upon usage, as a one-time charge, or monthly fee. These fees involve official checks and safekeeping, as follows:

Cashier's checks: These are also called **official checks** and are provided to deposit account holders of a bank when circumstances call for more certainty of payment. For a specified fee, a customer can purchase a cashier's check that, when presented to the payee, indicates that there is no risk in collection of the check since the funds have been paid to the bank for the check already. Cashier's checks will cost anywhere from $10–$30 per check. In addition, the customer must provide the amount for which the check is written. These checks will not be returned for insufficient funds.

Certified checks: Much like cashier's checks, a certified check can be purchased at the bank for a fee. Unlike a cashier's check, this is not a check drawn on the bank, or an official check. In this case, the customer is purchasing the bank's endorsement or verification that the face amount of the check exists in the account of the depositor. Once verified, the bank will stamp and sign the back of the check, guaranteeing the funds. The payee then does not run the risk of having the check returned, as the bank will absorb any loss from a balance deficiency. Again, the fee is a per-check fee in a range similar to that of a cashier's check.

Safe deposit box fees: Another service banks offer are safekeeping services, where customers can rent a box that is stored in the bank's vault. This is a secure location and designed for valuable documents or other assets that require the level of security a bank vault would provide. Safe deposit boxes are charged an annual or monthly rental fee for the box. Boxes are of various sizes: The larger the box, the higher the rental fee. Customers seldom shop based on safe deposit box fees. Once established, they typically pay these fees for the convenience and safety of their assets.

Summary

The service charges discussed in this section relate directly to the depository relationship that the customer has with the bank. Clearly, they are not the largest source of revenue; however, they can be significant, given the number of customers a bank has and the number of services they utilize. These are easily seen in the bank's income statement under "noninterest income." Of all the fees, overdraft fees may be the largest amount of these. All fees must be disclosed by law, anytime a change is made and usually on an annual basis.

Other Fee Services

Finally, the last of the most predominant fees that a bank assesses are for other services offered to consumers and businesses. These services are major areas of the bank that relate to businesses and customers. These services do not relate directly to depository accounts, per se, but are based upon the financial needs of the targeted groups. Banks strive to provide products and services that can meet all the client's needs. As the bank develops these products and services, they provide value to clients, making it convenient for them to provide "one-stop" shopping. All banks want customers to utilize their services to meet financial needs. As this occurs, the bank expands the share of wallet for their customers, which is highly valued. Pricing for these services is based upon percentage of balance managed as well as per occurrence.

In this segment of the chapter, we focus on two areas that provided significant noninterest income: cash (treasury) management services and wealth management services.

Cash Management Fees

Cash management, now called treasury management, fees and services are focused on meeting the financial needs of businesses. When a bank establishes a relationship with a business, usually for a loan, the business will have other financial needs. First, the business will need a checking (transaction) account for handling its payment transactions. For a business, these are usually more significant than the typical consumer and are very much valued by the bank.

Cash (treasury) managers are part of the commercial department and work in tandem with commercial lenders. Their primary objective is directed at obtaining deposits from large organizations and providing services that are beneficial to the needs of larger businesses, although business of other sizes avail themselves of some of these services as well. These services are designed to help the organizations to process payments and speed the usage of funds, as they are received more efficiently. To accomplish this, technology is one of the key ingredients, as will be seen in each of the services discussed. The services offered are provided for a fee, which is all a portion of noninterest income. In this regard, this department is a revenue generator by way of the services deployed. For this chapter, some of the primary services will be discuss below, but this is by no means exhaustive. Banks continue to evolve services that may be more unique to the needs of the specific client, but this will provide a good understanding of the types of services typically offered in this area of the bank. These services include:

- lockbox services
- remote deposit capture
- automated clearing house (ACH)
- cash vault services
- account reconciliation
- positive pay
- controlled disbursement
- direct deposit
- merchant card services
- wire transfer services

Lockbox services: Banks provide this service, which is accomplished by a special unit in the bank. This unit is part of either operations of cash management operations. The banks establish a special post office box (PO box) account. This PO box is available to the bank and is used to collect the hundreds of payments that large customers receive in the mail. The goal of the service, to the customer, is to process many payments as quickly as possible to speed up cash collection and availability of funds to the client. This is accomplished by the bank, accessing the PO box, and depositing the checks into the customer's account, which is at the bank immediately. This is done first, prior to any of the accounting entries made by the entity, so that the funds are immediately available. This makes the cash available much faster than the client could ever process these checks through their normal channels due to the direct deposit of funds into the client's account. In addition, post office boxes can be geographically set up in different parts of the country where people may be making payments, thereby reducing mail time to the PO box and speeding the collection and deposit of cash. This is sometimes called "remittance processing," and fees range from a few cents to a dollar per payment processed. This service is ideal for organizations such as counties, government, and other municipalities that are collecting property tax and other tax payments from citizens.

Remote deposit capture (RDC): In the past, merchants (e.g., retail businesses, restaurants, etc.) would typically collect payments at their place of business. These would include either cash or checks (excluding debit and credit cards, which utilize a different service). These items would physically be brought to the bank and placed in a night depository box for processing in the morning. RDC streamlines this for checks received by allowing the merchant to electronically scan and transmit the check to the bank several times throughout the day. By doing this, it would speed the process of collection of funds and placement into their account for availability. In the past, physical checks would be sent to a central processing center for scanning and transmission, which takes time. Remote deposit capture permits this to occur much quicker and therefore provides quicker availability of funds to the merchant. Banks would provide scanners to the merchant to process checks. Dependent upon the amount of the checks, these can be ones that process hundreds of checks relatively quickly. RDC became possible with the passage of Check 21, allowing banks to accept electronic images of checks. For a merchant, the cost of RDC is approximately $15 per month. Essentially, this is the same technology that is available to individual consumers, allowing individuals to deposit checks by taking a picture of the check and transmitting it to the bank.

Automated clearing house (ACH): Automated clearing house is a "funds-transfer" system that allows for the transfer of funds for payroll purposes, tax refunds, payment of bills, and other types of payments. ACH is run by the National Automated Clearing House Association (NACHA). Automated clearing house serves financial institutions, which allows bank clients to move money efficiently and quickly between accounts. Basically, bank clients (businesses or individuals) begin a direct payment or deposit and the bank then batches this with other ACH transactions and sends these to the Federal Reserve or clearing house throughout the day. As these transactions are received from the originating depository financial institution (ODFI), they are sorted and made available to the receiving or intended financial institution, known as the *receiving depository financial institution*

(RDF). Once this occurs the originator's and the recipient's accounts are adjusted and reconciled. The most common usage of this service is direct deposit of payroll checks into an individual's account. Fees for this service will range from 20 cents to $1.50 per transaction (or percentage of .5% to 1.5%) and/or monthly fees from $5–$30. There are other fees for returns as well. All these services and fees are outlined in the bank's fee structure.

Cash vault services: Similar to banks themselves, merchants receive cash payments and need a typical amount of coin and currency, daily, to conduct business. Retail organizations, restaurants, and others utilize cash every day. Dependent upon the size of the organization, it may be beneficial to utilize cash vault services to receive deliveries of cash daily, as well as to store it at the end of the day.

Account reconciliation: These are services that are designed to help the client to be more efficient with their time. Account reconciliation services provide reconciliation of a client's business checking account electronically. This allows for the upload of this reconciliation into the client's accounting system. The benefit of this service is that it provides third-party oversight of this process, which improves the accuracy and timeliness of this important function. This is particularly useful for large organizations that have many transactions and complexities that would preclude doing an effective job manually.

Positive pay: This service is designed to protect the customer from check fraud. The service is an automated process that compares checks issued by the organization with those that are presented for payment. This automated process makes it much more efficient to do this comparison regularly, and where there a difference, they are submitted to the organization for more in-depth analysis. This service is provided by the bank for the benefit of the client.

Controlled disbursement: Controlled disbursement is a service that is available only to companies. This service allows companies the ability to review disbursements in their account prior to it being made to plan more effectively and to take advantage of maximizing the interest earned on their funds. In addition, companies can also be selective on the assets that earn the most interest and control when and how much is disbursed from such assets to maximize earnings. Additionally, float is utilized in disbursements, taking advantage of the time it takes to get the disbursement cleared.

Direct deposit: Direct deposit is a service that allows corporations to make automatic payments directly into a checking or savings accounts. Corporations can obtain this service to automatically make payroll payments into employee accounts. This allows the corporation to hold onto the funds until payday and then automatically deposit it, allowing them to earn interest, if possible, on their account. This is extremely beneficial to large corporations where an extra day or two on a large amount of funds on deposit can be substantial throughout the year.

Merchant card services: Merchant card services allow customers to accept card (debit and credit card) transactions for payment at their stores. This service is a partnership between the merchant (customer) and the bank, with the bank providing the necessary electronic communications and the card-swipe terminals to facilitate the transactions. This is a definite benefit to the merchant, as most people utilize cards to make purchases, so this would facilitate increased sales. Merchants pay fees for these services on a transaction basis and through rental of terminals.

Wire transfer services: Wire transfer services permit the transmission of funds electronically to the recipient, quickly and efficiently. Customers must utilize these services through a bank utilizing the Fedwire (Federal Reserve Wire Network), among others, to electronically transfer funds. This is valuable for large transactions that are needed to be made securely and very timely. In addition, these can be timed to occur at designated predetermined times.

Wealth Management Services and Fees

Wealth Management is a relatively newer designation for a group of services that involve investment and trust management. In the past, these generally were considered trust departments, only. Now, banks have expanded this to include personal financial planning services, retirement planning, and tax management services. These are sold to individuals and businesses and can be a considerable source of revenue based upon the amount of assets under management. This can be as high as 25% of a bank's net income.

In general, wealth management departments charge fees based on the size of the assets. "Assets, under management" is the determinant for generating revenue. The bank will price these services as a percentage of the total amount in the accounts. This can be for an investment account and/or trust relationship. The primary areas of revenue generated include the following:

- personal trust management: Trusts are used as a means of managing funds and disbursing funds to designated beneficiaries. Customers come to banks offering these services accept funds (corpus), and structure the trust relationship, which there are many, and manage the funds. In general, these are charged based on the amount of money under management.
- investment management services: Much like an investment firm on Wall Street, banks provide investment management services to manage a portfolio of assets to achieve a particular return. These can be retirement funds, "nest eggs," that provide a regular income based upon the achieved return. As with trusts, the individual or corporation will pay a regular fee based upon a percentage of the total assets under management.
- employee benefit and retirement services: Another service or set of services relates to retirement and employee benefits. Corporations provide benefits to employees, such as stock options, 401(k) plans, and other defined contribution accounts that the company contributes to, in addition to the employee. These funds are managed in the wealth management area based upon the portfolio strategy they adhere to. Again, a fee is charged as a percentage of the balances managed.

- custody and safekeeping services: Finally, banks offering these services obtain fee income from safely and securely storing important and possibly negotiable documents in their vaults. These may be deeds, contracts, stock certificates, bond indentures, and many more. Fees would be assessed on a regular basis, based upon the volume of assets to be held in custody.

Summary

These last two areas that produce other fee income can be considerable in a bank. They are not based upon interest rate fluctuations and therefore carry less risk and can be very important to a bank in times of interest rate fluctuations when net interest margins are declining. There can be many more fee income areas within a bank, such as insurance services or others. Nevertheless, noninterest income is a significant piece of the profitability picture of a bank.

Noninterest Expense

The final area in this chapter relates to expenses that are part of doing business as a corporation. Banks, like other corporations, incur expenses to run the business. For a bank, these fall under the category of noninterest expenses. These expenses can be considerable and will be found on the bank's income statement. Noninterest expenses for a bank may be standard required costs (i.e., costs of doing business), and others can be considered more discretionary. Banks should judiciously utilize discretionary expenses, as they relate to contributing to revenue generation and growth.

In this last area, key operational and discretionary expenses will be explored to understand how they are used to effectively promote growth and profitability.

Core Operational Expenses

All banks have core operational expenses that they incur to run the business. These, for the most part, are not considered discretionary; however, they are areas that banks look to when interest rates fall and margins are narrowed. These can be very effective areas to look at to find economies to help to maintain the net income history. These are the primary areas and are not considered exhaustive, but proportionally, they are the most significant areas to consider.

Core operational expenses fall into a few areas, including:

- salaries and benefits
- equipment and technology
- branch management

Salaries and Benefits

Salaries represent the payment made to employees for their services. In addition to salaries, banks pay for a significant portion of employee benefits. These are substantial, usually 35%–40% percent of the total salaries. This makes salaries and benefits the largest of the noninterest expenses, representing approximately 60% of the total noninterest expenses. As previously indicated, these are not discretionary: Banks cannot avoid paying staff. However, this is generally one of the first places that banks look when the primary net interest income is declining. Banks attempt to obtain efficiencies by placing a hiring freeze on new positions or having a reduction in force due to the decline in volume of loans and other areas that require staff. Although not generally a desired area to cut expenses, it is significant enough that it would have a positive impact on the bottom line.

Equipment and Technology

Although these can be separated as individual accounts, or combined, they nevertheless represent a very substantial amount of noninterest expense. Banks are heavily laden with equipment. These include standard bank equipment, such as ATMs, cash dispensers, vaults, teller drawer systems, security cameras and systems, and a variety of other items that must be maintained and updated regularly. Banks have little choice regarding equipment expenses and often seek to obtain volume deals to optimize costs and expenses.

Similarly, information technology is a necessity in banking today, and it is costly. Standard technology equipment for a bank includes core data processing systems, computer hardware (e.g., desktops, laptops, file servers), software, network circuits, routers and switches, telephones, and web servers. Again, these are a cost of doing business and generally standard in the industry. Banks endeavor to optimize these costs through volume deals and upgrading only when necessary. Banks with a large branch network, obviously, are going to incur considerably more in technology costs.

Branch Management

Physical, brick-and-mortar branches are very costly. Branches must be maintained and cannot be allowed to decline due to lack of care, as this has an impact on the customer base. Branch expenses include utility costs, landscaping, snow removal, property taxes, decorating and maintenance, repairs, parking lot paving and repairs, roof repairs, and others. These can amount to millions of dollars annually dependent upon the size of the branch network.

Typically included in this area are other physical structures that the bank owns. These typically result from repossessed properties, or other real estate owned (OREO). Like branches, these properties must be maintained. Although the bank will actively be attempting to sell these properties, they must be maintained to hold their value so that the banks losses are minimized. This will include landscaping, repairs, maintenance, utilities, and all attendant costs of keeping the property up.

Discretionary Expenses

This last area is called **discretionary expenses** because a decision must be made as to whether to incur an expense, how much to incur, and to what value. In other words, these are expenses that can be incurred that would produce value to the bank. The student of banking should take care to understand how these might be different than core operational expenses. A strategy should be developed to utilize these to the fullest, and what impact they may have to the bottom line. Discretionary expenses involve four primary areas that can be instrumental to a bank's bottom-line if properly utilized: technology, branches, marketing and advertising, and training.

Information Technology

Aside from the technology mentioned under operational expenses, the utilization of technology can be an efficiency generator for the bank. Strategically, technology not only can be an enabler but also a means of reducing other costs. In general, it is good practice to have a strategy for the deployment of technology that can improve the productivity of employees (reduce costs) and/or increase revenues. Although it can be difficult to determine what to spend and where, a strategy of increasing costs for the sole purpose of improving operations can be a differentiator and can set a bank apart from its peers. This can be the deployment of fintech technologies that can improve the efficiencies of operations. Fintech have focused on developing streamlined, automated processes that can replace or enhance standard processes. For smaller community banks, these technologies can put them on par, technically, with very large banks. Without a strategy and focus for utilization of technology, the bank can become outdated and not competitive with peers. It is not advisable to spend money for the sake of spending money on technology, but it is wise to have a strategy for its utilization, which can make a big difference.

Branches

Similar to technology, branches should be considered as vehicles to attract deposits and customers to the bank, which can expand the revenue of the bank. This can go in either direction. Today, it is a known fact that the need for physical branches is declining based upon the deployment of mobile and internet banking. Banks should carefully consider whether branches are producing the value they need compared with the cost of maintenance (an operational expense). When they are not, the bank can consider selling the branch, shuttering the branch, and even demolishing the branch. This can amount to a considerable amount of cost savings on an ongoing basis, for even a nominal cost of demolition. Another consideration that banks can evaluate is a sale-leaseback of branches. If the bank owns their branches, structuring a deal to sell some or all the branches for an immediate cash benefit while leasing them back for a finite term, at a reduced cost, may be beneficial, especially when the future path for branches is diminishing.

On the contrary, another opportunity might be adding branches. Again, a key strategy is needed for this. Banks must carefully consider the need, the location, and what they hope to gain from the deployment of a new branch. Branches can cost as much as $5 million to build and therefore must be carefully considered. Building a branch in a geographic area where the opportunity to obtain new depository customers is high can create that opportunity if it offsets the costs of maintaining the branch. Another advantage of a branch in a new area is the establishment of a presence where none existed before. This creates awareness and the possibility of expansion. Nevertheless, there are significant opportunities involved, whether the bank is expanding or decreasing branches.

Marketing and Advertising

Another area of discretionary opportunity is marketing and advertising. Banks are highly competitive and must establish themselves as the preferred bank among potential customers. Investing in advertising and marketing will pay back effectively with more accounts, more deposits, and more loans. Of course, advertising alone will not do it: Competitive pricing is very important, as is technology. In addition, the service the bank provides is also a differentiator, and this story must be told. To do this, the bank must commit discretionary funds to marketing and advertising. Advertising can consist of billboards, radio, television, internet, and even social media.

Training

The last area of opportunity for discretionary spending is training. The more the bank can provide for ongoing training and improvement, the more effective and efficient the staff will be. Using the U.S. military as an example, which is arguably the best in the world, they train constantly. The more the bank trains, the stronger and more productive, as well as creative, the staff will be.

Summary

Opportunities exist within expenses. Banks should not view these as detrimental but rather as opportunities for improvement and efficiencies. Having an ongoing process or campaign that is continuously evaluating expenses and opportunities is a decided benefit to the bank. The student of commercial banking, when learning about the management of a bank, should carefully consider this area, especially the discretionary expenses that can be most effective in competing and gaining market share.

CHAPTER SUMMARY

Noninterest income and noninterest expenses do not generally get the attention that interest income obtains. However, as this chapter highlights, banks must have an active plan for these two areas if they are to remain competitive. This begins with a strategy and must be integral with other revenue-producing strategies on the interest income side. The combination of both will pave the way for the success of the bank. As banking becomes more competitive, this chapter becomes a critical ingredient in understanding how banks are managed.

Although the balance sheet is critical to plan for interest income, the lifeblood of the bank, managing the income statement as well is most important, below the net interest income line. Today, banks have many opportunities to expand noninterest income—more so than in the past—becoming more diverse and using this as a hedge against the uncontrollable, fluctuating interest rates.

END OF CHAPTER QUESTIONS

1. What is the purpose of lifeline banking?
2. Explain the nature of conditional pricing. How is it used, and how is it determined?
3. A cash management product that is focused on comparing withdrawal amount to verify that they match with actual results is called what?
4. Identify the three components of the cost plus profit margin pricing of deposits.
5. What is considered the largest of the noninterest operational expenses for a bank?
6. Define what is meant by the "unbanked" segment of the population.
7. What deposit service charge is assessed when a check is presented for more money than what is in the account?
8. Which of the services offered by banks for deposit accounts does not presently include a charged fee?
9. What is a check called that is endorsed with a stamp and signed by an officer of the bank?
10. The ability to deposit checks electronically, for both businesses and individuals, is called what?

CHAPTER 11

Measuring and Analyzing Results

Financial statements are the lifeblood for understanding the financial activities of a bank. Beyond this, there are very specific metrics that are used to assess and compare the performance of a bank. These metrics are used to communicate to the stakeholders of the bank (i.e., shareholders, customers, investors, employees, and market makers) what progress the bank has made over a given period. The metrics contained in this chapter have become some of the primary metrics from which banks compare themselves to their peer banks. This comparison is not only important to answer the question as to how competitive the bank is but also to use these as a foundation for reporting during quarterly earnings releases. The purpose of this chapter is to outline which of these metrics and ratios are most important and used for this purpose, specifically understanding what they are, what they measure, how they are calculated, and how they are analyzed. Additionally, the standard communication mechanism of the performance of the bank is the earnings release. This chapter will explore the nature of this important report, how it is composed, and the impact that it has on the bank's success.

Key Terms

Return on assets (ROA)
Return on equity (ROE)
Efficiency ratio
Net interest margin (NIM)
Asset quality
Nonperforming loans
Other real estate owned (OREO)
Texas ratio
Liquidity coverage ratio
Stable funds
Required stable funds
Static or dynamic gap
Interest sensitivity ratio
Capital adequacy ratio
Risk-weighted assets
Earnings release

Learning Objectives

By the end of this chapter, the student will:

- Understand how banks are measured.
- Learn the importance of forecasting performance objectives.
- Identify the key performance ratios that are important for banks.
- Know the components and importance of a peer analysis and the primary ratios used for comparison.
- Know the purposes of an earnings release: its timing, composition, and stakeholders.

How Bank Performance is Measured

Banks have many ratios that are used. These are quite numerous and serve to refine and point to specific areas that can help to analyze the effectiveness of a bank. Although there are many of these metrics, or ratios, this chapter is going to focus on the primary metrics that are considered most important and define the results of the bank most expeditiously. The most important ratios revolve around four primary areas, as follows:

- investment performance
- efficiency
- profitability
- risk

Each of these broad areas has a metric or two that is used to measure how well the bank is performing in relation to that category. In addition to this, banks will develop objectives for what they believe the target performance should be at the end of the year, or even at the end of each quarter. As a result, each year, as the bank plans for the coming year, the specifics of the plan cannot be written until the objectives are established for these performance areas. Once established, strategies can be developed to attain those objectives, and hence the details of a plan to be communicated to the staff.

Investment Performance

Commercial banks are corporations. As such, they are in business to create shareholder value and grow, much like any other corporation. In this regard, there are two aspects of performance that are most important to evaluate how effective the bank is in generating a return. Return, for a bank, is much like that of any other corporation: It is related to their ability to generate bottom-line net income. However, net income is generated based upon the resources (assets) the bank has available to them to generate revenue. The assets of a bank contain the accounts that produce the revenue for the bank, and therefore, analyzing how effective the bank is in doing this is of paramount importance.

The two primary areas that are considered in this category include **return on assets** and **return on equity**. Each of these metrics focuses on two very important aspects of the bank, how well assets are utilized to generate income and how well contributed funds are used to generate income.

Return on Assets

Banks accept deposits and make loans. In fact, the economic function that banks perform is making loans to businesses in the community to support the growth of businesses, resulting in job creation and production. Because the largest asset that a bank has are its loans, the return generated from these loans becomes the critical measure. As loans are the largest asset, they generate most of the revenue for the bank by way of interest income and therefore defines the metric.

Banks are often and regularly compared based on return on assets (ROA), for these reasons. All banks make loans, and therefore, comparing them on the effectiveness of this metric is a strong indicator of competitiveness and internal effectiveness of the bank.

The ratio of bank earnings, net income, is viewed in relation to the total assets of the bank. The actual calculation of the ratios is:

- formula:
  » (Net income / Total assets) = %

This results in a percentage, the higher of which is better. However, like all ratios, they are only as good as they are compared to past results and to the industry (peers). Only then do they have true meaning. Embodied within this ratio are management's ability to price loans effectively, manage their interest margin, use their staff of relationship managers and lenders to negotiate effective deals, and generate the maximum amount of income while mitigating risks to the extent possible.

Returns on assets can range, by bank, and certainly, there are other assets that are taken into consideration in the generation of income. It is always advisable to compare to a peer group of banks (similar size, markets, and geography) to gauge the meaning of the result. The reason banks and other corporations have assets is to utilize these assets in the production of income. Since banks rely on loans as their major assets, this becomes a very effective performance measure. This is based upon a percentage: The higher the percentage, the better.

- evaluation:
  » This is a comparative ratio and indicates the degree to which the total assets produce bottom-line income. Since the numerator is "net income," this is net of all expenses, including interest expense and noninterest expense. Therefore, this indicates how effective the bank is at utilizing its assets effectively to produce net income. So this tells the reader how effective the bank is at utilizing its assets, which tells a lot about the management of the bank.

Return on Equity

Return on equity (ROE) is like return on assets but is more focused on the return that investors are obtaining from their investment in the bank. This metric is designed more for investors, to ensure what percentage of income is earned from the amount invested in the bank. Banks are corporations; therefore, they have shareholders who contribute capital to the bank by way of equity (common stock). This ratio provides an understanding of how the bank is producing an effective return from the capital received.

Capital (equity) is a "source" of funds. This is the foundation for the "uses" of funds, which are assets. The money contributed by this investment allows the bank to purchase assets (buildings), make loans, invest in securities, and pay bills (cash). So how these funds are utilized to produce net income becomes an important consideration for investment in the bank. Although this is an important ratio, it is not the primary one for comparison purposes, as is return on assets.

The calculation of ROE of simple and like the ROA.

- formula:
  - (Net income / Common stock equity) = %

The numerator is bottom-line net income, as before, but the denominator is a bit more complex. Common stock equity (CSE) includes the following components:

- common stock
- additional paid in capital
- retained earnings

Ultimately, this is part of the capital structure but represents ownership in the bank. Retained earnings is included because this represents the impact of internal funding, or that net income has grown after the payment of dividends. When retained earnings is added to common stock, if the number is positive, common stock equity goes up, and so too does the book value of the bank—and subsequently book value per share. If this does increase, it creates shareholder value, which is the primary goal of any corporation. Therefore, this becomes a measure of earnings to the value (book) of the business. The goal is for the percentage to grow. Again, ratios are best assessed when compared to peers and over time. The higher the percentage, the better the performance.

- evaluation:
  - Since net income plays a role in both the numerator and the denominator, the higher the net income, the more impact on the percentage. The goal is to improve the percentage. As CSE grows, the percentage will grow only if net income grows to a sufficient level to increase the percentage. Since net income is a component in the retained earnings formula, it increases book value after dividends have been paid from this. The numerator, net income, is prior to the payment of dividends. When the percentage increases, the "value" of the bank is growing, and the value of the investment is being effectively deployed and utilized.

In conclusion, capital (common stock) is used to purchase assets; therefore, it is a measure of how well management has used these funds to produce the assets that have the greatest potential to produce the greatest amount of net income. The utilization of these assets is, then, measure by return on assets.

Efficiency

Efficiency is a key comparative metric for a bank. The reason that this is a consideration in the performance of a bank is so that there is an understanding of how well banks are attempting to utilize their assets in the production of revenue and, ultimately, income. Inefficient organizations eventually become impaired and impact their capital through erosion. The primary measure used for a bank is the efficiency ratio.

Efficiency Ratio

The **efficiency ratio** is designed to measure what it costs to produce $1 of revenue. Everyone knows it takes money to make money, and that is what this ratio is all about. The basic components of the ratio are the relationship between cost and income, and results in a percentage, based upon 100%. The higher the percentage, the greater the cost to produce revenue; therefore, decreasing this result is the objective. As with the other ratios, however, this should be compared to peers as well as over time to determine the level of improvement. So, in this case, a higher percentage is not desirable. Another way to look at the results is to view it as dollars. For example, a 60% efficiency ratio result would indicate that it costs 60 cents to produce $1 of revenue.

- formula:
  - (Noninterest expense / (Net interest income + Noninterest income – Provision for loan losses)) = %

Although the formula has a few more components, it basically is a ratio of expense to income. The numerator represents noninterest expenses, which are the operating expenses for the bank. The denominator consists of net interest income, which is interest income minus interest expense, the net income from loans. In addition, noninterest income is included, or fee-type income. Finally, the provision for loan losses is subtracted (taken from the bank's income statement). Therefore, the result is the percentage expenses represent in relation to the income produced—less provision for losses.

- evaluation:
  - As indicated, the result is a percentage. The higher the expense, the worse the bank is doing in relation to efficiency. Therefore, the goal is to reduce this percentage. Banks are often compared to one another using this ratio. Generally, efficiency ratios at or below 50% are considered very positive. This indicates that the bank spends 50 cents to produce $1 of income. When banks are efficient, they spend less to produce more income.

Profitability

Profitability for banks and corporations alike comes down to bottom-line net income. This indicates whether the bank is profitable and by how much. Anyone analyzing a bank's financial statement would certainly look to the income statement to see how well the bank is doing. Although important, for banks, a more important measure of performance and profitability relates to their major role as a lender. Since loans produce most of the income, understanding the net profitability resulting from this primary activity is most important.

There are many measures of profitability, the traditional of which would be the net profit margin. This is important for corporations, as it is a measure of the bottom-line net income in relation to sales (revenue). However, this is much more effectively accomplished by looking at interest income and interest expense as part of the loan production process. In short, the most effective and comparative ratio involves the amount "net" interest income and its relationship to assets, using the net interest margin.

Net Interest Margin Ratio

Net interest margin (NIM) is a major comparative ratios for banks and an excellent indicator of the profitability of the bank, through loan production. This is a percentage that indicates the amount of net income (interest income minus interest expense) produced to total assets. Interest income is essentially the primary revenue (sales) produced by the bank. Net interest income is the net profit that results, factoring in the cost of obtaining funds (interest expense from deposits). This amount is viewed in relation to the total earnings assets of the bank to produce the percentage. Earning assets refer to those assets that generate interest income for the bank. The higher the percentage, the greater the profitability and the performance of the bank. This is an important relationship since all banks make loans, thereby making this an excellent comparison point to determine how well the bank is doing.

- formula:
  - » (Interest income – Interest expense) / Total earnings assets = %

Banks are frequently compared based on the result of this ratio, from a peer standpoint. From an analyst viewpoint, it indicates how effective the bank is at obtaining the deposits to fund loans. This is a testament to the bank's pricing strategy, how well they priced loans to not only obtain them competitively but also to generate revenue. In addition, banks must price deposits effectively to obtain them, so the net interest income produced is a true measure of how well the bank achieves this in a highly competitive marketplace. Remember, there is only a finite amount of loan opportunities in a marketplace, and all banks in that marketplace are competing for those loans. So the larger the net interest income, the more effective the bank is, which will translate into a higher percentage when compared to the total assets (the bulk of which are loans) in the net interest margin.

- evaluation:
  - The goal is to produce a higher net interest margin, over time and in relation to peers and the industry. Historically, this percentage has ranged from 3%–4% and higher, but normally within that range. Again, this ratio focuses on the lending function and should be looked at in this context. It is an often-quoted metric, particularly in earnings releases, and to the marketplace as a key performance ratio.

Risk

This chapter is devoted to performance in general. However, it is difficult to truly analyze a bank without considering areas that may put the bank at risk. Risk is uncertainty, and uncertainty can impair a bank. Banks face many risks, which will be discussed in a later chapter, but in this segment, it is important to identify, at least, some of the major risk areas that impact the bank and can negatively affect the performance measurements previously mentioned.

Among the risks that are considered important for comparison with peers and for evaluation of the strength of the bank include the following:

- asset quality
- liquidity
- interest rate
- capital

Except for asset quality, which relates to credit risk, the remainder are considered financial risks. Within each of these areas, there are specific ratios that are the metrics that can be used to assess the strength of the bank. Each of these will be outlined in greater detail in the next chapter.

Asset Quality

Asset quality, as the name implies, is a measure of the quality of the assets on the bank's balance sheet. Since loans are the largest of the bank's assets, asset quality relates to risk attendant to loans, which is nonpayment, resulting in a loss. Loan loss is an important consideration in how well a bank analyzes and monitors the loans it makes. If losses are high, is this due to economic events or, comparatively, to the strength of the management (lending) practices the bank employs? From an analysis standpoint, this is a major consideration. If losses increase, these can ultimately erode capital levels in the bank, which will affect the bank's ability to be compliant and to remain in business.

As a precursor to loan losses, banks monitor **nonperforming loans**. These are loans where the client is not making their regular payments due to lack of cash flow and profitability. These loans are monitored closely to hopefully prevent them from becoming total losses, but they become an indicator of potential losses. For this reason, banks will compare to their peers on this basis. In the asset quality realm, three important ratios exist:

- asset quality ratio
- nonperforming loans ratio
- Texas ratio

<u>Asset quality ratio</u>: The asset quality ratio is the primary measurement of the quality of loans. It is a measurement of the amount of actual loans losses to total or average loans. This is based upon a percentage and is another ratio where the goal is to be lower, not higher. A lower percentage indicates that the asset quality is higher and less losses are being taken. Again, these are always relevant to performance over time and to peers to truly make the assessment.

- formula:
  - » (Loan losses / Total loans) = %

Obviously, less losses taken in relation to loans is the goal. This is the end product of the loan process, and a key measure, because it represents the actual amount of loans written off. This is a terminal event, and no further attention will be placed on these loans.

- evaluation:
  - » Asset quality is a relatively low percentage. Unless the bank has significant problems, this percentage should be less than 1%. As a measure of risk and the impact to capital, keeping the ratio low guards the bank from eroding its capital and putting itself at risk of going out of business.

<u>Nonperforming loans ratio</u>: This ratio is a preliminary ratio that provides a warning or "heads-up" of the potential for loan losses. Banks closely manage their primary credit risk, nonpayment. For this reason, the lending staff is continually analyzing the cash flow of the businesses that they lend to understand problems in advance and to remain close to the businesses that are having difficulty. In the next chapter, the various stages of nonperformance, and remedies, will be outlined in detail. However, for this purpose, the focus will be on those loans that are not making payments—that are, by definition, nonperforming. To effectively determine this ratio, the bank must have the systems to easily identify these loans and classify them as such.

- formula:
  - » (Nonperforming loans / Total loans) = %

In some cases, the denominator may also include **other real estate owned (OREO)**. The reason for this is that OREO property is property taken as collateral when the loan was written off as a loss. OREO properties are assets of the bank, like loans, and generally result from the loan process.

- explanation:
  - » The percentage that results from this metric should be higher than the asset quality ratio. The reason for this is that not all nonperforming loans will result in a loss. The plan is that the bank is negotiating with these loans, restructuring them, and hopefully resulting in a performing client, once again. In this regard, the percentage should not be extremely large but higher than the asset quality ratio. The distance between this ratio and the asset quality result is a measure of how effective they bank is at renegotiating and restructuring these loans into functioning loans.

Texas ratio: The final ratio is one that was used extensively during the financial crisis of 2008. The Texas ratio measures nonperforming loans as a percentage of ownership (capital) and loan loss reserves. This is a percentage, the higher of which is indicative of definite bank health issues. During the financial crisis, the Texas ratio was used to earmark banks that were at risk of failure. It was an indicator that the dollar amount of problem loans (non-performing) was exceeding the amount of tangible common equity, ownership capital. A high percentage would indicate the potential that the bank could not absorb these if they were to become losses and remain compliant and solvent.

- formula:
  - » (Nonperforming loans / (Tangible common equity + Loan loss reserves) = %

Nonperforming loans were the same as those discussed in the nonperforming loan ratios, as the numerator. Tangible common equity is common stock equity; common stock; retained earnings, not including intangibles (i.e., goodwill); and preferred stock. Finally, loan loss reserves are included in the denominator. This represents the provision for loan losses from the income statement.

- explanation:
  - » This is truly a bank health ratio and is an indicator of severe problems. Given the formula, when the result is greater than 100%, the amount of nonperforming loans exceeds the bank's tangible capital, including amounts reserving for losses. The higher this percentage, the greater the risk that the bank may not be able to cover its losses and would be at risk of failure.

Liquidity

Liquidity represents the funding side of the bank. All banks must be liquid, and now, as of Basel III, banks must adhere to a specific liquidity coverage rate. Liquidity is one of the primary financial ratios, and it is closely monitored by the asset and liability committee (ALCO) of the bank. The goal of liquidity is having enough and generating enough liquid assets that can be converted into cash relatively quickly so that the bank can cover its cash outflows. This is a risk area that must be monitored every day, throughout the day, so that the bank understands its liquidity position.

Liquidity involves understanding the cash inflows and cash outflows of a bank that occur regularly. Cash inflows result from the assets of the bank. This includes payments made on loans, loan payoffs, REPO repurchases, interest income received, sale of physical assets, sale of securities, and other transactions that result in cash flowing into the bank. Cash outflows result from the liabilities of the bank. These include customer withdrawals from deposit accounts, checks written on accounts, interest expense payments, maturities on debt instruments, repayment of loans, loan payments, and dividend payments. The difference between these two is the primary liquidity position of the bank, positive or negative. Banks strive to be in a net "positive" liquidity position. Another aspect of liquidity is high-quality liquid assets available. These include cash, government securities, and other marketable securities (Vermaak, 2017).

Liquidity is determined by two primary liquidity ratios:

- liquidity coverage ratio (LCR)
- net stable funding ratio (NSFR)

Liquidity coverage ratio (LCR): The liquidity coverage ratio is now a regulatory requirement for banks, as of Basel III. Liquidity for a bank is different than a corporation, which looks at the current ratio to determine if there are enough current assets to cover current liabilities. Banks, unlike businesses, deal in cash flow, and these cash flows occur continuously throughout the day. At the end of the day, the bank must be liquid. The liquidity coverage ratio is the primary ratio to determine this.

- formula:
  - » (High-quality liquid assets / Net cash outflows) = %

As stated previously, the numerator (high-quality liquid assets) are those that can be immediately turned into cash when needed. This means they must be almost the equivalent of cash. The components of high-quality liquid assets are as follows:

- high-quality liquid assets: These are clearly assets of the bank. Unlike cash inflows and cash outflows, these represent the balances in the following accounts on the balance sheet, and are not transactions:
  - » Obviously, cash is the first part of this group.
  - » Government securities (treasuries) are literally risk-free and have a ready market. These can be turned into cash almost immediately. Banks hold these rather than storing them

in cash because cash is a nonearning asset. By investing excess cash in these securities, the bank can not only earn interest but can also sell these quickly and redeem them for the needed cash.

» Other "marketable" securities would fall into this category, but the key is marketability, a ready market.

On the other hand, net cash outflows, the denominator, require a little more effort. Net cash flows is the difference between cash outflows and cash inflows and represents the cash activity of the bank for the given period (e.g., month, quarter, etc.). The components of each of these items is as follows:

- cash outflows: These are the liabilities of the bank. Cash outflows from the liabilities represent the following activities:
  - » withdrawals from deposit accounts (savings, checking, and time deposits)
  - » checks written and paid against checking accounts
  - » interest payments on interest-bearing deposit accounts
  - » interest payments on debt instruments (subordinated debt and notes)
  - » dividend payments on preferred and common stock
  - » interest payments on borrowing from other banks
  - » interest payments on borrowings from the central bank
  - » interest payments on securities sold under agreement to repurchase (REPOs)
  - » payments made for taxes due
- cash inflows: These are assets of the bank, excluding high-quality liquid assets, previously mentioned. Cash inflows emanate from the assets of the bank from the following activities:
  - » loan payments received from borrowers (including interest payments)
  - » interest payments received on investments (Treasury securities and others)
  - » interest payments received from money loaned to other banks
  - » interest earned on the purchase of securities held for repurchase (reverse REPOs)
  - » other cash received from the sale of fixed assets

According to Basel III, the total of cash inflows is capped at 75% of total cash outflows and cannot exceed this amount for usage in the calculation of net cash outflows.

- evaluation:
  - » The result of this formula is a percentage. According to Basel III, this must be greater than or equal to 100% to be compliant. In a sense, this is like a current ratio, as it demonstrates how well the bank can cover its cash flows (obligations for cash outflows). Since banks receive cash inflows regularly, by capping these at 75% of outflows, banks are held to a more stringent requirement to ensure adequate liquidity. The ratio percentage, then, indicates what percentage of the net cash outflows, after reducing them

by the cash inflows, are covered by the high-quality liquid assets. If they are 100%, or above covered, then the bank has the immediate liquidity to make sure they can handle the cash outflow obligations. If a bank were to be below this threshold, it would indicate that they could only cover a portion of the cash flows and put them in an illiquid state.

Net stable funding ratio: This other liquidity measure is relatively new. This ratio focuses more on **stable funds** that are available and those that are required, rather than the actual transactions themselves. Although the ratio looks at the relationship of assets to liabilities, once again, it emphasizes those funds that are deemed most stable and can be relied upon. In this regard, rather than relying on the coverage of net cash outflows from high-quality liquid assets, it compares the funds that can be counted on to be available to those that are necessary to be available or required.

- formula:
  - » (Available stable funds / Required stable funds) = %

Although a relatively simple formula, an understanding of both the components of the numerator and the denominator is important.

- available stable funds: These represent sources of funds for the bank and therefore emanate from the liabilities of the bank. Again, rather than look at cash flows, an assessment is made of the balance for the accounts indicated below. Banks will assess maturity levels greater than one year and less than one year and identify the balances associated with each. This will provide an indication of whether or not the funds have a likelihood of being available to the bank. Additionally, a weight factor is applied to the account balances to arrive at the amount used to determine total available stable funds. This weight percentage is determined by the Basel Committee on Bank Supervision and assigns stability weights of 100%, 85%, 70%, 50%, and 0% to these balances to arrive at the available stable funds, based upon the following:
  - » due to other banks: These are short term in nature (less than one year) and therefore carry a stability weight of 0%, indicating that the funds obtained cannot be relied upon.
  - » due to customers: Savings and checking accounts are not governed by maturity; therefore, the bank must determine the amount that would be expected to remain with the bank (stable funds) in the event of an emergency and those that would be less stable. Those amounts deemed "stable" would receive an 85% stability weight, generally, and those considered "less stable" would receive a weight of 70%.

Certificates of deposit and other floating rate instruments are governed by the maturity date. If greater than one year, these would receive a stability weight of 100%, and those less than one year would receive a weight of 50%, generally.

- » debt securities: These securities issued to raise funds, if greater than one year, would have a stability weight of 100%, whereas those less than one year would not be stable and would be at a weight of 0%.

   - subordinated debt: Subordinated debt is generally of a long-term nature, greater than one year, and can be relied upon and receive a weight of 100%.
   - equity capital: Equity, as well, can be relied upon and has a stability factor of 100%.
   - preferred stock: Those with maturities of greater than one year would receive a 100% weighting; otherwise, it would receive 0%.

- **required stable funds**: This portion of the calculation, or metric, is a bit different, although it, too, relies on percentage factor based upon its requirements. Required stable funds are those funds needed to support fewer liquid assets. For example, cash, as an asset, is highly liquid and does not demand stable funding by nature of its highly liquid status. Therefore, it will receive a factor of 0% and would not be included as requiring stable funds. Required stable funds are assets, some of which are less liquid than others. Virtually all assets are included in this determination but receive the factors indicated below in the determination of requiring stable funds.
   - cash and marketable securities: These are highly liquid; therefore, the factor applied is 0%, if the marketable securities are less than one year.
   - due from other banks: Maturities greater than one year would carry a 100% factor and less than one year at 0%, as payment is imminent and therefore liquid.
   - loans to customers: This will depend on the type of loan and the maturity. Generally, loans with maturities greater than one year will be factored at 100%, with less than one year at either 85% for retail loans or 50% for nonfinancial corporate clients.
   - marketable securities: These securities, if greater than one year, will carry a 5% factor.
   - corporate bonds: Those with maturities greater than one year will receive a factor of 20%; otherwise, it will be 0%.

In general, both the available and required stable funding rely on weights and factors that must be determined based upon maturity and stability. Therefore, these are applied by the bank based upon the Basel standards.

- evaluation:
   - Like the liquidity coverage ratio, the net stable funding ratio requires banks to be at or above 100%. The NSFR is a refinement of the LCR in that the concept of stability is a part of the assessment. Stability relates to the "core" accounts of a bank, or those that can be relied upon to remain in the event of a financial crisis. So this metric is geared more toward the impact on liquidity if a financial crisis were to occur again, as it did in 2008, and whether banks could remain liquid as a result. This is considered a stress-type assessment.

Interest Rate

One of the major challenges for every bank is to cope with interest rate fluctuations, which can occur beyond their control. The Federal Reserve bank ultimately controls the fluctuations in interest rates. When rates are changed by the Fed, they will impact all the lending rates by the increment of change. Since most of the revenue for a bank comes from interest income, declines in interest rates will affect their margins and create this risk.

Banks are affected by changes in interest rates from both an asset and a liability standpoint. Banks receive interest income and pay interest expense. As interest rates change, it can place the bank in an asset or liability sensitive state. Although remedies and the discussion of these sensitivities is defined in an upcoming chapter, there are a few ratios that are used to assess this sensitivity. These ratios include:

- static or dynamic gap
- interest sensitivity ratio (ISR)
- interest rate risk ratio (interest sensitivity gap ratio)

Static or dynamic gap: This calculation is not a ratio but rather a determination of the dollar sensitivity of the bank. Dollar sensitivity is determined by two items: the total amount of interest-sensitive assets and the total amount of interest-sensitive liabilities. The difference between the two identifies the sensitivity gap.

- formula:
  - (Sum of interest-sensitive assets – Sum of interest-sensitive liabilities) = $

Interest-sensitive assets are those assets that are sensitive to changes in interest rates, when rates change the rate applied to that asset changes, as a floating rate. The same holds true for liabilities that are sensitive to rate changes. For example, CDs are deposits that have an interest rate that is fixed, for a period. A fixed rate like this would not be deemed sensitive to interest rate fluctuations.

- evaluation:
  - A positive result, using the formula, indicates that the bank is considered "asset-sensitive," indicating that they have more assets that are affected by interest rate changes than liabilities. A negative result indicates the opposite, that the bank is considered "liability sensitive." Whether the bank is liability or asset sensitive will dictate the type of action the bank will need to take to remedy the situation, defined in a later chapter.

Interest sensitivity ratio (ISR): This ratio is designed to highlight, as a percentage, the relative sensitivity of the bank. Essentially, it identifies the interest sensitivity gap in percentage form.

- formula:
  - (Interest sensitive assets / Interest sensitive liabilities) = %

Interest sensitive assets and interest sensitive liabilities are the same sums determined when completing the "static gap" formula. The only difference is that they are being divided by one another.

- evaluation:
  - » Since this is a percentage, if interest-sensitive assets exceed interest-sensitive liabilities, the result will be greater than 100%—and less than 100% if the reverse occurs. Using this metric, then, indicates that a bank is asset sensitive if the percentage is greater than 100%, and if the bank is liability sensitive, then the percentage will be less than 100%. In both cases, the degree the percentage represents indicates how sensitive the bank is on either the asset or liability side. This understanding will help in determining what action the bank needs to take.

Interest rate risk ratio (interest sensitivity gap ratio): This ratio relies, in part, on the static gap calculation. The major difference is that this result is compared in relation to the assets. This will result in a percentage as well and defines the sensitivity level in relation to total assets, which sometimes may be an easier result to assess.

- formula:
  - » (Interest-sensitive assets – Interest-sensitive liabilities) / Total assets = %

This is somewhat a variation on a theme. This last ratio, however, may be a good combination of all, and a relatively easy metric to assess.

- explanation:
  - » Since this metric incorporates elements of the other two, it may be preferred. The analysis of the result is relatively easy to assess. If the result is a "positive" percentage, the bank is asset sensitive; if a "negative" percentage, the bank is liability sensitive. Calculating this percentage in relation to assets makes it easier to see how distant the percentage is from zero, which would indicate the degree of sensitivity. Since a result of zero indicates no interest-sensitivity risk, higher percentages can quickly establish the need for urgency.

Capital

Although the capital ratios represent risk to the bank, they also represent compliance risk. Capital represents the primary ownership and sources of funds for the enterprise. The evaluation of these ratios provides a sense of comfort or urgency about the bank's capital. Like the other areas, capital risk will be defined more fully in an upcoming chapter, but these ratios, nevertheless, are important for assessing a bank's level of risk to the underlying capital of the bank, the erosion of which can affect the bank's ability to remain in business.

There are four basic capital ratios that are computed and used by regulators to assess the capital adequacy of the bank:

- capital adequacy ratio (CAR)
- Tier 1 capital ratio
- Tier 2 capital ratio
- leverage ratio

Capital adequacy ratio (CAR): The capital adequacy ratio is also called the "total capital ratio." This combines all elements of the capital and determines its overall percentage as it relates to assets. This provides a gauge as to the degree that capital represents to the assets of the bank. Since capital provides the source of funds for usage by assets, it is important to understand this relationship. The formula for this calculation will require some explanation.

- formula:
  - (Tier 1 capital + Tier 2 capital) / Total "risk-weighted" assets = %

Beginning with the numerator in the equation, both Tier 1 and Tier 2 capital require explanation.

- Tier 1 capital: This is part of the capital structure and includes:
  - common stock and surplus
  - Treasury stock
  - retained earnings (undivided profits)
  - qualifying noncumulative perpetual preferred stock
  - minority interests
- Tier 2 capital: This is part of the capital structure but is more focused on debt capital and includes:
  - allowance for loan losses (up to 1.25% of risk-weighted assets)
  - mandatory convertible debt (qualifying preferred stock)
  - subordinated debt

The denominator is made up of assets; however, for this ratio, these are **risk-weighted assets** only. These are the assets on the balance sheet but multiplied by a factor that indicates the degree of risk inherent in the asset themselves. For example, business loans are quite risky and will have a factor of 100%. Therefore, all commercial loans will be included. Cash, as an asset, carries no risk; the factor is 0%. Therefore, when multiplied by the amount of cash, it will be zero and will not be included. More will be discussed in a subsequent chapter on this topic.

- evaluation:
  - » This is the primary ratio that is used to determine capital compliance by the regulators. As of 2019, the end of the phase-in from Basel III, a bank is adequately capitalized at 8% and well capitalized at 10%. When banks lower their denominator, take less risk in their assets, their capital ratio will improve, and the reverse will occur if they take on more risky assets. Therefore, this ratio is all about risk to the enterprise.

Tier 1 capital ratio: The Tier 1 ratio is like the capital adequacy ratio, but only includes Tier 1 capital in the numerator. The denominator remains the same.

- formula:
  - » (Tier 1 capital / Risk-weighted assets) = %

As indicated, for the numerator, Tier 1 includes all the following capital structure items, as indicated for the CAR.

- Tier 1 capital: This is part of the capital structure and includes:
  - » common stock and surplus
  - » Treasury stock
  - » retained earnings (undivided profits)
  - » qualifying noncumulative perpetual preferred stock
  - » minority interests

The denominator remains the same, risk-weighted assets; therefore, there is no change.

- evaluation:
  - » The Tier 1 ratio is designed to focus on the primary capital of the bank, core capital, and how this relates to total risk-weighted assets. To achieve compliance, banks are expected to be adequately capitalized at 6% and well capitalized at 8%. This is also an important ratio, from a regulatory standpoint, because this is the bank's primary capital.

Common equity Tier 1 capital ratio (CE1): Common equity Tier 1 is another hybrid capital ratio, more refined than the broader Tier 1 ratio. Common equity Tier 1 is focused on common equity, only, as the primary numerator.

- formula:
  - » (CET1 / Risk-weighted assets) = %

CET1, as the numerator, includes the items listed below. The denominator is risk-weighted assets, as in the previous ratios.

- common equity Tier 1 capital: This is part of the capital structure and includes:
  - » common stock and surplus

- » Treasury stock
- » retained earnings (undivided profits)

This ratio is designed to focus more on ownership capital, without minority interests and preferred stock. This is considered the bank's true core capital.

- evaluation:
  - » CET1 capital is obviously less than Tier 1 capital, as it includes fewer items. Therefore, 4.5% is considered to be adequately capitalized and 6% well capitalized.

Tier 2 capital ratio: Tier 2 capital is the other part of the capital structure, which includes more debt instruments. This is considered supplemental capital but nevertheless a source of funds.

- formula:
  - » (Tier 2 capital / Risk-weighted assets) = %

Tier 2 is defined as it was under the capital adequacy ratio (CAR). It includes the following components:

- Tier 2 capital: This is part of the capital structure but more focused on "debt" capital and includes:
  - » allowance for loan losses (up to 1.25% of risk-weighted assets)
  - » mandatory convertible debt (qualifying preferred stock)
  - » subordinated debt

As with the other ratios, Tier 2 capital is divided by risk-weighted assets again.

- evaluation:
  - » Seldom is Tier 2 a stand-alone metric for evaluation. Normally, it is included as a component of the total capital ratio (CAR). However, since it is secondary capital, the percentage is relatively low. In general, 2% is considered adequately and well capitalized.

Leverage ratio: Finally, the last ratio is called the "leverage ratio." This ratio is very similar to the Tier 1 capital ratio with the exception that the denominator is total assets, not risk-weighted assets. In most cases, this ratio will be lower than the Tier 1 capital ratio.

- formula:
  - » (Tier 1 capital / Total assets) = %

Tier 1 capital is the same as all others and includes the following components:

- Tier 1 capital: This is part of the capital structure and includes:
  - » common stock and surplus

- » Treasury stock
- » retained earnings (undivided profits)
- » qualifying noncumulative perpetual preferred stock
- » minority interests

The denominator is total assets. This is a more conservative application of the overall ratio.

- evaluation:
  - » The leverage ratio is a measure of core capital to total assets. This will diminish the capital percentage from that of the Tier 1 ratio. For this reason, adequately capitalized is 4% and well capitalized is 5%.

Summary

These represent the primary comparative and risk ratios. They are used to evaluate how well the bank is doing and to gauge how they are doing compared with peers. There are many more ratios that are not outlined in this chapter; however, these can be very detailed refinements that are much more focused. However, for the purposes of evaluating a bank, these represent the primary metrics to evaluate.

How the Performance of a Bank is Compared

Ratios are excellent tools to assess the performance and the key risks banks face. As with all ratios, these are best understood when evaluated over time and in conjunction with their peers. Banks regularly compare themselves with their peers based on many of these ratios, but also on few other metrics. To understand this, it is necessary to understand the nature of both the comparative ratios and what constitutes peers.

Comparative Ratios

Comparative ratios, generally, are ratios that when compared to peers can identify how well a bank is doing. In other words, they add meaning to the metric. Ratios, themselves, can be meaningful; however, this meaning is enhanced considerably when they can be compared to the competition. Banks are in a highly competitive industry, so attracting and retaining clients and performing well against the competition is most meaningful.

For comparative purposes, some of the ratios previously indicated in this chapter are included, but there are other metrics as well. A good peer assessment may include the following:

- total asset size
- total loans

- annualized loan growth
- ROA and ROE
- efficiency ratio
- asset quality
- nonperforming asset ratio
- net interest margin

As indicated, several of these ratios have already been defined, including ROA and ROE, the efficiency ratio, asset quality, nonperforming asset ratio, and net interest margin. These will not be discussed below for that reason. However, the other metrics are explained below.

Total Asset Size

One of the major factors that sets the perspective for a bank is their asset size. Asset size is important for comparative purposes because larger banks may have different results and may not be as comparable. In this regard banks strive to identify peers by asset size to enable a true comparison. Asset size typically falls within ranges, usually between certain intervals to define the similarities in operation.

Total asset size is the primary metric for comparing banks and defines them as community, regional, or money center banks. Since loans are the largest of the assets, asset size is the most important relational metric.

Total Loans

Beyond the total assets, understanding the total amount of loans provides an assessment of loans to the total assets. This too puts into perspective how one bank may compare itself to others. The loans, then, can be determined as a percentage of total assets to determine the loans-to-asset ratio. This will provide an assessment as to what level the bank has lent to its capacity. This can be a helpful metric from a competitive standpoint to see how competitive the bank will be for loans if they are at or near capacity.

Annualized Loan Growth

This is an important competitive metric. Understanding how fast a bank is growing its loans will indicate how aggressive they will be in pricing and obtaining customers. With this type of metric, it is important to compare ratios with ratios. If a bank is growing at an aggressive pace, an assessment of their asset quality may be indicative of the quality of their lending process. This explanation is valuable and may help to explain why your bank may or may not be competitive with growth. This can then be compared with ROA and nonperforming loans.

Overall, these key metrics can form the basis of an effective peer report.

Bank Peers

Bank peers should be carefully determined and can be very helpful in planning the bank's strategy. To be effective, peers must be determined based on a few key characteristics:

- market area
- size
- regulatory oversight
- competitors

Market Area

Market areas defines the boundaries and scope of the products and services offered. To truly compare one bank to another, understanding whether the peer falls within the same market area and breadth as your bank is important. The reason for this is that it is likely that you are competing for the same business. The selection of a bank that has a much wider market area would not be comparable to the metrics of your bank for many reasons. To do so could distort the performance of your bank and lead to incorrect actions. Understanding the market area will help to add validity to the comparison.

Size

When comparing to other banks, it is advisable to select banks that have a similar size in assets. This does not have to be exact, but within a reasonable range. Remaining within a comparable size puts resources into perspective. Banks of similar asset sizes have similar amounts of total resources that they could use in achieving performance. Banks much larger than the one to compare is not a fair assessment, as they may have more staff, more technology, and other advantages that would make it difficult to compare. The key is to put the comparison peer into perspective.

Regulatory Oversight

Regulatory oversight is also meaningful. Larger banks that may have more regulatory restrictions can be difficult to compare. Understanding who the regulators are, whether state or nationally chartered and whether they fall under the SIFI designations, can be important. The importance is to ensure an apples-to-apples comparison.

Competitors

The final area is an understanding of who the competition is: Who do the lenders see on the streets, and who competes for the same business in your locale? Having a strong intuitive sense of who the competition is also carries weight. In this regard, it may be clear that a major competitor could be a large nationally chartered bank. Although it may be difficult to compare from a performance ratios standpoint, they are nevertheless the competition and worthy of inclusion. Knowing the competition is half the battle when attempting to gain market share.

How the Performance of a Bank is Reported

Commercial banks are corporations. They have shareholders, investors, customers, clients, and other interested parties. They regularly report their earnings and performance to the stakeholders every quarter, and annually. Quarterly reports are developed to explain the financial performance of each quarter. These are called earnings releases.

Meeting Purpose

There are several reasons why earnings releases are conducted. There are very important to the market price of the bank's stock. Typically, all corporations develop earnings releases, and the marketplace gears up for "earnings season" when quarter-end nears. Beyond this, the specific purposes of the release include the following:

- to convey the financial outcome of the bank to the bank's market makers
- to paint a picture of the bank, highlighting key ratios and increases and decreases over the past quarter
- to explain the rationale behind the results to the investing public and the actions initiated that produced such results
- to field questions from the market makers to articulate the most positive outlook for the bank

Earnings Release

Earnings releases consist of the following activities and events that occur on a quarterly basis.

- quarterly report: This is a formal report to market makers and investors, as well as customers. The report itself is a detailed financial reports that consists of ratios and financial performance from one quarter to the next.
- live meeting: These are "live" meetings and are usually conducted as a teleconference, with key individuals dialing into the meeting. Meetings are typically recorded and posted on the bank's website for access by other stakeholders who are interested but could not participate in the live session.
- press release: Immediately following the session, a press release is given to the press for communication to the broader public. The press release provides an executive summary of the financial highlights that have occurred over the quarter.
- market reaction: Following the press release, there generally is an immediate market reaction to the report. This can be positive or negative but is quite important to the banks shareholders, as it will impact the market value of the stock.

Components of the Report

Although the formal report will vary by bank, it is important to understand the key features that would typically be on the earnings report. The sections can vary but are designed to convey the key metrics and events that have transpired at the bank. There are a minimum of five sections in the report:

- select quarterly highlights: This section of the report provides brief bullets of key performance ratios and metrics, highlighting increases or decreases over the prior quarter. These are literally single line entries on the first page of the report, without major detail behind them. They simply identify the improvement or decline. This quick reference provides the major thrust for the detail contained in the report. This is typically presented in an overview fashion from the chief executive officer (CEO).
- operating performance: The next segment of the report is the overall operating performance. This is typically delivered by the chief financial officer (CFO) and is a review of the balance sheet and income statement, focusing on earnings. This is a high-level review focusing on the key highlights and providing substance behind the results.
- loan portfolio analysis: This section is presented by the chief lending officer. The bulk of this section will be devoted to business loans, focusing on loan growth, asset quality, and nonperforming loans. The composition of the loan portfolio is an important ingredient, as this will highlight risk exposure areas that may not be immediately obvious.
- retail portfolio analysis: One of the key ingredients in this section is the effective generation of funding to the support of the lending process. Therefore, deposit growth and distribution of deposits is an important breakdown to establish the effectiveness of the retail unit. Additionally, the retail loan portfolio distribution and growth are an important point of discussion.
- capital management (risk) analysis: Compliance with capital requirements is an important report. The chief risk officer will likely report the status of the bank's capital adequacy to support loan losses and to perform effectively in a stressed environment. Whether the bank is adequately or considered well capitalized is an important consideration and item to report and discuss.

Participants

The composition of the individuals that participate in the earnings release includes both internal and external participants. These are generally the presenters and interested partners.

Internal (bank): The internal participants would consist of key officers of the bank that can best report on the content of the report. These will include the following:

- chief executive officer (CEO)
  - » The CEO usually sets the tone for the meeting and initiates the discussion by providing a synopsis of the results for the year. This is a broader overview focusing on the bank's

strategy and plans. Dependent on the results of the reports, the CEO's responsibility is to explain reasons for performance or nonperformance and provide an outlook of what will be done in the next quarter to rectify the situation.

- chief financial officer (CFO)
  - » This individual is the chief financial officer of the bank. Their job is to walk through the financial results of the quarter and provide detail for the results. This will include earnings highlights, earnings per share, and how that compared with what the marketplace was expecting. This would include performance of some of the key metrics and ratios outlined in this chapter as well as an outlook for the future by way of a pro forma.
- chief lending officer (CLO)
  - » The chief lending officer is typically present to discuss loan progress as well as loan quality. Since the bulk of the revenue is generated from making loans, the report from this executive is imperative, particularly based on loan growth to plans and charge-offs. The amount the bank is reserving for loan losses will be the subject of discussion as well, and reasons for increases or decreases. Questions will be posed for specifics, and these are best addressed by the officer in charge of lending.
- chief risk officer (CRO)
  - » In today's world, risk and compliance have become major considerations for all banks. For this reason, the CRO needs to be present to discuss compliance with capital standards and other risks the bank may be facing. If the bank has recently been exposed to robberies, fraud, and/or security breaches, these will be a topic of discussion at the meeting. The individuals listening will expect plans on how these might be mitigated and addressed in the future.
- other officers
  - » Dependent upon events that have occurred during the quarter, other officers may be in attendance. This may include the chief information officer for technology related issues or initiatives, the chief retail or deposit officer for discussing funding progress and priorities, and potentially the chief credit officer for discussing concerns of portfolio risk.

<u>External participants</u>: External individuals will join the meeting as participants or listeners. Although these can range from a wide group of individuals, they typically adhere to the individuals indicated below. These are very interested parties who will take the time to join via telephone or video conference.

- market makers
  - » Market makers create a market in the bank's stock. Therefore, they have a vested interest in the company. They also have expectations formed prior to joining the meeting. These expectations generally involve the earnings per share (EPS) expected. The

market typically anticipates what the bank will do, earnings wise, and uses this as the benchmark to gauge success. These are active participants in the meeting and will pose questions to the officers present. Since this is a live meeting, responses to these questions will be used to interpret responses from the officers and therefore are very important to the success of the meeting.

- investors/others
    - » Other investors will join and listen to the call. These are passive listeners and can pose a question but not necessarily in a live situation. Bank employees will listen, as will other customers and interested parties. This will be the remainder of the participants.

Goals

The goals of the earning release are very important to the bank, and for this reason, the bank should prepare effectively for these reports. These meetings will set the tone for how the marketplace views the strength of the bank. To be effective, clear goals should be established so that all parties understand what must be conveyed. These goals should adhere to, at a minimum, the following:

- Provide effective reasons behind overall performance.
- Instill confidence in the bank in terms of knowledge, control, and performance.
- Convey specific initiatives that may have had significant impact on the results.
- Discuss key strategic initiatives and the impact they will have on the future results of the bank.
- Obtain positive lift in performance of the bank's stock price.

It is always advisable, when preparing to meet in this format, to define the objectives and effectively plan to ensure everyone is ready to field questions and convey confidence.

Summary

The earnings release is a vital part of the bank's story. It sets the tone for what has happened and what will happen in the next quarter and the future. It will define the bank's strategies and plans and what the future holds.

CHAPTER SUMMARY

The performance of the bank is a critical part of understanding the operations of a bank. The ratios and metrics defined in this chapter can help to diagnose the effectiveness of the bank. These metrics are best understood when compared with peers and over time. In addition, they often can be dissected by viewing them in conjunction with other ratios.

The ability to calculate these ratios and understand them will help the student of banking to communicate as a banker. The components of the metrics will help to point in directions where the bank may need to improve, and the comparison to peers establishes the effectiveness of the results from a competitive standpoint. Because banking is so competitive, regular evaluation of these results can aid in honing the plans for the bank and subsequently produce the results that would be positively conveyed at the earnings release.

END OF CHAPTER QUESTIONS

1. Identify two of the five goals of the earnings release.
2. Define what "risk-weighted assets" represent.
3. What is the difference between Tier 1 and common equity Tier 1 ratios?
4. What is the objective of the asset quality ratio? Should this be higher or lower to show improvement?
5. What are the key parts of the earnings release?
6. What does the efficiency ratio tell the banker?
7. What are the four categories of key bank metrics to evaluate?
8. What percentage is considered well capitalized for a bank's capital adequacy ratio?
9. Name the key participants, internally, in an earnings release.
10. Which ratio is focused on the risk of fluctuating interest rates?

CHAPTER 12

Understanding and Managing Financial Risks

Commercial banks are financial entities. They deal in money and finance as their reason for existence. In addition to this, banks deal in risk. Risk is uncertainty, and since one of the major reasons for a bank to exist is to make loans, this is one of the biggest risks bank face. Nevertheless, beyond this, as financial entities, banks live in a world of risk that relates to the financial nature of their business. The elements that create these risks, for banks, center around the movement of money, cash inflows and outflows, fluctuations in the cost of money, which is interest rates, and the underlying foundation of the bank's value, capital. These represent all the primary day-to-day activities of a bank. Since this is what banks do, create risk, banks must understand and be able to manage these to remain in existence. These risks are significant, more so than others, and individually can create difficulties that could impair if not cause the demise of the bank. For this reason, banks have a major management committee, entitled "asset/liability committee," or ALCO, to monitor and manage these significant risks.

This chapter is devoted to these financial risks, specifically, due to their importance and the nature of the inherent risk they pose. It is important for the student of commercial banking to understand the stand-alone nature of these risks and imbed them in their minds as existential risks that require attention. Of the many risks banks face, the three financial risks that are the focus of this chapter include capital risk, liquidity risk, and interest rate risk, or interest sensitivity. Understanding

Key Terms

Capital
Core capital
Supplemental capital
Tier 1 capital
Undivided profits
Tier 2 capital
Risk-weighted assets
Basel Committee on Bank Supervision (BCBS)
Basel I
Basel II
Basel III
Capital buffers
Prompt corrective action
Stress tests
Basel IV
Internal ratings-based approach (IRB)
Bankers acceptances
Commercial paper
Negotiable CDs
Eurocurrency deposits
Net liquidity position
Sources of funds approach
Hot money
Vulnerable funds
Stable funds
Money position
Lagged reserve accounting (LRA)
Reserve computation period
Reserve maintenance period
Usury
Basis points (BPS)
Risk-free real rate of interest
Yield curve
Term structure of interest rates
Yield to maturity
Normal curve
Abnormal/inverted curve
Flat curve
Static "dynamic" gap
Net interest margin
Interest rate swaps
Loan sales
Loan securitization
Standby letters of credit
Interest rate caps, floors, and collars

Learning Objectives

By the end of this chapter, the student will:

- Identify and understand the meaning of financial risk.
- Know the three financial risks that banks face.
- Understand how to manage and mitigate the risks attendant to each of the financial risks.
- Learn the components and underlying tools, techniques, and methods used to understand and manage financial risks.
- Gain a deeper understanding of the components and origins of the metrics used to measure the risks.

the nature and background of these financial events and the risks they create is of paramount importance in the overall management of a bank.

Capital Adequacy Management and Risk

All corporations raise capital at the onset of the business. **Capital** represents the funds contributed by investors to provide the source of funding for the start of the company. It is a major part of the capital structure of the business and provides funding to purchase the assets necessary to conduct business. These funds are employed in a variety of ways to establish the mechanisms to produce revenue. Buildings must be purchased, equipment must be bought, bills must be paid, employees must be paid, and other investments must be made, all with the goal of generating revenue that will contribute to the growth of the original capital. This occurs through bottom-line net income, which, if positive and retained in the company, will increase the common stock equity of the firm and enhance the value of the stock.

This capital must always be protected so that common stock equity, or capital, is not eroded by losses the company may face. When this occurs, the value of the company will decline, and if this continues, it will eventually put the company and its shareholders at risk of failure. Therefore, capital is raised as a protective measure, which must be guarded, to ensure confidence from the public and other stakeholders, including customers, employees, owners, and suppliers.

Commercial banks are corporations and, generally, public companies. They have shareholders and function much the same as any other corporation as it relates to the management of its capital. The major exception to this is that banks are highly regulated by the government and must adhere to specific levels of capital to remain compliant. Since the bulk of the assets of a bank are loans, which themselves are highly risky, significant loan losses can result in an erosion of capital and not only cause them to be out of compliance with regulations but also put them at risk of failure. This section of the chapter will define the components and origins of these requirements and the need for effective and sustained management.

Overview

Understanding the nature of bank capital is an important ingredient for managing it. For this to occur, an understanding of the importance and rationale for the regulation of capital is necessary, leading to an understanding of what is consider "adequate" capital. To begin, for a bank, capital serves several purposes.

Absorbs Losses

Banks, and other companies, will have poor performing years. This may result in a financial loss (negative net income). Dependent on the amount of loss, this will reduce the common stock equity (common stock + retained earnings) of the bank. If the bank has considerable common stock equity (capital), it can absorb this loss without putting the bank at risk of failure. Therefore, having capital that is sufficient to anticipate and cover these losses without impairment to the bank allows the bank to regroup and make the changes necessary to correct this situation.

Cushions for Protection Against Risk

The adequacy of the capital can not only absorb losses but also provides protection to customers of the bank who deposit their hard-earned funds in anticipation of growth from interest. The risk to customers is the inability of the bank to pay back the deposit when demanded. Inadequate capital can cause the bank to run out of money to pay its depositors, resulting from a run on the bank. In addition, the level of adequacy maintained protects the FDIC from having to cover the losses that depositors might incur.

Promotes Public Confidence

Banks are public companies, corporations, that people invest in. To continue to grow and raise funds, having appropriate levels of capital helps to create shareholder value and instills confidence in the bank as a trusted financial partner. This is incredibly important for a bank, as this level of confidence is needed for the bank to attract depositors to the bank and for other services. That is a significant part of the funding that banks need to make loans. If confidence is eroded and the bank cannot attract deposits, it will ultimately decline, and likely fail.

Limits Excessive Asset Growth

Understanding how financial statements function is core to this purpose. Capital is a source of funds, and assets are uses of funds. Theoretically, capital provides the budget for capital expenditures and growth; in short, one cannot spend beyond the capital provided without raising additional capital. This provides a "cap" for the expansion of assets. For a bank, lending beyond the limits of what the bank could absorb in losses creates this protection, theoretically.

Reason for Bank Regulation and Supervision

As will be outlined in this chapter, the need for banks to hold a specific amount of capital necessary to absorb losses from times of economic upheaval created the specific thresholds by law. This is preventative and allows banks to continue lending in times of economic downturns to stimulate the economy. Nevertheless, this has created the need for regulation and the intense scrutiny that exists today.

Banks can fail for many reasons. Increased capital and maintenance of adequate levels helps to protect not only the bank but also the economy, but it does not guarantee that banks will not fail. In many ways, like most regulation, this is reactive in nature. The Basel Committee on Banking Supervision was formed for the purpose of focusing on capital as one of the major areas affecting the bank's overall health. This international accord allowed for more universal assessment to (a) limit the amount of bank failures; (b) maintain public confidence and trust in banks; and (c) limit the number of losses that the government may have to absorb as a result.

To accomplish this effectively, it was necessary to define what is considered "adequate" levels of capital and to mandate that these levels be maintained through regulation, universally. In addition, to ensure a functioning economy, maintenance of these levels may be subjected to regular stress tests to ensure that banks can continue to perform in adverse or extremely adverse conditions. Nevertheless, a sound definition of the components that make up "capital" had to be developed to ensure that all adhere to the same basic structure.

Components

To understand what bank capital consists of, the components must be defined. These include the actual capital structure accounts, how they are categorized, and the other attendant elements that create the measurement of adequacy, assets, and risk-weighted assets.

Core Capital

The capital structure of a bank, like that of most corporations, is comprised of both debt capital and equity capital. Within these broad categories, there are further divisions that group all capital structure components into two key divisions, **core capital** and **supplemental capital**. This is also called **Tier 1 capital**. This grouping of capital structure items includes all items that relate to the ownership of the bank from the issuance of common stock and, in general, capital that will be available and will not be paid down. In short, this is more permanent capital and is the foundation value of the bank. Specifically included in this group are:

Common stock and surplus: This is the ownership equity in the bank. These are shares of common stock purchased by investors. Surplus, or "additional paid-in capital" is the amount paid in excess of par value for stock, or at a premium. This, nevertheless, is part of common stock but may be recorded separately as "capital surplus" or "additional paid in capital." Regardless, it is still capital received.

Treasury stock: Treasury stock is common stock that has been repurchased by the bank in the secondary market. This is still considered common stock outstanding, but now the bank owns the stock. Banks and other corporations do this for a variety of reasons, some of which include stock incentive programs for employees, pension benefits, and other incentives.

Retained earnings: For a bank, as defined in Chapter 6, this is called **undivided profit**. Retained earnings are derived from the net income produced by the bank, less dividends paid out to common and preferred shareholders. It is what is retained in the bank to increase the value of the bank and as "internal funding" to be used for major capital expenditures without having to go to the external world for funding.

Qualifying noncumulative perpetual preferred stock: In general, this is preferred stock, which is considered quasi-debt because it is contractual and typically has a maturity. However, this type of preferred stock is a bit different from others. First, "noncumulative" means that the dividends that are required to be paid will not accumulate, in arrears. That is, if the bank is not doing well and cannot make dividend payments that year, they do not accumulate to be paid back later. These start over, fresh, each year with no requirement to pay missed dividends. The "perpetual" nature of these preferred shares places them in the core capital category because they will not mature but will remain outstanding if the bank is in existence. They also can be traded in the secondary market, like common stock.

Minority interests: Minority interests are ownership of stock in the company, common stock. These are isolated to account for those owned by others, as opposed to a parent company. In general, these are seen when there is a parent–subsidiary relationship, whereby the majority is held by the parent under common stock and the remainder by other investors, deemed the minority.

Supplemental Capital

Supplemental capital is also called **Tier 2 capital**. This division of capital is reserved for more of the debt-related types of capital structure and others. These are deemed "supplemental" because they may not exist in perpetuity but have maturities or will change or can change. In this regard, although they are a part of the total capital picture, they are more temporary in nature and may not be counted on for the long term. This is considered less secure than Tier 1 (core) capital because it may be more difficult to liquidate. Components of supplemental capital include:

Allowance for loan losses up to 1.25% of risk-weighted assets: Allowance for loan losses is a contra-account on the balance sheet and writes down the value of the loans (assets) based upon the possibility of loss. Since these are still considered outstanding loans, due to the bank, albeit with the possibility of loss, they could be liquidated (called) to produce funds to absorb losses. These are subject to a limit of 1.25% of risk-weighted assets, however.

Mandatory convertible debt: Mandatory convertible debt could be issued corporate bonds, which are required to be converted to common stock at a specified time. Obviously, once converted it would become a part of core capital, but until then, it is debt. These may be more difficult to liquidate depending on the value of the bank's stock price.

Qualifying preferred stock: This is the preferred stock, which is a hybrid instrument. It will have a maturity date, like a bond, and carries no mandatory conversion requirement prior to its maturity. Funds are available but less available from a liquidation standpoint than core capital. The qualifying nature of these refers to the taxability of the dividends it produces.

Subordinated debt: This is corporate bonds, which are defined by contract (a bond's indenture). These have a fixed maturity date and operate similarly to preferred shares.

These two divisions are the major category used throughout the capital adequacy measurement process and are important to understand.

Risk-Weighted Assets

Risk-weighted assets are the asset values of a bank multiplied by a percentage that indicates the degree of risk associated with the asset. Risk-weighted assets serve as the denominator for the capital adequacy metrics discussed in the last chapter. The reason these have been identified is because not all assets carry risk to the bank; therefore, they should not be included in the calculation (or not fully) for determining the level of capital adequacy. For example, cash is an asset, yet cash carries no risk of loss and therefore should not be included, because it is always available to the bank. On the other hand, loans are extremely risky typically, at the 100% level. They must be included in the denominator. When calculating the capital adequacy ratios, if a bank invests in less risky assets, the denominator will decline, therefore raising their overall capital ratios, which is good for the bank. In this regard, banks must carefully analyze how they invest in assets to avoid major concentrations in asset that carry 100% risk. This diversification of risk helps to improve the capital strength of the bank to absorb losses. Obviously, since banks invest mostly in loan assets, they may balance this by focusing on loan segments that carry less risk, like mortgage loans.

Another area that will increase risk-weighted assets is off–balance sheet items. These must be included and can carry significant risk. From a risk rating standpoint, assets are assigned to five categories of risk, ranging from 0%–100%. Risk assessments for loans are made based upon repayment, but also on the quality and value of the collateral. For that reason, mortgage loans carry less risk because the home is the collateral. Treasury securities held by the bank would carry zero risk because they are highly liquid and backed by the power of the United States government. These risk categories and levels were defined in Basel I and included the following:

- 0% risk: cash, government securities, central bank debt, and other governmental departments and organizations
- 10% risk: central bank debt of countries with high inflation in the recent past
- 20% risk: interbank debt
- 50% risk: residential mortgage debt
- 100% risk: private sector debt; real estate, plant, and equipment debt; capital instruments issued at other banks

Basel

Basel is a city located in Switzerland. It is the home for the **Basel Committee on Bank Supervision (BCBS),** which was formed in 1974. This committee was formed emanating from an international agreement on capital standards. One of the major purposes of the committee was to standardize banking practices throughout the world to ensure that that there was a set of common standards for all countries. This is an important consideration, given the global nature of the economy. The countries included in the Basel Accord are the United States, Belgium, Canada, France, Germany, Italy, Japan, the Netherlands, Spain, Sweden, Switzerland, the United Kingdom, and Luxembourg—in short, the major economic powers of the world. Without a set of common capital standards, impairment of major banks may have an impact on the economies in multiple countries.

As a result of these concerns, three separate agreements and standards have been developed over the years, and another one is in transition. These include Basel I, Basel II, Basel III, and now Basel IV, which is planned for implementation in January 2023. Each set of standards provided more control for various areas of risk that banks in the world face.

Basel I

Basel I established the first set of regulations under the Basel Committee on Bank Supervision (BCBS). The primary goal of Basel I was to minimize credit risk through the establishment of minimum capital requirements.

- year of adoption: 1988
- primary emphasis: capital

- created: Basel I was a landmark in many ways. It developed the original capital standards, many components of which continue to be in use today. Among its many developments included:
  - » original capital standards
  - » divided capital into two primary groups: core capital (Tier 1) and supplemental capital (Tier 2)
  - » defined for use risk-weighted assets and the five levels of risk to classify bank assets
  - » ratio of capital to risk-weighted assets
  - » established market risk as a consideration in addition to capital
- capital standards:

Level	Adequately capitalized
Tier 1 capital ratio	4.0%
Tier 2 capital ratio	4.0%
Total capital ratio	8.0%

- challenges and problems: There were several shortcomings from the first accord. These included the following and paved the way for the develop of Basel II standards.
  - » Other risks were not considered in this initial accord, including liquidity, market, operational, and others.
  - » There was no emphasis on the market value of assets, only the book value.
  - » No attention was given to the differences of banks and their risk profiles.
  - » Banks found ways to bypass these standards, which created more risk in the system, which defeated its purpose.
  - » Inaccurate estimates, on the part of the banks, could lead to excessive risks.

Basel II

Basel II expanded the initial capital requirements established under Basel I. It established additional items and refinements, as it learned from the shortcomings of Basel I. Although these refinements did not occur for 16 years, they established a more focused framework, helping banks to not only understand the standards but also to reduce stress. This occurred through the three-pillar framework, which helped to standardize regulatory variations across countries.

- year of adoption: 2004
- primary emphasis: capital + credit risk
- created: Basel II focused on a gradual phase in and was more sensitive to risk. Specifically, the developments of Basel II included:

- three-pillar framework
  - minimum capital requirements
  - regulatory supervision and assessment of procedures
  - market discipline, through use of disclosure requirements for banks' risk exposure for uses of financial statements
- It considers the credit rating of bank assets in determining risk weights. If a bank has a higher credit rating for the asset, the lower the risk weight for purposes of the capital ratio calculation.
- It divides the bank's capital into three tiers, as opposed to the two in Basel I. The higher the tier, the less debt instruments, such as subordinated debt, are permitted to be included.
  - Tier 1: most strict, shareholder equity + disclosed reserves + retained earnings + innovative capital instruments
  - Tier 2: Tier 1 + various other bank reserves + hybrid instruments + medium- and long-term subordinated loans
  - Tier 3: Tier 2 + short-term subordinated loans

- capital standards:

Level	Adequately capitalized
Tier 1 capital ratio	4.0%
Tier 2 capital ratio	4.0%
Tier 3 capital ratio	8.0%

- challenges and problems: As with Basel I, the BCBS learned that Basel II did not address all levels of risks banks might face, and even though this was a gradual phased-in set of standards, it was preempted by the financial crises of 2008, precipitating the need for a more refined set of standards. Nevertheless, the main shortcomings included:
  - There was no measurement of operational risk.
  - Regulator competence was raised as a shortcoming, especially since this was one of the pillars of Basel II.
  - There was an inability to quantify the various risk exposures into a total risk exposure for a bank.
  - There was concern that smaller banks may be unable to address the risk assessment needs of their banks.

Basel III

In 2008 the global financial crisis was underway. This major upheaval caught most financial institutions off guard and was a true test for Basel II and its predecessor. Although the prior two Basel Accords made effective inroads into the understanding of the strength of banks and what elements were most important to manage them (i.e., capital and credit), they, unfortunately, were inadequate to prevent the financial system and the economy from imploding. Capital standards were designed as a hedge against bank failures, among other things, but as the financial crisis progressed, it became obvious that not only was this ineffective to prevent failures but also that other financial risks needed attention as well, such as bank liquidity. Nevertheless, urgent action was required, and **Basel III** became the replacement for Basel II, preempting its full implementation.

- year of adoption: 2009
- primary emphasis: capital + liquidity
- created: Basel III, like Basel II, required a phase-in period for the increased capital standards required. This gave banks some time to build up the capital such that the requirements themselves did not put smaller banks at risk of failure. Given the imminent knowledge of what was occurring during the global financial crisis, Basel III expanded on and defined a number of requirements designed to, once again, protect the financial sector and to avoid economic upheavals in the future, as was occurring at that time. These focuses included:
    - emphasis on preventative measures to avoid global economic meltdowns
    - defined minimum capital standards, by tiers:
        - Tier 1 as core capital (equity and reserves) that is shown on a bank's financial statements to provide a buffer that permits the bank to continue to operate, considering economic challenges
        - Tier 2 as supplementary capital (unsecured subordinated debt with maturities of at least five years)
        - Total capital was defined as the combination of both Tier 1 and Tier 2 capital, although each carried a separate (not combined) compliance level, as shown in the chart below.
    - defined a phase-in period from 2012–2019
    - segregated banks by size and for the first time identified banks that manage enough of the financial resources in the country to be deemed "systemically important financial institutions" (SIFI) banks. In this regards, these larger banks would be subject to higher capital requirements (surcharges from 1.0%–3.5%) to strengthen them, as they were deemed "too big to fail," which would perpetuate any economic crisis if they could fail. These additional amounts, or **capital buffers**, are conservation buffers for larger banks to provide additional cushions to avoid disruption in operations.
    - introduced the leverage ratio, which was calculated like the Tier 1 ratio, but used total assets, rather than risk-weighted assets, as the denominator. This placed more of a focus on how much money a bank can lend, in relation to its common stock equity or capital. Banks were required to report this at the start of 2015.

- » introduced **prompt corrective action (PCA)** for supervision, which allowed regulators to cite banks for unsafe or unsound practices and require them to have an immediate capital restoration plan. Banks in this category would be precluded from:
  - ▹ paying dividends or other distributions of capital
  - ▹ acquisitions
  - ▹ opening new lines of business
- » Regulators identified banks based upon their level of capitalization in relation to these standards, and to act. The categories of capitalization included (see specific percentages in the tables below):
  - ▹ well capitalized
  - ▹ adequately capitalized
  - ▹ undercapitalized (below adequately capitalized)
  - ▹ significantly undercapitalized
  - ▹ critically undercapitalized
- » introduced liquidity standards for banks to be held to. This required threshold was designed to preclude banks from borrowing too much to meet their needs. The liquidity coverage ratio (LCR) was used for this purpose.

• capital standards (as of full phase-in at 2019):

Level	Adequately capitalized	Well capitalized
CE T1 capital ratio	4.5%	6.5%
Tier 1 capital ratio	6.0%	8.0%
Tier 2 capital ratio	2.0%	2.0%
Total capital ratio	8.0%	10.0%
Leverage ratio	4.0%	5.0%

• capital standards (as of full phase-in in 2019, with conservation buffers):

Level	Adequately capitalized	Well capitalized
CE T1 capital ratio	7.0%	9.0%
Tier 1 capital ratio	8.5%	10.5%
Tier 2 capital ratio	2.0%	2.0%
Total capital ratio	10.5%	12.5%
Leverage ratio	3.0%	4.0%

• liquidity standards (as of 2019):

Level	Threshold
Liquidity coverage ratio (LCR)	100.0%

- challenges and problems: In general, Basel III has been effective in the definition of risks and requirements that banks face, particularly as they were learned during the financial crisis. The introduction of formal **stress tests** and the requirements of Dodd-Frank refined and operationalized many of these standards and have been effective. Banks today are subjected annually to these stress tests, and although portions of Dodd-Frank have been rolled back, banks have generally been able to strengthen and were well prepared for the events that occurred during the 2020 COVID-19 pandemic. Nevertheless, Basel IV has evolved, with new requirements planned.

Basel IV

As indicated, a new Basel accord has emerged, **Basel IV**. New standards have been devised and are planned for implementation in January 2023. Many of these are refinements previously agreed upon but are defined to continue to strengthen the financial sector and continue to prepare for other global economic impacts that may occur in the future.

- year of adoption: 2017
- primary emphasis: capital + leverage ratio + risk weights
- created: The focus of Basel IV is to ensure that bank capital requirements are not reduced too low based upon internal estimates, which is permitted using the **internal ratings-based approach (IRB)** for credit risk. Credit risk involves nonpayment of loans and subsequent loss to the bank. As banks take losses from credit risk, these must be absorbed by the bank through capital. Therefore, refinements through internal estimates can effectively lower capital requirements, and Basel IV provides limitations to this. In addition:
  - » Under the IRB, banks using this approach must categorize exposures in asset classes and develop risk parameter estimates that more specifically estimate the risks. These predictive measures include probability of default (PD), loss given default (LGD), and exposure at default (EAD), as well as maturity (M) for the bank's portfolio. From this, banks can then calculate the risk-weighted assets, which, if lower, could raise their capital ratios. Basel IV provides limits to the reduction in capital that could occur as a result.
  - » a standardized floor of 72.5% for the capital requirement if the bank utilizes the standardized approach, which defines credit risk based upon the external credit rating of the entity involved.
  - » a reduction in the risk weight for low-risk mortgage loans
  - » a higher leverage ratio for globally systemically important banks (G-SIBs) of 50% of the risk-adjusted capital ratio
  - » an increase in disclosure of financial metrics and other reserves
- capital standards: There are no specific changes to the capital ratios defined, and phased in, under Basel III. However, the leverage ratio for G-SIBs will increase by 50% of the risk-adjusted capital ratio. This would likely move this to approximately 9.25% adequate to 10.25% well capitalized.

Level	Adequately capitalized	Well capitalized
CE T1 capital ratio	7.0%	9.0%
Tier 1 capital ratio	8.5%	10.5%
Tier 2 capital ratio	2.0%	2.0%
Total capital ratio	10.5%	12.5%
Leverage ratio	9.25%	10.25%

- liquidity standards:

Level	Threshold
Liquidity coverage ratio (LCR)	100.0%

- challenges and problems: With a phase-in by January 2023, challenges can occur during the interim, although not yet known. These can include the impact from the pandemic of 2020, which is yet to be seen in terms of loan losses resulting from this event. Although different than the financial crisis of 2008, the effects of government intervention (stimulus) are yet to be determined fully.

Ratios

Although the capital ratios, their formulas, and evaluation were included in Chapter 8, they are included here for convenience. Capital ratios are compliance ratios, but certainly can be viewed as performance ratios. The goal is to retain and grow capital through profitability, so in this regard, it can be a measure of strength and successful operations to maintain levels at adequate to well-capitalized levels.

- total capital, or capital adequacy ratio (CAR)
  - » (Tier 1 capital + Tier 2 capital) / Risk-weighted assets = %
- Tier 1 capital ratio
  - » (Tier 1 capital / Risk-weighted assets) = %
- common equity Tier 1 capital (CET1)
  - » (Common equity Tier 1 capital / Risk-weighted assets) = %
- Tier 2 capital ratio
  - » (Tier 2 capital / Risk-weighted assets) = %
- leverage ratio
  - » (Tier 1 capital / Total assets) = %

Management and Compliance

As indicated previously, regulators are required to take prompt corrective action (PCA) if banks become deficient in their capital ratios. Regulators routinely perform safety and soundness exams, at least annually for banks. Using their CAMELS rating system, the "c" relates to capital, and the exam focuses on the bank's current capital ratios. Banks must be compliant; otherwise, they risk heavy scrutiny from the regulators, requiring plans to quickly bring capital to adequate levels, if possible. Dependent upon the degree of capitalization, this may result in the regulators officing in the bank's headquarters and monitoring whether or not the bank can raise the capital to acceptable levels. In the extreme event where this is not possible, the regulator will initiate plans to close the bank and attempt to find a buyer of the bank's loans and deposits, if possible. Any undercapitalized situation (below the adequately capitalized level) is a concern, but how far below will determine whether the bank can recover. Depending upon the urgency of raising capital, there are several methods that banks can employ to raise their capital levels. In many ways, these are the typical means used to increase capital, as a source of funds, when needed, but care must be taken to ensure that the net result is not to leave the bank in such a weakened state that survival will be improbable for the future.

Raising Capital Externally

External sources of attracting and raising capital would be the more immediate and typical means of raising capital, although it does involve obtaining willing participants, which could take time.

Sell common stock: Issuing the bank's common stock is the most typical means of raising capital, albeit not the first priority. When faced with an urgent need to raise capital, this is not typically a stock issue to the public, but more likely the attraction of a significant partner that is willing to put up the capital to salvage the bank. This will involve effort, focusing on already existing shareholders that have a significant stake in the company and want to ensure that the value of their shares does not diminish. In the extreme circumstance where capital cannot be raised and the bank fails, shareholder value will be zero. Shareholders, obviously, are not willing to see their shares (their investment) become worthless, so they may be willing to invest further to help the bank recover and protect their investment. Unfortunately, if the bank has not been performing well in the recent path, shareholders may have already sold their shares to cut their losses. Nevertheless, this is a means of raising capital and will require some convincing on the part of the CEO to do this.

If there is a less urgent need, a stock issue can be appropriate if there is enough demand for the stock and the price is right. Equity capital is of value, as there are no requirements for payment of dividends, like debt, so the only obligation that exists is to create shareholder value through stock appreciation. Unfortunately, in the marketplace, stock issues, in general (for a nonspecific purpose), are viewed as a sort of last resort to raise funds. It can be dilutive to other shareholders and is indicative of the fact that other sources do not exist for the bank due to their credit rating or lack of other avenues of funding. Therefore, this is not the most positive method to use, but it is available.

Selling preferred stock: Another avenue for raising capital is a preferred stock issue. Preferred stock is much like corporate (subordinated) debt and is considered quasi-debt. Unlike common stock, preferred stock is contractual, and dividends are required to be paid, much like interest. The issuance of preferred stock is equity, which is ownership in the bank, although with limited to no voting ability. It does have a higher claim on dividends than common stock and has a higher claim on assets than common stock, in the event of liquidation. This can be attractive to investors, although the fixed dividend itself is also an attractor if the bank is perceived to be stable enough to make payments. Preferred stock can be perpetual or nonperpetual, meaning it will have a maturity. The latter makes this level of funding temporary. Therefore, when raising this type of capital, the time that the capital is needed must be taken into consideration, as these funds will be required to be paid back at some time. For this reason, perpetual preferred stock make be the best direction, albeit with consideration of the dividend expense.

Issuing debt capital: Corporate debt is the issuance of corporate bonds or subordinated (junior) debt. The issuance of debt is part of the capital structure under liabilities, rather than shareholder equity, as the previous two sources were. In this regard, the bank would be obligated to make fixed interest payments regularly per the terms of the bond's indenture (contract). Although this is a definite source, bank debt is rated by the rating agencies. If the bank is struggling financially, their bond ratings may be lower, such that they may be riskier to investors. Nevertheless, this is a source of needed funds that can be obtained; however, there will be floatation costs (underwriting) to issue this, fixed contractual interest payments that must be paid regularly, and the principal must be paid back at maturity. Finally, this would be considered part of Tier 2 capital, supplemental, for the reasons indicated above. Since Tier 2 is part of the total capital ratio, this can help to bring the capital adequacy ratio into compliance. However, it will not have bearing on Tier 1 or common equity Tier 1 capital.

Selling assets and leasing facilities: Another way to ultimately increase capital is to consider selling assets. Assets, or fixed assets, are typically physical facilities. For a bank these include branches and other real estate owned (OREO). The sale of assets will generate cash and reduce fixed assets, an asset transaction. This creates funds for which the bank can use to generate income, pay bills, and make investments. The sale of such assets, in addition, may create gains that are income to the bank, which will have the effect of potentially increasing common stock equity through increasing net income. This may raise the numerator of the capital adequacy ratio and help with capital compliance. Since bank branches are needed to conduct business, the bank may not wish to sell them outright—if owned—if they still need them. An option to address this is to sell the physical property under agreement to lease it back. This is called a sale-leaseback transaction and is a means of unlocking needed funds in physical assets.

Stock for debt securities swaps: The bank could swap common stock for current debt issues to avoid the contractual interest payments and the payback of principal at maturity. This will require incentive on the part of the investors. By swapping these securities, the bank could increase its Tier 1 capital. This would be beneficial to meet Tier 1 and common equity Tier 1 requirements but would have no effect on the total capital ratio, as this includes both Tier 1 and Tier 2 capital. Nevertheless, it may provide benefits to the bank, which may be considered.

Raising Capital Internally

Internal funding is considered "organic," which means that it is generated internally through the operations of the bank. This is always a goal, and if net income is increased, making it positive, it will raise the value of capital. The challenge is that if the bank is not doing well, net income is probably negative and would require additional funding and investments to turn that around. If the bank improves its net income, all or a large portion of this would be "retained" by the bank. This is called "retained earnings," or "undivided profit." If net income is higher and a greater portion retained, this is part of the numerator for both total capital and Tier 1 capital. By increasing the numerator, all else being equal, the capital ratio will go up, which is the goal.

Reduce Risk-Weighted Assets

Another option for banks struggling to raise their capital ratios is the focus on the denominator side of the equation, risk-weighted assets (RWA). Considerations of the amount of risk in the assets that the bank invests in can be a means of producing a higher capital ratio. To do this, the bank can reconsider investing in assets that carry little to no risks. As previously discussed in Basel II and III, assets are classified by risk, and these are defined levels per the Basel Committee on Bank Supervision. The bank could consider reallocating asset investments that are defined to be less risky. By doing this, the total amount of risk-weighted assets will decline and the capital adequacy and Tier 1 ratios for the bank will increase. To consider this, the bank should look specifically to the following:

- investment in government securities: These investments carry zero risk, as the securities are fully backed by the United States government.
- investment in interbank loans: Loans to banks are less risky, given the type of organizations involved. These carry a risk factor of 20%, much less than concentrations in loans.
- types of loans: Most loans will carry a risk factor of 100%, for the most part. However, evaluating the types of debt is a consideration. Potentially, higher concentrations in mortgage

loans could be beneficial, as they carry a risk factor of 50%. This, of course, is going to depend upon the bank's strategy and plans for loans since loans are the major source of revenue.

- risk estimates of loans: Since banks have large concentrations in loans, rather than utilize the risk ratings previously defined, banks can utilize the internal ratings-based approach (IRB) to estimate the risk of specific loan assets based upon more defined metrics and analytics, as well as collateral, which would provide more certainty of recovery and therefore lower the risk factor involved. By lowering the risk factor, with sound logic and metrics, the total risk-weighted assets would ultimately decrease and therefore raise the bank's capital ratio.

Summary

Capital adequacy is a major financial risk and poses an existential risk to the bank. This is both from an inability to cover sustained losses and from a regulatory standpoint. From the latter standpoint, declining capital ratios will get the attention of the regulators in advance, and they will be closely monitoring the bank's actions to rectify the levels. Regardless, continued losses will continue to erode the capital to the point where the bank simply cannot continue to do business and will fail. However, the failure of poorly managed banks, in themselves, will occur and is not the major focus. When many banks across the globe are at risk due to poor management, economic upheavals, or other events, the need for a broader set of standards becomes a necessity. When banks are at risk, they cannot lend money, and when this occurs, the economy will decline. The advent of the Basel Accords through the Basel Committee on Bank Supervision has become a major effort to address this most critical financial risk. Unfortunately, this is not the only existential risk that banks face financially: The next sections will outline two further risks that carry this level of urgency and impact.

Liquidity and Funding the Bank

Liquidity is a need for all organizations. The major emphasis of liquidity is the ability to satisfy current obligations, which is monitored for most organizations using the current ratio. However, for commercial banks liquidity takes on much greater intensity simply because the bank is a reservoir of cash and their products and services are money-based, financial in nature. At a basic level, banks take in cash and pay it out;, therefore, their ability to satisfy these demands for cash, when needed, becomes the definition of liquidity for a bank. A major consideration of this definition is "ready access" to cash. As an example, if a customer were to go to a supermarket to buy food and there was no food or not enough food available, this would be a major problem. Supermarket customers expect access to food whenever it is needed. It is the same concept with banks. Customers expect banks to have cash, and when they go to a bank, they expect to be able to access cash whenever they need it. If it were not available when a customer enters a bank, this would create considerable concern because customers place their money in a bank for safekeeping. This negative event is so egregious that it could cause a run on the bank. A *run* is when there is public panic that the bank does not have the cash and many of the customers immediately go to the bank to obtain their money. When the bank does not have enough cash, it must close its doors, with the likelihood of reopening doubtful. For this reason, banks must be liquid, always, because it is unknown when and how much will be needed from customers throughout the day, every day. This typically is the first indicator that the bank is in trouble.

Sources of Funds

Banks obtain funds from a variety of sources and use these funds to conduct business and manage obligations. To understand bank liquidity, it is necessary to know these sources and uses of funds, in detail. These sources and uses, ultimately, create the cash inflows and cash outflows that the bank must manage to always ensure the liquidity of the bank. Understanding the nature of these will help in the management of a bank because they do occur spontaneously but must be cultivated and managed. This is where the bank's plans, objectives, and strategies play a critical role. The sources of funds available to banks are many. These are liabilities to the bank because they consist of funds given to the bank requiring an obligation of repayment. The primary and secondary sources of these funds are outlined below.

Bank Deposits (Primary Source)

Bank deposits are the largest amount of liabilities on a bank's balance sheet. These represent customer funds that have been given to the bank not only for safekeeping but also to generally receive income, via interest, to grow these balances. This is a cash inflow to the bank, which are subject to withdrawal upon demand. Deposits represents one of the components of the bank's definition, taking deposits subject to withdrawal on demand. Deposits are highly competitive; banks must actively advertise and price deposits effectively to attract them. Once bank deposits are obtained, they must do an effective job of providing services to these customers to retain them. In addition to marketing these products, the bank will have a relatively large retail staff comprised of personal bankers and tellers to obtain and service these accounts. The primary depository accounts fall under the following categories:

- checking accounts: transaction accounts used for making payments. All businesses and consumers need a checking account as the primary source for debit cards, ATM transactions, and writing checks. These are funded by consumer deposits through direct deposit of payroll checks and other receipts. Checking accounts do not typically pay interest, with the exception of NOW and money market accounts.

- savings accounts: These represent more discretionary funds on the part of consumers. They pay interest and are designed to not be used regularly, like checking accounts, but tend to remain relatively constant.
- time deposit accounts: Time deposits are interest-bearing accounts that are usually for specific terms, as with certificates of deposit (CDs) and individual retirement accounts (IRAs). These deposits pay higher interest rates and are more investment-related than the other two and are relatively stable for periods of time.

Nondeposit (Secondary Source)

Since bank deposits are highly competitive and must be priced and marketed effectively to be obtained, banks must also have back-up sources of funding that are less dependent upon the competition. These funding sources provide a cushion for the bank to meet their needs and objectives. The sources of these funds will come from both the money market (short term) and from the capital markets (long term). Additionally, secondary sources are more readily attainable or more within the control of the bank and are generally not subject to withdrawal upon demand. These include:

Interbank deposits: These are borrowings from other banks in the federal funds market, using excess reserves on a relatively temporary basis. Banks will cultivate and establish relationships with other banks for these reasons. By making loans to other banks, relationships are built that, when needed, the bank can utilize to raise funds. These relationships are typically with upstream correspondent banks. These borrowings can be very short term or longer, including:

- overnight loans: returned within 24 hours
- term loans: longer term for specified terms of several days, weeks, or months
- continuing loans: These are autorenewable loans with correspondent banks.

Repurchase agreements: These are a temporary type of borrowing. In this case the bank will sell government securities owned to another bank. This is on a temporary basis for a specified term, whereby the selling bank agrees to buy the securities back at the end of the term. Interest is charged to the selling banking for the term the funds are used.

Central bank borrowings: These are borrowings from the Federal Reserve bank's discount window. These are high-interest-rate loans and are generally used as a last resort. The types of available include:

- primary credit: short term to banks with solid financial positions. The rates are a bit higher than the federal funds rate.

- secondary credit: higher interest loans for banks not qualifying for primary credit
- seasonal credit: generally, for longer periods of time, to meet seasonal needs of small- and medium-sized banks.

Federal home loan bank loans (FHLB): These are borrowings from a government-sponsored entity (GSE). Advances can be obtained from this entity by utilizing home mortgages as collateral. There are 11 regional FHLBs in the country. This is an excellent source of immediate funds and is highly desirable to cultivate and build a relationship with. Advances can be short term to long term.

Banker's acceptances: These are items that are purchased by businesses to provide a guarantee of payment at a specified date or maturity. Banks receive the funds for the banker's acceptance and ultimately will pay this to the party to whom it is intended. These are liabilities to the bank until paid, but it is a source of funding for a short-term period, usually between one and six months. In a sense, this is like the purchase of a cashier's check where funds are given to the bank for the check and then the check is given to the payee. The bank guarantees the payment.

Commercial paper: This is another short-term money market instrument. It is unsecured and pays a fixed rate of interest. It is issued by banks and large corporations to raise temporary funds. This is a quicker and less complex way to raise temporary funds without having to raise more traditional funds. It is often issued at a discount, and both principal and interest are paid at maturity.

Negotiable CDs: These are also known as "jumbo CDs" and have a minimum face value of $100,000. Maturities are short term, withing a few weeks to one year. These are not repaid until maturity.

Eurocurrency deposits: These are funds held by banks as deposits from depositors outside the country. These again are short-term to medium-term funding for the bank and escape reserve requirements and other interest rate obligations.

Floating rate notes: Floating rates notes are variable rate short-term bonds issued by banks. Interest is tied to benchmark rates, such as the federal funds rate or other benchmark rates. These can be advantageous to banks dependent upon the direction of the variable rate. Nevertheless, these are others instruments for raising funds.

Subordinated debt: Subordinated debt are corporate bonds. Debt instruments in the capital structure scheme is debt and can carry maturities of medium to long term. Interest is fixed by contract (indenture) and is subordinate to other instruments in the liquidation process. Nevertheless, interest must be paid and is an obligation of the bank.

Equity issues: Finally, banks can create stock issues, common and preferred stock. These are long-term instruments and are part of shareholder equity. In the case of preferred stock, dividends generally must be paid by contract and may or may not have maturities. Common stock, on the other hand, can pay dividends, but it is not required, so there is less of an obligation on the bank's part. These generally are last resort funding sources, particularly for common stock, as they can be dilutive to existing shareholders. Costs will be incurred for underwriting to issue these instruments.

Uses of Funds

Banks use the funding they receive from the liabilities identified previously for a variety of reasons. These generally relate to cash movement and are focused in two key areas.

Making Loans (Primary Use)

A bank's major purpose is to make loans. This represents the largest of the bank assets. When a bank makes a loan, it must payout, in cash, the loan amount to the borrower for their specific needs. Therefore, the bank must have the cash to do this, which comes primarily from the deposits received, among others. These loans will be in a variety of segments, which will include both business (commercial) loans and consumer loans, consisting of:

- commercial and industrial loans
- real estate construction
- agribusiness loans
- consumer installment loans
- credit cards
- residential mortgage loans

Satisfying Current Obligations

Cash is used to "satisfy" a variety of needs. These generally involve obligations or demands that the bank must address. These are typical obligations that are necessary to run a business, but since the bank deals in cash, they will involve a variety of other uses, including:

- paying salaries
- paying bills
- meeting withdrawal requests of depositors
- paying interest
- paying dividends

Liquidity Position

Understanding the components of the liquidity needs of the bank is paramount to understanding the nature of this risk, so much so that Basel III has developed a required threshold. The liquidity position is relatively simple to determine but must be managed very frequently. Banks are in the business of money; therefore, cash is flowing in and out of the bank every day, every hour, and every minute. Maintaining a positive liquidity position is therefore the goal, and this can only be closely monitored with sophisticated software systems so that the liquidity position and potential demands can be seen and addressed quickly. Often, banks will maintain a liquidity cushion, levels beyond which will trigger action.

Liquidity is based upon cash flows: cash inflows and cash outflows. It is the difference between these two that results in the **net liquidity position**. This is the sum of the sources of cash minus the uses of cash, as indicated in Table 12.1.

Table 12.1 **Net Liquidity Position Calculation**

	Sum of supplies of cash
-	Sum of demands for cash
=	Net liquidity position

To understand this simplistic formula, an understanding of the "supplies" of cash and the "demands" for cash is required. Keeping in mind that these all represent cash inflows and cash outflows that occur frequently.

Demands for Cash

Demands for cash occur frequently for banks. These occur predominantly from cash outflows. These include:

- withdrawal of funds from customer deposits
- loan proceeds paid to customers from loans made to customers
- repayment of nondeposit borrowings (e.g., FHLB, commercial paper, etc.)
- expenses paid for operations, including taxes, salaries, and so on
- dividends paid to shareholders
- interest paid on deposits and other borrowings

Supplies of Cash

Supplies of cash occur regularly as well. These are cash inflows and result from a variety of transactions, as follows:

- deposited funds from customers for checking, savings, and time deposits
- revenues from the sale of nondeposit services
- loan payments from borrowers (principal plus interest)
- sale of bank assets (physical properties)

- borrowings from the money market
- borrowings from other banks and the central bank

These supplies and demands of cash occur throughout the day. To effectively manage the liquidity position, the bank must be able to project or anticipate these supplies and demands of cash. Given the appropriate software, projections can be easily made from the bank's historical patterns. This forms the basis for developing an optimal cushion, which requires effective management and monitoring techniques.

The most significant challenge in understanding the net liquidity position is to be able to identify supplies of cash from demands for cash. This is determined by analyzing the transaction and determining whether it is a cash inflow or a cash outflow. This is best illustrated in the example below.

Example 12.1 Net Liquidity Position

Assume that a local regional bank has recorded the following transactions during a given period. What is the bank's net liquidity position?

- deposits received of $25 million
- loan payments received of $5 million
- nondeposit service payments of $15 million
- dividend payment of $8 million
- withdrawals from deposits of $12 million
- sold 3 branches for $10 million
- new loans made included $25 million

Solution:

Supplies of cash

- deposits received = $45 million
- loan payments received = $15 million
- sold 3 branches = $10 million
- TOTAL SUPPLIES OF CASH = $70 million

Demands for cash

- nondeposit service payments = $15 million
- dividend payments made = $8 million
- withdrawals from deposits = $12 million
- new loans made = $25 million
- TOTAL DEMANDS OF CASH = $60 million

NET LIQUIDITY POSITION = **$10 million**

As illustrated, the bank is liquid, at the amount of $10 million. However, this is not static and will change very quickly; therefore, the bank must have the tools to plan for this.

Management Techniques

Managing liquidity requires careful monitoring. Although the basics are relatively simple, the goal is to always know the liquidity position of the bank at any point in time and to plan for changes. Although there are many ways to manage liquidity effectively, there are two techniques that are highlighted to demonstrate how this can be monitored: the sources and uses approach and the structure of funds approach.

Source of Funds Approach

The **source of funds approach** focuses on forecasting anticipated loans and deposits for a given period. Deposits are liabilities and represent sources of funds, while loans are assets and are uses of funds. Although this does not account for all cash inflows and outflows, the concept addresses the vast majority of these because of the magnitude of deposits and loans.

Banks plan and therefore have a good idea of what anticipated loans and deposits will be over a future period. This could be determined based upon historical results but also based upon planned objectives for new business.

Table 12.2 **Sources and Uses Approach**

1. Estimate the amount of deposits anticipated over a period (e.g., 6 months), month by month.
2. Estimate the amount of loans anticipated over the same period, month by month.
3. Determine the change in each from the prior month (+/−).
   a. If deposits increase, this is a source of funds (+), and if they decrease, this is a use of funds (−).
   b. If loans increase, this is use of funds (−), and if they decrease, this is a source of funds (+).
4. Add the sources of funds and uses of funds and determine the liquidity "deficit" or "surplus."

This approach provides the estimates necessary for planning liquidity. If liquidity deficits are indicated, the bank can plan appropriate funding levels to ensure that a positive liquidity position is available.

Structure of Funds Approach

The second approach that could be used focuses on percentages rather than estimating changes in loans and deposits. Under this approach, deposits and other sources of funds are categorized into three groupings, based upon what percentage will leave the bank. Once this is determined, the bank can anticipate and project the amount of funding it will need to make up for the attrition and apply this against the other demands for cash. Although this approach can be used, it must be based upon the historical patterns of the bank's accounts, and then tracked for accuracy.

Hot money: Hot money is made up of liabilities (deposits) that are considered volatile—that is, they do not have loyalty and will leave the bank. Hot money is extremely volatile, and customers in this category will shop rates and move frequently. Certificates of deposit can be a good example of accounts in this area, where rates can be most competitive. Deposits in this category can be quite high—up to 95%. In determining the optimum balance of deposits that will remain, the number of deposits in this category would be multiplied by 1%–95%.

Vulnerable funds: These funds are also volatile but not as much as hot money. Like hot money, a percentage is determined of the amount that will leave the bank. Again, the bank would need to determine this, but it could be as much as 30% of these funds.

Stable funds: The last category represents the most loyal funds. This grouping would fall under the category of "core" deposits. These are deposits that typically do not move and can be counted on. Although this is the case, some fallout does occur in this areas, so an assumption of 15% could be applied.

Making the calculation based upon the percentages for the types of deposits determined and then summing the results will indicate the number of deposits that can be counted upon. From this the bank can then estimate its cash outflow needs and determine whether there will be a deficit or surplus of liquidity.

Measurement

Measuring liquidity involves two primary ratios to measure the level of risk. Both metrics have been outlined in Chapter 8, but the formulas are included here for convenience. Both metrics are utilized under Basel III, and both require a result of 100% or greater.

Liquidity Coverage Ratio (LCR)

(High-quality liquid assets / Net cash outflows) = %

- high-quality liquid assets
  - cash
  - government securities (treasuries)
  - other "marketable" securities
- net cash outflows
  - (Cash outflows – Cash inflows); cash inflows are capped at 75% of cash outflows.

- cash outflows: These are the liabilities of the bank. Cash outflows from the liabilities represents the following activities:
  - withdrawals from deposit accounts (savings, checking, and time deposits)
  - checks written and paid against checking accounts
  - interest payments on interest-bearing deposit accounts
  - interest payment on debt instruments (subordinated debt and notes)
  - dividend payments on preferred and common stock
  - interest payments on borrowings from other banks
  - interest payments on borrowings from the central bank
  - interest payments on securities sold under agreement to repurchase (REPOs)
  - payments made for taxes due
- cash inflows: These are assets of the bank, excluding high-quality liquid assets, previously mentioned. Cash inflows emanate from the assets of the bank from the following activities:
  - loan payments received from borrowers (including interest payments)
  - interest payments received on investments (Treasury securities and others)
  - interest payments received from money loaned to other banks
  - interest earned on the purchase of securities held for repurchase (reverse REPOs)
  - other cash received from the sale of fixed assets

Net Stable Funding Ratio

(Available stable funds / Required stable funds) = %

- available stable funds: These represent sources of funds for the bank.
  - due to other banks
  - due to customers
  - debt securities
  - subordinated debt
  - equity capital
  - preferred stock
- required stable funds: Required stable funds are those funds needed to support fewer liquid assets.
  - cash and marketable securities
  - due from other banks
  - loans to customers
  - marketable securities
  - corporate bonds

Reserve Requirement

One cannot discuss bank liquidity without discussing the reserve requirement. The reserve requirement is an imposed maintenance balance by the Federal Reserve system that all member banks must adhere to. The reserve requirement originated with the Federal Reserve Act of 1913. This act required banks to hold a percentage of deposits, in reserve, at the Federal Reserve without the ability to use the funds. In this regard, when determining optimal liquidity for the bank, banks must first ensure that they are meeting reserve requirements; otherwise, they would be in violation of the act. However, the funds are included in the calculation of liquidity but cannot be used.

The reserve requirement is designed to promote safety in that these are earmarked funds that would only be used in an emergency to cover excess customer withdrawals. It is also a tool of the Federal Reserve system to raise or lower the money supply in the economy. Over the years the thresholds and amounts have changed but remain a key requirement of the Federal Reserve system. Banks must actively manage this amount, which is called the **money position** of the bank. The role of money position manager requires that enough reserve be maintained regularly in accordance with the requirements but also to ensure that an excess is not maintained but rather the minimum requirement, so that all excess funds are invested at the higher rates of return.

Components

The components of the reserve requirement begin with the percentage of deposit accounts (dollar amount) that must be maintained. The following is the type of accounts involved in the calculation.

- included: transaction deposits (checking, NOW, and money market accounts)
- excluded: nontransaction reservable liabilities (nonpersonal time deposits, eurocurrency liabilities)

Although these funds cannot be used by the bank, they do earn interest. This began in 2008 and is generally paid at the upper level of the federal funds rate. However, like required capital, these funds are not available for usage by the bank for other investment purposes.

Calculation

Since balances on the bank's books change frequently and since a fixed amount must be maintained, how the balance is to be determined was defined through **lagged reserve accounting (LRA)**. This approach consisted of two periods in the process of determining the balance, the **reserve computation period** and the **reserve maintenance period.**

Reserve computation period: This first part computes the amount to be held in reserve. This is accomplished by determining the average amount of transaction deposits, including vault cash, over a two-week period. The two-week period begins on a Tuesday and ends on the Monday two weeks later, or 14 days. Once the balance is determined, the percentages defined in the formula outlined in the next section produce the amount to be held.

Reserve maintenance period: The amount determined must then be maintained, on reserve, at the Fed for a 14-day period, following the reserve computation period, which will take place from Thursday to the Wednesday two weeks later. In this way a static amount is held over this two-week period and does not fluctuate until the next reserve computation period recalculates the new amount. Therefore, the reserve amount is recalculated 26 times per year for all member banks, determined by the money manager at the bank.

Formula

Finally, a formula has been derived for use during the reserve computation period. This formula is based upon bank size thresholds and defines the percentages of transaction deposits required. The result of this formula is known as the "legal reserve requirement." This becomes the amount, net of the average amount of vault cash, that is the required to be held at the Federal Reserve. The formula for this calculation is included in Table 12.3. Although this is a tool used by the Federal Reserve to affect the money supply, the percentages are not frequently changed, although they could be. However, the threshold levels do change regularly, and those shown in Table 12.3 are the latest from 2020.

Table 12.3 **Reserve Requirement Calculation**

Net transaction accounts (millions)	**% Requirement to be reserved**
$0 to $16.9 x	0%
+ $16.9 to $127.5 x	3%
+ More than $127.5 x	10%
= Legal reserve requirement	
· Average vault cash	
= Required amount to be maintained at the Fed	

Clearing Balances

In addition to reserves, banks can also hold additional amounts at the Fed. These additional amounts can earn credit from the Fed and can be used to pay for services that the member bank obtains from the Fed. Services might include usage of Fedwire, the Fed's wire transfer system; automated clearing house; and other services used and to cover checks or debit items drawn against them. Some banks will do this if they are regular users of the services.

These credits are calculated based upon the amount of money maintained in the clearing balance held in the two-week reserve maintenance period. The formula for this calculation is contained in Table 12.4.

Table 12.4 **Clearing Balance Credit Calculation**

Average clearing balance
× Federal funds rate
× 14/360
= Credits

Summary

Liquidity is one of the most important financial risks a bank can face. As indicated, a run on a bank is an event that is feared universally throughout the banking industry. Banks never want to be in a situation where they cannot manage withdrawals and ultimately must close their doors. This has tremendous negative reputational risk for the bank, as the trust in the bank would be immediately eroded. To avoid this and ensure adequate amounts, bank staff will develop liquidity cushions that are closely monitored daily such that anything close to the cushion threshold will result in immediate action. Today, with the technology and systems available, banks can monitor their historical patterns and continue to hone the cushions so that they effectively ensure against a crisis. Liquidity is part of the regular agenda of the asset liability committee of the bank so that it gets high-level attention on a regular basis, and of course, it is now part of the regulatory requirements for liquidity coverage and net stable funding ratios, as defined by Basel III.

Interest Sensitivity

The last of the financial risks is that which results from the usage of interest rates. It is well known that banks are affected by and use interest rates as a major part of their business. Interest, technically, is the cost of money, and it changes on a regular basis. All interest rates are affected by changes in the federal funds rate, which is one of the monetary policy tools the Fed uses to manage the economy. Since banks rely on interest rates to produce revenue to the bank and as one of their major expenses, fluctuations, or movements, in these rates create the financial risk to the bank—the definition of interest rate risk. Banks, more than others, are most sensitive to fluctuations in interest rates. When the Fed lowers interest rates, the bank will lose revenue, which, unless made up elsewhere, will reduce the bottom-line net income of the bank. Of course, the opposite can occur in a rising rate environment. The challenge, and the risk, is to attempt to forecast what interest rates will do in the future.

Interest rate fluctuations can have a significant impact on the banks in terms of net income, the market value of trading accounts, impact on other sources of income and expenses, and, ultimately, the economic value of the bank. Therefore, this is another major financial risk area that is a regular topic of discussion in the asset and liability committee of the bank. When banks formulate their annual budgets, they begin with a sales forecast. This forecast will project the amount of revenue the bank will generate from interest income; therefore, understanding what interest rates are likely to do becomes an important consideration.

This last section in the chapter will highlight how banks attempt to forecast interest rates, manage interest rates, and mitigate the risks attendant to interest rate risk.

Understanding Interest Rates

Most individuals understand interest rates at a basic level, from the rate that is quoted, and paid, on a loan or interest paid to the individual from a savings account. Although, interest rates are percentages that are applied to loans and deposits, in general, to produce the cost or earnings that will be generated and accrue to the bank or individual, they nevertheless are the price of credit. Credit refers to loans, or borrowing, and for any extension of credit, whether to a consumer via a loan or to the bank via deposits, it is the price that will be paid, or compensation, for the usage of these funds. Sometimes interest rates have negative connotations, as can been seen all throughout history. This is known as **usury**. This is the practice of charging unusually high interest rates, beyond the norm, to enrich the lender unfairly. In most cases, and certainly in the United States, the Fed and the marketplace will keep interest rates, generally, within reason due to competition and free enterprise. However, perceptions of interest rates can be negative, and banks may be the brunt of these negative perceptions because they are the ones charging these interest rates, even though the Fed controls these through monetary policy, which is not widely understood by the populace. Nevertheless, interest rates are the lifeblood of the bank and can make the difference of remaining in business or not—hence, the risk.

Banks will be sensitive to interest rate fluctuations in different ways. This will be based upon the composition and balances in assets and liabilities on their balance sheets. Therefore, to effectively manage the risks attendant to interest rates, banks must understand their sensitivity.

Language and Components of Interest Rates

Typically, interest rates are spoken of as percentages, with at least two decimals. The increase or decrease of interest rates, however, is spoken of in **basis points (BPS)**. Basis points are an easy way to clearly discuss the level of change in interest rates. A basis point is the equivalent of 1/100th of a percentage point, or .01%. This is the equivalent of 1 basis point. So if interest rates are at 3.25% and increase by 1 basis point, the new rate would be 3.26%. Obviously, this is not a significant change, but when there is a 100-basis point increase, that is significant. Using the last example, if rates are presently at 3.26%, this

100-point increase will result in a new rate of 4.26%, a large jump. As another example, the Federal Reserve has recently moved the federal funds rate in 25 basis point increments, up or down, moving from 1.00% to .75%, to .50%, to .25%.

Components

Most of us are familiar with what is called the "stated rate." This is typically what is quoted to us when we are attempting to obtain a car loan, a student loan, or other type of loans. This is also called the **nominal rate**. However, interest rates, as will be discussed more fully in later chapters, are built based upon a base rate with added premiums. The components and determination of the interest rates are made up of these components.

Risk-free real rate of interest: The actual risk-free rate of interest is calculated at the nominal rate of interest minus the inflation rate (Nominal rate – Inflation rate). The meaning of risk-free real rate of interest is somewhat theoretical, but it is the minimum return an investor would demand, with no inflation and no risk. Since this is not the real world, it becomes more theoretical, but it does establish the foundation for interest rates.

As a way to determine what is considered the risk-free real rate of interest, it is suggested that the appropriate current U.S. Treasury rate that conforms to the duration of the investment be used. This would be the nominal rate. For example, if this were an investment that had a duration of 10 years, the U.S. Treasury note rate could be used as the nominal rate. If, for example, this was 1%, then the risk-free real rate of interest would be 1% because zero inflation is the premise for the real rate of interest and risk-free, which is U.S. treasuries. Therefore, this is the return investors would demand for their investments, at a minimum.

Risk premiums: In the construction of interest rates, risk premiums are then added to the risk-free real rate of interest to compensate for added risk. These premiums are determined in basis points and are added to this rate. Some of the more prominent risk premiums include:

- default risk: Higher risk borrowers, based upon analysis of their credit worthiness, would pay more to obtain the loan, presumably because they carry more risk.
- inflation risk: In the likelihood, based upon analysis, that inflation will occur, a premium may be added to compensate for movement in inflation and therefore more costs.
- maturity risk: This is also called "term" risk. The longer the term of the loan, the greater the risk to the lender; therefore, more compensation would be required to compensate for this risk.

Managing Interest Rates

Banks live by interest rates, and for that reason, they are continually focused on what rates are doing in the marketplace. This is a critical function and involves many parts in truly managing interest rates. Understanding each of the following will provide a sound basis for managing interest rates for the bank. These include four areas:

- asset/liability committee oversight
- strategies for asset/liability management
- forecasting interest rates
- determining the interest sensitivity of the bank

Asset/Liability Committee Oversight

The asset/liability committee (ALCO) of the bank is one of the critical management committees that all banks have. This committee meets on a frequent basis and is comprised of the CEO, chief financial officer, chief lending officer, chief retail officer, and potentially others. The purpose of this committee is to focus on the assets and liabilities of the bank, as they relate to the generation of interest income, the payment of interest expense, the funding needs and liquidity of the bank, and the levels of capital maintained at the bank—in short, financial risk. As it relates to interest sensitivity and risk, the committee is continually monitoring interest rate forecasts and fluctuations and how they are impacting bank profitability. When fluctuations occur, or economic upheavals, changes will have to be made in terms of positioning assets and liabilities to put the bank in the best position possible given these fluctuations. The committee also monitors the level of sensitivity of the bank is and what strategies will be deployed to compensate for this. Overall, this committee is a dynamic and action-oriented committee and must be prepared to make decisions as the environment changes. The frequency of meeting and timeliness and quality of decisions will be instrumental in the management of interest rates.

Yield Curves and Forecasting Interest Rates

Each year, the bank will begin their planning process by forecasting their sales, or revenues. For a bank, this is predominantly interest income. In order for the bank to budget effectively, they must understand the direction of interest rates. The asset/liability committee will also need to understand that and to monitor this for making effective decisions throughout the year. A critical tool to help with this understanding is the **yield curve** or **term structure of interest rates**. This tool provides bankers with a glimpse of the future of interest rates and inflation rates and investor expectations about the economy and their related decisions. The yield curve is a graphical depiction of the direction of inflation and interest rates. The yield curve is made up of several components, and it is important to understand how to read it.

Debt security composition: The chart utilizes debt instruments that have a similar risk profile so that they can be easily compared and decisions can be made. Good examples of securities to use would be U.S. Treasury securities. Treasury securities consist of short-term T-bills, medium-term T-notes and long-term T-bonds and therefore are good candidates. However, other similar, related short-, medium-, and long-term corporate bond issues would be effective as well.

Relationship between interest rates and maturity: The yield curve plots the maturity (term) of the debt security against its yield at each maturity interval, for a specified time. It is the relationship between the yield and the maturity that will dictate the shape of the curve.

Yield to maturity: The curve is based upon yields. Yields are determined as the "yield to maturity" (YTM) at that point in time of the security based upon its maturity. Yield to maturity is the discount rate that equates the current sales price with the expected future cash flows for its maturity. Cash flows are based upon the coupon rate paid on the bond, and the term is the remaining amount of time to maturity. Yield to maturity is equal to the cost of debt and the market rate of comparable bonds; therefore, this is an effective assessment of the return anticipated from the specified security. When YTM is higher, the price of the bond is sold at a discount (less than par value) because the coupon rate is likely lower than the going market rate of interest, so the market will not buy the security because they will receive less of a cash flow, so it must be sold at a discount. This will create a higher yield because if the bond is sold below par, at maturity the par value will be paid, along with interest throughout the remaining term, enhancing the yield.

Point in time assessment: Yields are plotted at a specified time. This is a specific day so that it can be compared with other dates.

An example of a yield curve is shown in Figure 12.1.

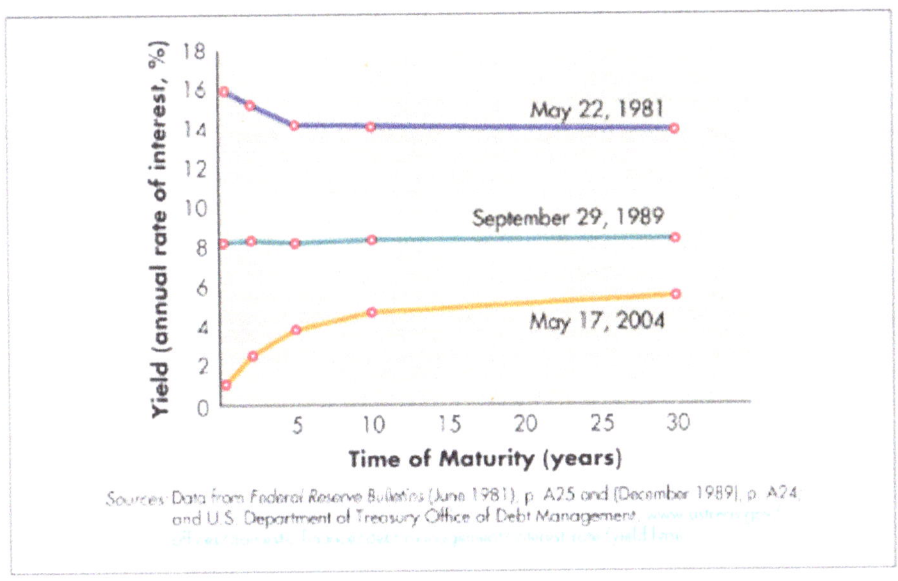

FIGURE 12.1 Yield Curve

Understanding and Interpreting the Yield Curve

Having discussed the components, it is important to analyze and interpret the yield curve itself. Once yields are plotted, for a specific point in time, a line can be drawn to plot the yields in relation to the maturity for the security. Once this is plotted, a specific direction, or slope, can be determined. Looking at Figure 12.1, three different slopes are illustrated, at three different points in time. Each slope direction is meaningful and provides an expectation of the future.

Upward sloping: This is a normal curve, the characteristics of which include:

- Longer term rates are higher than shorter term rates. This is indicative of the fact that there is more perceived risk in longer term securities, which would reflect a normal conclusion.
- This reflects expectations of higher interest rates and higher inflation. The reason for this is that investors are demanding higher returns for longer terms to compensate for the risk, but they are optimistic about the future, anticipating that rates will go up. This usually occurs when inflation is rising, which will drive down the price of the security, but the overall yield increases in return.

Downward sloping: This is an abnormal/inverted curve. Characteristics of this direction include:

- Inflation is declining. As inflation drops, interest rates will decline to stimulate the economy.
- This is a more pessimistic view, indicating signs of recession or economic decline. Therefore, yields on maturities will decline, as securities are sold at premiums due to the falling interest rates. The expectation is that the economy is slowing down.

Flat: This is a flat curve. There is no slope; therefore, there is no change in yields from short term to long term. Characteristics include:

- Short-term yields remain the same as long-term yields, indicating interest rates are stable (no increases of decreases), and the same holds true for inflation (i.e., status quo).
- This is neither optimism nor pessimism. In this regard, there are no expectations about future changes or changes to the economy. It is stable.

Impact to Banks

The yield curve is an important tool for bankers, especially since they deal in interest rates. However, to truly understand the impact of the yield curve evaluation from a banker's perspective, it is necessary to put it into the language that bankers and others will relate to.

Relationship to interest rates: Although the slope of the curve provides expectations of the economy, and inflation, the curve provides an assessment related to profitability. This relationship is the spread, or the difference, between long-term and short-term interest rates.

This will have a relationship to the net interest margin, or the degree of profitability from the lending process. Further:

- long-term rates: apply to loans and securities, which generated interest income for the bank
- short-term rates: apply to deposits, which generate "interest expense" for the bank

The difference between these two is net interest income.

Relationship to the slope of the curve: Since short-term rates relate to interest expense and long-term rates to interest income, the distance between these two provides a sense of the potential margin of profitability, dependent upon the direction of the curve.

- upward sloping curve: Long-term rates are higher than short term, indicating a higher profitability margin since long-term rates relate to interest income and short-term to deposits.
- downward sloping curve: Short-term rates (interest expense) are higher than long-term rates (interest income), indicating a lower margin and the potential for less profitability.

Relationship to the net interest margin ratio: As discussed in Chapter 8, the net interest margin ratio is one of the primary metrics used to assess profitability for a bank. This is the difference between interest income and interest expense in relation to total assets. The goal is for this to be positive and increase over time. Dependent upon the shape of the curve, this can be an indicator of profitability for the future and may require banks to plan different strategies to address what they see.

- upward sloping curve: Positive net interest margin, profitability, interest income (long-term rates) exceeds interest expense (short-term rates). The degree of difference between these two will raise or lower the net interest margin.
- downward sloping curve: Negative net interest margin, loss in profitability, interest expense (short-term rates) exceeds interest income (long term rates). The bank will need to plan for other means of revenue production (fee income) and/or reduce expenses.
- flat curve: Neutral, interest income (long-term rates) equal interest expense (short-term rates)—therefore, break-even. Since this would produce no net interest income, as with the downward slope, the banks should be planning a focus toward other avenues of revenue generation and/or expense reduction. Since this represents the status quo, the outlook is stable, but there is no margin for profitability.

The goal for bankers is to interpret what the yield curve is telling them. This provides an "outlook" or environment in which they will be operating. Since banks have a variety of products that pay or receive interest, they are diversified enough that the curves indicated above are not an absolute prediction of what will happen to the bank, but more an indicator of the environment. From this information, the bank can develop their strategy, armed with this information based upon the outlook. For this reason, yield curves are very telling to bankers and help them to be able to hone their plans to accommodate the future.

Strategies for Asset/Liability Management

How to manage fluctuations and environment changes results from strategies that the bank has adopted for implementation. Three basic strategies exist or have been employed by banks to manage interest sensitivity. These strategies will dictate the action plans necessary to respond to situations based upon this orientation. These strategies include

- asset-focused strategy
- liability-focused strategy
- funds-focused strategy (Rose & Hudgins, 2013)

Asset-Focused Strategy

Assets are the source for generating revenue for the bank. These must be managed and forecasted during the planning process and are deemed to be within the control of management. For example, the growth of loans, which is a major asset, is a function of well-trained staff (commercial lenders), tools, support staff, and communication. The presumption is that management will establish a forecast (objective) for the growth of loans at the end of the year and that this is controllable and will likely be attained. In contrast, management does not believe they can control the growth of deposits and that this falls under the marketplace and competition and outside of their control. Therefore, less attention is placed on the deposit generation side (liabilities) and more on asset side. With more emphasis on assets, the bank drives the growth of the bank more proactively, with the belief that they can control these effectively. However, with less emphasis on the deposit or liability side, growth objectives may be curtailed if funding is not well managed and deemed to be outside of their control. This could create more risk of nonachievement if the funding is not achieved from deposits or other liabilities, which creates more uncertainty.

Liability-Focused Strategy

In contrast to the asset-focused strategy, this strategy focuses more on funding and deposit generation, with the belief that these can be controlled through monitoring growth, volumes, the marketplace and competition, and other measures that will allow them to actively control the growth of funding. Liquidity and funding are a critical objective of the bank and the major source of funding for loans. For this reason, an emphasis is placed on the liability side as the priority for management. This does not mean that assets are not controlled or anticipated; they are, but to a lesser degree. This would indicate a more acute need to make sure the bank is well funded and can provide the necessary funds for making loans. Therefore, loans could grow to the extent that the bank provides the funding, rather than leading with the loan objective at the onset. Although this strategy is important for achieving the funding needs of the bank, it may create more risk on the achievement of revenue needs of the bank from asset growth.

Funds-Focused Strategy

This is a balanced strategy and focuses on both assets and liabilities, equally, as manageable and controllable. This strategy tends to mitigate the risks on either side of the balance sheet by balancing the focus. In so doing, management can not only forecast growth but can also temper this growth by what they believe they can achieve in funding. This more equitable strategy helps to manage more realistically what is controllable and reduce the risks that may occur on either side. Liabilities are not only funding sources for loan growth but can also generate interest expense, so these considerations must be understood in tandem. Assets are revenue source, but unrealistic objectives cannot be achieved without the underlying funding. Therefore, to achieve a more realistic result, the balanced strategy would presumably reduce the risk attendant to an overemphasis on assets or liabilities management.

It is clear from these strategies that banks must actively manage their assets and liabilities to ensure the performance desired. Since both liabilities and assets are affected by interest rate fluctuations, it is necessary to understand the ramifications of these fluctuations. This depends on the direction of the interest rate fluctuations (up or down) and the concentrations of assets and liabilities and whether the interest rates involved are fixed or variable. This sensitivity is crucial to the bank's ability to determine what must be done.

Measuring the Bank's Sensitivity to Interest Rates

With the backdrop of the prior sections on managing and understanding interest rates, the bank must now look to see where their exposure lies regarding interest rates. As indicated previously, the yield curve provides a direction or insights of the direction of rates and expectations for the economy. Since banks are very much focused on their net interest margins, they must understand where their sensitivity to interest rates lie.

To accomplish this, the bank's assets and liabilities are assessed. Both assets and liabilities are affected by interest rate fluctuations. Assets generate the bulk of the revenue from interest income, and liabilities generate the largest portion of expense from interest expense. Each asset and liability may or may not be affected by interest. This depends upon the makeup of the balance sheet. For example, loans are assets and generate interest income from the interest rates charged. When interest rates change, this can either reduce or increase the amount of income the loans generate. Further, if rates are fixed and interest rates in general increase, the bank will earn less than what they could for new loans, a lost opportunity. The same holds true for interest expense. If interest rates increase, then the bank may pay more interest expense. If they have fixed rates on CDs for customers that are high and rates drop again, they will be paying more interest than they need to in the current market.

Given these scenarios, banks must understand how many of their assets are subject to interest rate fluctuations and how many of their liabilities are subject to interest rate fluctuations. This means analyzing each account and determining whether it earns interest income or pays interest expense and then summing the interest-sensitive assets and summing the interest-sensitive liabilities. As another example, cash is an asset. However, it is not subject to interest rate fluctuations, as there is no relationship to interest rates; therefore, it is not included. Standard checking accounts do not typically pay interest; therefore, they would not be included in interest-sensitive liabilities.

Dollar Interest-Sensitive Gap

The difference between the sum of interest-sensitive liabilities and the sum of interest-sensitive liabilities indicates the type of interest sensitivity the bank has. This is known as **static (dynamic) gap**. This result represents the dollar gap between interest-sensitive assets and interest-sensitive liabilities, as shown in Table 12.5.

Table 12.5 **Static (Dynamic) Gap**

$ interest-sensitive assets – $ interest-sensitive liabilities = $

The result of this calculation will indicate the following for the bank:

- positive result = asset sensitive
- negative result = liability sensitive
- zero result = no sensitivity

This is truly the first step in understanding interest sensitivity. Once it is known, this will provide the bank with the knowledge of what they may need to do to mitigate this interest risk, which will be discussed later. Whether the bank is asset or liability sensitive is important but does not in itself indicate whether the bank is performing well or not; it is simply an indicator. The reason for this is that if a bank is liability sensitive, it means they have more accounts influenced by interest rate fluctuations than assets. Although this will affect interest expense, in a declining rate environment this could be positive for the bank dependent upon the nature of the liabilities the bank has and their terms. Banks must not only know whether they are asset or liability sensitive but must also understand the direction of interest rates—hence, the yield curve—to truly determine what action they must take.

Although this is the first step to understanding interest sensitivity, there are a few other metrics that are used to measure this.

Interest Sensitive Gap Ratio

This is another metric used, which calculates the interest sensitivity as a percentage rather than in dollars. The formula for this is contained in Table 12.6.

Table 12.6 **Interest Sensitivity Gap Ratio**

($ interest-sensitive assets – $ interest-sensitive liabilities) / Total Assets = %

This ratio is often used as percentage, as it puts this in relation to total assets so that the degree of sensitivity can be determined. Much the same as in the static gap, the results are analyzed as follows:

- greater than zero % = asset sensitive
- less than zero % = liability sensitive
- equal to zero = no sensitivity

Interest Sensitivity Ratio (ISR)

The last measurement of sensitivity that is also used looks at the gap as a ratio, rather than a percentage. Dependent upon the user, this may be easier to use and/or assess. This ratio is called the interest sensitivity ratio (ISR) and is illustrated in Table 12.7.

Table 12.7 **Interest Sensitivity Ratio (ISR)**

$ interest-sensitive assets / $ interest-sensitive liabilities = Ratio

Although this ratio arrives at the same result, it does so in relation to 1, as follows:

- greater than 1 = asset sensitive
- less than 1 = liability sensitive
- equal to 1 = no sensitivity

Net Interest Margin

Probably the most important ratio, the measurement that is used is the net interest margin. Although this relates to the degree of profitability from the lending function, it is based upon the interest rates and interest rate risk. In this regard, understanding asset and liability sensitivity will point the bank in a direction of awareness. Understanding this will have a bearing on the overall margin that is obtained from the lending function, which is affected by interest rates. Simplistically, loans produce interest income, and deposits incur interest expense. However, are the rates variable or fixed, and what are the maturities of these accounts, both assets and liabilities? These are critical considerations in managing profitability and interest rate risk. So, although the sensitivity ratios create awareness on the part of the bank, it is what they do with this knowledge that allows them to manage the net interest margin and profitability effectively. The **net interest margin** is a measure of their success in managing this. This metric was identified as one to the primary comparative ratios in Chapter 8, and it is very important to the bank overall. The calculation, displayed in Table 12.8, includes many of the same elements we have been discussing in this section: interest income produced from assets (longer term rates) and interest expense produced from liabilities (shorter term rates).

Table 12.8 **Net Interest Margin**

($ interest income – $ interest expense) / Total assets = %

Net interest margin cannot be discussed enough and is the culmination of the bank's ability to manage interest rates and mitigate the risk of fluctuations in interest rates. It is for these reasons that careful records and regular monitoring of the bank's position relative to interest rates will go a long ways toward profitability.

Overall, the importance of this section relates to the original determination of which assets and which liabilities are sensitive to interest rate risk. The bank's systems should be able to capture these accounts, sum them, and provide an ongoing assessment of the level and type of interest sensitivity that exists. Armed with this knowledge, the bank can plan for and build a structure for mitigation.

Mitigating Interest Rate Risk

Mitigation is the process of reducing or limiting the amount of risk the bank faces. For the purposes of this section, that is interest sensitivity or interest risk. Unfortunately, it does not eliminate this risk completely. There will always be rate fluctuations that are unanticipated, and changes to the bank's balance sheets by way of new types of loans, new depository accounts, and other accounts, and concentrations, which will impact the bank's exposure. For these reasons, banks must carefully manage the process and focus on remedies that can be used to mitigate the risks they face now and have these available as the environment changes.

There are several tools that can be used to mitigate this important financial risk:

- interest rate swaps
- loan sales
- loan securitization
- standby letters of credit
- interest rate caps, floors, and collars

Interest Rate Swaps

Among these tools, **interest rate swaps** have emerged as a means of equalizing or compensating for interest risk exposure, but they can be rather complex to understand. This tool first emerged in the 1980s and is a creative way to address the sensitivity of a bank (asset or liability) by partnering with another bank or entity wishing to do the same. In short, it is a contractual relationship and is "off balance sheet." In other words, the financial transaction that occurs, because of the contract, has no bearing on the accounts and amounts in the balance sheet. The results will only affect the results in the income statement. Therefore, this is a means of addressing an imbalance in asset or liability sensitivity and the impact this might have to the income statement if left alone. By establishing a financial arrangement with a third party, the transaction will take place as with any other contractual relationship, but hopefully for the betterment of both parties. Banks may find themselves liability sensitive and based upon their estimates of interest rate movement may erode their net interest margin. To avoid this degradation, which would affect their profitability, the bank would arrange a financial transaction to trade the payment or receipt of fixed or floating rate amounts with another individual who might be in the opposite situation. Essentially, the two parties agree to exchange interest rate cash flows. Interest rate swaps are comprised of several components and consist of nomenclature unique to this instrument.

Contract: Agreement between two parties, called counterparties. These parties agree to:

- pay a fixed rate of interest and receive a floating rate of interest
- receive a fixed rate of interest and receive a fixed rate of interest

Notional amount: This is the dollar amount that the contract will be based upon (usually the dollar gap of sensitivity).

Principal: No principal changes hands. This is simply an exchange of interest payments for a period, and only the net amount of interest changes hands.

LIBOR: the index used for swaps is the London Interbank Offered Rate

Off balance sheet: The transaction does not impact the balances on the balance sheet; only the income statement is affected.

Term: Contracts range from 1–15 years in duration.

The process for the initiation and the workings of an interest rate swap will generally occur in the following sequence. This is broad, and some contracts may have more complexity, but this will provide the reader with a general sense of the how these typically flow:

- Determine the static or dynamic gap (interest sensitivity gap) for the bank from a review of the balance sheet and the determination of asset or liability sensitivity.

- Identify the notional amount that the contract will be based upon. This will usually be the static gap previously identified.
- If a negative gap exists (liability sensitive), the bank will pay more interest than it receives, and the net interest margin will decline.
    - If the bank expects interest rates to rise:
        - Execute the swap.
        - PAY fixed rate of interest and RECEIVE floating rate of interest on the notional amount.
    - If the bank expects interest rates to decline:
        - No action is needed, there is no need for a swap.
- If a positive gap exists (asset sensitive), the bank will receive more interest than pay; therefore, the net interest margin will increase.
    - If the bank expects interest rates to rise:
        - No action is needed; there is no need for a swap.
    - If the bank expects interest rates to decline:
        - Execute the swap.
        - PAY floating rate of interest and RECEIVE fixed rate of interest on the notional amount.

For the purposes of the contract, the fixed rate paid or received is based upon the interest rate swap curve rates, and the floating rate paid or received is based upon the quarterly LIBOR rate.

A handy table is included in Table 12.9 for ease in determining the appropriate actions for interest rates swaps.

Table 12.9 **Interest Rate Swap Table**

Expectation	Rate type	Negative gap	Positive gap	Impact
Rates will go up.	Fixed	Pay fixed.	Do nothing.	Fixed rates remain constant, floating rates go up, and net impact is positive.
	Floating	Receive floating.	Do nothing.	
Rates will decline.	Fixed	Do nothing.	Receive fixed.	Fixed rates remain constant, floating rates go down, and net impact is negative.
	Floating	Do nothing.	Pay floating.	

As previously indicated, interest rate swaps are one of the tools used to mitigate interest rate fluctuations, and risk. As can be seen, during the process the exchange of interest rates with another party can put the bank in a positive situation, which can impact its bottom-line net income. Beyond this there are other benefits of this important tool.

- Fee income can be earned from the arrangement. This is part of the contract and can be helpful in times of declining interest margins.
- It ultimately protects the balance sheet of the bank. This is determined from the static gap and keep the bank in the correct position to capitalize on rising rates over a period.
- It literally compensates for the negative situation the bank may be in without doing anything. The existence of interest rates swaps has had a significant impact on the bank's ability to mitigate this important risk.

Loan Sales

Loan sales is the ability of the bank to sell loans in the secondary market and remove the loan from its balance sheet. By doing this, the bank has eliminated the risk from interest fluctuations for these assets. The details of this risk mitigation concept include (Rose & Hudgins, 2013):

Loan types: Mortgage loans are among the most sold, although other types may also be sold.

Organizations involved: Fannie Mae and Freddie Mac (government-sponsored entities) typically engage in purchasing loans, whereby they bundle them into securities. Wall Street investment banks have been involved in these transactions as well, particularly during the financial crisis of 2008.

Reason/benefits: The obvious benefit is that it eliminates the interest rate risk for the loan, as it is no longer on the balance sheet. In addition, the bank receives the proceeds from the sale, which they can, in turn, lend again and presumably at more attractive rates. A third benefit is the bank can retain servicing rights on the loan. This is a source of fee income for the bank, without the risk of interest rate fluctuations. This can positively affect the capital ratio by lowering the risk-weighted assets, unless reloaned.

Risks: Transactions of this nature will gain regulator attention and scrutiny. Loans sold may be those most attractive, leaving the remaining portfolio at higher risk, proportionately.

Loan Securitization

Another interest risk mitigating technique, like loan sales, is that of loan securitization. This technique, as the name implies, involves bundling loans in securities. The bank would "pool" assets (loans), which become collateral for the securities that are produced; these then would be sold to investors.

Loan types: Mortgage loans, credit cards, and other high-quality loans are bundled; these may become collateralized mortgage obligations (CMOs), among others (Rose & Hudgins, 2013).

Organizations involved: investors

Reason/benefits: The primary benefit is the removal of the loan from the balance sheet, like loan sales. As loans are removed, the interest risk is removed as well. The bundled securities are then sold to investors with proceeds going to the bank, which can be reloaned. Interest income is paid to the investors, as is principal repayment at maturity. This creates a source of funds for the bank.

Risks: Because the loans that are used are at a higher quality, the remaining loans in the portfolio are riskier. Additionally, the bank becomes an underwriter, with all the attendant risks involved.

Standby Letters of Credit

Standby letters of credit are the issuance of a promise to pay a third party in the event of default on the part of the borrower. This is not a loan and therefore is an off-balance sheet item, considered a contingent liability on the part of the bank. These instruments are analyzed like a loan by the bank to ensure that the borrower is credit worthy. They are an interest risk mitigation technique since there is no financial transaction or payout of proceeds and therefore no interest rate risk (Rose & Hudgins, 2013).

Reasons for usage: Since no funds have been paid out, there is minimal costs of issuance (no insurance fees are incurred and other items). Customers requiring these need a guarantee that the money is available for the project or obligation to be started.

Benefits: This is a source of fee income to the bank, without the risk of nonpayment; therefore, it is risk-free revenue with no concern for interest rate fluctuations, because no funds have been paid out. The likelihood that funds would be required is relatively low since this is insurance that the payment will be made inevitably. Therefore, it is low risk and revenue generating.

Risks and mitigation: The primary risk is that the standby letter of credit will be required, and this will become a loan. This then becomes part of the interest rate risk that banks face and, additionally, creates credit risk. Furthermore, these can have an impact on capital requirements, as well as garnering the attention of the regulators—therefore, a higher level of scrutiny. Ultimately the bank could sell participations in this standby to mitigate and diversify the risk attendant to this.

Interest Rate Caps, Floors, and Collars

These tools provide protection that will mitigate the risk of significant fluctuations in interest rates affecting interest income and expenses. By providing boundaries, or limits, the risk is reduced to the limits established, which can be better calculated and built into the loan agreements (Rose & Hudgins, 2013).

Interest rate caps: Cap are the upper limit, or ceiling, where the interest rate cannot exceed beyond. In the case of floating rates on liabilities, the bank can be protected from rates rising above a specified limit, thereby minimizing its exposure and thusly the risk.

Interest rate floors: Similar to caps, floors are limits at the opposite end. These provide the outer boundary, on the downside, when interest rates decrease significantly. This protects the bank and allows them to ensure that a minimum return can be obtained from the loan when rates decline.

Interest rate collars: A collar is both an upper- and lower-limit restriction. It provides protection on the high side as well as the low side and identifies the returns that could be available to the bank in a rapidly changing interest rate environment. This allows the bank to establish and measure the risk that they would be comfortable taking.

These restrictions and limitations must be built into the loan agreements of the bank and agreed to by the customers. In many cases these would be reasonable to obtain the loan; therefore, they become effective risk mitigators of interest rate risk.

Summary

Interest rate risk can be challenging to manage, especially given the circumstances that can affect interest rates. The financial crisis of 2008 and, more recently, the pandemic of 2020 are excellent examples of events that have triggered interest rate fluctuations rapidly and for sustained periods of time. For these reasons, bankers must be on their guard to monitor and prepare for these fluctuations and be active in attempting to forecast these. More recently, negative interest rates have been discussed. Whether these would ever become a reality or not is left to be seen but nevertheless continues to challenge the need for effective interest rate risk management.

CHAPTER SUMMARY

Financial risks continue to be the major risks that banks face. These risks, individually, can impact the bank's ability to function and put them at risk of failure. From inadequate capital levels that make absorbing losses impossible as well as noncompliance with regulations, to runs on the bank from a lack of liquidity, or loss in profitability for inadequate analysis and management of interest rate fluctuations, these are the significant financial risks that banks face. Although there are more risks that banks must contend with, there is more latitude for recovery of these in the event they occur than there is for the financial risks. For these reasons, banks must be proactive in their approach and management of financial risks, which is the reason that this chapter has been fully devoted to understanding them.

END OF CHAPTER QUESTIONS

1. Identify the differences between Tier 1 and Tier 2 capital.
2. What is the reserve computation period, and what is its duration?
3. Name the three types of curves that may be seen in a yield curve and what they tell you about the future.
4. Is the issuance of loans to borrowers considered a cash inflow or a cash outflow?
5. Identify two risk mitigation tools that could be used to minimize interest rate risk and briefly explain how they are used.
6. What is the primary difference between the Tier 1 capital ratio and the leverage ratio?
7. What was the primary focus(es) of Basel III?
8. What is meant by "hot money" in the liquidity management approach?
9. What are the components of the net liquidity position calculation?
10. What is the primary comparative interest rate metric used to manage interest rate performance?

Figure Credit

Fig. 12.1: Source: www.ustreas.gov/offices/domestic-finance/debt-management/interest-rate/yield.html.

Managing Credit Risks

Although not one of the crucial financial risks, the making of loans to borrowers is one of the major risks that a bank can face. Making loans to customers is the primary role of the bank, and loans are risky. As assets, they are part of the denominator in calculating overall capital adequacy, as outlined in the previous chapter. As illustrated, these assets carry a risk rating generally at the 100% level. Since the largest asset for a bank is loans and they carry significant risk, it receives major attention from everyone. Whenever a merger or acquisition takes place, the first thing that buyers look at in conducting their due diligence is the quality of the loans that are on the books of the target bank. The reason for this is simple: If the quality of the loans is lacking, the greater the probability of losses, which would have to be absorbed by the capital of the acquiring bank. In short, if the loans become losses, it can dramatically affect the acquiring bank's profitability and defeat the purpose of the merger or acquisition, if not put them at risk of failure. As part of the annual safety and soundness exam conducted by the regulators, this is a major portion of the exam and falls under the "a" in the CAMELS rating system, for "asset quality." In short, loan quality is vital to a bank and can ultimately cause an erosion of capital and put the bank at risk. Although not as acute as the existential risk posed by financial risks, credit risk may evolve more slowly, due to the nature of the process, but carries the same ultimate impact. Too many bad loans pose the

Key Terms

- Credit risk
- Term
- Tenor
- Amortization
- Cash flow
- Underwriting
- Loan policy
- Nonperforming loan
- Financial statement spread
- Going concern
- Pro forma
- Uniform cash flow analysis (UCA)
- Earnings before interest taxes depreciation and amortization (EBITDA)
- Loan structuring
- Prime rate and LIBOR
- Risk mitigant
- Security
- Perfect
- Personal financial statement
- Loan review
- Loan workout
- Credit scoring
- FICO system
- Asset quality

Learning Objectives

By the end of this chapter, the student will:

- Understand the definition and nature of credit risk.
- Know the dimensions and magnitude of credit risk.
- Learn the process of underwriting loans.
- Identify mitigation factors to reduce credit risk.
- Know how both commercial and consumer loans are analyzed and the components of each.
- Identify the tools used to analyze consumer loans, including the FICO system.
- Learn and understand the key measurement tool for measuring asset quality.

same existential threat to the bank, and one need only look at what happened during the financial crisis of 2008 to understand this.

Nevertheless, making loans is why banks exist. It is their primary product and generates the highest amount of revenue for the bank. This chapter outlines the nature of credit risk and how banks manage and mitigate this risk through the underwriting and monitoring process. For these reasons, banks build sales forces to compete and make loans to businesses and consumers, but they also build staff and processes to analyze potential borrowers and build departments and mechanisms to monitor, rate, and, ultimately, work out struggling loans—all with the goal of managing and mitigating credit risk.

Understanding Credit Risk

Credit risk results from the lending process. Like all risks, it emanates from uncertainty, and in this case, that uncertainty is whether the loan will be repaid or not. Therefore, **credit risk** is the loss that results from nonpayment of the loan. The exposure to credit risk is significant for a bank because it is the largest of all assets of the bank.

A major tenet in investment management is diversification. Business loans, the largest segment of loans, are, in a sense, investments in the companies that need funds. In many cases, loans are needed for the business to take on new products, expand, or to research new ventures. In this regard, the bank is investing in the company. So, in many ways, the process of analyzing the credit worthiness of the business is akin to the analysis that may take place when evaluating investing in a company's stock. Therefore, a relatively deep financial analysis of the company in question must occur. However, for a lender, it is not with goal of creating shareholder value but, rather, loan repayment. When an investment is not producing the returns desired, the stock could be sold. However, when a business is struggling, the bank cannot simply sell the loan, especially if the business is not doing well. So, although the primary risk is nonpayment of the loans, there are several dimensions of this risk that establish the magnitude of the risk for the bank. Banks seldom put all their eggs in one basket. They diversify their risk. This is accomplished by developing segments of lending that can spread the risk so that the bank will not be significantly impaired if one major loan segment is affected by events in the economy. Examples of this are the savings and loan industry in the 1980s that had huge concentrations of mortgage loans (these entities were not well diversified by design) and the concentration in real estate loans during the financial crisis. Both examples spelled doom, certainly for the savings and loan industry but also for commercial banks, with considerable bank failures during the financial crisis.

Beyond these examples, credit risk occurs from the nuances of the diverse aspects of the portfolio, creating differing levels of risk from several sources.

Products: Banks offer a variety of different loan products to both businesses and consumers. These products have different risks associated with them based upon the nature of the product. Term loans and mortgage loans have significant amounts of collateral secured to mitigate these risks, whereas credit cards have no security. Each product has a different level of credit risk.

Borrowers: Each borrower is different. Each business type has different industries they are part of, with different analysis aspects for consideration. In addition, consumers range widely in financial strength, patterns, and behaviors. Small businesses and large businesses have differing needs, with either simplistic or extremely complex structures. This creates the need for lenders to be extremely knowledgeable about a variety of businesses and consumers to be effective and minimize risk.

Activities: Businesses vary in the activities they perform or are engaged in. These activities can differ significantly from one another and create other dimensions and sources of risk. For example, agribusiness loans, which are farm loans, are significantly different than a manufacturing entity. Real estate and construction loans can be for apartment complexes, business offices, or plants. The activities that these businesses perform create their own level of risk, as there will be many different types of threats to these activities. Changes in economy, industry events, and even the changes in behavior, such as those seen in the pandemic of 2020, can create threats to the activities of these businesses, which, in turn, creates credit risk to the bank.

Geography: Finally, where the business or consumer is located can create risk. Businesses in far-off locales where the bank may not have a presence or an ability to closely monitor the business creates even more risk. In addition, the geography itself creates the risk. Hurricanes in Florida each year in the late summer and fall can impair a business relatively quickly and without warning. This threat does not exist in the Midwest, for example. Distance, earthquakes, hurricanes, tornados, flooding, and snow all may be more prevalent in certain geographies, each creating additional risk to the companies that the bank may do business with.

Overall, credit risk is significant, and it is incumbent upon the bank to implement effective policies and procedures and educate staff and arm them with the tools necessary to mitigate these risks to the extent possible. The only way this risk can be eliminated is to not make loans, which is not optional, given a bank's purpose. Therefore, banks must minimize this risk as much as possible. Those that are effective in doing this excel and prosper. However, the primary mitigatory of this risk is sound credit analysis and underwriting practices.

Lending Basics

Lending in a bank typically follows two forms, commercial (business) loans and consumer loans. These distinct categories of loans, although quite different in analysis and risk, are combined to form the largest asset on the balance sheet, loans. Banks devote distinct departments to each of these categories due to the different skill sets and processes needed. These departments include commercial lending and retail lending. Before delving into the analysis of each, there are some common aspects that are important to understand in the process

- elements of repayment
- underwriting process
- loan policy
- risk mitigation and management (Keusal, 2015)

Elements of Repayment

Because repayment is the risk involved in a loan, it is important to understand some of the key components of repayment attendant to loans. These elements are important aspects of both business and consumer loans relative to repayment.

Term

Term is the duration of the loan agreement, or when the loan matures and must be paid off. This may define the period from which interest is computed on the loan to be repaid. This period is specified in the loan agreement, along with the interest rate. During this period, both principal and interest payments will be made to pay off the loan.

Tenor

Tenor refers to the amount of time remaining before the loan becomes due, or matures. For example, if loan had an original term of five years and three years have passed already, the loan tenor is two years.

Amortization

Amortization is an accounting term for the write down of an asset. Loan amortization is similar, as it defines the process in which the principal amount of the loan is paid back. Amortization includes both principal and interest payments made on the loan, with interest portions of the payment larger in the early period of the loan and principal portions larger in the later periods of the loans. The loan term and amortization period can be different, but generally, they are the same.

Source

The major source of repayment for all loans is **cash flow**. For a business, this comes from operations, which generate revenue. For consumers, this comes from salaries and other sources of regular income (e.g., pensions). Cash flow is by far the most important aspect in the lending process, as this is how the loan will be repaid.

Underwriting Process

Underwriting is the process of deciding whether to lend money to a person or business after assessing all the risks attendant to the deal. This attention to the known risks stems from an analysis of several areas, which are standard and will apply, to some degree, to both business and consumer loans. Nevertheless, these items must be evaluated and executed during the process.

Loan Customers

Banks make loans to businesses and consumers. Although prospective customers may walk into a bank or contact a bank seeking a loan, in some cases the bank must solicit business in the marketplace. Underwriting, by definition, begins at this stage that can be called "business or loan development." This is more appropriate on the business side, but potential consumer customers are also solicited through advertising and a presence in the community. Loan customers are sought because the bank does not generate this significant revenue source unless loans are made. The risk inherent in this process is the origin of the potential clients, and what sources are used to produce these prospects.

Character and Sincerity

For business and consumer loans, character and sincerity are the major foundations for any loan. Banking is a people business, and lenders must understand who they potentially will lend money to. To determine this, it is necessary to meet and talk with the potential borrower and understand whether there is serious intent to repay the loan. In addition, the character of the individual or the business officer involved is also important. Are they of sound character, upright in the community, run an honest business, and are the type of individual that could be trusted to honor their obligation? Obviously, this cannot fully be determined by reading it on a piece of paper; bankers must meet and talk to the individuals to gain a solid level of comfort for these important areas. This may take some time, but that is part of the process and helps to cultivate a solid relationship.

Credit Record

For both businesses and consumers, an evaluation of the prospect's past credit history is important, especially if the bank has never done business with the prospect before. This can be a credit bureau report or other business reports that identify how well the prospect has paid other debts in the past (whether they have filed for bankruptcies or have had other bad debt). These reviews help to solidify the sincerity of the prospect by validating whether they have honored their obligations in the past. History is very helpful in predicting the future patterns as it relates to repayment.

Financial Condition

Financial condition involves reviewing a customer's financial statements, if a business, or reviewing a personal financial analysis for consumers, or their application finances. The objective of the financial condition review is to validate that that there is adequate cash flow produced, free of current obligations, to repay the loan. For a business this becomes more complex, and these will include multiple financial statements. For consumers this will generally be found in the credit application and somewhat in the credit bureau report. However, bankers must validate this information to be certain it exists and is available. This process will uncover other debt the prospect has and whether there is sufficient income (revenue) to pay that debt and any new debt planned. Additionally, since loans are typically for a period of several years, it is important to assess what the forecast may look like in terms of ongoing revenue generation in order to be confident that repayment will occur. As previously stated, cash flow is the most important consideration for both businesses and consumers to verify and ensure that it is currently sufficient and will be in the future.

Assess and Mitigate Risks

During the evaluation process (prior steps), the lender will identify certain risks that may be prevalent now or in the future. These can be economic downturns, competition in the marketplace, changes in customer behaviors, loss of job, and poor financial management. A list of potential risks should be made and then prioritized in order of severity. This is the first step. Once determined, each risk can then be evaluated for mitigation. Mitigation will conform to the risk and can include obtaining collateral in the event the loan is not paid, obtaining cosigners and guarantees from third parties who will be responsible for payment if not paid by the borrower, and other restrictions and requirements that may be built into the loan agreement that can minimize the risks determined. It is incumbent upon the lender to be effective in minimizing the risks and to protect the bank from loss in all cases.

Loan Agreement and Disbursement

The loan agreement outlines all the terms, interest rate, maturity, collateral, covenants, guarantees, and other terms identified in the process. This is the borrower's opportunity to review the arrangement and determine if they agree. If not, these become negotiable points in the deal and must be worked out to proceed. Once this is done, the agreement can be executed by both the borrower and the bank. This becomes the legal document behind the deal. At this juncture, the loan funds are disbursed to the borrower. This will either be physically in a check, a payment directly to the individual the client plans to pay (e.g., a car dealer), or, for businesses, a checking account is opened at the bank and the monies deposited in it.

Monitoring Compliance

Once a loan is made, the process does not end: Often, this is the start of a lengthier assessment. All loans need to be monitored, particularly business loans, as the loan amounts are usually significant. Monitoring involves many steps, but the most important is a regular review of financial statements for business customers. Monitoring continues until the loan is paid off and is the responsibility of the lender, particularly with business loans.

Loan Policy

All banks have a **loan policy**. The importance of the policy, for risk mitigation, is that it provides the "rules" for the bank for lending money. This is important. Otherwise, as new lenders are added from other organizations, there would be no limitations of what they could do. This would create tremendously more risk to the bank. Banks must carefully consider the ground rules that go into a policy to define this. Some of the more important components included in the loan policy are identified below.

Lines of Authority

Lenders do not have unlimited authority. Nor does the bank, which has a legal lending limit. The policy, therefore, identifies the dollar amount of authority each level of lender would have before they are required to obtain sign off at the next level. Every lending officer in the bank, including the CEO, would have a lending authority level. In addition, the policy will establish guidelines for presentation of the loan at the credit committee for approval.

Collateral Guidelines

Guidelines for the types and amounts of collateral will be defined based upon loan amount and the type of loan. Collateral is an important risk mitigatory, and the bank will want to define what collateral is acceptable. Not all banks accept all types collateral, which is based upon risk. Therefore, this is established in advance by the bank.

Loan Rates/Terms of Repayment

Lenders have authority to negotiate terms and rates, but only within specified guidelines. These will be outlined in the policy and updated on a regular basis. It behooves the lender to know the specifications when negotiating so as not to commit to something that will not be approved. Furthermore, loan operations will use the policy to monitor adherence to the guidelines and note any exceptions.

Quality Standards

The quality of loans refers ultimately to the level of losses taken to the overall portfolio. This is calculated for the bank but can also be calculated for each lender's portfolio. These standards, or levels, are defined in the loan policy. In addition, other qualitative standards relative to the analysis are defined in evaluating the loans, as well as maintenance of documentation. All loans have a credit file, which now is mostly electronic. This houses all related documentation. The loan policy may specify the structure and order of the documents in the file, in addition to what should be included in the file.

Limits

As indicated, all banks have a legal lending limit, and this is defined with the policy. The limit is unique to each bank and is set by the FDIC and the OCC. The legal lending limit defines how much money can be lent to a "single" borrower. This limit is 15% of the bank's capital. If the loan is secured, the limit extends to 25%, with an increment of 10%. The bank, through its policy, may restrict this further and, if so, will define this in the loan policy.

Trade Area

An important consideration is the boundaries. As may be recalled, geography is one of the dimensions that creates greater magnitude in credit risk. For this reason, each bank will define their trade area, the geographic area within which they will lend money to customers. For the reasons specified earlier, banks are careful not to extend their reach beyond where they feel they can manage and monitor effectively.

Problem Loans

Invariably, some loan recipients will have difficulty paying back the loan. Although certainly not desired, this does occur. The loan policy defines the procedures lenders must use to monitor and detect problem loans. When this occurs, the bank provides procedures for how to classify and what to do with the loans at each level. Ultimately, a loan may be delivered to the workout area, where specialists are available to work with the clients and potentially restructure the loan to obtain payment.

Risk Mitigation and Management Tools

The tools that are available to lenders throughout the process of making loans are many. These tools are specifically used to evaluate and monitor loans. All are designed to provide information and/or analysis in the process of underwriting toward the minimization of credit risk. Many of these have been discussed; however, this provides a good outline of the primary tools of risk mitigation.

Loan Policy

As previously outlined, this provides the rules and guidelines, as well as boundaries, for lending.

Six Cs of Credit

These are the six primary considerations used to evaluate the credit worthiness of an individual or entity (Keusal, 2015). These are defined more fully in the next section.

Financial Analysis

These are the personal and corporate financial statements that are provided for preliminary analysis and ongoing monitoring. These will include ratio analysis and cash flow analysis statements, in addition to application data.

Loan Structuring and Documentation

This includes the "pricing" of the loans, type of loan, loans terms, risk analysis, and the specific loan documentation that is required, which may include collateral documentation and others.

Loan Agreement

This is the primary legal document. It includes the promissory note and defines all terms and requirements of the loan. This must be agreed to by the client and the bank and included as part of the loan documentation.

Monitoring

This is a process for periodic financial analysis and follow-up, with alert mechanisms to inform the lender when specific events or late or missed payments occur. These mechanisms are established and monitored by other support staff but directed to the lender so that they may follow up with the client.

Workout and Loan Review

These are two separate support areas and functions. Loan review is a department that evaluates and "rates" loans based upon their current level of risk to the bank. Since they are independent of the lender, they provide an objective view and assessment of the credit.

In the event the client has increased in risk and has had trouble in making payments and is deemed a **nonperforming loan**, the loan may be referred to the workout area to attempt to restructure the deal to prevent a loss and obtain payment, albeit with modified terms.

Consumer Loan Application

For consumer loans, the primary document for evaluation is the credit application. This contains a wealth of information, including bank accounts, job position and status, current and past addresses, references, cosigners, and other information. This application forms the basis for most of the information about a consumer client. In some cases, a personal financial statement will be required, all of which become part of the important documentation for the client.

Credit Bureau and FICO

As part of the analysis, understanding the client's past payment history and previously extended credit is a critical part of determining whether the client has performed well on other accounts. This history may indicate patterns for the future and becomes an important ingredient in the process.

Predictive Analytics

Many banks now rely on other metrics that are used to provide internal risk ratings of loans. These include metrics based upon the bank's portfolio to predict exposures in the portfolio and predict the likelihood of loss for customers. These can be very helpful when looking ahead and attempting to forecasts losses. These include metrics such as probability of default, loss given default, and exposure at default.

Credit Scoring

Scoring is tool that relies on establishing weights to portions of a consumer loan application. The sum of the weights is then used to quickly determine if the loan should be approved or rejected outright. This is used to handle large volumes and can be somewhat predictive as to which customers can or cannot receive immediate approval. Dependent upon the amount of loans the bank wishes to approve, they can raise or lower the total point values for approval whenever they like, making credit easier or harder to obtain, depending upon their needs. Credit scoring also limits the amount of application to judgmentally review, as these can be labor intensive.

Six Cs of Credit

The last area for understanding credit risk are the six Cs of credit. It is important for the reader to understand these important considerations because they apply to all loans. These are basic tenets of lending and consist of six items that should be well understood and considered whenever anyone is contemplating a loan. Although there are many items considered thus far in this chapter to understand credit risk, this provides a basic framework for consideration that can easily be adopted and applied in both commercial and consumer loans (Keusal, 2015).

Character

This is part of getting to know the customer and focuses on understanding whether the prospect has a serious intent to repay the loan and demonstrates the integrity to provide this level of confidence. In addition, character also relates to the specific purpose of the loan itself—whether the reason makes logical sense and fits with the need of the individual or business. In other words, is it appropriate?

Capacity

When talking to a potential client and attempting to understanding the needs conveyed, it is important to decipher whether the individual has the authority to negotiate with and execute the loan. For business loans, it is important to ascertain whether the party in discussion with the lender has the legal authority to bind the company to the loan agreement. Usually only designated individuals in the firm may execute contracts and deals; therefore, it is incumbent upon the lender to ensure that this is the case. The same applies for a consumer loan. The individual who is signing the loan must be of the age to legally be responsible for the loan. This should not be taken for granted.

Cash

The ultimate source for repayment of the loan is cash flow. This cannot be said enough: If the cash flow is not there, the loan will not be repaid according to the terms of the agreement. For consumers this will be the individual's income and whether it is sufficient to handle their current obligations and the loan payment. For businesses it is the same, but it is more complex to determine.

Collateral

In most cases collateral will be needed to "secure" the loan. Collateral minimizes the risk of nonpayment by providing an asset that the bank will own, upon default, and can liquidate for cash to make the loan whole. Collateral must be perfected in the process, which means the bank has a legal claim to the title in the event of default and can take ownership. The other consideration is the value of the collateral and whether it will remain the same throughout the term of the loan.

Conditions

The lender must be aware and understand how current and future economic conditions might affect the borrower's business, or the borrower individually. Some businesses are very sensitive to economic events and upheavals, and these must be considered as risks when considering a loan. This awareness it important, as it permits the lender to monitor specifically for these events. A good example of this is loans to foreign countries. A key conditional consideration is "country risk," or the economic climate of the country that could impair the ability of the borrower to repay. For individuals, the type of job an individual has may be more sensitive to changes in the economy and may not be mainstream enough to continue in adverse situations. A job loss can put the loan at risk of repayment, as demonstrated by the financial crisis of 2008 and the pandemic of 2020.

Control/Competition

This is a newer items to the list of Cs, but an important one. Does the loan meet the requirements and guidelines specified by the bank's loan policy, and would it be sensitive to regulatory pressure in the event of changes and modifications? Considerations should always be given to regulations, particularly since regulators will look at loan quality each year in the safety and soundness exams. Competion is intense in the marketplace and loans must be competitively priced and negotiated in such as way as to obtain the business, while minimizing the risks to the bank (Keusal, 2015).

These tenets of loan underwriting provide an effective foundation when considering any loan. Meeting these needs, in general, will go a long ways toward minimizing credit risk and improving and maintaining the quality of the loan portfolio.

Analyzing Credits for Decision Making

Now that credit risk has been firmly established, the analysis of credits provides the steps that will evaluate the credit worthiness of potential borrowers. This is by far the most important aspect of the lending process. If banks do not make loans, they do not take risks; however, they will not make any money and will go out of business. Therefore, each potential loan, whether business or consumer, must be analyzed fully to make sure that the loan is made with full knowledge of the client's finances and ability to repay. Credit analysis is the process of performing these functions and gaining the necessary knowledge.

This section will outline how business and consumer loans are analyzed, identifying the key components of the process and highlighting the differences. Before beginning, one of the major differences between business and consumer loans is volume. Consumer loans generally are of higher volumes (i.e., number of loans) than commercial. However, commercial loans, in the aggregate, are of a higher dollar amount, individually and collectively. Therefore, they create more risk. The volume involved and the dollar exposure creates the difference in analysis of these loans.

Commercial Credit Analysis

Commercial credit involves making loans to businesses. This is clearly an economic function and provides the funding for business growth, jobs, and general prosperity in the community and the country at large. When banks stop lending to businesses due to risks that may be involved, it slows the growth and recovery of the economy, as we have seen in the recent past.

Since businesses are complex and varied, detailed steps must be taken during the credit analysis process to get the loan approved. These functions differ from consumer loans, as will be clear later in the chapter.

A major part of the analysis of commercial loans will center around the information that will be contained, ultimately, in a loan package that will be presented to the credit committee for approval. Once a prospect has been identified and a need established, credit analysts will begin this process of compiling information for decision making. These will include the following:

- financial condition analysis
- loan structuring
- identifying risks
- developing mitigants for the risk
- loan documentation
- loan review and workout

Financial Condition Analysis

The financial condition of a business is found within the financial statements of the entity. Whenever a prospect is to be analyzed, the first request is to obtain financial statements so that the financial analysis can begin. A true financial assessment of a business will require a minimum of three levels of analysis:

- analysis of balance sheet and income statements
- analysis of cash flows
- analysis of financial ratios

Analysis of Balance Sheet and Income Statements

When requesting financial statements on existing companies, the objective is to obtain historical information for the past three to five years. This is of considerable importance to understand the financial trends of the company: whether they are improving, declining, or stable. However, dependent upon the size of the company, it is always desired to have "audited" financial statements. These provide an independent assessment of the validity of the amounts contained on the statements, which eliminates some of the risk in the analysis. However, this is not always possible, and the bank may receive company-prepared statements.

To compensate for this, banks have templates that they have established that allow analysts to transfer and display the provided statements in ways that are more comparable and highlight items for analysis. The templates and the process are known as a **financial statement spread.**

The analyst is looking to evaluate the trends over the years to determine the level of revenue growth that has occurred and whether the company is profitable. These are important considerations, as the bank wants to ensure that the company is considered a **going concern.** An example of a financial statement spread template is shown in Figure 13.1.

The analysis of financial statements is the primary tool of the credit analyst. In addition to historical information, a future forecast, or **pro forma**, is highly desired from the customer. If the customer does not provide this, the analyst may produce this based upon a potential sales growth percentage and project this. Pro formas are projected based on the "percentage of sales" method, in general. This method determines the percentage of sales for each of the cost items in the income statement for actual historical amounts (see Figure 13.1 to see where these percentages are located on the income statement). Once a historical average or most recent actual percentage is determined, these percentages are held constant over the future projection and project the cost items based on the new sales amount. In this regard, as the sales amounts increase over the forecast years, costs and expenses will increase in relation to the fixed percentage determined, as shown in the example in Figure 13.2.

The pro forma allows the analyst to determine how the company will perform over the next five years, which will be very important in determining whether the company will be able to repay the planned loan.

Finally, analysts sometimes develop "scenario analysis" pro formas. This is a type of stress test in that it reflects the best-, likely-, and worst-case scenarios based upon three levels of sales growth. For example, a worst-case scenario might be that there is zero sales growth in the future. This helps the analyst to frame the risk and paint a picture of the likelihood of the payback.

INCOME STATEMENT	Prior Year	2017	2018	2019	2020	2021
Revenue		13,300	14,892	16,443	19,149	21,311
Growth %			12.0%	10.4%	16.5%	11.3%
Cost of Goods Sold		10,712	11,717	12,620	14,585	16,064
% of Sales		80.5%	78.7%	76.8%	76.2%	75.4%
Gross Profit		2,588	3,175	3,823	4,564	5,247
% of Sales		19.5%	21.3%	23.2%	23.8%	24.6%
General & Administrative Expenses		801	938	991	1,185	1,361
% of Sales		6.0%	6.3%	6.0%	6.2%	6.4%
Operating Profit (EBIT)		1,787	2,237	2,831	3,379	3,887
Interest Expense	#REF!	33	29	69	74	86
Net Other Expense (Income)		-305	2,439	-398	-598	-398
% of Sales		-2.3%	16.4%	-2.4%	-3.1%	-1.9%
EBT		2,059	-230	3,160	3,903	4,199
Tax Expense	563	674	-239	1,092	1,144	1,380
Tax Rate		32.8%	103.8%	34.6%	29.3%	32.9%
Net Income (EACS)		1,385	9	2,068	2,759	2,819
Dividend Expense		513	629	783	929	1,178
Divident Payout Ratio		-37.0%	7146.6%	37.9%	33.7%	41.8%
Net Income		872	-620	1,285	1,831	1,641
Operating Income		1,787	2,237	2,831	3,379	3,887
Depreciation		581	656	748	934	1,030
Amortization		0	0	0	0	0
EBITDA		2,367	2,893	3,580	4,313	4,917

BALANCE SHEET	Prior Year	2017	2018	2019	2020	2021
Assets						
Cash	#REF!	2,037	3,234	1,844	1,611	2,263
Marketable Securities	0	0	0	0	0	0
Inventories	#REF!	1,242	1,111	1,091	1,306	1,379
Accounts Receivable	#REF!	486	561	631	719	769
Other	#REF!	435	565	603	716	350
Total Current Assets	#REF!	4,200	5,471	4,169	4,353	4,761
PP&E	#REF!	2,659	3,201	3,519	4,088	4,534
Other		1,361	2,845	3,065	4,005	5,035
Capitalized Financing Fees						
Goodwill						
TOTAL ASSETS		8,219	11,517	10,753	12,446	14,330
Liabilities						
Accounts Payable	#REF!	398	492	534	684	731
Notes Payable	0	0	0	0	0	0
Accruals						
(OLDCO) Line of Credit	#REF!					
(OLDCO) Current Maturities of Long Term Debt		0	0	0	3	404
(OLDCO) Other	#REF!	1,812	4,886	2,505	2,966	3,412
Total Current Liabilities	#REF!	2,210	5,377	3,039	3,654	4,547
(NEWCO) Subordinated Debt						
(NEWCO) Senior Debt						
(OLDCO) Long Term Debt	#REF!	895	1,657	2,441	2,973	3,892
TOTAL LIABILITIES		3,105	7,034	5,479	6,626	8,439
Shareholder Equity						
Preferred Stock		6	2	2	2	7
Common Stock		5,109	4,480	5,272	5,818	5,884
Additional Paid in Capital		0	0	0	0	0
Retained Earnings		0	0	0	0	0
TOTAL SHAREHOLDER EQUITY		5,115	4,482	5,274	5,820	5,891
TOTAL LIABILITIES & SE		8,219	11,517	10,753	12,446	14,329

CASH FLOW STATEMENT	Prior Year	2017	2018	2019	2020	2021
CASH FLOW FROM OPERLATING ACTIVITIES						
Net Income		872	-620	1,285	1,831	1,641
- Depreciation and Amortization		581	656	748	934	1,030
- Changes in Working Capital		-517	148	-7	-153	-75
- Other		189	3,074	-2,381	461	446
Net Cash Provided by Operations		1,124	3,258	-355	3,073	3,041
CASH FLOW FROM INVESTING ACTIVITIES						
Capital Expenditures (Purch. PP&E)		-974	-1,411	-818	-1,881	-2,223
Net Cash from Investing Activities		-974	-1,411	-818	-1,881	-2,223
CASH FLOW FROM FINANCING ACTIVITIES						
Line of Credit (revolving)		0	0	0	0	0
Long Term Debt (Current Maturities)		-233	521	160	-967	-572
Subordinated Debt						
Senior Debt						
Net Cash Provided (Used) by Finance Activities		-233	521	160	-967	-572
NET CASH FLOW		-82	2,367	-1,013	224	247
Beginning Cash Flow		2,051	2,037	3,234	1,844	1,611
Ending Cash flow		1,969	4,404	2,221	2,068	1,858

FIGURE 13.1 Financial Statement Spread Template

INCOME STATEMENT	Prior Year	2017	2018	2019	2020	2021	Objectives	2022	2023	2024	2025	2026
Revenue		13,300	14,892	16,443	19,149	21,311		23,442	25,786	28,365	31,201	34,322
Growth %			12.0%	10.4%	16.5%	11.3%	10.00%	10.0%	10.0%	10.0%	10.0%	10.0%
Cost of Goods Sold		10,712	11,717	12,620	14,585	16,064		17,582	19,340	21,274	23,401	25,741
% of Sales		80.5%	78.7%	76.8%	76.2%	75.4%	75.00%	75.0%	75.0%	75.0%	75.0%	75.0%
Gross Profit		2,588	3,175	3,823	4,564	5,247		5,861	6,447	7,091	7,800	8,580
% of Sales		19.5%	21.3%	23.2%	23.8%	24.6%		25.0%	25.0%	25.0%	25.0%	25.0%
General & Administrative Expenses		801	938	991	1,185	1,361		1,500	1,650	1,815	1,997	2,197
% of Sales		6.0%	6.3%	6.0%	6.2%	6.4%	6.40%	6.4%	6.4%	6.4%	6.4%	6.4%
Operating Profit (EBIT)		1,787	2,237	2,831	3,379	3,887		4,360	4,796	5,276	5,803	6,384
Interest Expense	#REF!	33	29	69	74	86		174	154	134	114	94
Net Other Expense (Income)		-305	2,439	-398	-598	-398		-469	-516	-567	-624	-686
% of Sales		-2.3%	16.4%	-2.4%	-3.1%	-1.9%	-2.00%	-2.0%	-2.0%	-2.0%	-2.0%	-2.0%
EBT		2,059	-230	3,160	3,903	4,199		4,655	5,158	5,709	6,314	6,977
Tax Expense	563	674	-239	1,092	1,144	1,380		1,396	1,547	1,713	1,894	2,093
Tax Rate		32.8%	103.8%	34.6%	29.3%	32.9%	30.00%	30.0%	30.0%	30.0%	30.0%	30.0%
Net Income (EACS)		1,385	9	2,068	2,759	2,819		3,258	3,610	3,996	4,420	4,884
Dividend Expense		513	629	783	929	1,178		1,303	1,444	1,599	1,768	1,953
Divident Payout Ratio		-37.0%	7146.6%	37.9%	33.7%	41.8%	40.00%	40.0%	40.0%	40.0%	40.0%	40.0%
Net Income		872	-620	1,285	1,831	1,641		1,955	2,166	2,398	2,652	2,930
Operating Income		1,787	2,237	2,831	3,379	3,887		4,360	4,796	5,276	5,803	6,384
Depreciation		581	656	748	934	1,030		1,383	1,883	2,133	2,508	1,375
Amortization		0	0	0	0	0		0	0	0	0	0
EBITDA		2,367	2,893	3,580	4,313	4,917		5,744	6,680	7,409	8,312	7,759
						4						

BALANCE SHEET	Prior Year	2017	2018	2019	2020	2021	Objectives	2022	2023	2024	2025	2026
Assets												
Cash	#REF!	2,037	3,234	1,844	1,611	2,263		10,000	10,000	10,000	11,270	13,934
Marketable Securities	0	0	0	0	0	0	0	0	0	0	0	0
Inventories	#REF!	1,242	1,111	1,091	1,306	1,379		1,662	1,828	2,011	2,212	2,433
Accounts Receivable	#REF!	486	561	631	719	769		873	960	1,056	1,162	1,278
Other	#REF!	435	565	603	716	350	350	350	350	350	350	350
Total Current Assets	#REF!	4,200	5,471	4,169	4,353	4,761		12,885	13,138	13,417	14,994	17,995
PP&E	#REF!	2,659	3,201	3,519	4,088	4,534		4,150	4,267	3,133	2,125	1,750
Other		1,361	2,845	3,065	4,005	5,035	5,035	5,035	5,035	5,035	5,035	5,035
Capitalized Financing Fees								0	0	0	0	0
Goodwill								0	0	0	0	0
TOTAL ASSETS		8,219	11,517	10,753	12,446	14,330		22,070	22,440	21,586	22,154	24,780
Liabilities												
Accounts Payable	#REF!	398	492	534	684	731		752	827	910	1,001	1,101
Notes Payable	0	0	0	0	0	0	0	0	0	0	0	0
Accruals							0					
(OLDCO) Line of Credit	#REF!							6,169	4,701	1,770	0	0
(OLDCO) Current Maturities of Long Term Debt		0	0	0	3	404		404	404	404	404	404
(OLDCO) Other	#REF!	1,812	4,886	2,505	2,966	3,412	3.412	3,412	3,412	3,412	3,412	3,412
Total Current Liabilities	#REF!	2,210	5,377	3,039	3,654	4,547		10,737	9,344	6,496	4,817	4,917
(NEWCO) Subordinated Debt								0	0	0	0	0
(NEWCO) Senior Debt								0	0	0	0	0
(OLDCO) Long Term Debt	#REF!	895	1,657	2,441	2,973	3,892		3,488	3,084	2,680	2,276	1,872
TOTAL LIABILITIES		3,105	7,034	5,479	6,626	8,439		14,224	12,428	9,176	7,093	6,789
Shareholder Equity												
Preferred Stock		6	2	2	2	7	7	7	7	7	7	7
Common Stock		5,109	4,480	5,272	5,818	5,884	5,884	5,884	5,884	5,884	5,884	5,884
Additional Paid in Capital		0	0	0	0	0	0	0	0	0	0	0
Retained Earnings		0	0	0	0	0		1,955	4,121	6,519	9,171	12,101
TOTAL SHAREHOLDER EQUITY		5,115	4,482	5,274	5,820	5,891		7,846	10,012	12,410	15,062	17,992
TOTAL LIABILITIES & SE		8,219	11,517	10,753	12,446	14,329		22,070	22,440	21,585	22,154	24,780

FIGURE 13.2 Financial Statement Forecast

Analysis of Cash Flows

The second part of a financial condition analysis is a detailed look at cash flows. As indicated many times in this chapter, cash flows are the source of repayment of the loan and therefore are of vital importance to the analyst. Loan payments are made with cash, as are other obligations. Cash is generated initially from revenues, but the ultimate cash flow is what remains after payment of cost of goods sold and general and administrative expenses, in general. The analysis of cash flows is conducted by taking both the historical and forecasted (pro forma) data from the financial statement spread and transferring it into a **uniform cash flow analysis (UCA) statement**. This statement arrays accounts in such a ways as to highlight the bottom-line available cash flows after all transactions. This identifies for the analyst whether the company is producing cash flows and, after payment of existing debt obligations, has positive cash flow remaining. An example of a UCA cash flow statement for two years of actual historical data and five years of forecast is illustrated in Figure 13.3.

UNIFORM CREDIT ANALYSIS (UCA) CASH FLOW

	2020	2021	2022	2023	2024	2025
NET SALES	19,149	21,311	23,442	25,786	28,365	31,201
Change in Account Receivable, Inc. (Dec.)	-88	-50	-104	-87	-96	-106
CASH FROM SALES	**19,061**	**21,261**	**23,338**	**25,699**	**28,269**	**31,096**
Cost of Goods Sold	-14,585	-16,064	-17,582	-19,340	-21,274	-23,401
Change in Inventories	-216	-72	-283	-166	-183	-201
Change In Accounts Payables	151	46	21	75	83	91
Change In Other Payables	461	446	0	0	0	0
CASH PRODUCTION COSTS	**-14,189**	**-15,644**	**-17,844**	**-19,431**	**-21,374**	**-23,511**
GROSS CASH PROFIT	**4,872**	**5,618**	**5,494**	**6,268**	**6,895**	**7,585**
SG&A Expenses (Net of Depreciation)	-251	-331	-117	233	318	512
Change in Prepaids	0	0	0	0	0	0
Change in Accruals	0	0	0	0	0	0
CASH OPERATING EXPENSES	**-251**	**-331**	**-117**	**233**	**318**	**512**
CASH AFTER OPERATIONS	**4,621**	**5,287**	**5,377**	**6,501**	**7,213**	**8,096**
Miscellaneous Cash Income	598	398	469	516	567	624
Income Taxes Paid	-1,144	-1,380	-1,321	-1,489	-1,689	-1,894
NET CASH AFTER OPERATIONS	**4,075**	**4,306**	**4,525**	**5,528**	**6,092**	**6,826**
Interest Expense	-74	-86	-425	-350	-214	-114
Dividends Paid	-929	-1,178	-1,233	-1,389	-1,576	-1,768
FINANCING COSTS	**-1,002**	**-1,264**	**-1,658**	**-1,739**	**-1,790**	**-1,882**
NET CASH INCOME FROM OPERATIONS	**3,073**	**3,041**	**2,867**	**3,789**	**4,302**	**4,944**
Long Term Debt Reduction CMLTD	-3	-404	-404	-404	-404	-404
NET CASH AFTER DEBT AMORTIZATION	**3,069**	**2,637**	**2,463**	**3,385**	**3,898**	**4,540**
Capital Expenditures	-1,881	-2,223	-1,000	-2,000	-1,000	-1,500
Change in Intangibles	0	0	0	0	0	0
Change in Long Term Investments	0	0	0	0	0	0
FINANCING SURPLUS/(REQUIREMENT OR DEFICIT)	**1,188**	**415**	**1,463**	**1,385**	**2,898**	**3,040**
Change in Short Term Debt	0	0	6,274	-1,385	-2,898	-1,991
Change in Long Term Debt	536	1,323	0	0	0	0
Change in Equity	546	66	0	0	0	0
TOTAL EXTERNAL FINANCING	**1,082**	**1,389**	**6,274**	**-1,385**	**-2,898**	**-1,991**
CASH AFTER FINANCING (Change in Cash)	**2,270**	**1,804**	**7,737**	**-0**	**0**	**1,049**

FIGURE 13.3 UCA Cash Flow Analysis

A quick way in which bankers view whether cash flow exists in the company is to look at the **earnings before interest taxes depreciation and amortization (EBITDA)**. This indicates whether or not positive cash flow exists for the company, which are warning signs to the bankers as to whether their primary risk, nonpayment, would exist or not.

As one views the UCA cash flow statement, if the amount indicated on the line "net cash after debt amortization" is positive, this is a good sign of the generation of enough cash flows to cover obligations. Nevertheless, this is an integral part of the analysis of financial condition and speaks directly to credit risk.

Analysis of Financial Ratios

The final part of the financial condition analysis is the calculation and review of financial ratios. Financial ratios are extremely telling about a company, and they highlight very clearly areas where the company is doing well and not so well. From a consulting standpoint, ratios are very effective for pinpointing areas where the company should concentrate to improve their performance. From an analyst standpoint, this is also true, but for different reasons. The analyst will highlight areas of concern, how these may be used to determine more risk that the company might represent to the bank, and whether it is negative enough to warrant not lending money. Of course, since banks are in business to make loans and take risks, some ratios that are negative could be used to add premiums to the pricing (interest rate) to accommodate for the risk, increase collateral, and/or apply covenants in the loan agreement. Nevertheless, ratios are an important part of the analysis, an example of which is contained in Figure 13.4.

As shown in the example, ratios are not every effective, unless one can view trends—whether they are moving up or down—and compare them to industry (peers). If both are available, ratios can be very interpretive. Trends tell the analyst whether or not the company is improving, and the industry provides relevance (how well they are doing compared with their peers). As indicated in the illustration, there are five categories of ratios that are important: liquidity, debt, activity, profitability, and market. Combined, these paint a very effective picture of the company and its importance. A detailed understanding of the financial ratios is beyond the scope of this text; however, it is important to know that this is an integral part of the overall financial condition analysis.

Loan Structuring

As part of the analysis of commercial loans, the next major section is called **loan structuring** and defines the "structural elements" of the evolving loan deal. Structural elements are critical to the deal and are defined based upon the completion of the financial condition analysis. As the financial condition is determined, the analyst can now begin to build the deal based upon those results. As part of this analysis, there are four main parts of loan structuring, including

- type of loan
- repayment period
- pricing
- risk mitigants (Keusal, 2015; RMA, 2020)

Type of Loan

After the need for the loan and the amount needed have been established from the customer, the analyst will determine what the appropriate type of loan is for the need. Loan types, or "facilities" as they are called, fall into a few major categories to fit different needs. These include term loans, lines of credit, construction loans, and bridge loans.

Term loan: A term loan is structured based upon a fixed rate of interest for a specified term. These loans are designed for major equipment purchases (e.g., machinery, truck fleet, etc.), also called capital expenditures. These loans are typically secured by the asset that is purchased from the loan proceeds.

Ratio Analysis

Category	Ratio	Actual 2018	2019	2020	2021	Growth	Average	Industry	Result
Liquidity	Current Ratio	1.02	1.37	1.19	1.05	-13.85%	1.31	1.00	1.00
	Quick Ratio	0.81	1.01	0.83	0.74	-13.66%	0.95	2.00	0.00
Activity	Inventory Turnover	10.54	11.57	11.16	11.65	7.80%	10.71	10.00	3.00
	Avg. Days Inventory	34.62	31.55	32.69	31.32	-7.24%	34.50	1.00	2.00
	Avg. Collection Period	13.76	14.01	13.71	13.17	-0.32%	13.59	1.00	2.00
	Average Payment Period	15.32	15.44	17.12	16.60	5.18%	15.61	1.00	3.00
	Asset Turnover	1.29	1.53	1.54	1.49	-2.09%	1.49	1.00	1.00
Debt Ratios	Debt Ratio	61.08%	50.96%	53.24%	58.89%	0.12	52.39%	65.74%	1.00
	Times Interest Earned	78.23	40.97	45.84	45.04	35.33	52.94	51.10	1.00
	Debt to Equity Ratio	1.57	1.04	1.14	1.43	23.94%	1.16	1.00	0.00
	Financial Leverage	2.57	2.04	2.14	2.43	10.92%	2.16	1.00	3.00
Profitability	Gross Profit Margin	21.32%	23.25%	23.83%	24.62%	6.06%	22.50%	24.59%	3.00
	Operating Profit Margin	15.02%	17.22%	17.64%	18.24%	7.94%	16.31%	16.30%	3.00
	Net Profit Margin	0.06%	12.58%	14.41%	13.23%	6.17%	10.14%	12.31%	3.00
	Earnings Per Share	$0.01	$1.38	$1.86	$1.93	20.22%	1.22	1.00	3.00
	Return on Assets	0.08%	19.23%	22.17%	19.67%	3.95%	15.60%	13.20%	3.00
	Return on Equity	0.20%	39.21%	47.41%	47.85%	15.30%	32.35%	38.93%	3.00
Market	Price Earnings Ratio	25.00	28.45	31.42	28.39	2.12%	28.59	21.82	2.00
	Book Value per Common Share	$2.98	$3.52	$3.92	$4.03	4.26%	3.57	1.00	3.00
	Market to Book Ratio	12.41	11.15	14.89	13.59	17.75%	11.82	1.00	3.00
	Dividend Yield	1.13%	1.33%	1.07%	1.47%	0.91%	0.01	1.00	2.00

FIGURE 13.4 Financial Ratio Analysis

Line of credit: Lines of credit are not outright payments of loan proceeds but rather a designated limit that the company borrows against, up to that limit, as the needs arise. These usually are designed for companies that require seasonal lines of credit to increase their cash flows during the down portion of their season. Retailers can fall into this category. The company can draw on the line of credit, like a credit card, during the term for which the line of credit is granted. Primarily, these are designed for working capital.

Construction loans: Construction loans are real estate loans where funding is required during the construction phase of the project. This is a temporary need, as construction projects will generally last from 6 months to a year or more. During this period, the borrower will need to pay contractors for the various parts of the project when due. As this need arises, the borrower will draw on the construction loan for the amount the contractor (e.g., a carpenter contractor) requires. As each contractor completes their work, they are paid from the construction loan. During this period, the borrower pays interest only on the monies borrowed. When the project is complete, the total amount that has been borrowed will be rolled over into a more permanent loan, such as a mortgage loan, and regular payments will be made over the term of the deal.

Bridge loans: Bridge loans are, as the name implies, a "bridge" from one period to another. These are short-term loans and are made to advance funds to a borrower that is needed now to receive a windfall at a specific period. These are opportunistic type loans, and funds would be used for the company to take advantage of an immediate opportunity that will, in turn, produce a significant financial opportunity at a specified time. Once the event producing the opportunity occurs, the entire loan, plus interest, is paid off from those proceeds. Dependent upon the length of the time between the loan and the event, the borrower may need to make interest-only payments; otherwise, they will be bundled into a final "balloon" payment at the end.

Repayment Period

Each type of loan will require a repayment period and terms. These will be outlined in the loan agreement. These will be determined in consideration of the financial condition of the company and in conformity with the requirements of the bank's loan policy. For example, if a term loan is structured, the loan term will likely relate, somewhat, to the life of the asset. In addition, the pro forma financial statement and cash flow analysis will be instrumental in determining the length of the term. This will depend upon the strength of the company. Lines of credit are defined for a specified time as well, whereby the company can on the line as they need the proceeds to pay contractors. Construction loans will generally be short term in nature based upon the time required to build the structure, and bridge loans are very short term, triggered by the opportunity event occurring.

In addition, the amortization period will be defined, which will establish the repayment of principal and interest. This amortization period can be different than the overall loan term, dependent upon the need. Repayment terms are negotiable, to a degree, and will be based upon the amount of risk it creates for the bank. Obviously, the longer the repayment period, the more risk the bank takes. Nevertheless, these are established in concert with the financial condition of the company and their ability to repay the loan in a timely manner.

Pricing

Pricing commercial loans was outlined more fully in Chapter 9. However, as a structural element, this establishes the cost of credit. Again, the analyst will take into consideration the guidelines in the loan policy and build the price in accordance with external indices, such as the **prime rate** or **LIBOR** (transitioning to SOFR), with additional premiums added for default and maturity risk, as well as profitability premium. Pricing is used to compensate the bank not only for the cost of the loan (from funding) but also for risk that they accept. In a highly competitive environment, bankers may have to negotiate stringently with the client to retain the business and keep it from going elsewhere. It behooves the bank to make loans, but if the price becomes too low, the loan will not contribute well to profitability and the attainment of the interest rate margin. Therefore, pricing is both a science and an art; the more experience one has in negotiating price, the greater the success in securing the deal.

Risk Mitigants

As indicated, many times, all loans have risk; it is a matter of how much risk. As part of the credit analysis, the analyst must identify these additional risks that are attendant to the borrower. These risks will be uncovered during the financial condition analysis and in conversation with the borrower and their staff. These risks must not only be identified but also be prioritized. It is always advisable in the prioritization process to categorize these as primary, secondary, and tertiary risks. Once they are identified, the analyst must then focus on determining what **risk mitigant** is appropriate to each level of risk (primary, secondary, and tertiary).

Risk mitigants are designed to limit the inherent risk identified based upon the tool used. Three basic risk mitigants are available to the banker: collateral, loan covenants, and guarantees. Each of these are designed to provide the bank with greater surety that the loan proceeds will ultimately be returned:

- collateral: Collateral, also called **security**, is the attachment of an asset such that if the loan is not repaid the bank will take ownership of the asset and liquidate it to obtain the proceeds to pay back the loan. As part of the process of obtaining collateral, the lender must **perfect** their interest in the asset. This, legally, allows the bank to obtain title to the asset and take ownership in the event of default.
  - Collateral is an effective deterrent to nonpayment. Borrowers seldom wish to lose their assets and will strive to ensure payments are made. This gives the lender an advantage and is the reason why collateral is popular. Several types of collateral exist. The most used include:
    - physical inventory of the client
    - real and personal property (e.g., buildings, equipment, etc.)
    - accounts receivable due the client. Once singed over to the bank, the bank receives repayment from the company's clients.
    - Personal guarantees can form the basis as collateral as well.
- loan covenants: These are written agreements that are very specific and relate to the specific risk identified. Loan covenants can be positive or negative and can have financial or nonfinancial implications. These are designed either to restrict the company from doing something or require the company to perform certain tasks. The nature of these is to limit the company's ability to act without restraint or consultation on the part of the banker. The reason for these is that the analyst has identified a risk from the financial condition analysis whereby if the company were left unimpeded, their actions could dramatically increase the risk to the bank. Covenants must be adhered to as part of the deal, and if not, the bank can call the loan. Examples and a comparison of these are identified below:
  - positive covenant: This is a "requirement." The company must perform certain actions that are defined in the loan agreement. These can be financial or nonfinancial. A

positive financial covenant may be to make loan payments 5 days prior to the due date. A nonfinancial covenant may be to require the bank to produce quarterly, audited, financial statements to the bank.

» negative covenant: These are restrictions or constraints to the borrower. The company cannot perform certain activities or conduct other types of business. A negative financial covenant may be that the bank cannot have its current ratio fall below 2.0 at any time. A negative nonfinancial covenant may be that the company cannot merge or acquire another company during the term of the loan.

- guarantees: Guarantees are fallback mechanisms. They can be viewed as collateral in a sense because the guarantor provides a guarantee that the loan will be repaid if the company does not repay it. Guarantees can be either corporate or personal. A corporate guarantee may come from a parent company of the subsidiary, guaranteeing coverage of the loan. A personal guarantee may come from a principal of the firm. This could be a chairman or CEO. This means that they have the funds, individually, to cover the loan in the result of nonpayment. When a personal guarantee is obtained, the analyst will require verification of their ability to repay by requesting a personal financial statement (PFS) as well as recent tax returns to validate this. A further analysis of the parent company will likely be required, as well for the corporate guarantee.

Risk mitigants can go a long way in dramatically reducing the risks of a loan. These are considered a major part of the loan structuring process.

Loan Agreement

The loan agreement is not a part of the credit analysis; however, it does embody the requirements of the loan and is important to understand. This is a detailed legal document, and once it is executed by both the borrower and the bank, the commitment is bound. Many of the items defined in the previous section are included in the loan agreement, and this would be the first place to look to understand the terms of the deal. Loan agreements can, at a minimum, include the following items:

Promissory note: This establishes the acceptance of the terms and outlines the promise to pay the loan back in full, with all interest defined. Legally, this is the binding agreement that provides the offer and acceptance necessary for a contract to occur.

Loan commitment agreement: This section provides the detail of what has been committed to the borrower from the bank. This will establish the amounts, the pricing, and other terms that have been committed in the deal.

Collateral: As discussed, this is the security involved in the loan. This establishes what the collateral is, the value of it, and any requirements on the part of the borrower to maintain the collateral.

Covenants: This defines both the constraints and the requirements that are made of the borrower, based upon the risks determined.

Borrower guarantees and warranties: Personal and corporate guarantors are identified, with any appropriate detail, as well as what they warrant as it relates to coverage of the loan.

Events of default: This defines exactly what will occur in the event payments are not made, identifying any grace periods, penalties, and other events that will occur and at what interval if the borrower is slow to repay or does not repay. It defines what will happen and when.

Monitoring and Disposition

As part of addressing the credit risk attendant to commercial loans, monitoring is a major part of the process. This occurs from both the lending officer but also from other independent parties within the bank. Disposition results from when the monitoring process has not produced positive results and the loan continues to not perform (i.e., payments are not made). So, even after having done all the up-front work to analyze the potential borrower and prevent or mitigate risk, this process is ongoing all the way to the end.

There are two separate departments that are involved in this process: **loan review** and **loan workout**.

Loan review: Loan review is a proactive function in the bank in which it takes it upon itself to assess and rate existing loans, periodically, to provide an independent assessment outside of the sales area. This is a proactive function because it is a self-policing of the loan process to identify further risks and track progress of loans that may be struggling. Banks have a well-structured set of ratings that this department utilizes to determine risk, and these are reported to management and the board of directors. Some of the primary functions of this group include:

- conducting qualitative reviews of loan performance, periodically, throughout the year, according to a specified schedule
- monitoring loans for compliance with the loan policy of the bank, assessing current financial condition, and evaluating the sufficiency and availability of collateral and other documentation, including the credit file
- prioritizing the loans they review by the largest loans made as well as those struggling to make payments more frequently than others (again, proactively making sure that these loans are monitored more often for action)
- The standard loan review schedule, or routine, may be interrupted based upon economic conditions. In the event of a financial crisis, reviews may be accelerated (and for specific types of loans or industries).

Loan workout: Loan workout is more the "reactive" side of risk management. At this stage, the loan is not making payments and it has, by default, been turned over to a specialized group who work only with these types of loans. This is a last-effort attempt at putting the borrower back on track, which is not always successful. Nevertheless, it is a final attempt to mitigate the credit risk attendant to these loans. The functions and activities involved in risk management for this group include:

- They will closely monitor the warning signs of these struggling loans to determine what action must be taken.
- Their goal is to attempt to obtain full recovery of the loan, through restructuring the deal and working out arrangements to pay at less stringent terms, if this will potentially prevent a loss.
- They are independent of the lending department due to the sensitivities of salesforce and their clients. Working out loan arrangements for recovery can be aggressive, and at this stage, the goal is not necessarily to salvage the relationship but more so to obtain full recovery of the loan.
- Even after a loan is written off as a loss, this group will send these loans to external legal firms and agencies who can continue to attempt recovery of any monies, usually taking 33%–50% of the recoveries.

Summary

Analyzing and mitigating the risks of commercial loans is intense, from start to finish. Because the future cannot be predicted, it is incumbent on the bank to mitigate this risk as much as possible before proceeds go out the door. Banks employ many individuals in the business loan groups to do this work of analyzing the financial condition, structuring the deal, outlining and agreeing to the terms, reviewing and monitoring the loans, and attempting a workout of the loans—all designed to mitigate credit risk for this important area. The reason for this intensity lies in the size of the individual loans. The loss of a single large commercial loan can be very detrimental to the bank. Although the volume of commercial loans will not be as high as consumer loans, their average size is considerably larger than a consumer loan. The loss of a single commercial loan can be the equivalent of multiple consumer loans—hence the focus.

Consumer Credit Analysis

Consumer loans are, generally, loans to individuals and households. These are sometimes called "personal" loans and represent the extension of credit for specific household or individual purchases where ready cash may not be available. The individual balances on these loans, except for some of the residential mortgage loans, are much smaller than business loans. However, collectively, they can represent a sizeable amount of outstanding loans on the balance sheet. Individual customers and households are more numerous than the number of business relationships that a bank may have. However, from a priority and a risk standpoint, they do not generate as much revenue (interest income) and the balances, individually, do not pose as much risk to the bank in default. Nevertheless, consumer loans are quite important to the bank.

Unlike commercial loans, the evaluation of a consumer loan is much different, with some similarities but without the intensity of analysis. Consumer loans are analyzed and made by the retail staff in a bank, by personal bankers. These individuals will assess the potential borrowers for credit worthiness, but the process will require some differences. Consumer loans, like commercial loans, are subject to credit risk, or nonpayment of the loan. This has not changed. The assessment of these risks, however, requires different skills and even involves some automation. To understand the credit risk and mitigate this, it is important to understand, first, the primary types of consumer loans.

Types of Loans

Although there are many variations of consumer loans, the primary types that are offered by banks fall into three categories:

- personal loans
- residential mortgage loans
- credit cards

Personal Loans

Personal loans are generally "installment" loans; that is, payments are made in installments throughout the life of the loan, per an amortization schedule. The typical type of consumer loans includes auto loans, appliance loans, debt repayment loans, student loans, boat loans, furniture loans, and other types of loans for needed items in the household. These loans are typically structured in relatively short terms: three to five year terms are not unusual. From a further structuring standpoint, these loans are usually secured by the asset purchase. For auto and boat loans, the car or boat form the basis of the collateral, which is subject to repossession if not paid. For other physical asset loans, some type of collateral will be identified.

Personal loans, with collateral, help to mitigate risk. However, they can be risky because it is fully based upon an individual's financial strength, which can change frequently. These loans are usually priced according to published rates that are fixed, but available publicly. Rates are seldom, if ever, negotiated. Losses on personal loans occur at different schedules than commercial loans.

Residential Mortgage Loans

Mortgage loans, individually, are considerably larger than personal loans. Although mortgage loans are secured by property, they nevertheless have a significant amount of risk. However, as a general rule, mortgage loans may have less of a percentage risk in the calculation of risk-weighted assets, based upon Basel standards. As a result, this is a consideration when determining the amount of mortgage loans to make, from a capital adequacy standpoint. With a lesser percentage risk, the capital ratio would increase, all else being equal. These represent loans to individuals for the purchase of a home, their personal residence. The loans are also secured by the value of the home itself. Since most homes tend to appreciate, over time, this collateral can a very effective risk mitigator in the event of non-payment. For this reason, they carry less risk. Mortgage loans have terms of 15–30 years, so they are long term in nature, presenting some maturity risk to the bank. Mortgage loans can be a considerable portion of the consumer loan portfolio, by their individual balances, and dependent upon the bank's strategy. Nevertheless, when payments are not made, the bank can foreclose on the mortgage and take ownership of the home. When this occurs, the bank will attempt to sell the home and recover the balance of the loan, if possible. Foreclosed mortgages result in OREO property, which must be maintained by the bank until sold. This is a costly venture for banks because they do not want the asset to lose value; however, until sold, maintenance costs can be high. Foreclosure of mortgages are an absolute last resort on the part of the bank. Bankers will work closely with borrowers to avoid this terminal event.

Another aspect of mortgage loans are home-equity loans. Individuals can borrow against the equity they have in their homes to free up needed cash for other expenditures. Equity in a home is the difference between the fair market value of the home and the amount owed. In a time of rapid appreciation, this can create sizeable equity amounts that can be borrowed against. When the loan is made, it is secured by the home itself and now becomes a part of the total amount owed. For example, if a home is valued at $400,000 in today's market and the individual owes $200,000 remaining on the mortgage loan, they have $200,000 in equity in the home. Presumably, if they sold their home, they would have a $200,000 gain after paying off the loan. Rather than sell the property, many people wish to unlock this equity and use it to enhance their home by remodeling, expanding it, adding a pool, or other initiatives. By taking out a home-equity loan and receiving the total equity value of $200,000, they have the cash to use, although now the amount owed is $400,000. The risk to the borrower is whether the home continues to appreciate. If it does not and declines in value, the borrower may find themselves owing more on their home than it is worth. This is known as being "underwater." This is exactly what happened to many homeowners during the financial crisis of 2008.

Credit Cards

Unlike the prior two consumer loans, credit cards are totally unsecured and carry a significant amount of risk. These are like a line of credit in the commercial realm. Once credit is granted, the bank would assign a credit limit to the borrower. The borrower may then purchase goods and services up to that credit limit. The balance on the account can be paid off completely or it can be paid in monthly payments and continue to revolve. This means that only a portion will be paid, and the individual will carry an outstanding balance. Because these are unsecured and risky, banks charge a high interest rate to accommodate for the risk and assess penalties for late payments.

Credit cards are a way of life today: Almost everyone has one, or many. This clearly is large portion of the consumer debt that is monitored relative to economic forecasts. They do provide a considerable amount of freedom, and credit limits can grow as high as $50,000 or more.

Evaluating the Consumer Loan Application

The consumer loan application is the primary analytical document that is obtained for consumer loans, including credit cards. This takes the place of the financial statements for commercial loans and is the starting point for assessing the credit worthiness of the borrower. Some of the applications will be more extensive than others, depending upon the loan. Mortgage loan applications are notorious for information, more so than for a furniture loan or other smaller borrowing need. However, to analyze consumer loans, there are several considerations that are typical in all circumstances. These include:

- character of the borrower
- application review and analysis
- credit bureau report
- cosigner

Character of the Borrower

The six Cs of credit equally applies to consumer loans as it does for commercial loans. Among these, the most predominant are character, cash, and collateral. The character of the borrower is an assessment the personal banker will ultimately have to determine during the discussion of the need for the loan and based upon responses in the application. Does the loan make sense as a legitimate need for the individual, and does the potential borrower have a serious intent to repay the loan? These are judgement calls on the part of the personal banker, but with experience, the banker can become very adept at making this assessment.

Cash, or cash flow, is critically important as well. The borrower will have to demonstrate this by providing evidence of a job and an income that is sufficient to make payments. Finally, collateral is also very important, and most consumer loans will be secured by some asset in the process, except for credit cards.

Application Review and Analysis

As indicated, the primary document for credit analysis of consumer loans is the application. This contains the legal agreement embodied within it and is signed at the time of application. There are several mandatory items the personal banker will look for in assessing whether the individual is credit worthy, based upon their information. The typical application will always include the following items for assessment:

- job/occupation
- income levels
- residence stability
- home ownership or rental
- savings and other deposit balances
- outstanding debt

Job/occupation: Since consumer loans are an extension of credit, the potential borrower must have a job that produces income from which payments will be made. The banker will assess how long the individual has been at their current job. Longevity is important because it indicates stability, which relates to less risk. For example, individuals who have been on their jobs for several years are more favorable than someone who has been working their job for less than one year. Applications usually request a former job if an individual has been at their job for less than one year or so, and this is an important assessment, as it is known that people will switch jobs. If the individual remained at their last job for several years, that is to their benefit. If, however, the last job was also short term, or there are gaps between employment, that is a sign of instability of income source. The type of occupation can make a difference as well. Professional positions, managerial positions, and trade specialists, such as electricians or plumbers, will be more favorable in the analysis than unskilled positions, but that depends upon the length of time on the job. Duration creates stability, and that is sought in an application.

Income levels: Applications request income levels via a chart or outright. This is the cash flow that is required as one of the six Cs of credit. If the amount of income is not perceived to be enough to cover principal and interest payments, the loan will be rejected. This can be all sources of "regular" income. Although there is no UCA cash flow analysis that is performed to analyze this, bankers will attempt to validate employment and income levels before the loan is made.

Residence stability: How long the applicant has remained at their current residence is another indicator of stability. Like job duration and status, information regarding the current residence will be required, and if it is short term, a prior address and duration will be requested. If this is a longer term, the assessment will be made on that basis. However, if that too is short term, this will become a stability issue and will work against approval.

Home ownership or rental: In addition to stability, the type of residence is important. If the borrower owns or is buying their home, these can be additional points or pluses for the borrower. Although many people rent, renting does not connote a sense of permanence. Leases are short term, and it is relatively easy to unbundle from a rental lease without major loss. If one owns a home, this is much more difficult. For these reasons, the type of residence will indicate risk.

Savings and other deposit balances: Applications usually ask the borrower for their bank and what types of accounts and balances they have. Balances in accounts, particularly in savings or other time deposits, indicate the availability of other funds that can be used to make payments. It also tells the banker more about the borrower, that they are frugal and can budget well enough to put money aside for future needs. This is very positive and can make a difference if there is weakness in other areas.

Outstanding debt: Lastly, the bank will want to know what other debt the borrower has. Do they have a mortgage, a car loan, or other loans? In addition, they will want to know the monthly payments required to service the debt, as well as the outstanding balances owed. This debt is taken into consideration in addition to the request for the new loan. This may be indicative of pyramiding of debt, which creates significantly more debt.

Credit Scoring the Consumer Loan Application

The elements contained in the consumer credit application previously outlined are analyzed in two formats. The first format was implied in the last section, which is a judgmental assessment. In this format, a lender would analyze all the information and decide based upon their intuitive evaluation and feel for the credit, much like a commercial loan would ultimately be made. These are time consuming, and with considerable volume, given the amount of retail customers, they can require considerable human effort and time to complete. Additionally, given different bankers making the analysis, there can be inconsistencies in the decisions.

To combat these drawbacks, a methodology known as **credit scoring** evolved several decades ago that has streamlined this process considerably, saving both time and human effort and increasing the consistency of decisions. Credit scoring utilizes all the elements of the application and the credit bureau to assign scores based upon customer responses on the application. Therefore, when an application is received, a computer or an analyst can use a scoring key and assign point values to the responses. In this regard, weights are established for each category (i.e., residence stability, job stability, etc.), and then an actual point value is assigned to ranges of responses. For example, a person who is on the job less than one year may receive 0 points; on the job between one and three years, maybe 5 points; and greater than three years, 10 points. This is determined by the system utilized but with bank input to tailor the scoring to their portfolio needs. Credit scoring dramatically reduces personal judgment and leaves the decision to the range that will indicate approval or denial. This will manifest in three levels of decision, as follow:

- approve outright: total score over a specific threshold
- reject outright: total score under a specific threshold
- judgement review: Total scores that fall in between these two upper and lower thresholds will be set aside for a judgmental review since the score is marginal and can go either way.

Scoring is beneficial to the bank not only for its efficiencies but also for its flexibility. If the bank sets thresholds too stringently, they may not approve the amounts they would like to for their objectives, or they may be seeing more losses coming from the portfolio, which necessitates raising the threshold. Either way the bank has flexibility to manipulate the scores to achieve the goals they desire.

Credit Bureau

The credit bureau is almost always consulted when extending consumer credit. Items on the application are important and should be validated, but the credit bureau is an excellent source to understand the borrower's payment patterns, outstanding debt, employment, and any derogatory information. Credit bureaus, such as Experian and Equifax, provide a service that is available to the banks and other extenders of credit. This is a good source to validate information contained on the application, and then some. Credit bureaus will identify all places where the individual owes money and will provide a 12-month history of payments (missed or late) that provides the banker with a sense of their payment patterns, which is the primary risk the banker is trying to address.

Credit bureaus also indicate whether there have been any judgements filed for non-payment or whether the individual filed bankruptcy. It also reflects recent inquiries—that is, others who are checking the credit bureau for similar reasons. Too many inquiries are negative, indicating that the individual is seeking credit from several other sources that may be turning them down. The credit bureau can reflect the current reported employment, so this is another means of validating application data. In short, the credit bureau is a wealth of information and provides much information that can help mitigate the risk in the analysis process.

Cosigners

Cosigners are sometimes required to extend credit. If the analysis proves that the information is weak and the bank is reluctant to provide the loan, they may request a cosigner. A cosigner is not a guarantor, but an equal party to the loan. This means that if payment is not received, the bank can contact the cosigner and ask for payment. If the loan goes into default, the cosigner is equally and legally responsible for the debt and will be held accountable—this means reporting this to the credit bureau for both parties. Care should be taken if one is considering being a cosigner on a loan, due to the legal responsibility. For a bank, however, the cosigner would have to be evaluated similarly from an application and credit bureau. If they are deemed financially stronger, this can bode well for making the loan.

The FICO System

The credit bureau is an integral part of the analysis of consumer credit, as outlined in the previous section. However, over the last several years, this has gained greater attention for consumers through the FICO score and merits special attention. The **FICO system** was originated by the Fair Isaac Corporation. This system provides lenders, as well as consumers, with a single score that indicates the individual's history in debt repayment and other credit-related issues. This score is now available to consumers so that they can manage their credit rating and enhance their overall score. Prior to this, it was difficult for consumers to obtain this information, let alone understand it. With a specific score, it becomes much easier to determine the strength of an individual's credit.

The FICO score is based upon specific information that is contained in the credit bureau reports in five areas and weights this information to arrive at a total score (see Table 13.1).

Table 13.1 **FICO Score Factors and Weightings**

Factor	Weight (%)
1. Payment history	35%
2. Amount of money owed (total outstanding balances)	30%
3. Length of borrower's credit history (over 10 years)	15%
4. Nature of new credit requested	10%
5. Types of credit borrower has already used. Not all debt is the same (e.g., real estate, credit cards, auto loans, etc.).	10%

When viewing the weightings, one can see that the total amount of outstanding balances on all debt will make a difference on the borrower's overall score, as will payment history. This totals 65% of what the score is based upon to provide an indication of how the score is determined and how it can be managed.

The FICO score ranges from 300–850, with average scores at 675 and a median of 710. Table 13.2 illustrates the percentages of consumers that fall within the ranges and the meaning of these scores. When viewing this chart, it is surprising to note that 88% of consumers have "fair" to "poor" credit. This not only highlights the need for self-awareness and management for consumers but also highlights the risks involved in consumer credit. For that reason, repayment, obviously, is most important, from a weight standpoint, and is the very factor that creates credit risk.

Table 13.2 **Distribution of FICO Scores (source: Experian)**

FICO Score	Meaning	% Consumers with score
800 +	Exceptional	1%
740-799	Very Good	2%
670-739	Good	8%
580-669	Fair	27%
579 and below	Poor	61%

Risk Measurement

The last section of this chapter outlines how credit risk is measured for the bank. Although this metric has been discussed in the last chapter, it merits a bit more detail. All loans possess credit risk, which is a combination of all commercial and consumer loans combined. Although each category can be measured separately, and even within lending segments, the metric used is often compared with peers on a total loan basis.

As has been defined throughout this chapter, credit risk results from nonpayment of loans. More specifically, this is the loss resulting from nonpayment of loans. Therefore, it is important to understand the number of losses taken in relation to total loans. Since loans are assets, this metric refers to the quality of the loans, as it relates to loan losses—hence, the **asset quality** metric. Asset quality is a percentage and relates the dollar amount of losses to total loans in percent form. The formula for this is shown in Table 13.3.

Table 13.3 **Asset Quality Calculation**

($ amount of loan losses / Total loans) = %

Most performance ratios and measures indicate that performance is positive (improving) if the percentage grows (is higher). This is not true regarding asset quality, and the reader should take special note of this. If a bank is showing improvement in asset quality, the percentage is decreasing. The goal is for this percentage to be as low as possible. In general, it should be a relatively low percentage, less than 1% or 2%, but the objective is for it to decline.

As the analysis of loans deepens, presumably, a better quality of loans will be produced, and losses should decrease. For this reason, the analytical functions defined for both commercial and consumer credit are most important and can be quite effective in the improvement of loan quality.

CHAPTER SUMMARY

Risk mitigation from a credit risk standpoint demands a considerable amount of resources and is, by no means, a guarantee. The purpose of the chapter has been to inform the reader of all the aspects of what creates credit risk and what can be done to mitigate it. For banks, considering the size of loans on their balance sheets, this is a sizeable risk and one that is not immediately obvious. Whether or not a customer will pay their loans will not be evident instantly, and it may take a while for it to become obvious that the risk will materialize. This is not only the nature of risk, which is uncertainty, but also the nature of underwriting loans. This function is both a science and an art. The science aspect of underwriting lies in the processes, procedures, metrics, and other tools and can be learned and applied. For this reason, credit analysts go through training and an apprenticeship period before they are in the position to make loans. The "art" aspects of underwriting come with experience and judgement. As time progresses, lenders not only see many business forms but have also been exposed to economic downturns and other events that have helped them to learn over time. Seasoned lenders can intuitively know where to look for information and judge the impact more so than someone going through the mechanics of the process. Although credit risk stands alone as an important risk for the bank, in terms of asset quality, this becomes an indicator that can dramatically affect capital and therefore creates the risk of erosion of capital both from a coverage standpoint and from a compliance standpoint. Nevertheless, credit risk, in addition to the financial risks defined in the prior chapter, frame much of the risk picture for a bank and define the necessity of risk mitigation.

END OF CHAPTER QUESTIONS

1. What is the range of scores in the FICO system?
2. Identify the three aspects of analyzing the financial condition of a business for credit.

3. What are the top two determinants (factors) in developing the FICO score for an individual?
4. Define what credit risk is.
5. Identify at least three key elements that are contained in a bank's loan policy.
6. What is the primary source for mitigating credit risk?
7. What are the typical types of collateral that a bank may seek from the borrower?
8. Name the six Cs of credit and briefly identify what they represent.
9. Identify the two types of loan covenants and what they do.
10. Name at least three evaluation items in a consumer loan application.

CHAPTER 14

Managing Other Forms of Risk

By now it is relatively clear that banks face many significant risks. One need only look at bank's 10-K and 10-Q reports to understand the litany of risk factors identified at the start of the report. The past two chapters have identified the most pervasive and consequential risks that banks face, for which two major committees of the bank are dedicated, ALCO and the credit committee. Unfortunately, it does not end there. Many other risks face the industry. These risks, if manifested, can trigger financial and other more significant risks, so it is very important to understand the nature of these inherent risks and know the ramifications. This provides a level of respect for these, which is appropriate, and from which awareness is the major requirement.

The purpose of this chapter is to create awareness of all other risks. For the entry-level student of banking, a basic awareness and understanding of what these risk factors are and what they represent is important. A more in-depth study of each of these risks, however, is beyond the scope of this text. Nevertheless, a thoughtful discussion of the remaining risks banks face will aid the reader in understanding the complete picture for managing a bank and mitigating its risks.

Range of Risks Facing Banks

Unfortunately, commercial banks face many risks. The financial and economic nature of banking is at the root of many of these risks. Although many of the more

Key Terms

Operational risk
Natural threats
Technology
Internet
Voice over IP (VOIP)
Service level agreements (SLAs)
Cybersecurity
Compliance risk
Reputation risk
Strategic risk
Litigation risk

Learning Objectives

By the end of this chapter, the student will:

- Understand the complete framework of risk banks face.
- Differentiate between financial and credit risks and all other remaining risks.
- Define the other risks banks face and what factors affect them.

significant risks that banks face have been outlined in the last two chapters, there is value in having a mental picture of the risk landscape.

One way to view all these risks is to picture it as a wheel. To manage a bank effectively, it is necessary to manage and mitigate "all" risks. When one of the risks is not well managed, it will distort the circular nature of the wheel, and it will not roll effectively. To avoid this ineffective functioning, banks must have awareness, plans, and a process to manage these risks. There are a total of 10 risks that all banks face. These include:

- capital risk
- liquidity risk
- interest rate risk
- credit risk
- operational risk
- technology risk
- compliance risk
- reputation risk
- strategic risk
- legal risk

Figure 14.1 depicts these risks in the wheel analogy previously referenced. This chart is color coded to differentiate between the financial and credit risks from the other risks banks face. Although these are the total risks, this chapter provides and overview of those risks other than financial and credit.

Other risks are less directly focused on the financial implications that have already been discussed and more on the activities involved that create these risks.

Factors Affecting Other Types of Risks

Other risks within the scope of the risk profile of banks are those that relate to bank activities that create these risks, or the lack thereof. These risks may not immediately pose a major threat to the bank, but the continuance of each can ultimately lead to financial and other risks that can be a more immediate threat to the bank. The focus of this section is on these other risks, which include:

- operational risk
- technology risk
- compliance risk

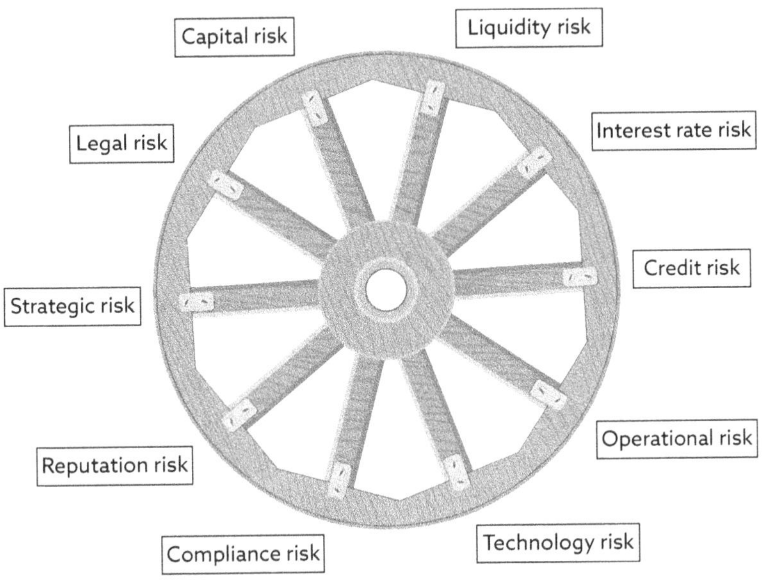

FIGURE 14.1 Breadth of Risks

- reputation risk
- strategic risk
- legal risk

Operational Risk

Definition

Operational risk is the risk of loss from failed internal processes and procedures, human errors, and external events. Each of these items creates risks from which loss of revenue or income can result. These can occur from incorrect system algorithms, data entry errors, incorrect procedures, failed equipment, and other external events and threats.

Activities Creating Risks

Banks have many operational areas where risks evolve. These generally occur from people-intensive areas where various policies and procedures can occur. Activities that will affect these include:

- loan operations: booking commercial and consumer loans; processing payments; producing loan documentation; processing and perfecting collateral
- deposit operations: deposit account opening; inadequate reconciliations; incorrect data entry; improper validation of information

- other operations: Other operating areas where risk may emanate include trust operations, credit operations, facilities management, and other departments where human error and system functionality can play a role.

Threat Sources

These threats can be both internal and external and create the risk in these areas.

- fraud: fraudulent access and usage of systems by internal employees
- third parties: third-party vendor failures and errors that are relied upon by the operational area
- natural threats: **natural threats** that can disrupt processing, such as fires, floods, snow, hurricanes, tornados, and other natural threats that can destroy legal documents, office equipment, and systems, creating outages that will put the bank at risk of loss
- suppliers: disruption of suppliers and sources of materials and supplies

Risk Mitigation

There are several ways to mitigate operational risk:

- policies and procedures: Effective policies and detailed procedures can be an excellent deterrent to errors and discrepancies that can put the bank at risk of issues. These should be audited to ensure they are up to date and adhere to all regulations and laws.
- training programs: It is important to have a training department or program that ensures that employees are aware of the latest regulatory changes and updates in software systems to avoid inaccuracies. Training, unfortunately, has become discretionary; however, the more frequent and effective the training, the more the quality of output and delivery will be enhanced.
- contingency planning: The development of effective back-up and disaster recovery plans can minimize the time to restore operations in the event of a disaster. Contingency planning procedures should be developed and regularly tested to ensure they work effectively.

Technology Risk

Definition

The primary risk from **technology** is the loss and uncertainty that evolves from usage of the **internet**. External hacking threats are not a matter of whether they can or cannot get in to the bank's systems; it is a matter of whether the bank is targeted or not. If so, they will get in. Although other system failures and outages create risks, the internet poses the greatest threat.

Activities Creating Risks

Banks rely on many systems and technological tools in the execution of bank functions. Examples of these include:

- web browsing: Usage of the internet by literally all employees in the bank presents significant risks. These can result in malware, phishing, social engineering, trojan horses, and other information capture and disruption.
- email usage: lack of encryption of sensitive data; response to phishing attempts providing sensitive information
- network printing: Most employees in the bank print documents to network printers. Given their interconnectivity, they can create risks of unauthorized access.
- telephone usage: Today many phones are part of the overall network, such as **voice over IP (VOIP)**, which can create risks to the bank.
- smartphone usage: This risk is similar to that created by other technical devices that are connected to the internet and may have interconnectivity with other systems within the bank.

Threat Sources

There are several sources of threat related to technology risk:

- website outages: Disruption of the bank's web presence can pose immediate threats to the business dependent upon the duration of the outage.
- network outages: These can impair the ability of clients to access electronic systems and/or internal employees reaching the host or other computers. These can affect printing, telecommunications, access to data, and other information.
- hackers: These provide the greatest threat to the bank. When breaches occur, they can be monumentally disruptive and even cause a bank to fail.
- employees: Employees can create threats internally to the bank through sabotage of equipment and unauthorized access to sensitive information.
- third-party or internal core system outage: Many banks outsource their host or mainframe computing. The reliance on a central system creates a significant vulnerability if the outage is sustained. Information would be unavailable to clients and employees. Reliance on third parties creates significant third-party risk, as outages would be outside of the bank's oversight and control.

Risk Mitigation

There are ways to mitigate technology risk:

- back-up sites: "Lights out" back-up sites provide locations that contain duplicate hardware, software, and network and are used when the bank's primary systems are impaired. These sites are designed to switch immediately and "fail-over" to the back-up site.
- system patching: Software patching protects systems from existing vulnerabilities determined. These relate to known vulnerabilities and require all systems to be updated with the latest patches to avoid these risks.

- antivirus systems: Another preventative measure is the implementation of antivirus software to prevent computer viruses and disruption in the bank. Antivirus software must be updated frequently to be effective.
- third-party agreements: Policies for evaluating and managing third-party relationships can establish effective standards, including **service level agreements (SLAs)**, to ensure that third parties do what they say. This establishes discipline and monitoring of third-party relationships to obtain the levels of service required.
- cybersecurity assessments, awareness, and monitoring: **Cybersecurity** is complex and changing every day, given the number of cyber threats occurring. This is why it is important to engage cybersecurity experts to evaluate the bank's risk profile and tailor recommendations that can help the bank to prevent risks and define actions that must be taken in the event of a breach.

Compliance Risk

Definition

Compliance risk is the risk of penalty, loss, or closure resulting from inadequate adherence to regulations and laws while executing the bank's critical functions.

Activities Creating Risk

There are several areas of activities that create compliance risk:

- finance: not managing capital adequacy, liquidity, and reserve requirements; errors and inaccuracies in external reports, such as the 10-K and 10-Q, that violate disclosure requirements
- operations: adherence to privacy requirements in access to client information, as well as other standards
- technology: information security and cybersecurity risks that would expose the bank to hacking and other cyber threats
- credit: lack of adherence to Truth in Lending laws
- deposits: lack of adherence to Truth in Savings laws

Threat Sources

There are two main sources that create compliance risk:

- employees: lack of attention, understanding, and adherence to defined regulations and laws
- systems: inadequate and outdated systems and programs that may not have the latest compliance standards updated

Risk Mitigation

There are several strategies that can be used to mitigate compliance risk:

- internal compliance reviews: the development of a department that performs periodic compliance reviews in sensitivity and reports these to management and the board of directors

- internal audit: inclusion in audits; procedures for reviews of sensitive areas that would be reviewed during a regulatory exam to ensure internal compliance
- external audits and third-party reviews: external audits procedures to review sensitive areas for compliance violation; hiring other third parties for independent review and assessment in specific technical areas
- training and education: developing a culture of compliance through education and training that is updated regularly to create awareness of laws and regulations, and the requirements for same
- policies: establishment of formal and updated policies that are communicated to all employees regularly for adherence

Reputation Risk

Definition

One to the biggest risks that banks face is that of impairment to their reputation, or **reputation risk**. This is the risk of loss involving negative publicity, inaccurate information, lawsuits, penalties, and publicity resulting from fraudulent and unsavory business practices, as well as a bank's ethics.

Activities Creating Risk

There are certain activities that are most likely to create reputation risk:

- business practices: The bank's functions and procedures can impair the level of trust, such as a lack of adherence to privacy or inaccuracies in account management. These can be most functions within the bank, and therefore, this makes the risk much more pervasive.
- website hacking: Cyber threats can create reputation risk through lack of accuracy, trust, and exposure of clients to risk. When doubt is created in the minds of the clients, impairment will ensue.

Threat Sources

There are several sources that create reputation risk:

- hackers: External hackers can create inaccuracies in information such that clients will no longer feel comfortable in relying on it. In addition, outright theft of monies from accounts will create a lack of integrity of systems and therefore mistrust.
- unethical employees and managers: Employees and managers may attempt to defraud clients through unsavory practices that are not only unethical but also illegal. An excellent example of this is Wells Fargo.
- disgruntled employees: Employees who are passed over for promotion or receive poor performance reviews may seek to communicate inaccuracies about the bank externally through

electronic and social media channels that can expose the bank to doubt and create a lack of trust.

- weak protection of systems: Systems that are improperly patched or do not include virus protection can expose the bank to disruption, particularly for externally facing devices, such as a website. The extent of the disruption can create negative feelings about the bank to its detriment.

Risk Mitigation

There are several methods of mitigating reputation risk:

- code of conduct: Having a defined and updated code of conduct that all employees must review and sign, annually, helps to establish boundaries and the importance to appropriate conduct.
- ethical training and standards: Training is an absolute must for bank employees to be effective. Training should occur regularly and be included as a mandatory requirement.
- management oversight: Management should be more focused on seeking out fraud within the organization. The hierarchy and reporting lines should be set up in such a way that permits that level of oversight to avoid situations that can put the bank at significant risk.
- social media policies: Given the preponderance of social media today, to protect themselves, a bank needs to have a social media policy. This defines what employees may and may not do and how these can translate into impairment of their employment if abuse occurs. This should include statements relative to leaking corporate information.

Strategic Risk

Definition

Literally all businesses face strategic risk. Banks, however, must be focused on this not only for themselves but also as they evaluate companies for business loans. **Strategic risk** is the risk of poor performance (earnings) and losses resulting from inadequate or lack of effective planning and attention to the economy and marketplace and its indicators.

Activities Creating Risk

There are several activities that create strategic risk:

- strategic planning: Processes for planning for the future may be flawed and not adhere to effective processes due to a lack of understanding or training or when it is abdicated to others in the organization not adept at the process.
- budgeting and capital expenditures: Each year banks plan for the next year by developing a sales growth objective and the capital costs needed to meet these objectives. A lack of

appropriate dollar allocation to the plans will cause the objectives to not be met. Furthermore, the commitment of significant dollars to capital expenditures that do not adhere to effective capital budgeting analysis can greatly impair shareholder value.

- communication and execution: If plans are not effectively communicated throughout the organization, execution will be limited or nonexistent. Again, this can impair the achievement of the objectives.

Threat Sources

There are several sources of strategic risk:

- education and experience: Strategic planning requires understanding, training, and experience. Without these, strategic planning will be considerably inadequate. The bank should ensure that managers are trained and experienced in strategic planning by making strategic planning a process, as opposed to a one-time event.
- planning structure: Planning should be an organized structure within the bank. Individuals should be designated as planning directors, and a strategic planning committee should be clearly defined. This is a group that should be specifically designated, familiar with one another, and meet periodically to plan and monitor strategically.
- measurement: A lack of measurement tools can be detrimental to the planning process through lack of awareness of the results. Strategic planning defines objectives to obtain. Without knowing the progress toward attainment, the likelihood of achievement is greatly diminished.

Risk Mitigation

There are several ways to mitigate strategic risk:

- consistent process for decision making: Strategic planning must be a regular process rather than ad-hoc events. This process should call for regular sessions, analysis of progress, and ongoing monitoring for modification. The greater the consistency, the greater likelihood that the success will be assured.
- metrics for assessment: Defining and regularly reporting progress to objectives helps to manage where progress is deficient and allows for actions toward attainment. Without these it is like not having a map or GPS to get someplace quickly. Metrics allow for corrections to be made to get back on track, if needed.
- clear roles and responsibilities: Understanding the roles and responsibilities is critical. Not everyone can be the driver of the strategic plan. Competing strategic plans will serve only to ensure that the goals will not be attained. It is very important to define these roles in order to obtain the power of the organization moving toward one goal, and in one direction.

Litigation Risk

Definition

Litigation risk is the risk, once again, of loss resulting from deviation from contractual agreements, lawsuits, and inadequate contract development and structuring, rendering them unenforceable.

Activities Creating Risk

There are several activities that are most likely to create litigation risk:

- account opening: Deposit account opening requires the development of applications and agreements to establish the legal basis of the terms of the agreement. If agreements are not properly executed, it can create risks to the bank in terms of holding clients accountable to terms.
- loan documentation: Part of loan documentation includes loan agreements, which define the terms and the legal obligation for repayment with the client. Out-of-date standardized documents can put the bank at risk of not being able to hold clients responsible for the terms. Many loan documents are now prepared with unique specifications for more complex deals. Although these are prepared by attorneys, they will not be standardized and could miss key requirements of the bank.
- operations: Operations and support areas of the bank work with many third parties. Each of these requires the development of an operating contract. Often, contracts may be executed by managers within the department for expediency; however, the manager may not have the legal authority to bind the bank. This can put the bank at risk of an inability to hold them to the terms since the contract is not binding.

Threat Sources

There are several sources that create litigation risk:

- employees and management: Internal employees and management can be sources of threats. Employees may have disagreements with management, from a human resource standpoint, for dismissals and other issues, resulting in lawsuits due to unfair labor practices. Managers also can create the threat by actions they take regarding their employees that may trigger lawsuits, as well as taking liberties with contracts, violating terms, and putting the bank at risk of actions.
- lack of legal review: The lack of legal resources in the bank, or from outside counsel, creates threats from inadequate legal language, due to a lack of consultation with an attorney.
- clients: Clients can initiate actions against the bank for discrepancies in account handling of terms and conditions as well as misperceptions of interactions with bank employees.

Risk Mitigation

There are several strategies for mitigating litigation risk:

- third-party risk management: Banks should have a third-party risk management policy for the handling of third-party suppliers and other organizations. These policies define the rules for legal contracts, attorney reviews, and evaluation of the financials of third parties. This will ensure consistency in handling and mitigate many of the risks attendant to these relationships.
- education: Bank managers must be educated in legal risks and the complexities associated with contracts and adherence to third-party risk management policies.
- lines of authority and execution: Similar to the usage of a loan policy, the bank should establish clear lines of authority for initiation and execution of contracts so that it is clear with all managers who has responsibility for working with contracts and third parties.

CHAPTER SUMMARY

Banking can be a risky business. As defined in this and the last two chapters, the management of a bank requires a deep understanding of these risks and the creation of a culture of risk management. One of the fastest growing areas in banks is risk management, predominantly because of the myriad of risks that banks face. Similarly, regulators have intensified their focus on risk management, requiring that all manager have an ability to assess the risk of situations and develop strategies for mitigation. Understanding the other risks banks face helps to complete the risk picture and expand the awareness of management to risks that can translate into financial impact via loss. Many of the risks in this chapter may not have immediate repercussions for the bank; however, the expansion of cyber risk can. A significant breach can create financial risk through reputation risk, impairing capital and ultimately causing the bank to fail. In this regard, no risk can be minimized in terms of attention. For this reason, understanding that other risks exist and having a framework for understanding the complete range of risks will aid the bank in keeping the "wheel" round and rolling effectively ahead.

END OF CHAPTER QUESTIONS

1. What risk requires the development of social media policies as a risk-mitigation initiative?
2. Third-party risk management is associated with what risk?
3. Identify some of the sources of threats associated strategic risk.

4. What is the total number of risks that banks face, as defined in this chapter?
5. What are some of the activities that create operational risk for a bank?
6. Patch management is a risk mitigation technique for what risk?
7. A code of ethics can be an effective risk mitigation technique for reputation risk. What is the goal of this technique?
8. What role do capital expenditures play in managing strategic risks?
9. Define how the account opening process creates risks for the bank.
10. Identify the six other risks banks face, and explain what the risk of each is.

Figure Credit

Fig. 14.1b: Copyright © 2011 Depositphotos/lapotnik.

REFERENCES

American Bankers Association. (2014). *Principles of banking* (11th ed.).

American Bankers Association. (2018). *Legal foundations in banking.*

American Bankers Association. (2018). *Quick reference guide to banking laws and regulations* (12th ed.).

Bank Holding Company Act of 1956, 12 U.S.C. § 1814 *et seq.* (1956).

Baumohl, B. (2008). *The secrets of economic indicators* (2nd ed.). Wharton School Publishing.

Belasco, K. S. (1991). *Earnings enhancement handbook for financial institutions: Proven techniques for managing float, reducing noninterest expenses, and increasing non-interest income.* Bankers Publishing Company.

Boyes, W., & Melvin, M. (1991). *Economics.* Houghton Mifflin Company.

Center for Financial Training. (2017). *The U.S. banking system* (3rd ed.). South-Western Cengage Learning.

Choudhry, M. (2011). *An introduction to banking, liquidity risk and asset-liability management.* Wiley.

Fazio, J. (2017). *This might be a dumb question but ... how does money work?* CreateSpace Publishing.

FirstB@nk. (2017). *SimArch user manual.* Ziegfried Vermaak.

Hallman, G. V., & Rosenbloom, J. (1987). *Personal financial planning.* McGraw-Hill Book Company.

Hull, J. C. (2018). *Risk management and financial institutions.* Wiley.

Investopedia. (n.d.). *Laws and regulations.* https://www.investopedia.com/laws-and-regulations-4427769

Keusal, A. (2015). *Breaking into banking: Cracking the code on launching a successful career in commercial banking.* CreateSpace Independent Publishing Platform.

Koch, T., & MacDonald, S. (2015). *Bank management* (8th ed.). Cengage Learning.

Kolari, J., & Gup, B. (2017). *Commercial banking: The management of risk.* Textbook Media Press.

Lehmann, M. (2005). *The Irwin guide to using the* Wall Street Journal (7th ed.). McGraw-Hill.

Little, J., & Rhodes, L. (1980). *Understanding Wall Street.* Liberty Publishing Company.

Melton, W. (1985). *Inside the Fed.* Dow-Jones Irwin.

Prochnow, H. (1981). *Bank credit*. Harper and Row.

Ritter, L., Silber, W., & Udell, G. (2009). *Principles of money, banking, and financial markets* (12th ed.). Addison-Wesley.

Rose, P., & Hudgins, S. (2013). *Bank management and financial services* (9th ed.). McGraw-Hill Irwin.

Rose, P., & Marquis, M. (2011). *Money and capital markets* (11th ed.). McGraw Learning Solutions.

Sayari, K., & Shamki, D. (2016). *Journal of applied finance and banking*. International Scientific Press.

Trennert, J. (2015). *My side of the street*. St. Martin's Press.

Waupsh, J. (2017). *Bankruption: How community banking can survive fintech*. Wiley.

ABOUT THE AUTHOR

Dr. Kent S. Belasco is the Director of the Commercial Banking Program and Assistant Professor of Finance at Marquette University. Prior to joining Marquette, he spent over 37 years in banking with Citicorp, Exchange National Bank, Deloitte and Touche, and First Midwest Bank. Dr. Belasco is a Certified Public Accountant in Illinois and has authored numerous publications on bank productivity, bank systems management, staffing and project management. He received his doctorate in business education from Northern Illinois University and is originally from Chicago, Illinois. He currently resides in Long Grove, Illinois, with his wife, Carol, and daughter Sarah.

www.ingramcontent.com/pod-product-compliance
Lightning Source LLC
Chambersburg PA
CBHW080416280126
38902CB00017B/1337